Politics, Ideology,

and Literary

Discourse in

Modern China

POLITICS, IDEOLOGY, AND LITERARY DISCOURSE IN MODERN CHINA

Theoretical Interventions and Cultural Critique

LIU KANG AND XIAOBING TANG, EDITORS

Foreword by Fredric Jameson

Duke University Press   Durham and London   1993

© 1993 Duke University Press
All rights reserved
Designed by Cherie Holma Westmoreland
Typeset in Melior with Eras display
by Keystone Typesetting, Inc.
Library of Congress Cataloging-in-
Publication Data appear on the last printed
page of this book.

Liu Kang, "Subjectivity, Marxism, and
Cultural Theory in China" first appeared
in *Social Text* 31/32 (1992).

Xiaobing Tang, "The Function of New
Theory," first appeared in *Public Culture*,
vol. 4, no. 1 (Fall 1991), © University of
Chicago Press. Reprinted by permission.

CONTENTS

Foreword   Fredric Jameson   1

Introduction   Liu Kang and Xiaobing Tang   8

PART ONE
Problematics of Subjectivity and Modernity

Subjectivity, Marxism, and Cultural Theory in China   Liu Kang   23

The Subjectivity of Literature Revisited   Liu Zaifu   56

Split China, or, The Historical/Imaginary: Toward a Theory of the Displacement of Subjectivity at the Margins of Modernity   Ching-kiu Stephen Chan   70

Narratives of Modern Selfhood: First-Person Fiction in May Fourth Literature   Lydia H. Liu   102

Female Subjectivity and Gender Relations: The Early Stories of Lu Yin and Bing Xin   Wendy Larson   124

PART TWO
Representation, Realism, and the Question of History

Ideologies of Realism in Modern China: The Hard Imperatives of Imported Theory   Theodore Huters   147

Lu Xun, Shen Congwen, and Decapitation   David D. W. Wang   174

Red Sorghum: Limits of Transgression   Tonglin Lu   188

PART THREE
Cultural Critique and Ideology

    Narrative, Ideology, Subjectivity: Defining a Subversive Discourse in Chinese Reportage   *Yingjin Zhang*   211

    Anxiety of Portraiture: Quest for/Questioning Ancestral Icons in Post-Mao China   *Yuejin Wang*   243

    Resisting Writing   *Li Tuo*   273

    The Function of New Theory: What Does It Mean to Talk about Postmodernism in China?   *Xiaobing Tang*   278

    Postscript   *Leo Ou-fan Lee*   301

    Index   305

    Contributors   315

Politics, Ideology, and Literary Discourse in Modern China

FREDRIC JAMESON

Foreword

The eclipse of the avant-gardes (including the political ones) has often been taken to be a more than accidental characteristic of the postmodern turn; less often remarked is the concomitant substitution—for the great avant-garde manifestos and indeed for the very conception of the great individual master text or statement—of the anthology, the collective symposium, as the generic expression of the emergence of new concerns and new fields or objects of study. It is something that can now, over a longer history, be most dramatically witnessed in feminism, where, after the initial salvos of Kate Millet and before her Simone de Beauvoir, feminist literary theory began to emerge in the form of successive anthologies, a process instructively documented by Jane Gallop in her *Around 1981*. Black literary theory followed much the same pattern, as did Black feminist literary theory; more recently Chicano studies has also begun to constitute itself by way of just such collections. In fact, these anthologies map a problematic rather than articulating a set of positions, laying down norms, or issuing guidelines. This replacement of the cultural-political line by the conception of the problematic (conceived as constituting its object fully as much as merely recognizing or reflecting it) is a current historical symptom that can be read as a depoliticization and the annexation of praxis by the academic as much as a liberation from sterile doctrinal questions and arguments.

Most recently, two new areas have convulsively surfaced in precisely this way. Called cultural studies and postcolonial studies respectively, they both essentially project their struggle on the terrain of the academy—in the form of questions of curriculum and specialization, tenure, canon, what counts as scholarly work, and who has the power in the universities and the foundations. Both also seek legitimation by an appeal to larger political movements or tendencies, those of multiculturalism and anti-imperialism, respectively. Finally, both are to a certain extent the sociological expression of distinctive newly emergent sociological strata. A series of anthologies and theoretical collections studs the course of each, although these now seem to follow each other in more rapid succession than the historical moments so powerfully marked in Jane Gallop's narrative.

All of this also seems to have something to do with high theory, which we have been told is dead (along with Marxism and "modernism," the modernization theories, that seem to have been so intimately related to it), replaced by more pragmatic or empirical, historical (neohistorical?), and reformist or micropolitical projects. But this detheorization (much like de-Marxification and de-Maoification, perhaps even deregulation) would seem to be greatly exaggerated, if not the result of a misunderstanding, for it can perhaps better be grasped as the exchange of a theorizing whose vehicle is the avant-garde manifesto for one whose essential structure is that of the problematic itself. A problematic remains a theoretical entity, but one that must be grasped in a different way from the traditional representational or philosophical one.

Still, however theory is to be judged, its emergence as a historically original fact is linked in fundamental ways to the emergence of all the new movements mentioned above as well as to the constitution of a general academic left intelligentsia after the failure of 1960s activism. That even the most seemingly apolitical forms of Theory—semiotics, for example—were socially, historically, and biographically related to left political movements could be documented and offers a very interesting subject for future research in cultural and intellectual history. I have in mind, however, a more basic relationship—namely, that for all of us involved in theory in the first days it was Theory itself (of whatever type)—that was in and of itself political insofar as its practice marked a break from the by then canonical procedures of the New Criticism; its adoption signaled an immediate affinity with other younger scholars, like a masonic handshake. Later on the great ideological divisions began not so much to influence as to reveal their latent presence within theory itself, but that division was less one between left and right—since the Right, with a few exceptions, has always seemed constitutionally hostile to theory as such—as between the left and the commitment of liberals and liberal humanists to forms of theory that did not raise troublesome political issues. Meanwhile, all the conceptual innovations themselves became acquisitions and passed into a more general academic koine at the same time that they began to fan out from literature departments and to initiate the same general process in the other disciplines.

Yet when "theory" arrived in those new spaces—and this is my point in telling this story—politicization had already taken place. It could not repeat the same evolutionary process in any innocence. The two stages—theory as politics and the politicization of theoretical positions—were henceforth collapsed—in short, in its new terrains, "theory" confronted the peculiar historical and structural phenomenon of "uneven development" or "nonsynchronicity," as it has variously been called.

But nonsynchronicity in terms of development has an equivalent or opposite number in space for which we do not have a term, and this phenomenon is also at work here. Indeed, the story I have told is a North American one and, if not "postcolonial" in any honorific or meritorious sense, it is certainly peripheral to the degree to which the United States was always on the receiving end of all these theories, which, if not mainly French, were certainly continental European, even when for the most part intermediated by the British cospeakers (who have in the meantime themselves become Europeans). The result was that Theory here was always un-American, in virtually the full range of the various traditional meanings of this epithet, so that it was predictable, at the end of the theoretical period, that native theoreticians would begin to reaffirm some properly American tradition (Peirce, pragmatism, Dewey) and urge us to cease whoring after foreign gods.

We therefore need a global or geographical term for the ways in which chronological nonsynchronicity manifests itself in a spatial and even a national form: immense systemic "anxieties of influence" sweep through the various national questions, when they are not eating away at the very heart of "nationalism" itself, whatever that may be. But the problem with this word (in search of a concept)—inextricably intertwined with the problem of the spatial loops we are trying to theorize here—is not only that it binds us into a sterile opposition between the nation-state and the transnational powers and structures that offers an intolerable antithesis (since, mostly, no one really likes either, but everyone is capable of making powerful arguments on either side); at that point the arguments are pitched to slip down the slope of moralizing and of "taking sides" and making just such judgments. To take up the estimable example of Johannes Fabian's conception of the "co-eval"—of a nondominatory relationship between unequal cultures or social formations—it certainly has the merit of solving the ethical problem and embodying an ideal, but only at the price of doing away with the problem altogether (merely the result of our bad, Western, center/margin thinking), whereas it was the problem that we needed to retain for analysis. The problem of unequal relations was in fact the reality, whereas our own thinking (including the wishful kind) is perhaps less important. But the knee-jerk invocations of "power" are not very useful either: we need here something like a geometry of these relationships (which remain relationships of subordination and hierarchy), something that seems already latent and undeveloped in Gramsci's conception of the unequal prestige of a given linguistic and cultural area that plays a decisive role in the construction of hegemony. Here the conception of the national culture (with its mysterious links to economic and political power, which are never direct, as witness Greece or France) is modeled as something like a force of gravity whose laws and more complex manifestations now demand codification. But it is necessary to add that such a geometry will have to be non-Euclidean, in order to accommodate phenomena on the order of nonsynchronicity or even of Freudian retroactivity (*Nachträglichkeit*): it will have to allow for the "outsider principle," in which the theoretical newcomer suddenly restructures a whole problematic that had become a weary prison yard for old theoretical pros. Finally, it will have to model the leap-frogging effect of the dialectic itself, where (at least until recently) economic modernization suggested the advantage of brand-new plants over the pioneering factories. But the "non-Euclidean" dimension of these figures lies in the fact that the issue of "foreign" theory and outside or international influence that was for earlier theory an external matter, at best an accident of form, now enters the content itself to be added to theory's objects of study, creating in the process a new theoretical field.

This process can be observed in the present collection of essays, one of the richest and most stimulating I have encountered in recent years and one that at once begins to pose all kinds of new questions and problems for that "Western theory" it prides itself on having assimilated. My sense is that with this younger generation of literary theorists in the China field we are well beyond the debates on Western influence that were painful and crippling in the early years of the century in China and whose contaminations still seem detectable in the debates of many other "Third World" cultures.

There are surely many reasons for this possibility of making a fresh start from a starting point that only too often in the past proved to be a cul de sac. First of all, younger scholars from the People's Republic of China (particularly since the fading away of their own orthodoxies) do not have to deal with the same weight of tradition (including the Chinese classics fully as much as the prestructuralist or "pretheoretical" Western literary ones), as do their colleagues in Hong Kong or Taiwan (in their very different ways), let alone students in Third World countries with intellectual and educational traditions inherited from the European colonizers. As for the traditions of premodern national culture, socialism clearly broke the mould of those patterns, only later on obligingly breaking the mould of its own (Maoist) ones. China thereby finds itself in a situation evidently unique in the world today, in which, despite unparalleled discouragement among the intellectuals, the collective hope invested in the various (socialist and nonsocialist) paradigms of modernization remains intact, while none of the dogmatisms is henceforth exempt from doubt and skepticism. Intellectuals confront opportunities and can have a sense of mission instructively different from obtains in Eastern Europe, where a dogmatic belief in Western political and economic paradigms is coupled with an utter loss of hope in the prospects for modernization as a total social process.

Second, it might be interesting to adduce in this work the relative distance of the stance of Chinese scholars from the "postcolonial" one elaborated in other cultures. Indeed, it seems possible that in China the catchall category of "the West" does not have the same function as do conceptions of the "center" or of "Eurocentrism" in other geographic and cultural areas. Perhaps the United States must be included far more centrally, since it is from the United States rather than from Europe that these intellectuals "import" their theory, which is however not North American in origin. But the cultural prestige of the United States does not include the high-cultural or philosophical achievements we associate with Europe, and is indeed mainly a mass cultural one, involving dangers and imperialisms of a different kind to which the People's Republic of China is both less and differently exposed.

Finally, New Theory in China arrives simultaneously with postmodernism, including the various internal literary postmodernisms (of which the omnipresence of Mo Yan in these pages is, for example, one sign). Unlike modernism, however, which was specifically Western and marked as an import, postmodernism in its very nature can be and always is home-grown, its pluralist celebration of difference constituting an immediate authorization of local cultural production over imports, whether from the outside or from the national power centers themselves. Nor can the theory of postmodernism be said to be Western exactly, for it arrived in Europe as an import in its own right and in the peripheral areas initially derived from the peripheral and hitherto un- and antitheoretical area of architecture.

Of greater interest in the present context is the way in which the various ideologies of the postmodern have encouraged and enabled new reflections on subjectivity and have produced new debates on "the subject"—debates that may themselves be obligatory or a required part of the general postmodern problematic but can scarcely be said to have frozen over into dogma or doxa. For every celebration of the decentered subject, for example, there can be found an equally powerful celebration of "identity." The question of subjectivity in the postmodern is therefore an immense playing field for dialectic in the Platonic sense (and perhaps in some other ones).

The way in which, in the climate of a certain bureaucratic Marxism, the claims of subjectivity are pressed as an urgent political matter is a recurrent episode in the revolutionary tradition most recently recapitulated in the West by that moment in which Sartre's foregrounding of consciousness, the revival of Gramsci, and the insistence by Raymond Williams and others on the cultural dimension of Marxism all coexist (paradoxically, the rumors of Maoism that reached the Western left during this period seemed to provide fresh theoretical and political ammunition for this particular struggle). But the consciousness-and-culture debate in post-Mao China is rehearsed in original and stimulating new ways from which "the West" (if there still is such a thing) certainly has something to learn but from which other disciplines (and other national cultures) also have much to learn. Above all, the center has something fundamental to learn from what it seems ludicrous to call a "margin," for the essential feature of the constitutive blindness of what we can still call (at least in this respect) the center is its repression of all those collective and political urgencies within itself that are identified as "nationalisms" when they appear in the various Others. The remarkable and remarkably various Chinese interrogations of the psychic subject that can be found in the present pages, however, have found it impossible to deal with this issue without conjoining it with the in fact inseparable problem of the collective or national or group subject, a problem from which, on my view, the psychic or subjective or individual version is in fact derived. This anthology, then, constitutes a formidable intervention into a range of debates on subjectivity and identity that, however multicultural internally, have rarely taken into account the possibility of real and productive difference outside, in other social formations, and even in other modes of production.

LIU KANG AND XIAOBING TANG

Introduction

1

This volume is the product of a conference held at Duke University, on October 26 to 28, 1990. The conference, with the general title of "Politics and Ideology in Modern Chinese Literature," was the first annual meeting of the American Association for Chinese Comparative Literature (AACCL) and attracted some forty scholars and critics from across the world. The meeting at Duke brought together scholars and critics from three distinct backgrounds: scholars of Chinese literature in the United States, writers and critics from mainland China and Hong Kong, and a number of Chinese graduate students who, having come to the United States in the early 1980s, have begun to form a noticeable intellectual and professional presence in their field. This historic convergence of separate intellectual traditions turned out to be highly productive. Papers read and discussed at both plenary sessions and individual panels covered a wide range of topics and represented various political agenda and theoretical approaches, such as feminism, psychoanalytical criticism, poststructuralism, narrative analysis, Marxist critical theory, and new historicism. To a certain extent, these new theoretical interests reflect the transformation that the study of modern Chinese literature is currently undergoing.

The significance of the Duke conference lies beyond its immediate academic context. Because of the strong presence of Chinese writers and critics who arrived in this country after the Tiananmen Incident in 1989, discussions at formal sessions as well as outside regular meetings gained a sense of urgency and relevance. The heated exchange at a special roundtable discussion in Chinese testified to a general mood of what Edward Said has called, in a different context, the commitment to "worldliness and change."[1] In the spirit of worldly commitment and intervention, participants in the Duke conference reached a consensus that it was time to engage in a comprehensive reexamination of modern Chinese literature not only in terms of its local political and ideological traditions and determinations, but also against the larger background of world historical experience of modernity and postmodernity. To accomplish such a goal, it was felt, a new critical discourse and cultural strategy is needed to reinscribe a specifically determined indigenous cultural experience. The enormity of this task is obvious. Indeed, one of the remarkable features of the Duke conference was an acute awareness of both the power and limits of languages and paradigms with which we conceptualize and articulate our experience. The three central themes that generated the most interest attest to this search for a new language: the problematic nature of a theory of subjectivity, representations of modernity in the Chinese context, and the question of cultural critique. All these recurring topics point to the difficulty of either achieving or inventing an authentic, at least inalienable, discourse for modern Chinese consciousness. As a particular form of this consciousness, modern Chinese literature and literary criticism, especially in the contemporary period, can be said to have moved constantly in two opposite directions. On the one hand, they turn toward the future and embrace modernity as an ideology for change. On the other hand, they look back to the past with ambivalence and even nostalgia, claiming radical iconoclasm against tradition and in the same breath hoping to resurrect certain forms from the past so as to escape from the imposingly strange modern age.

In contemporary Chinese literature, the search for a new language is expressed by literary experiments that include modernist techniques and a return to traditional narrative forms; such a search is better reflected in debates over terminology of literary criticism. In the second half of the 1980s there was an outburst of interest in "culture," specifically traditional cultural forms. Yet, curiously enough, what has now been termed the "culture fever" of the 1980s was indirectly fueled by an impassioned interest in new theories and methodologies. Western theories of postmodernism and poststructuralism were embraced by Chinese literary critics with great enthusiasm at the same time that "three new theories" (system theory, cybernetics, and information theory) from the natural sciences were eagerly being applied to the study of literature. Understandably, the strategy of importing Western theories en masse has been motivated primarily by a pragmatic consideration (the same strategy underlay most May Fourth intellectuals' zeal for a "bright, advanced, and humane Europe"): namely, to confront the Chinese reality, and, in many cases, to claim radical or what Lin Yü-sheng has described as "totalistic" iconoclasm in the face of all old models and traditions, Chinese as well as Western.[2] One fruitful way to examine twentieth-century Chinese history, it appears to us, is to retrace and examine the persistent problem of language.

The seemingly perennial Chinese anxiety over "Westernization" and "modernization" is compounded by the current debates about postmodernity that have been going on in other intellectual and institutional milieux. The discourse of postmodernity puts into question all the fundamental assumptions about culture, history, and the accepted notion of self and the other. Chinese critics, including most authors contributing to this volume, find themselves not only caught between the two readily accessible models of cultural relativism and evaluative universalism, but also torn by the tension between "old models" and new theories. As is obvious from this volume, political intervention tends to bring to crisis these two related but different lines of intellectual orientation: while some authors find it highly relevant to further a mandatory critique of the official literary and cultural practice and politics in China, others tend to tackle the equally compelling task of dismantling ideological constructs such as "modernity" and "subjectivity" from a global perspective. A constant worry shared by participants in the conference can be stated as follows: Are we using new theory as a superior vantage point of intervention only to speak the language of yet another master?

The chapters in this book inevitably reflect the problems of reinventing a critical discourse that would come to grips with the issues concerning theory in general and historical narratives in particular. A major objective of our intervention is to challenge our accepted notions and to see in what way we can construct a different narrative of the Chinese experience of modernity through the medium of literature. But we must constantly be aware of possible pitfalls, since the established paradigm has largely been predicated on a convenient division between an undifferentiated "West" and a homogenized "China." In other words, we must caution ourselves against the danger of turning our own inquiries into either an ideological foreclosure or a form of nativist politics. On a close examination, binary thinking still appears to be the dominant mode when we realize that some of our inquiries are inextricably based on an opposition between, for instance, the historical and the imaginary, truth and fiction, realism and lyricism, or, finally, longing for the future and nostalgia for the past. Binary thinking by itself does not necessarily constitute a problem, but it does indicate the extent to which we need to be aware and critical of our own intellectual heritage. In such a spirit of painful and necessary self-doubt, authors in this volume have raised more questions than offered ready solutions.

2

The present volume does not intend to offer a comprehensive chronological study of modern Chinese literature. Nor do the authors focus solely on rejecting or even invalidating "old models." On the contrary, authors are primarily concerned with exploring implications of major theoretical constructs such as "subjectivity," "representation," and "modernity." All three of these concepts, as indices to prevailing ideologies of culture, history, and society, have irretrievably implicated themselves, either with their presence or through their negation, in modern Chinese literary discourse and thereby have determined the latter's social relevance. In this sense, literary discourse is an ideal site for an investigation into both a real and an imaginary encounter with history. History is not to be displaced, but history is accessible to us only through specific and very often distorted "textual forms."[3]

In their attempt to recapture the Chinese experience in its historical specificity, some authors strategically take contemporary Western theories as a point of departure. This revisionist gesture often helps release new energies in those appropriated theoretical formulations. The continual return to the topic of subjectivity reveals the degree to which many of the authors included in this volume are involved in contemporary debates about identity, selfhood, and otherness. For instance, the vocabulary and conceptual frameworks with which authors such as Stephen Chan and Lydia H. Liu discuss subjectivity and modernity are decidedly steeped in contemporary Western theoretical discourse. Others, like Liu Kang and Wendy Larson, engage in historical and archival analyses. As Liu Kang indicates in his essay "Subjectivity, Marxism, and Cultural Theory in China," while subjectivity as a "liberal humanist" concept has been under assault in the Western context, particularly in the antihumanist, poststructuralist tradition, it nonetheless acquired an emancipatory significance in China in the mid-1980s. If the decentering of the subject has indeed become a central trope for the postmodernist scenario in the West, it is because, as some thinkers argue, reification and commodification of the most private and emotive spheres of human experience have reached their present proportion. In China, the formation of subjectivity has a different political thrust. Liu Kang sets out to recontextualize the debate about *zhuti xing* (subjectivity) in the 1980s by first tracing the issue back to the staunch but unorthodox Marxist theorist Hu Feng's formulation of "subjective fighting spirit" in the 1940s. Hu Feng's intent then was to contend for a site of revolution and resistance at the level of subjective experience, which as a cultural arena had been either ignored or suppressed by the official ideology of collective class struggle and national salvation.

In the 1980s theorists Li Zehou and Liu Zaifu inaugurated a heated discussion of subjectivity within a Marxian framework. Their initial reflections crystallized a cultural ethos of "recovering" the once-denounced humanist values and "returning" to the May Fourth project of cultural enlightenment. However, the politics underlying the debate that ensued are quite obvious. The discourse of subjectivity, as Liu Kang argues, can be seen as a self-conscious effort to redefine the intellectual as an autonomous and self-regulating subject. By advocating a humanist, autonomous literature of subjectivity, Liu Zaifu effectively challenges the literary orthodoxy that has always valorized a revolutionary collective identity at the expense of individuality. Thus his theorization of a "literary subjectivity" makes a pivotal political insurgence. As Liu Zaifu's essay "The Subjectivity of Literature Revisited" illustrates, his purpose is to move beyond the "dualistic" mode of thinking while retaining the fundamental "ontological" and "axiological" thrust of his thoroughly dialectical conception of subjectivity. Liu's exposition becomes more trying as he moves on to grapple with the existential meaning invested in "subjectivity" in modern times. He posits a forward-looking "subjective force" that is the hallmark of modernity. This "subjective force" expresses the subject's desire for self-fulfillment and self-realization, which he terms *duixiang xing* (objectifiability), as opposed to *zhuti xing* (subjectivity). At this point, Liu Zaifu actually goes beyond a critique of institutionalized denial of subjectivity and addresses, in his own terms, the issue of modernity.

If Liu Zaifu's reflections on *duixiang xing* as the project of modernity and his critique of traditional "dualism" are symptomatic of the twofold movement toward both past and future, then Stephen Chan's "Split China, or, the Historical/Imaginary: Toward a Theory of the Displacement of Subjectivity at the Margins of Modernity" resituates the problem of subject formation within contemporary, if not specifically poststructuralist, terrains. Chan's strategy is to examine the poststructuralist terms and concepts that he will subsequently employ to prepare for a Chinese textuality in which "subjectivity" is to be constituted. After fully gauging the difficulty at the theoretical level, he turns to read Mo Yan's novel *Thirteen Steps* in order to retrieve the repressed or displaced subjectivity at the level of the unconscious. The volatile, traumatic movement of becoming "Chinese" is captured by Chan in the very form of his own suggestive prose and the logic of his argument. In his own words: "My essay represents not so much coherent arguments on my part for arriving at a conceivable analytical paradigm as some personal notes toward an alternative critical imagination through which the fragmented body of text—any text—would manifest itself in dreams."

In her critical reading of two first-person narratives by Lu Xun and Yu Dafu, Lydia H. Liu focuses on the experience of disillusionment resulting from modern Chinese intellectuals' frustrated quest for *ziwo* (self). She draws us deep into the labyrinth of ethics and even ontology in Lu Xun's "Regret for the Past" and explores the repressed narcissistic desire of the I-narrator in Yu Dafu's "Reminiscences on Returning Home." Her reading is sustained by a feminist critique of *masculinism* as well as by a historical analysis of the intellectual context of the 1920s and 1930s. Liu highlights in her chapter the complex and often conflictual relationship between a determinedly modern conception of an individual self and the reality of modern life. Her intervention raises questions about the understanding of modernity as well as about the discourse of individuality, abundant in writings from the May Fourth period.

This ideological quest for a modern self during the May Fourth period is most of the time voiced from an assumed male perspective, while efforts to articulate a feminine identity have often gone unheard. Wendy Larson ventures into this field by offering historical and formal analyses of stories written by two women writers, Lu Yin and Bing Xin. Her reading shows that Lu Yin and Bing Xin, and to some extent Ding Ling, constructed their fictional worlds from a unique female perspective, very often through the preferred form of letters and diaries. These formal devices give shape to an oppositional female subjectivity that acknowledges as legitimate the emotive, "female-voiced" lyrical tradition and offers a glimpse of an alternative selfhood at variance with what is postulated by the dominant ideology of the modern nation-state.

It is by now obvious that our reexamination of the modern discourse of subjectivity has a double vision: it is a critique that specifically situates itself in the context of modern China while drawing on the antihumanist tradition in contemporary Western theoretical formulations. Closely related to this development then is a questioning of realism and representation, for if the subject is recognized as constituted and problematic, its claim to realistic representation and eventually to truth has to be taken with a grain of salt. In fact, Marston Anderson has already begun this work in his 1990 book *The Limits of Realism: Chinese Fiction in the Revolutionary Period*. In his critical analysis of the fate of realism in modern China, Anderson tells the story of how various impediments (social and moral) that the discourse of realism encountered eventually led to its relinquishment: "In working with the mode, Chinese writers and critics had come increasingly to understand that realism did not naturally lend itself to the activism and populism that Chinese radicals felt the times demanded."[4] Thus critical realism, when its imperatives are faithfully followed, reveals its own limitation and vacillates between a withdrawn "individualism" and a "revolutionary collectivism."

Theodore Huters' essay in our volume picks up the issue of representation where Anderson left off. Further pressing Anderson's argument about the limits of critical realism, Huters calls attention to a series of contradictions inherent in what he calls the "anxiety of the Real" in modern Chinese literature. First, there is the confusing entanglement of realism and modernism as conflicting literary movements (for instance, state-realism versus unofficial modernism), which Huters attributes to a "peculiar convertibility of the [political] contexts." Second, a "historical contingency" creates a paradoxical situation where Chinese writers encounter a Western "universal" discourse of representation only to be reminded of a silenced and nullified Chinese "universal" discourse in the past. The need for universality as a rhetorical device for legitimation then makes it necessary for Chinese writers to mask the alien origin of the new, imported universal discourse. Huters further probes the complicitous relationship between politics and literature in modern China by examining the conflation of two attributes of realism: a "critical spirit of the modern" and a "supreme faith in the powers of representation." He concludes that the politics of (national) salvation and a deeply embedded utopianism in modern Chinese realist works have only intensified the social and cultural crises. A "perfect metaphor" for this intensification is found in Mao Dun's two short pieces of realistic fiction that he analyzes here.

Between the anxiety of the Real that Huters describes and the impediments to critical realism, David Wang intervenes to examine another dimension of the realist discourse, namely, the representational chain that links the body to language. Overloaded with guilt and moral anxiety, Lu Xun's realistic fiction, for instance, actually undermines the signifying chain of realism by grounding the representation of Chinese reality on the thematic of decapitation, which then serves as a metaphor for "the mutilated condition of the meaning system that makes Reality what it is." Motivated by Lu Xun's literature of rupture and anxiety, Shen Congwen, argues Wang, renders the decapitation motif in a unique and displaced "lyricism" that grasps yet more forcefully the complexity of human emotions and motivations. Wang's reading of these two writers' different representations of the "break" or decapitation further develops, albeit in a revisionist vein, C. T. Hsia's argument that modern Chinese writers are all burdened with a "moral obsession." Yet while Hsia reproaches those writers for their lack of transcendent power to overcome their parochialism (a blame that Huters in his essay identifies as coming from Hsia's own "determination to pursue successful representation"), Wang's reading in effect recuperates a representational power in Shen Congwen's lyrical realism that requires the reader to take a mobile perspective and to weave together "all sensory impressions."

It is in Mo Yan, the contemporary novelist known for his *Red Sorghum* series, that the linkage between literary representation and the body is given a new spin. Stephen Chan, as we have seen, deploys Mo Yan's almost volatile text to advance his thesis of a split and fragmented body of text, but Tonglin Lu sees in Mo Yan's often extravagant, sometimes grotesque representations of the female body an intentional manipulation and transgression of the official "socialist realism." On the one hand, Mo Yan resorts to a carnivalistic celebration of the body that has a decidedly revolutionary significance as a subversion of what the critic Li Tuo and others have termed "the Mao Style." On the other hand, as Lu demonstrates, Mo Yan's work also epitomizes a deeply rooted nostalgia for a "natural" and prerevolutionary community. Such writings by Mo Yan seem to move in precisely the two directions that we identified at the outset. The central concern and obsession—an obsession that is historical rather than moral—has to be the memory of the recent revolution. Indeed, contemporary Chinese writings can only articulate their historicity when the massive revolutionary experiences of the twentieth century find themselves represented and reflected upon in all types of emplotments and formulations. This is also true for literary criticism. Besides Li Zehou and Liu Zaifu, we find a whole group of young critics (Chen Pingyuan, Qian Liqun, Huang Ziping, Wang Xiaoming, Ji Hongzhen, Chen Sihe, and others) whose work echoes, although in a different form and at a separate level, the same critical reconfrontation with a historical revolution. It is noteworthy that the Chinese critics began to probe the issues of collective memory and the writing of history with little recourse to poststructuralist thinking and theorization. Their initial critical impulse was more like a reaction, an effort to resist the official representation or outright distortion of either the past revolution or the everyday lived experience.

3

It is undeniable that the "cultural reflection" in the aftermath of the Cultural Revolution (1966–1976) became possible only with a postrevolutionary mentality. But very often this intellectual reflection goes beyond a simpleminded rejection of terroristic, authoritarian social control and violence, and actually reaches the difficult philosophical moment of rethinking modernity. Through various forms of "cultural reflection," such as the "Searching for Roots" and "Educated Youth" literature as well as the debate about subjectivity and discussions on the "tradition/modernity" dichotomy,[5] the modernist desire for domination over nature and human destiny is being critically revalued, with the project of socialism being shown as a sublime expression of that utopian longing for modernity. Also the effort of rethinking history, tradition, or simply the retrieved and reinvented memory of a collective or personal past begins to address the present in a different voice and to produce a creative tension. Most noticeably, in the highly experimental fiction of the late 1980s, such as Su Tong's fictional genealogy and Ge Fei's continual reimagining of the imagined past, we find a strong expression of the nostalgic, and no less revolutionary, yearning for history. This history is evoked not only through a painful questioning of "master narratives" such as those of national identity and collective movements, but also by means of reconstructing the micronarratives of personal memoirs, fantasies, and testimonies.

One narrative form that falls between the collective master narratives, on the one hand, and personal testimonies, on the other, is reportage. Yingjin Zhang's chapter on Chinese reportage, which constitutes what he calls a "subversive discourse," examines a literary genre that vacillates between conformist propaganda and subversive writing; cases in point are writings by Liu Binyan, Qian Gang, and Hu Ping. On close examination, the "textuality" of reportage is quite complex and presents a transgression of accepted categories of fiction and history. It is also informed by the implacable tension between official ideology and the experience of everyday life. The ultimate challenge for the reportage writers, however, is to voice their own "subjectivity" in a mode of writing that is supposed to be impersonal and objective.

Just as Yingjin Zhang's critical vocabulary is largely taken from Althusser, the following essay is another case in which Western theory is expanded, if not brought to crisis, by being tested in a different cultural context. In "Anxiety of Portraiture: Quest for/Questioning Ancestral Icons in Post-Mao China," Yuejin Wang situates Luo Zhongli's "photorealist" or "superrealist" images of impoverished Chinese peasants against the general intellectual background of cultural reflection. Luo Zhongli's iconographic portrait of a father figure bespeaks the need to confront the father-leader-despot icon as a Chinese cultural residue. In cinematic spectacles of Grandma and Grandpa, as Wang also observes, the moving camera presents the past/present, self/other relationship in a shifting and dynamic way, which nevertheless ends up magnifying a rather immobile icon—a single portrait. Wang's chapter on contemporary art and cinema, like Yingjin Zhang's on reportage, is an example of ideological analysis that carefully poses important questions and highlights some of the fundamental contradictions of contemporary Chinese culture. Both projects are strong evidence that more extensive cultural critique has to be conducted from an interdisciplinary approach. The divergent writing styles witnessed in Zhang and Wang, on the one hand, and in Li Tuo and Liu Zaifu, on the other, highlight the problem of language once again. Li Tuo's brief piece, beautifully translated by Mary Scoggin, presents an interesting alternative case of how Western theories and theorists can be incorporated into a writing that sets as its task to revolt against the Mao style.

Finally, in his review of recent interactions between Chinese and Western critical theories and, moreover, of the general cultural dynamic in contemporary China, Xiaobing Tang establishes a historical connection between locally engaged discourse such as "subjectivity" or simply "theory" and its global context. Tang argues that the attraction of "postmodernism" for a new generation of Chinese writers and critics has its own historical and cultural implications. The "function of new theory," in other words, is to constitute a forceful cultural critique in its own right. This is yet another way of defining the task of critical intervention, or "the act of insurgency." The point, in the final analysis, is to critically uncover the complexity of political and ideological commitment and contradictions that underlies and simultaneously propels every instance of cultural imagination and production. As Edward Said puts it, "criticism belongs in that potential space inside civil society, acting on behalf of those alternative acts and alternative intentions whose advancement is a fundamental human and intellectual obligation."[6]

We would like to thank Duke University Press for publishing this volume, and to thank Mr. Reynolds Smith in particular for his patience and enthusiasm. We would also like to thank professors Fredric Jameson, Leo Ou-fan Lee, and Arif Dirlik for their support at various stages of this project. The Center for Critical Theory and the Asian/Pacific Studies Institute at Duke University, Chicago Multi-lingual Graphics, Inc., the China Times Cultural Foundation in Taiwan, and the Henry Luce Foundation contributed to the Duke conference. We are grateful to all the participants in the Duke conference, whose involvement either directly or indirectly helped make the book a collective effort. Besides the authors who contributed to this volume, participants in the conference included Sung-sheng Yvonne Chang, Chen Xiao-mei, Kirk Denton, Arif Dirlik, Edward Gunn, Huang Ziping, Fredric Jameson, Jeffrey Kinkley, Leo Ou-fan Lee, Li Lee, Peter Li, Perry Link, Hsiao-peng Lu, Christopher Lupke, Meng Yue, Mau-sang Ng, Richard Trappl, Marshall Wagner, Wang Ban, Jing Wang, Wang Xiaoming, Philip Williams, Yenna Wu, Xie Mian, Harry Haixin Xu, Ye Yang, Michelle Yeh, Michael Yetman, Zhang Longxi, Zhang Xudong, Zhao Heping, and Zhong Xueping. It has been a long but very pleasant experience working with all the contributors to this volume. We, as editors, only hope that the final volume has done justice to all the effort each author has put into writing his or her essay. In 1992 while we were preparing this volume, Wu Beiling, then vice-president of the AACCL and instrumental in the success of the conference, passed away after a long, courageous struggle with cancer. Finally, we wish to express our appreciation for the institutional support that we have enjoyed from the Department of Comparative Literature at the Pennsylvania State University and the Department of Oriental Languages and Literatures at the University of Colorado.

We owe the most, perhaps, to Marston Anderson for his understanding and encouragement. Without his firm initial backing, this book may never have come into being. It has been our deepest regret to realize that Marston, whose sudden death in 1992 deprived our field of a brilliant scholar and a sensitive critic, will never see this volume in its book form; for this reason, we would like to dedicate this book to the memory of Marston Anderson.

Notes

1. Edward Said, "Traveling Theory," in *The World, the Text, and the Critic* (Cambridge: Harvard University Press, 1983), pp. 233–234.

2. See Lin Yü-sheng, *The Crisis of Chinese Consciousness: Radical Anti-traditionalism in the May Fourth Era* (Madison: University of Wisconsin Press, 1979).

3. Fredric Jameson, *The Political Unconscious: Narrative as a Socially Symbolic Act* (Ithaca: Cornell University Press, 1981), p. 82.

4. Marston Anderson, *The Limits of Realism: Chinese Fiction in the Revolutionary Period* (Berkeley: University of California Press, 1990), p. 200.

5. See, for instance, Gan Yang, ed., *Dangdai Zhongguo wenhua yishi* (Contemporary Chinese cultural consciousness), introduction by Gan Yang (Hong Kong: Joint Publishing Co., 1989).

6. Edward Said, "Secular Criticism," in *The World, the Text, and the Critic*, pp. 29–30.

PART ONE

Problematics of Subjectivity and Modernity

LIU KANG

Subjectivity, Marxism, and Cultural Theory in China

Subjectivity as a humanist concept has been under assault in the current debates about contemporary "postmodern" culture in the West. Its fate in China, however, seems to have taken just the opposite direction. Following the resurgence of the humanist May Fourth (1919) tradition in literature and the arts in the wake of the Cultural Revolution (1966–1976) and the subsequent debates in philosophical and economical circles about modernization, the concept of subjectivity has gained a centrality in recent debates about culture in China, starting in the mid-1980s. The May Fourth Movement, a watershed in modern Chinese history, was initiated by the demonstration of Beijing students against the government's humiliating concession to Japan after World War I. It then turned into a nationwide cultural movement for a radical break with the Confucian tradition, as well as for a transformation of Chinese culture into a modern and global one.[1] As Western humanist values of "democracy" and "science" were hailed as liberating forces by May Fourth intellectuals, radical social theories such as Marxism and anarchism made a tremendous impact, ultimately leading to the establishment of the Chinese Communist Party in 1921.[2] The Chinese communists under Mao, however, gradually abandoned the humanist goals of the May Fourth Movement in the course of their struggle for and consolidation of power. The recent debate about China's cultural heritage and about the problems of tradition and modernity can be seen as a strong critique of Mao's legacy through the recovery and continuation of the incomplete cultural enlightenment of the May Fourth Movement.

The debate has taken place largely in the realms of literature, history, and philosophy, but its impact has been felt in many sectors of social life. A central issue in the debate has been the place of subjectivity in Marxist cultural theories. Despite the fact that Chinese Marxism, preoccupied with political and economic struggles, has never had a separate cultural theory, the problem of subjectivity has remained central to Marxist literary thought. For instance, Hu Feng's theory of a "subjective fighting spirit" in realism, formulated at a critical juncture of the Sino-Japanese War (1937–1945), linked the concept of social revolution with that of individual consciousness. In the 1980s, Li Zehou, a leading philosopher and cultural critic, and Liu Zaifu, a major literary theorist, who is now in virtual exile in the U.S., initiated a resurgence of interest in subjectivity.

Hu Feng's task in the 1940s had been to stake out a site of revolution and resistance at the level of subjective experience and consciousness, an area that the Chinese Marxist ideology of class struggle and national salvation deliberately ignored or suppressed. In Hu Feng's view, subjectivity is a key to realist representation, a mediation of political reality and lived experience. As such it pertains to the aspect of cultural critique as a major objective of the May Fourth New Culture Movement, for the question of subjectivity is as much a preeminent instrument of rejuvenating China's culture as it is a relentless critique of the Confucian tradition that subsumes subjectivity and consciousness within an ethic of universal kinship and communality. To be sure, Hu Feng's theoretical work is eminently representative of the May Fourth enlightenment project. Unfortunately, the debate in the 1940s ended in a virulent political assault on his deviant and "counterrevolutionary" stance. The increasing attacks against bourgeois subjectivism and idealism, and various forms of "revisionism," such as Lukácsian theory and Western Marxism as a whole, further consigned subjectivity to the enemy camp of anti-socialist ideologies.

Only after Mao's extremist "Cultural Revolution" had undone its own myth of creating a brand new cultural formation could the once-stifled voice of May Fourth humanism and its enlightenment project of cultural critique again resonate in China. In the realm of culture, Li Zehou's and Liu Zaifu's initial reflections on subjectivity in the late 1970s and early 1980s crystalized a cultural ethos of "recovery" and "return": a recovery of once-denounced humanist values and a return to the May Fourth enlightenment projects. In this respect, the connection between the two debates over the span of some forty years becomes apparent.

In what follows, I will begin with a brief account of Hu Feng's theory of the 1940s in order to recapture the historical specificity of the question of subjectivity in Chinese Marxist thought. I will then move to the cultural debates of the 1980s, focusing on Li Zehou's appropriation of idealist German philosophy and historical materialism, and on Liu Zaifu's reinvention of humanist and Marxist aesthetic thinking in their respective undertakings to reconstruct subjectivity in Chinese culture. This historical recontextualization is necessary, for later debates can be fully comprehensible only in the light of the earlier ones. I will argue that while Hu Feng's theory of subjectivity bears an urgency of political commitment directly supportive of the politics of cultural activity during the War of Resistance, in the theories of Li Zehou and Liu Zaifu of the 1980s there is an aestheticizing and depoliticizing tendency, which attempts to distance cultural activity from political reality by valorizing culture over and above other aspects of social life. This tendency, akin to that of contemporary Western cultural theories and Western Marxist theories in particular, must be contemplated within the global perspective of contemporary cultural reconfigurations. By tracing these thinkers' appropriations of Marxist categories in reconstituting subjectivity, I hope to bring this experience to bear on present Western theory. I want to demonstrate, through this rather rudimentary and less-than-adequate description of the debates, that categories such as subjectivity, culture, and consciousness have a very complex relationship with politics and cannot be reduced or attributed to an all-encompassing "culturalism." These recent debates on culture must be examined with respect to China's historic emergence as a new social formation following the long process of political pluralism and economic decentralization over the last ten years. The suppression of this civil society in the wake of the 1989 Tiananmen crackdown indicates the vulnerability of the cultural domain and the interdependence of political, economic, and cultural spheres.

I

Hu Feng had always been at the forefront of controversy and debates in left-wing literary circles. His writings, as Theodore Huters puts it, "came increasingly to chronicle the internal dynamics of the leftist literary scene itself," and "there was to be no debate in literary circles after 1938 in which Hu Feng did not take an active role."[3] In the debates of 1936, Hu Feng insisted that May Fourth new literature, inspired by the realist literature of the West, was the only correct mode of expression in educating and mobilizing the masses. In the next debate regarding national forms, which took place in 1939 and 1940, Hu Feng stood up firmly again to defend the May Fourth legacy of realism. The proponents of national forms promulgated a populist and nationalist literature for the sake of war propaganda, whereas Hu Feng insisted on the absolute necessity of May Fourth realism to demystify the traditional Confucian ideology and enlighten the masses (*hua dazhong*), rather than popularize (*dazhong hua*). As both Li Zehou and Liu Zaifu acknowledge, the questions of national forms and of May Fourth realism are essentially an issue of enlightenment and cultural critique. The masses, composed mainly of illiterate peasants, need to be educated and enlightened by intellectuals armed with revolutionary consciousness.[4] But politics cannot be ruled out in considering this literary debate. The real agenda of the proponents of the national forms was to rally the peasants around Mao's revolutionary army through traditional and popular forms of entertainment. In his refusal to compromise the goal of transforming Chinese culture with the expediency of communist propaganda, Hu Feng revealed his nonconformist political stance.

The debate on subjectivity in 1945 was a continuation of these previous discussions. The earlier controversies over national forms and Western influences, enlightenment and popularization boiled down in the subjectivity debate to the philosophical question of subject-object relationships in literary representation. This debate took place largely in the noncommunist territory of Sichuan and Hong Kong, three years after Mao's *Yan'an Talks* codified Chinese Marxist literary criticism. Almost the whole leftist literary circle, both in the Communist-controlled area and outside it, became involved in the debate. The issue was not settled until several years after the establishment of the PRC. Not surprisingly, the settlement came in the form of political repression. When Mao sensed the real threat that Hu Feng's aberrant position might pose to his cultural and literary orthodoxy, he intervened by denouncing Hu Feng as the captain of an anticommunist, counterrevolutionary clique. After the ruthless political assaults against the "Hu Feng clique" that swept across the whole country, Hu Feng was arrested in 1955. Thereafter the issue of "subjectivity" only received negative characterizations in literary history, and Hu Feng and all his colleagues were either imprisoned or banished from cultural circles. The official rehabilitation of the "Hu Feng Event" would come as late as 1987.[5]

Hu Feng's theory of "subjective fighting spirit" was mainly concerned with the problems of form and representation in the realist mode. By concentrating on the relationship between subjective experience or class consciousness, on the one hand, and representation, on the other, his theory encompasses critical problems of ideology and hegemony, body and desire, domination and resistance. "Subjective fighting spirit" for Hu Feng serves as a powerful weapon to combat both "subjective formulaism"—gongshi zhuyi, which means dogmatic adherence to literary "formulas"—and the "objectivism" then in vogue. The Japanese invasion and the national crisis caused writers to have an emotional crisis. A subjectivism prevailed that did not lead to truthful representation of social reality but to formulaic, stereotyped literary work. It remained divorced from the concrete world and individual lived experience, and derived its inspiration only from abstract idealism and romantic sentimentalism. At the same time, the ethos of national defense and political imperative was so overwhelming that the writer "felt himself completely given over to the demands of the time and found solace in a state of selflessness."[6] Objectivism thus dominated literary work, preventing the writer from realizing the broad significance of the war in its daily events. "Objectivism" appears to be a coded term in Hu Feng's usage, like "naturalism" in Lukács's vocabulary, referring to the narrow-minded, partisan, and utilitarian views of art held by the commissars of the Red Army's propaganda teams.[7] Hu Feng finds that "subjective formulaism" and "objectivism" are but two sides of the same coin. He argues that only a "subjective fighting spirit" can lead to realism: "The unity or combination of subjective spirit and objective truth has produced a militant new literature. We call it realism."[8] There is an eminent Hegelian overtone in Hu Feng's emphasis on the unity of the subjective and the objective in the consciousness of the individual as a way to grasp the totality of meaning. The "subjective fighting spirit" hence bears a striking resemblance to Lukács's "class consciousness." Just as Lukács insists that proletarian class consciousness is the only way to ensure that the proletariat overcome alienation and reification through comprehending social reality as a historical totality, so Hu Feng regards "subjective fighting spirit" as the foremost means for understanding social reality and realizing the potential of the people, which he ascribes to realist literary representation. It is no coincidence that Lukács, too, takes the literary form of narrative as the most privileged means of achieving revolutionary class consciousness.[9]

Realism serves as a powerful ideological critique and counterhegemonic strategy. In his seminal essay of 1944, "Situating Ourselves in the Struggle for Democracy," Hu Feng emphasized the combative character of the creative process by which an authentic work of realism is produced. He calls this process the "interfusion of the subject with the object," a term synonymous with social life itself in his vocabulary.[10] The "interfusion" of the author's self with the object-Other by which subjectivity is constituted is made possible only through revolutionary practice, which includes "opposing fascism and feudalism, lashing out at all forms and measures of slavish ethics, unearthing the potential power of the people, and articulating the people's desire and struggle for liberation" (22–23). The key to the successful constitution of revolutionary subjectivity is the power to combat the "spiritual slavery" of the masses and to uncover their revolutionary potential: "Although their [the people's] desires or struggles of life embody the demand of history, they take on myriad and malleable forms as well as complicated and tortuous paths. Although spiritually they were given over to liberation, the scars of thousands of years of spiritual slavery are always inherent or expanding in their mind. If the writer does not want to drown in the ocean of such a sensuous existence when engaging himself deeply into it, he has to foster a critical power in combating the content of their life" (21). Hu Feng locates "spiritual slavery" at the internal, unconscious level of sensuous existence, as an ensemble of cultural constituencies of domination through consensus rather than coercion.[11] The "subjective fighting spirit" thus takes on a counterhegemonic character, in the sense that its task is to combat the deeply embedded and internalized cultural values installed over thousands of years by the holders of power. This is precisely the primal objective of the May

Fourth enlightenment project of cultural critique, to which the Li Zehous and Liu Zaifus of the 1980s were to return with a deep sense of belatedness and vengeance.

Yet this subjectivity of resistance stems from the sensuous and bodily experience of the masses. In the same 1944 article, Hu Feng characterizes the dialectics of the formation of revolutionary subjectivity as a "struggle of one bloody mark after one scourge," the passion and affliction incurred in the course of artistic creation being "not simply the reaction to pressures of the time or burden of life, but the internal process of conscious expansion, accompanied by the pain of the body" (22). Literary representation, or realism, is entwined with this bodily experience and made possible only through the "passionate expansion," spiritual "embrace," and "penetration" of this powerful subjective experience, will, and feeling into its object of representation. In a somewhat phenomenological or Hegelian synthesis of subject-object relations, Hu Feng describes the genesis of artistic creation as "stemming from the struggle with the real life of flesh and blood. The real life of flesh and blood, of course, means the sensuous object." "The struggle with the real life of flesh and blood is a process of embodying, and absorbing the object, as well as a process of overcoming, and critiquing the object. . . . The critique . . . must grasp the social significance of the object from its concrete, lively, and sensuous experience, and instill into this experience the author's positive, affirmative, or negative viewpoint" (18–19). Four years later, in a much longer and more elaborate treatise, "On the Path of Realism" (1948), Hu Feng made the most explicit connection between subjectivity, sensuous experience, and reality: "The Real as such is simply the glowing and painful historical content in which flows the people's burden, awakening, potentiality, and desire and longing for life; . . . the author must internalize this historical content and make it his own subjective demand."[12]

In Hu Feng's theory of "subjective fighting spirit," the dialectic of domination and resistance can be resolved through transforming people's desire and potential for liberation from the state "in-itself" into the state "for-itself."[13] Hu Feng links this transformation with the question of literary form. The so-called national forms of the vernacular tradition are the bearers of the old ideology, or "spiritual slavery." Therefore the transformation of people's mind and the uncovering of revolutionary potential can only be realized by adopting new forms of May Fourth realism: "When feudalist culture (popular culture) still exerted its power through the 'sluggishness of history,' the urban class emerged in China as a powerful material force, and this class led a great literary revolution."[14] While Hu Feng's outright denunciations of popular culture and "national forms" may seem elitist, what he underscores is the notion that form and ideological content are inseparable and that form is a true bearer of the author's subjectivity. He wrote: "Form is the rational expression of objective reality *unified with the author's subjectivity*" (Hu Feng's italics).[15]

Hu Feng's subjectivity in literary creation is essentially a social agency of revolution and resistance. It is a thoroughly historical and political concept, free from transcendental universals. He insists on a critique of traditional culture as the essential task of modern enlightenment, refusing to subjugate cultural critique to the political agenda of popularization and massification. In the 1980s, Li Zehou hailed Hu Feng as one of the foremost Chinese Marxist thinkers who insisted on the theme of enlightenment as an absolute task for Chinese social revolution and transformation.[16] However, in the same essay, Li Zehou, reflecting on the failure of Hu Feng's theory to exert any major impact on the cultural and literary scene, acknowledges the ultimate determination of political reality. In a comparison of Hu Feng's theory with Mao's *Yanan Talks*, Li Zehou concedes that Mao "talked about literature and the arts from a sociopolitical perspective, which is higher than the laws of literature and the arts per se" (85). Mao's view, therefore, triumphed and dominated the Chinese cultural domain for the next three or four decades. The triumph of the theme of "national salvation" over "enlightenment" since the late 1930s is, according to Li Zehou, a "great sacrifice" that China has undergone in its way to modernization. The fundamental task for the 1980s was to renew the discontinued May Fourth enlightenment project of cultural critique in order to reconstruct Chinese culture in the future. This, of course, is occasioned by that "higher" level of political reality in post-Mao China.

II

The culture debate of the 1980s was as much a strong reaction to and negation of Maoist cultural policy as a passionate desire for the reconstruction and revitalization of Chinese culture. The scale and style of the debate, mostly occurring from 1985 to

1989, were such that the expression "culture fever" most vividly conveys their emotional dimension. However, under the prevalent optimism and hope for China's reconstruction that characterizes the theoretical works of the Li Zehous and Liu Zaifus, the creative works of writers and artists, and also the student movement at Tiananmen Square in the spring of 1989, there has been a very complex political reality fraught with contradiction and confusion. The cataclysmic Cultural Revolution not only shattered the entire social formation, but it also scrambled those ideological codes fundamental to the operation of the Party and state. One of the serious consequences was a legitimation crisis in China's social life, especially in the realm of culture and ideas. In the 1980s, however, a crucial development in Chinese political reality was the emergence of a civil society in this realm. With the ending of the Cultural Revolution, institutional changes and development gradually and steadily took place in cultural domains. If the earlier debates, such as the so-called Emancipation of the Mind movement of 1979, still bore a strong official imprint, then the recent cultural reflections of Li Zehou, Liu Zaifu, Jin Guantao, Su Xiaokang, and so forth, have a much more independent character. The debate about culture was kindled by a host of intellectuals striving to obtain independence or at least a semiautonomous status from the Party's control.[17]

The incipient social formation of civil society is both a solution to and an outgrowth of the legitimation crisis in post-Mao China permeating every sector of social life.[18] A major part of this crisis concerns the identity of Chinese "cultural workers" or intellectuals, as a consequence of the separation of cultural activity from the Party's political agenda. Having been simultaneously captives as well as guardians of the Party cultural apparatus for decades, intellectuals now feel immensely liberated from its fetters and, as such, are disoriented as to their new social identity in an increasingly open, commodified and contradictory society, where power still remains in the hands of the Party. There is, then, an urgent need to establish a new identity, an independent and autonomous rationality for intellectuals themselves. This identity must be sought in the Lebenswelt, or cultural system, resistant to bureaucratic control and autonomous from the power structure of domination and subordination. Subjectivity thus becomes a key issue to the new rationality in post-Mao China. Put in the context of institutional changes occurring over the years, reflections on subjectivity can first of all be seen as a self-conscious effort to redefine the intellectual self as an autonomous, self-determining, self-regulating, and free subject.

The philosopher Li Zehou took up the burden of recovering the independent subject. Li Zehou (1930–) studied at Peking University's philosophy department. He first made himself known in the late 1950s by his polemical articles on aesthetics against Zhu Guangqian, then China's leading aesthetician. Li Zehou has worked at the Institute of Philosophy at the Chinese Academy of Social Sciences since the 1950s, where he is now a senior researcher. As perhaps China's most important Marxist thinker in the post-Mao decade, Li Zehou has authored in the last fifteen years a number of highly influential books and articles on philosophy, aesthetics, Chinese classical philosophy and intellectual history, art criticism, and literary criticism. Since the late 1970s, he has emerged as an eminent intellectual leader, whose status and influence in China is probably comparable to that of Sartre in France. Li's appeal to the younger generation—college students in particular—is enormous. Many consider him a "mentor of spiritual enlightenment."[19] He earned this honor by first of all breaking new ground in the study of Marxism, the foremost subject of learning in China. He went all the way back to Marx's intellectual origins, German idealist philosophy, to search for a solid theoretical ground for a Marxist theory of subjectivity. This ground is to be sought in Kant, rather than in Hegel, for Kant laid the ultimate foundation for modern "self-reflection" of subjectivity, Nature, and society. In 1979, Li Zehou's *Critique of the Critical Philosophy: A Study of Kant* (hereinafter *Critique*) was published. A second revised edition came out in 1984, with the appendix of his important 1981 lecture "The Philosophy of Kant and the Theses on the Construction of Subjectivity." *Critique*, Li Zehou's major philosophical work, is a critique of Kantian philosophy from the historical materialist point of view of "practice." The main goal is to spell out a Marxist practical philosophy, which would lay the philosophical foundation for a notion of subjectivity as the main conceptual framework with which to examine Chinese culture and history. The book is difficult. Li admits that "probably my book is really affected by the style of *The Critique of Pure Reason*, notorious for its repetitiveness, monotony, and obscurity."[20] But, surprisingly, the first edition of 30,000 copies sold out quickly, and the second edition of some 40,000 copies was as popular as the first edition on the market. The book indeed induced a "Kant Fever" of no small scale in China's intellectual circles. (In order to comprehend the magnitude of the interest in theory and philosophy and the impact of Li Zehou's work, one must take into account the intellectual hunger of the post–Cultural Revolution generations. The author of this article is a product of that particular intellectual environment.)

Li Zehou tries to establish connections between historical materialist categories and Kant's reflections on human rationality and consciousness. The emphasis on historical materialism, as he later acknowledged, was aimed at Maoist radical idealism and subjectivism, which violated the inevitable law of History.[21] Kant, according to Li Zehou, for the first time places the issue of subjectivity at the center of philosophical thought by examining three essential constituents of human nature: knowledge, will, and feeling, in his three critiques of epistemology, ethics, and aesthetics. The a priori representations or concepts of understanding in Kant's first critique, the *Critique of Pure Reason*, function as a mediation between human mind and sensory data. The transcendental synthesis forms the kernel of Kant's "Copernican Revolution," which reconciles the idealist insistence on speculative consciousness as the sole resource of understanding and the empiricist dependence on sense perception for knowing the world. Kant tries to establish a rationality that redefines man's troubled relationship with Nature, the relationships between reason and sensuousness, mind and matter. The way Kant solves this problem is, in short, to give man a superior legislative power over Nature. Kant's second critique, in the realm of ethics, concludes by postulating a moral Law as a pure form of universal legislation. Man's supremacy over Nature is then guaranteed with the inscription of rationality in ethics. The second critique, therefore, reinforces Kantian rationality in the domain of ethics and will, approximating more closely the relationship between the phenomenal and the noumenal worlds, and glancing over once again the unknowable and mysterious *ding-an-sich*.[22]

Kant's greatest contribution to the philosophy of subjectivity is, in Li Zehou's view, his reflections upon the complex formation of human rationality. These reflections lead to an "anthropological ontology of subjectivity," as opposed to the various "idealist ontologies based on experience [desire], language, or logic" (258). Hence, the Kantian "anthropological ontology of subjectivity" will serve as a point of departure for a Marxist theory of subjectivity. Drawing on historical materialist assumptions, Li Zehou separates subjectivity into a material and a psychological component. He calls the former the world of science and technology, the latter "cultural-psychological formation" (*wenhua xinli jiegou*) (94, 209, 258, 429). Li Zehou insists on the determination of the material component and the secondary character of the psychological, for he considers the distinction of base/superstructure central to historical materialism. But his original and creative move is to place great emphasis on the constitutive character of "practice," defined as material production and the practice of tool making, rather than "praxis," which is used most frequently in Western Marxist writings to include theoretical and cultural productions. Engels characterized man's tool making as the defining feature of man's humanity which separates man from Nature and constitutes his subjectivity and self-consciousness. But how exactly subjectivity is constituted through tool making and material practice is not explained. Kant, on the other hand, uncovered the complex process of the constitution of subjectivity. However, Kantian philosophy is known for its eclecticism, compromising materialism with idealism. In order to overcome Kant's idealist impasse and to restore Kantian rationality to its "true" material basis, the reinvention of a historical materialist concept of practice is necessary.

Significantly, Li Zehou's reinterpretation of historical materialism appears in a negative characterization and critique of Western Marxism. He mounts his severe criticism of the Frankfurt School and Western Marxism in the chapter on "Kantianism in Social Theories":

> [In] Western Marxism . . . some stress the priority of thought, and some consider cultural revolution and cultural critique more important preconditions for economic reform and political revolt. Some, like Marcuse, escaped to aesthetics, or, like Habermas, to education, as their shelter of "revolutionary" or reformist theories. Therefore they like to use the term "praxis" to include man's every activity, as opposed to historical materialism. (362)

In defense of historical materialism, Li Zehou insists that "practice must be defined in terms of the use and making of tools, in order to unify the philosophy of practice and historical materialism" (362). Western Marxism, as Li Zehou puts it, "severs [the Marxist] philosophy of practice from historical materialism," with serious practical consequences in political reality. Drawing on the Chinese lessons, he admonishes:

> The Chinese Great Leap Forward of 1958 was indeed a grand practice. But it violated the historical law and had only negative consequences. Though a philosophical presupposition may look far removed from reality, it in fact always has significant bearings on social reality. The Cultural Revolution was another grave instance. The momentous student movement of the 1960s in the West did not yield any accomplishments either. (363)

It is thus no coincidence that Sartre, Althusser, and other Western Marxists touted the Chinese Cultural Revolution as a great praxis because of the fundamental affinity of "impetuous, petit-bourgeois ethical utopianism" inherent in Maoist radical leftism as well as Western Marxism (362). Clearly, Li Zehou's critique of Western Marxism is based primarily on the historical experience of Chinese Marxism, Maoist subjective idealism, and voluntarism in particular. His emphasis on tool making and material practice is also reflected in post-Mao China's overriding concern with modernization projects.

Contrary to the Western Marxists' fascination with the young Marx's Hegelian conception of the overcoming of alienation as the ultimate end, Li Zehou sees a genuine historical materialist solution to the future of humankind in Marx's formulation on the humanization of Nature in the *Economic and Philosophical Manuscripts*. In this document Marx suggests that it is the material practice of man that constitutes a humanized Nature, thereby leading toward man's complete and fully developed subjectivity.[23] Li Zehou seizes on Marx's formulation and further elaborates on how practice finally humanizes Nature. Here he draws not only on Kant, but also on the cognitive philosophy of Piaget and on Wittgenstein's theory of language game as social practice.[24]

Key elements of Li Zehou's theory of subjectivity are the concepts of "internalization" (*neihua*) and "sedimentation" (*jidian*). The notion of *neihua* is derived primarily from Piaget. Although the term *jidian* has a far more influential currency, it is largely a variation of the concept of internalization based on Piagetian theory of cognitive and affective development (53–55, 76–79, 119, 425–426). Li Zehou gives Piaget a prominence unparalleled by any other twentieth-century Western thinker in his system of thought:

> I value Piaget highly, because he almost repeats in the micro-field of child psychology what Marx and Engels discovered in the macro-world of history in the nineteenth century: it is not a priori internal rationality, nor

> logic and linguistic grammar, but practical and operational activity [sic], that forms the basis and origin of a human being's intellect, reason, and thought.²⁵

> Piaget . . . notices the key determination of [physical] action and operation in the formation of logical thinking as well as the whole open structure of cognition. He thus provides the important materialist basis for a scientific description of cognitive origin and development.²⁶

It is interesting to note that Habermas, whose "reformist" position is rejected by Li Zehou, also draws heavily on Piaget in his rationalist social analysis, which is eminently Kantian. Habermas rules out the radical contingency of the world in his communicative reason and favors a vision of political order based on a somewhat idealized classical model of bourgeois stability. The appeal to Piaget is indeed very curious and symptomatic. It may represent a tendency within contemporary Marxism to resuscitate certain materialist positions from rationalist and scientist models without confronting the unnerving issue of identity and nonidentity in materialism that the Frankfurt School philosophers brought up in their rethinking of Freud's psychoanalysis.²⁷

As regards the other key concept, "sedimentation," an effort to integrate rationalist discourse with historical materialism is also evident. According to Li Zehou, the material practice of man gives birth to his ability for symbolic production—i.e., language—and, in the meantime, this material practice has internalized man's sensuous experience into a psychological deep structure at the level of unconscious. In other words, the material practice has made possible a very long, complex process by which man's sensuous experience, his intuitive faculty of conceptualizing, knowing and understanding—the categories of time and space in Kant's parlance—has sedimented, or congealed, into a rational, cultural-psychological formation (*wenhua xinli jiegou*).

Li Zehou's "cultural-psychological formation" roughly corresponds to the notion of "unconscious."²⁸ But there is a fundamental difference between his "cultural-psychological formation" and the Freudian "unconscious": Li Zehou's psychic formation is a thoroughly rational and cultural product, while in Freud and Lacan the "unconscious" signals an irreconcilable hiatus between cultural constraints and natural instincts and drives. In Lacan's view, only the mediation of the symbolic, that is, of language, can establish rational order to the chaotic and undifferentiated unconscious, but at a high price: the formation of subjectivity through the mediation of language involves essentially repressive processes of condensation and displacement, whereby the Real is absent and can never be fully grasped. Li Zehou, relying on Piagetian, biologically oriented cognitive and developmental psychology, denies the decisive role of linguistic mediation. For his sedimentation process, rationality always has its full presence of totality. The mediation of the symbolic does not appear critical in the constitution of subjectivity.[29] The notions of sedimentation and cultural-psychological formation are a development of the Marxian notion of the humanization of Nature. Although Kant described this process with great phenomenological rigor, supplemented by Hegel's historical and dialectic reflections, it is historical materialism that brings out the convergence of subjectivity, nature, and history.[30]

The seeds for the final convergence, or completion, of a thoroughly anthropomorphized and psychologized subjectivity, however, were sown by Kant in his third critique, on aesthetic judgment. Li Zehou regards *The Critique of Judgment* as the keystone of Kant's philosophical arch: "As a middle point between Rousseau and Hegel, the social Man is the true center, the true point of departure and basis of Kant's thinking."[31] *The Critique of Judgment* constitutes Kant's wholesale resolution of the contradictions, antitheses, and antinomies between the particular and the general, sensuousness and rationality, Nature and society, freedom of will and law of morality. In the two preceding critiques, Kant had wrestled with those antinomies strenuously without a successful resolution. Since Kant's goal is to prove that man is the final purpose of Nature in his complete freedom, only aesthetic judgment can fulfill this objective. Aesthetic judgment is the moment whereby man's meditation of his own purposiveness without utilitarian purpose is fully realized. This realization amounts to nothing less than the ultimate fulfillment of man's self-regulating, self-referential, autonomous, and free subjectivity, which coincides perfectly with the final purpose of Nature. The Kantian aesthetic not only guarantees the universality of man's freedom, but also establishes the condition for the complete humanization of Nature or naturalization of Man.

This condition, obviously, lies at the heart of Marx's *Economic and Philosophical Manuscripts*. Marx's fundamental propositions are that humanness comes into being through humanizing Nature, and that the exercise of human senses, powers, and capacities is an absolute end in itself. In his seminal lecture of 1982, "The Philosophy of Kant and the Theses on the Construction of Subjectivity," Li Zehou uses aesthetic subjectivity not only as the master trope to define his whole theoretical enterprise, but also to constitute the paramount paradigm for a creative transformation of Chinese culture.[32]

Having recovered the crucial link between Kantian aesthetic subjectivity and Marxian humanized Nature through hypostatizing the concept of practice, Li Zehou then proceeds to examine a wide range of cultural issues in China. He has demonstrated, through rigorous analyses of Chinese classic texts of philosophy, ethics, and art, that Chinese traditional thinking exhibits a highly sophisticated practical or pragmatic rationality. This rationality represents a sober, optimistic, pleasure-oriented, and aesthetic view of life. In contrast to the Judeo-Christian cultural assumptions of the fundamental conflicts of desire, sinfulness, and redemption, as well as to the hedonist legacy in the West, the pleasure-oriented Chinese classical philosophy takes delight in the *rational* life itself. This rationalist worldview interfuses sensuous experience with a naturalist rationality, embodied by the principle of "unity of man and heaven (*tian ren he yi*)." In this sense, classical Chinese thinking is also essentially aesthetic: it takes the unity of sensuous experience with the rational order of the universe as its ultimate goal, to be fulfilled in a profoundly psychological and internalized mode of life. The stress on harmony and equilibrium, however, has its negative aspects. It severely hinders the development of man's capacity to conquer Nature and to realize his own humanity. Furthermore, as history evolves toward the modern period, traditional rationality lapses into an ossified doctrine. Chinese society is gradually eroded by the presence of the powerful Western modern world. The West, with its advanced science and technology, and more open, dynamic social structures, outshines China's ancient civilization.

Li Zehou's account of traditional culture then moves to its modern phase, where the drama of intense conflicts between Chinese tradition and Western influence unfolds. His most famous formulation about China's painful struggle toward modernity is the "dual variation of enlightenment and national salvation."[33] Briefly, his point is that the May Fourth Movement as the turning point in modern China started from a cultural critique, an enlightenment movement aimed at transforming Chinese ways of life into modern forms already existing in the West. However, this cultural enlightenment ended up in a political struggle for national salvation, when the country was besieged by imperialist invasions and domestic corruption. The enlightenment themes of individuality, subjectivity, freedom, and democracy were then superseded by the militant imperatives of collective class struggle mandated by the predominant theme of national salvation. The success of communist revolution in China reinforced the militarism and hierarchy of the national salvational movements. The high cost is the absolute subordination of the individual to the state, reinstituting the tradition that May Fourth iconoclasts set off to challenge.[34]

The incomplete project of the Chinese Enlightenment ought to be fulfilled, as Li Zehou suggests, by reinscribing the May Fourth thesis of "Westernization" in a Marxist vein, which radically alters the ideological content of the original concept. This proposition of "Western substance–Chinese function" (xiti zhongyong) is very controversial. It is opposed to the early reformist formulation of "Chinese substance–Western function" (zhongti xiyong). The fundamental difference between the two theses, Li Zehou argues, lies in the different definition of "substance"—ti. Li Zehou's ti, on the one hand, has a broad meaning of social existence, including both material, scientific-technological society and cultural-psychological formation. On the other hand, the Chinese ti that the old reformists insisted on preserving is merely Confucian ideologies and its cultural systems. As Li Zehou himself admits, the definitions and arguments about ti and yong, including his own thesis, are extremely imprecise and can be very misleading. His point, however, is to argue that what constitutes ti in modern times is nothing less than a subjectivity fully spelled out, if not completely realized, by the development of the modern West and its thinkers. Li Zehou's powerful plea is to create a modern Chinese subjectivity by revitalizing the classic rationality of "unity of man and heaven" based on the Marxian humanization of Nature.[35] He harshly censures the "pessimism, antihistoricism and antipsychologism" in modern Western thought, including analytical philosophy, structuralism, phenomenology, psychoanalysis, and the Frankfurt School of Marxism (1986:296). Education and psychology, as Li Zehou predicts, will replace the language-centered humanistic pursuits of the twentieth century in the near future, in order to fully restore humanness to humankind.[36]

Having thus outlined the main features of Li Zehou's thoughts on subjectivity, I will make a few observations. I have said that historical materialism is central to Li Zehou's whole project of cultural reflection. His unflagging insistence on a Marxist, dialectical, and historical materialist method is evidenced first of all by his consistent cross-examination of social thought, on the one hand, and concrete political conditions and historical experience, on the other. Another distinct characteristic is a passionate yearning for cultural reconstruction and regeneration. His tireless endeavor to promote a constructive Marxism does not simply stem from his personal conviction. It reflects the general ethos of China in its postrevolutionary era, which is characterized by a combined optimism for the future, deep remorse for the agonizing past, and strong anxiety about the disoriented present. Its optimistic, constructive spirit makes Li Zehou's cultural Marxism an attractive alternative to the ultra-leftist legacy of Maoism.

However, as I have said, an essential dimension of the generally forward-looking ethos of the time is a determined desire of recovery and return: return to the May Fourth humanism and enlightenment, return to the Chinese cultural tradition, and return to classic Marxism. Despite his appropriations of certain modern conceptions from, say, Wittgenstein, Piaget, and Clifford Geertz, Li Zehou's reflections remain locked in the categories of classical German thought. The term "reflection" (*fansi*) has a preeminent currency in the recent Chinese debate about culture, and the metaphysical connotation of the term is unmistakably reminiscent of classical German philosophy. By "metaphysical" I mean the paradoxical lack of self-reflexiveness in what is designated by some as a "cultural self-reflection" movement. This movement by and large remains oblivious to the specific historical contexts in which the conceptual models on which it relies were generated. In Li Zehou's case, the metaphysical dimension lies primarily in his relentless privileging and absolutizing categories of the aesthetic. And despite his frequent appeal to hermeneutical paradigms for interpreting culture and tradition, his arguments about modern Chinese history do not seem to transcend the old historicist paradigms of tradition versus modernity, Westernization versus Chineseness, or Western impact and Chinese reaction.

Furthermore, I think his insistence on historical materialist categories is problematic. First of all, fundamental here is the distinction of man from Nature defined by mankind's ability for tool making. But this distinction has been discredited by recent anthropological discoveries.[37] Li Zehou, however, seems to prefer the old definition of Engels, rather than heeding new counterarguments. Li Zehou rejects Western Marxist notions of "praxis" because the term includes cultural and theoretical work as part of material production. This rejection is based on what he believes to be the absolute value of the base-superstructure distinction for historical materialism.[38] There is at least some confusion, if not outright misunderstanding, in his insistence on the base-superstructure distinction. In the late capitalist society of the West, the information revolution has broken down the barrier between tool-making material production and communicative and informational production, so that materialist practice (or praxis) has to take into account the destabilized and restructured relationship between economic infrastructure and cultural and ideological superstructure. The long history of political and ideological interference and overdetermination that have negatively affected China's socioeconomic growth perhaps induced Li Zehou to reinforce the classic Marxist tenet of the ultimate determination of the economic base and to dismiss the Western neo-Marxist revision of the original distinction of Marx and Engels. What is curious and paradoxical, though, is Li Zehou's own rationalist "culturalism," which tries to reintegrate the Kantian aesthetic subject, Marxian humanization of Nature, Piagetian developmental psychology, and Confucian *ren* (benevolence) and *tian ren he yi* (unity of human being and heaven) into a final grandiose resolution of the dilemma of China (explicitly) and the contemporary world (implicitly). At any rate, the historical materialist distinction of base-superstructure seems to be dissolved or undermined by Li Zehou's own predominantly culturalist resolutions.

Second, his theory refuses to grant any ontological immanence to language and insists on the absolute secondary character of symbolic production of language as a result of material tool making. His position contains insights indispensable to a critique of the idealist language philosophies prevalent in the West. But by denying the materiality of linguistic and symbolic production as the mediation of the subject–object relationship, a crucial link in cultural production is missing.[39] Third, the anthropomorphic impulse in his stress on the humanization of Nature as the ultimate end simply ignores what Freud has revealed: nature has persistently refused to be subsumed entirely by civilization. A notion of subjectivity has to take into account this profound nonidentity of nature, discovered by Freud but neglected by Marx. As Fredric Jameson puts it, following the insights of Adorno, subjectivity must be characterized as "violent eclipse of the subject itself" in the moment of the subject's encounter with "that baleful fearful thing henceforth called Nature."[40]

Serious questions thus arise in respect to Li Zehou's relentless privileging of rationality. A Kantianism relying exclusively on rationality cuts across the whole of Li Zehou's thought, from the Chinese classical tradition to the future of Chinese culture. His account of rationality precludes the problematic terrain of the unconscious as an antagonistic Other to the rationality of the Subject. Both Kant and Freud discovered that subjectivity is predicated on the split and conflict between desire and sensuous experience, on the one hand, and law and reason, on the other. A rationality unifying the two essentially incompatible domains cannot be achieved simply by a prelinguistic, tool-making material practice that causes the former to congeal into the latter. In fact, Li Zehou's laborious effort to wed Piagetian cognitive psychology with historical materialism betrays a serious internal contradiction. At least it does not seem to lead to a tenable alternative either to the poststructuralist aporia of linguistic predeterminations or the dominance of the Lacanian Symbolic.[41] The dismissal of important recent discoveries concerning language is a very serious flaw in Li Zehou's thinking. What he has belabored painstakingly to demonstrated in the constitution of subjectivity, namely, the process of internalization and sedimentation, errs at the critical moment where the antagonistic nature is embodied in symbolic and linguistic practices. Li Zehou himself, however, is acutely aware of this lack of engagement on the part of Chinese thinkers with the Western contemporary psychology of language, power, and history.[42]

Surprisingly, his historical materialist and dialectical method seems to be suspended when he comes to define subjectivity and the humanization of Nature in exclusively aesthetic terms. Aesthetic subjectivity from Kant to Marx has had strong political bearings. The Kantian universal subjectivity, however versatile and ambiguous, is, as Terry Eagleton puts it, a projection of the late-eighteenth-century German middle class, "in image if not in reality, as a truly universal subject." This bourgeois subject has posed "an ideological challenge to the ruling order" and served as a "counter-strategy to the political dominance."[43] Li Zehou is not unaware of this political and ideological specificity of the Kantian notion of aesthetic subjectivity. But when he applies it to the Chinese condition, he seems to bracket the historical particularity of the concept by valorizing the aesthetic over the political.

Despite Li Zehou's strong reservations about the Frankfurt School, he actually practices a kind of supradisciplinary critique analogous to cultural criticism. His is a mixture of psychology, intellectual history, aesthetic theory, art criticism, and anthropological analysis (his psychological interventions, however, remain the weakest). He tries hard to shy away from direct political involvement. He also maneuvers his often aberrant propositions adroitly to comply, at least superficially, with the official decrees of the so-called construction of material civilization and spiritual civilization. The Party has launched incessant campaigns to combat "Western bourgeois spiritual pollution" and lately "capitalist peaceful evolution" by promoting "socialist spiritual civilization," namely the official Marxist ideology. Very often the slogans of these ideological campaigns are thinly veiled charges against unorthodox thinking. Thus, Li Zehou's constructive way of promoting and protecting cultural criticism is altogether admirable, given the intense political pressure under which he has worked. But it also betrays a certain degree of naïveté and idealism, common to Li Zehou's colleagues and students. Although Li Zehou's writings, especially his numerous occasional essays, are charged with a strong sense of commitment, fundamental to his thinking is a sustained psychological meditation operating at high levels of abstraction. In Liu Zaifu's literary theory of subjectivity, the inherent contradiction between political engagement and a depoliticizing and aestheticizing tendency is most evident.

III

"On the Subjectivity of Literature," the manifesto of Liu Zaifu's project to overhaul Chinese Marxist literary criticism, appeared in 1985. At that time, literary criticism in China stood at an intersection, bewildered by the busy traffic of new styles and trends, yet unable to locate its own position in the cultural coordinates of the post-Mao era. The dominant Maoist criticism was much despised and maligned. By 1985 the terroristic "literary criticism" of the Cultural Revolution was no longer popular. But Chinese criticism under the straitjacket of Soviet "socialist realism" suffered a fatal deficiency: its embarrassing inability to engage literary texts as literature, rather than as political and ideological documents. Liu Zaifu's critical study of Lu Xun, published in 1979, shows his self-conscious attempts to do away with the sociological platitudes. Inspired by Li Zehou's thinking on subjectivity, Liu Zaifu wrote his landmark essay on literary subjectivity, which ignited an enormous controversy in critical circles. Under the leadership of the liberal-minded Party secretary general Hu Yaobang and premier Zhao Ziyang, who were then backed by China's paramount leader Deng Xiaoping, Liu Zaifu was appointed director of the Institute of Literary Research, Chinese Academy of Social Sciences, and the editor-in-chief of *Literary Review* (*Wenxue pinglun*), the leading scholarly journal in the field. With such powerful positions, Liu was expected to be a spokesman for the Party's literary policy. But his subjectivity essay contained unmistakable criticism of the Party's interference in the realms of literature and the arts, while advocating a humanist, independent literature of subjectivity as an alternative. The Party loyalists smelled a whiff of dissent and deviation in Liu's work. The majority of Chinese writers and critics, on the contrary, hailed the article for its bold challenge to the Party's literary orthodoxy.

Liu Zaifu acknowledges his indebtedness to Li Zehou on many occasions. However, the difference between their philosophical and methodological points of view is quite remarkable. If Li Zehou's propositions on subjectivity are resonant with Kantian presuppositions, Liu Zaifu's theoretical framework has a much stronger Hegelian bent. Liu Zaifu is most explicit about his objectives of dialectical recovery or return: a recovery of creative subjectivity and a recovery of literature itself ("return to the subject and return to the text," so to speak).[44]

The effacing of the individual subject in official Marxist criticism is politically and ideologically determined in ways that cannot be explained in purely literary and cultural terms. As a reaction to Maoist rejection of individualism, Liu Zaifu's aesthetic reconstruction of subjectivity must be seen as an ideological strategy. From an Althusserian view, the aesthetic is ideological. The aesthetic centers the human subject in an imaginary relationship to a pliable, purposive reality, thereby granting it a delightful sense of its immediate, sensuous, and concrete experience.[45] By equating the aesthetic with the essence of the human being and then defining literature as that which embodies the level at which the human being understands itself, Liu Zaifu's formulation endows the aesthetic with a power to transgress the border of the imaginary and the real, thus challenging the notion of aesthetic representation. As for his theory, the sociopolitical reality of China that denies the very existence of subjectivity is not real; the real is the aesthetic being, or the subject in Liu's terms, which has been totally alienated and must therefore be reconstructed by literature and the arts. Liu Zaifu writes: "The significance of the thesis that 'literature is the study of human beings' (wenxue shi renxue) is self-evident, for it restores the practical subjectivity of mankind and spiritual subjectivity in the realm of literature. The enrichment and development of subjectivity marks the progress of history. As a study of human beings, literature develops itself at a pace paralleling the level at which human beings understand themselves."[46] In Liu Zaifu's frame of reference, "the progress of history" as a Marxist teleology maintains the romanticist utopianism that characterized the young Marx in the *Economic and Philosophical Manuscript*. Liu Zaifu transfigures Marxian utopian vision into the contemporary world, asserting that

> mankind nowadays has already left the immediate daily process of labor behind them. Labor and aesthetic activity come to unite into one, and human nature has continued to enrich, develop and perfect itself. . . . Never has the self-consciousness of human subjectivity as a whole become so manifest. Human beings are longing to modernize themselves as they demand the modernization of society. (6:15)

Liu Zaifu thus elevates subjectivity to an ontological immanence never accorded to it by Chinese orthodox Marxist criticism.

Liu Zaifu emphasizes the emancipatory function of the aesthetic experience of reading. From a Schillerian-Marxian perspective of aesthetic education, he describes the aesthetic experience of reading as a process by which man realizes his free, complete, and self-conscious being. Reading is equated with the unfolding of humanity and human essence of freedom and self-consciousness (7:3). For many years in China, aesthetic judgment was subordinate to the cognitive function of literature and the arts in the interest of political propaganda and ideological indoctrination. Liu Zaifu's aesthetic experience of reading as a return to humanity challenges the Maoist politicization of reading in China's official Marxist criticism.

After "On the Subjectivity of Literature," Liu Zaifu published several books and numerous articles, further developing his view of literary subjectivity. In a book coauthored with the young critic Lin

Gang, *Tradition and the Chinese Person* (1988), the emergence of individualist values and subjectivity is identified as the hallmark of Chinese modernity.[47] His historically accurate description of modern Chinese intellectual development, however, gives way to an aestheticized account of universal subjectivity, following Li Zehou's theory, as the ultimate goal of China's project of enlightenment and modernity. Also, Liu Zaifu characterizes modern and contemporary Chinese literature as essentially a process of discovery of humanity and human subjectivity at different historical junctures. He views literature as part of a profound cultural reflection upon Chinese tradition. The centrality of this cultural reflection is the question of subjectivity.[48] Liu Zaifu's theory of subjectivity constitutes a cultural theory from which to study modern Chinese literature. In a 1986 interview, he proposes cultural studies as a new approach to modern Chinese literature as opposed to the dominant political and sociological approaches. He contends that the most important feature of modern Chinese culture is the transformation of cultural conceptions, characterized by recognition of the primacy of individuality and subjectivity.[49]

Liu Zaifu's theory of subjectivity rests on a humanist view of subjectivity embedded in Hegelian metaphysics. He criticizes theories of mechanical reflection by valorizing creative subjectivity and literature as an embodiment of the human essence of freedom. But Liu Zaifu is keenly aware of the immense incompatibility between historically different social conditions and abstract systems of thought. At the heart of his theoretical reflection is a distinction between politics and culture. As I indicated earlier, much of Li Zehou's and Liu Zaifu's works were intended to stake out or relocate an autonomous site for the displaced intellectuals themselves. In this respect, their philosophical and literary reflections can be seen as strategies of reterritorialization in post–Cultural Revolution China. Such a project necessarily entails a staggering degree of difficulty and of internal contradiction. What is remarkable about Liu Zaifu's thinking, then, is a high degree of self-consciousness of the internal contradictions in his own thoughts. This is another major difference between Liu Zaifu and Li Zehou. Li Zehou's more carefully wrought and rigorously argued statements within a systematic framework often conceal their enormous difficulties and logical inconsistencies.

Liu Zaifu's critical reflexivity has to do with his unique sensitivity to contradictions. In a recent essay, Liu admits that one of his main objectives is to counter the dominant philosophical discourse in China, namely, "the dualism of mind and matter." This "dualism" refers specifically to historical materialism. Liu Zaifu strives to combat this historical materialist viewpoint.[50] But, ironically, dualism also characterizes the thinking habits in which Liu Zaifu is deeply entrenched. He has wrestled with this dualistic mode throughout his work. His book of prose poems, *Tragic Songs of Quest*, is replete with contradictory romantic yearnings for love, harmony, universality, not to mention trepidations about strident reality.[51] In Liu Zaifu's theoretical musings, antagonistic dichotomies seem to permeate every corner of life: at the level of social life, there are binary oppositions such as politics/culture, tradition/modernity, Westernization/sinification; at a theoretical level, those of mind/matter, feeling/reason, conscious/unconscious, cut across his work. One of his famous formulations is the "dual composition of literary character." He insists that a literary character is not a homogeneous monad, but possesses complex, dual characteristics. In another celebrated essay, "On Desire," Liu Zaifu deals with conflicts between human instincts, desires, and social orders and norms.[52] A careful reading of Liu Zaifu's major statements on subjectivity indicates the hybrid resources of his theoretical arguments.[53] His main frame of reference, however, remains that of the traditional Marxist categories, and his classic literary examples come primarily from nineteenth-century European romanticist and realist works and the classical Chinese tradition.[54]

The prime impulse of Liu Zaifu's aestheticizing enterprise is a desire to counter the political dominance of theories of reflection and representation with an aesthetic theory of subjectivity. His generation of intellectuals has become disillusioned with politics, and they try to distance themselves from it as much as possible. Yet politics inevitably intervenes at the very moment of depoliticization. Liu Zaifu tries to transcend politics by proposing aesthetic universals, but his aesthetic enterprise betrays the political intent he is unwilling to acknowledge.

IV

The project of Li Zehou and Liu Zaifu to a large extent continues Hu Feng's thinking. The differences between Li Zehou, Liu Zaifu, and Hu Feng lie primarily in the politics underlying their respective theories. While all of them insist on the May Fourth tradition of enlightenment and realism, Li Zehou and Liu Zaifu wish to stake out a territory of culture in which the enlightenment theme and Western individualist and humanist values are privileged. Hu Feng, by contrast, was more determined to put May Fourth realism and the enlightenment theme to the test in the battleground of lived, sensuous experience. His account of the creative process in which a militant, oppositional subjectivity takes shape grasped the historical difficulty and complexity of the issue. He also made tireless efforts to relate the theoretical and epistemological question of subjectivity to the practical issues of realism and form. Owing to historical limitations, however, Hu Feng's solutions and conclusions were partial and incomplete. Although he paid close attention to the problem of mediation of form, his theory fell short of probing the complex discursive formation in representing subjectivity. How the subjective fighting spirit can actually combat the feudalist popular culture and "spiritual slavery" and create a new, alternative revolutionary discourse is never clear in Hu Feng's theory. Neither Li Zehou nor Liu Zaifu successfully engages the problems of form and language in his reflections on subjectivity. Nevertheless, the central concern of both Li Zehou and Liu Zaifu is a formal one: it has to do with the structure of perception or the form of aesthetic experience, be it psychological (in the case of Li Zehou) or ontological (in the case of Liu Zaifu). There is generally a lack of self-consciousness of the formal constraints in their own cultural reflections. Both exhibit a strong aesthetic inclination in their conceptualization of culture, literature, and subjectivity.

The aestheticizing impulses of Li Zehou, Liu Zaifu, and other contemporary Chinese cultural critics seem to parallel a tendency in contemporary Western cultural theories. The tendency in the West is to model social and historical analysis on aesthetic modes and increasingly to distance cultural and literary criticism from social engagement.[55] In the West, it is a question of the paradoxical phenomenon of escalating interpenetration and fragmentation of social life. It has bewildered Western intellectuals and made radical social engagement increasingly difficult. The recent debates about modernism and postmodernism have touched on fundamental issues in contemporary late capitalist society, but the debates themselves remain confined within the academy, with little impact upon social and political life. Such is also the fate of Marxist cultural theory in the West. The political and ideological consequences and effects of academic cultural criticism, then, have become the central preoccupation among many critics, especially those who identify with Marxist critical approaches.

In China, the recent bloodshed at Tiananmen Square serves as a powerful reminder of how politics—that is, political struggle at the level of power structures, institutions, and daily life—has been entangled with every single instance, be it cultural, economic, or otherwise. Compared to this Chinese experience, the debate in Western academia as to which side of culture is more important, the rhetorical or the pragmatic, often seems trivial and inconsequential. I do not mean to belittle the important insights generated by recent theoretical debates in the West. But I think the obsession with language and discourse in the realm of culture has obscured more grievous issues in the nonlinguistic social practices. Yet, Chinese cultural critics can benefit from Western cultural theories in terms of rethinking the questions of ideology and power, domination and resistance, science and ethics. What can be learned from Western cultural debates and theories is a new way of looking at the relationship between culture and politics. Cultural practices are inseparable from politics. Indeed, cultural events should be seen as political interventions. Just as the 1966–1976 "Cultural Revolution" is indisputably a political intervention of Mao's faction *within* the Party and the state, so too are the Chinese civil society and cultural debates of the 1980s forms of political intervention of the forces *outside* and against the Party and state.

Contemporary Western critical theories are shifting their attention increasingly to critiquing modern Western ideological myths such as "modernity," "democracy," and "humanism." These Western assumptions are also deeply embedded in the attempts of Chinese thinkers such as Li Zehou and Liu Zaifu to establish a new cultural myth for the future of China by disengaging Marxism from its political contexts and aestheticizing, or culturizing, Marxism. But the humanist, aesthetic "essence" of Marxism that the Chinese thinkers try to recover is precisely the kind of ideological myth that is now subject to rigorous demystification. We then must ask ourselves: what shall we do, both in China and elsewhere, to carry on the project of cultural critique in this postrevolutionary age?

Notes

For their helpful comments, I would like to thank Tom Beebee, Daniel Gross, Fredric Jameson, Li Lee, Anders Stephanson and Xiaobing Tang.

1. For references on the May Fourth Movement, see Benjamin Schwartz ed., *Reflections on the May Fourth Movement* (Cambridge, 1973), and Chow Tse-tsung, *The May Fourth Movement: Intellectual Revolution in Modern China* (Cambridge, 1960). A more substantive critical evaluation of the May Fourth Movement from the point of view of intellectual history is Lin Yü-sheng's *The Crisis of Chinese Consciousness* (Madison, 1979).

2. See Arif Dirlik, *The Origins of Chinese Communism* (Oxford, 1989).

3. Theodore Huters, "Hu Feng and the Critical Legacy of Lu Xun," in Leo Ou-fan Lee, ed., *Lu Xun and His Legacy* (Berkeley, 1985), p. 142.

4. Li Zehou, "Ji Zhongguo xiandai san ci xueshu lunzhan" (Notes on three scholarly debates in modern China), *Zhongguo xiandai sixiang shi lun* (Essays on modern Chinese intellectual history) (Beijing, 1987), pp. 76–87; Liu Zaifu, "Wusi wenxue qimeng jingshen de shiluo yu huigui" (The loss and recovery of the enlightenment spirit of May Fourth literature), in Lin Yü-sheng, Li Zehou, et al., *Wusi: duoyuan de fansi* (May Fourth: pluralist reflections) (Taipei, 1989), pp. 92–122.

5. In January 1945, Shu Wu's article "Lun zhuguan" (On subjectivity) and Hu Feng's "Zhishen zai wei minzhu de douzheng limian" (Situating ourselves in the struggle for democracy) were published in the literary journal *Xiwang* (Hope) in Chongqing, with Hu Feng as its editor. These two articles inaugurated the subjectivity debate. Hu Feng's "subjective idealist" views were then under fierce attack by orthodox communist critics. In a report at the 1949 Congress of Chinese Cultural Workers held in Beijing, China's foremost leftist writer, Mao Dun, summarized the debate as follows: "They [Hu Feng and his colleagues] on the one hand stressed the defects of the people caused by feudalist rule and took as their fundamental task to combat these defects of the people. On the other hand, they valorized uncritically the individualistic and spontaneous struggles of the people. They regarded these struggles as healthy primitive vitality and as the driving forces of history, rather than the conscious struggles of collectivism.... These are in fact petit-bourgeois fantasies departing from the real life of the people. The discussions of literary subjectivity must therefore boil down to the problem of the writer's ideological standpoint and attitude, as raised in Comrade Mao Zedong's *Yanan Talks*. If a writer cannot totally abandon his petit-bourgeois standpoint in order to become one with the people, then the issue of literary popularization cannot be fully resolved" (quoted from Wang Yao, *Zhongguo xin wenxue shi gao*—A history of Chinese new literature, Shanghai, 1982: 596–597). Ironically, by 1949, Mao Dun, once the main proponent of May Fourth realism, had given up creative writings and assumed the official

post of cultural minister in the new government, only to recant the "petit-bourgeois flaws" in that same realist tradition.

6. Hu Feng, "Wenyi gongzuo de fazhan ji qi nuli fangxiang" (The development of literary and artistic works and the objectives of their endeavors), in *Niliu de rizi* (The days of adverse tides) (Chongqing, 1944), p. 7.

7. Hu Feng, "Zhishen zai wei minzhu de douzheng limian" (Situating ourselves in the struggle for democracy), *Xiwang* (Hope); *Lun xianshi zhuyi de lu* (On the path of realism) (Shanghai, 1948).

8. Hu Feng, "Xianshi zhuyi zai jintian" (Realism today), in *Zai hunluan limian* (In the chaos) (Chongqing, 1943); "Realism Today," English trans. by Paul Pickowicz, in Kai-yu Hsu, ed., *Literature of the People's Republic of China* (Bloomington, 1980), p. 64.

9. For an explication of the connection between narration and class consciousness in Lukács's theory, see Fredric Jameson, *Marxism and Form* (Princeton, 1971), pp. 160–205. The relation of Hu Feng to Lukács and Western Marxism in general warrants a separate, more detailed treatment than what can only be schematically suggested in the present discussion.

10. Hu Feng (1944), p. 20.

11. Cf. Gramsci's notion of "hegemony." As a Chinese Marxist theorist, Hu Feng independently arrived at a similar concept of "hegemony" as a cultural form of domination. Under the similar circumstances of war and revolution, both Gramsci and Hu Feng insisted on revolutionary practice as the fundamental path leading toward mankind's liberation.

12. Hu Feng (1948), p. 41.

13. Ibid., p. 87.

14. Hu Feng, *Lun minzu xingshi wenti* (On the question of national forms) (Chongqing, 1940).

15. Ibid., p. 77.

16. Li Zehou (1987), p. 76.

17. Official and semiofficial institutions in literature and the arts, such as the Institute of Literature Research of the Chinese Academy of Social Sciences, headed by Liu Zaifu, and the Chinese Cultural Academy, led by Tang Yijie, became new centers of independent thinking. Periodicals such as the highbrow *Dushu* (Reading), *Beijing wenxue* (Beijing literature), and *Shanghai wenxue* (Shanghai literature), academic journals like *Wenxue yanjiu* (Literature Studies), *Shehui kexue zhanxian* (Front of social sciences), and *Dangdai zuojia pinglun* (Review of contemporary writers) carried articles that challenged fundamental precepts of the official cultural and literary policies. The 1989 Democracy Movement in China that ended in bloodshed was directly linked to the emergent civil society, where ideas of democratic society and individual freedom were spawned. Little of the literature hitherto about the 1989 Democracy Movement, however, has discussed the relation between the two from theoretical perspectives. A recent discussion in

English of Chinese Marxist thought between 1978 and 1986 is Bill Brugger and David Kelly, *Chinese Marxism in the Post-Mao Era* (Stanford, 1990). But as the authors of this book acknowledge, the debates in aesthetics and literary theory as well as the important developments since the mid-1980s, remain unexplored.

18. For a recent discussion of civil society in post-Mao China presented by one of its most prominent figures, namely, Su Shaozhi, the former director of the Institute of Marxism-Leninism–Mao Zedong Thought at the Chinese Academy of Social Sciences, see Su Shaozhi, Barry McCormick, and Xiao Xiao-ming, "The 1989 Democracy Movement: A Review of the Prospects for Civil Society in China," *The Chinese Intellectual*, vol. 6, no. 3 (1991), pp. 8–16. Also see Xiang-lin Xu, "Civil Society Versus Monopolistic Party-State: The Political Crisis in Post-Mao China," *Political Science and International Studies* (April 1991), pp. 23–28.

19. See Leo Ou-fan Lee, "The Crisis of Culture in China," *Chinese Intellectual*, vol. 7, no. 1 (1991), p. 25.

20. Li Zehou, *Pipan zhexue de pipan* (Critique of the critical philosophy), (Beijing, 1984), p. 438.

21. Ibid., p. 439.

22. Gilles Deleuze's *Kant's Critical Philosophy* (Minneapolis, 1984), pp. 49–50, pp. 68–75, offers a critique of Kant's anthropomorphic tendency that serves as a good reference for Li Zehou's characterizations of Kant. Also see P. van De Pitte, *Kant as Philosophical Anthropologist* (The Hague, 1971).

23. Karl Marx, *Economic and Philosophical Manuscripts*, Coletti, ed. (1975), pp. 351–354.

24. Li Zehou is mainly interested in Wittgenstein's later thoughts on the interrelation of language and social practice. But he is quick to point out the basic difference between Wittgenstein and Marx: the former errs precisely in prioritizing language over social practice. See Li Zehou 1984, p. 57; 1986, p. 284. Ironically, it is the same later Wittgenstein who reversed his early notion of the determination of prelinguistic reality over the structure of language and placed greater emphasis on language as a constituting force rather than a constituted entity. For Wittgenstein, language and social practice are inseparable, whereas Li Zehou insists on the absolute determination of material practice over language. See Susan Easton, *Humanist Marxism and Wittgensteinian Social Philosophy* (Manchester, 1983), pp. 83–96; and David Rubinstein, *Marx and Wittgenstein* (Boston, 1981).

25. Li Zehou, *Zou wo ziji de lu* (Take my own path) (Beijing, 1986), p. 286.

26. Li Zehou (1984), p. 55. For an introduction to Piaget's developmental psychology, see Jean Piaget, *Genetic Epistemology* (New York, 1970), preface; also see his *The Principles of Genetic Epistemology* (New York, 1972), especially chapter 3.

27. I owe the point on Habermas' connection to Piaget to Fredric Jame-

son, who has kindly offered his incisive comments on this. For a deconstructive critique of Habermas' Kantian rationalism and his appropriations of Piaget, see Michael Ryan, *Politics and Culture: Working Hypotheses for a Post-Revolutionary Society*, chapter 1, "Critical Theory and Social Policing" (Baltimore, 1989), pp. 27–45. Terry Eagleton also maintains that "it is possible to see in Habermas' ideal speech community an updated version of Kant's community of aesthetic judgement." See his *The Ideology of the Aesthetic* (Oxford, 1990), p. 405.

28. Li Zehou (1984), pp. 56–58, 160; 1986, pp. 281–296, 274–280.

29. Li Zehou (1986), pp. 84–290. For the Lacanian notion of the unconscious, see Lacan, *Ecrits* (New York, 1977), pp. 2–7, 192–199. It must be added that aside from his reliance on Piaget, Kant, and Marx, Li Zehou labors to relate the psychologically oriented Confucian notion of *ren* (benevolence—as it is inadequately rendered in English) to the process of sedimentation and the constitution of "cultural-psychological formation." Briefly, Li Zehou interprets *ren* as a psychological internalization of *li* (propriety, rite), the external rules governing human behavior, which are derived from the rules and regulations of the rituals of ancestor worship. Fundamental to these two pivotal concepts in Confucianism—*li* and *ren*—is the emphasis not so much on the corporeal pleasure of sexuality and its attendant tension and guilty conscience, epitomized by the Oedipal complex, as on kinship, parental love and care, related essentially to procreative, anthropological, and biological aspects of sexuality. As the development of the highly sophisticated and elaborate Confucian system of *li*—rites and rituals—indicates, sexuality has from very early on been rationalized and anthropomorphized in Chinese society. Apparently, this has certain significant bearings on Li Zehou's almost complete disregard of Freud in his discussion of sedimentation and cultural-psychological formation, since Freudianism always looks suspect in view of the Confucian rationalist psychology (reinterpreted, of course, through Li Zehou's appropriation of certain Western models).

30. Li Zehou (1984), pp. 114–118, 325–351, 413–421; also see Kant, *Critique of Judgement* (Oxford, 1973).

31. Li Zehou (1984), p. 367.

32. Ibid., pp. 422–437.

33. The term "dual variation"—*shuangchong bianzou*—is borrowed from the lexicon of musicology.

34. Li Zehou (1987), pp. 7–50. For an English explication of some of Li Zehou's concepts of modern Chinese intellectual history, see Li Zehou and Vera Schwarz, "Six Generations of Modern Chinese Intellectuals," *Chinese Studies in History* (Winter 1983–84); also see Vera Schwarz, *The Chinese Enlightenment* (Berkeley, 1986), which has a similar analysis of China's modern intellectual enlightenment.

35. Li Zehou 1987:311–341; 1986:219–222.

36. Li Zehou 1984:437; 1986:281–296.

37. Serge Moscovici, *Society Against Nature* (London, 1976), pp. 27–39.

38. Li Zehou (1984), pp. 199–203, 360–365.

39. For a critique of traditional historical materialism, see Stanley Aronowitz, *The Crisis in Historical Materialism* (Minneapolis, 1990), especially chapter 3.

40. Fredric Jameson, *Late Marxism: Adorno, or, The Persistence of the Dialectic* (London, 1990), p. 215.

41. Li Zehou admits that "Piaget's final resolution in his genetic epistemology lies in biology rather than in history" (1984:55). But he does not discuss further how to overcome this inherent gap between biological and genetic models of human psychology and the historical consciousness of mankind. On the one hand, some critics point out that ultimately it is language, or symbolic formation, that seems to provide a meeting ground for Piagetian biological, developmental models and Freudian psychoanalysis. See Hans Furth, *Knowledge As Desire: An Essay on Freud and Piaget* (New York, 1987). Fredric Jameson, on the other hand, tries to recover from Lacanian notions of subject formation a Utopian site for reinscribing subjectivity into history. See Jameson, "Imaginary and Symbolic in Lacan: Marxism, Psychoanalytic Criticism, and the Problem of the Subject," *Yale French Studies* (1977), pp. 338–395.

42. Li Zehou (1984), p. 444.

43. Terry Eagleton, (1990), pp. 19, 27.

44. Liu Zaifu, "Zouchu duduan lun: Zhongguo dangdai wenxue pinglun shiji mo de zhengzha" (Beyond totalitarianist theories: the fin-de-siècle struggles of contemporary Chinese literary criticism), keynote speech at the Conference on Politics and Ideology in Modern Chinese Literature, Duke University, Oct. 1990.

45. Louis Althusser, "Ideology and Ideological Apparatuses," in *Lenin and Philosophy* (London, 1971); Eagleton (1990), pp. 98–99.

46. Liu Zaifu, "Lun wenxue de zhuti xing" (On the subjectivity of literature), *Wenxue pinglun* (Literary review) (Beijing), 1985, 5:13, 6:14.

47. Liu Zaifu and Lin Gang, *Chuantong yu Zhongguo ren* (Tradition and the Chinese person) (Hong Kong, 1988), pp. 309–320.

48. Liu Zaifu, "Zhongguo xiandai wenxue shi shang dui ren de san ci faxian" (Three discoveries of humanity in modern Chinese literature), in *Liu Zaifu ji* (Selected essays of Liu Zaifu) (Harbin, 1988), pp. 225–237.

49. Ibid., 181–195.

50. Liu Zaifu, "Zailun wenxue zhuti xing" (Rethinking the subjectivity of literature), *The Chinese Intellectual*, vol. 6, no. 3 (1991), p. 73.

51. Liu Zaifu, *Xunzhao de beige* (Tragic songs of quest) (Hong Kong, 1988).

52. Liu Zaifu, *Xingge zuhe lun* (On dual composition of literary character) (Shanghai, 1986).

53. Liu Zaifu has borrowed freely from existentialism and phenomenology to reinforce his ontological characterization of the aesthetic subjectivity. He is receptive to archetypal criticism, structuralism, reception theory, and psychoanalysis, engaging Heidegger, Freud, Lacan, and Derrida. In a recent article, Liu Zaifu writes: "Subjectivity is not simply consciousness . . . it is being itself." "Subjectivity is first and foremost a question of ontology rather than epistemology." "The highest value is man's ontological value of being . . . no matter whether it exists in the temporal form of 'present' or in the 'past,' the highest value of his being is always already embodied in the meaning of being here and now." By treating literature as "the symbolic world of man's spiritual freedom," Liu Zaifu actually repeats Heideggerian aesthetic existentialist propositions on literature and the arts. Liu Zaifu also suggests that human subjectivity has a dimension of opposition and transcendence over cultural and symbolic constructs, which will enable him ultimately to overcome the aporia of the language prisonhouse and cultural constraints he himself has built. It will therefore remedy the Lacanian "extreme pessimism" (1991:72–85).

54. Chen Yangu and Jin Dacheng, "Liu Zaifu xianxiang pipan" (A critique of the Liu Zaifu phenomenon), *Wenxue pinglun* (Literary review) (Beijing), 1988, 2:20–23.

55. Some British critics have consistently criticized the aestheticizing tendency in Western postmodernist thinking. See Terry Eagleton, "Capitalism, Modernism and Postmodernism," in *Against the Grain* (London, 1986), and "From *Polis* to Postmodernism," in *The Ideology of the Aesthetic* (Oxford, 1990). Also see Steven Connor, *Postmodernist Culture* (Oxford, 1989).

LIU ZAIFU

The Subjectivity of Literature Revisited

A period of nationwide debate opened among literary critics with the publication of my "On the Subjectivity of Literature."[1] In the midst of this debate, Chen Yong, with his article "Methodological Problems in the Study of Literature and Art," published in the journal *Red Flag*, made a politically oriented critique of my position. (He considered my views to be "possibly detrimental to the fate of socialism in China and also to the fate of Marxism in China.") After this critique it was impossible to contain the debate to scholarly discussion. To avoid the inevitable political entanglements, I did not take up this issue directly with my opponents, nor did I develop my original thoughts on the subjectivity of literature. Today, the problem of subjectivity has become an important dispute in literary circles in China, and, as I find myself in a more free and peaceful scholarly environment, I take up the problem as an academic question once again.

The Category of Subjectivity and the Transcendent Character of Literature

Subjectivity (*zhuti xing*) is not the same as the Subject (*zhuti*).[2] The subject refers to the human being (*ren*) or to humanity (*renlei*). Customarily included would be the individual subject (geren zhuti), or the individual, the collective Subject (qunti zhuti), a grouping of ethnicity, nationality, class, party, or organization, and the Subject of humanity (renlei zhuti). From a sociological point of view, Subjectivity takes its basic forms in individual Subjectivity, collective Subjectivity, and human Subjectivity.

Subjectivity describes the essential force within the Subject that is exclusively human and is manifest in the Object world (duixiang shijie).[3] Subjectivity is not only a function of subjective consciousness, but the entire essence of the Subject's existence. Therefore, Subjectivity is the essential human force that is intrinsic to the Subject's existence and embodied in the Object world. Every scholar who discusses the Subject can give Subjectivity a new definition, but the discussion of the Subject and Subjectivity will be meaningless unless it is rooted in this basic meaning.

In English the term "subject" stands in opposition to the word "object." However, dictionaries edited by Chinese scholars frequently translate the English word "subjective" as subjectivism (zhuguan zhuyi) or subjective agency (zhuguan nengdong xing), making it impossible to separate notions of Subjectivity and subjective agency. As the notion of Subjectivity has been widely used in a variety of contexts, it has become vulgarized and confused with subjectivism, subjective agency, and the spirit of subjective engagement (zhuguan zhandou jingshen). Actually these notions are not at all alike. My opponents invariably get confused on this very basic point.

Subjectivity has extension and intension. Its intension refers to inner determination or the features that structure the human Subject's existence as such; its extension covers the Subjectivity manifest in the relationship between subject and object within the Subject, i.e., Objectifiability (duixiang xing), which is a function of the Subject's existence. In the actual world, Subjectivity and Objectifiability are separated, but humans are capable of unifying the Subject with the Object as well as Subjectivity with Objectifiability by fully developing Subjectivity. One of the central issues of Subjectivity in literature is precisely the problem of unifying Subjectivity with Objectifiability.

Modern philosophy is different from classical philosophy in that the former no longer treats the world as substance (as in ontological naturalism [ziran benti lun]). It has abandoned this notion of substance and has come to see the world as a meaningful Object. Marx considers the world a product of "humanized nature" and an Object of human action. The world is thus an Objectification (*duixiang hua*) of essential human forces, a world of meaning. Without understanding Objectification there is no way of understanding Subjectivity.

Objectifiability is the demand and capacity on the part of the Subject to create its own Object world. This demand and capacity are proof that human beings are Objectifying organisms, striving to realize themselves by creating an Object world and turning the external world into evidence of their own Subjective powers. That is to say, the Subject's material needs and creativity can only be realized by acting upon a specific Object. Even an illusion requires the imagining of fictive Objects. Apart from the creation of Objects, Subjectivity cannot be established and cannot be realized. Subjectivity relates itself to the world through Objectification, thus establishing and realizing itself. Praxis, therefore, is the essential activity of humans. The Objective world is Subjectified (*zhuti hua*), or turned into an Objectification of essential human force. This Subjectification strips the world of any "thing-in-itself" quality, and therefore, the world exists only as an Object for the Subject. Objectification inevitably leads the Subject to incorporate the Object and regard it as part of itself, eliminating the distinction between the Object and the Subject. This kind of integration is the ultimate orientation and fullest realization of Objectification. Literature and art represent attempts to approach this ultimate state.

Insofar as its extension is concerned, Subjectivity constitutes the link between Subject and Object, and thus brings together humanity and the world. In terms of intension, Subjectivity is the fundamental attribute that differentiates humans from the world and primarily from animals.

There are several different levels of human nature and also multiple layers within human Subjectivity. Such levels of Subjectivity could be delineated indefinitely, but an elementary division can be made into three general levels according to a complex matrix of consciousness, linguistic signs, and cultural symbols. The lower level of Subjectivity is what has not yet been shaped into consciousness, symbols, and culture. The middle level of Subjectivity is what has already been shaped by consciousness, symbols, and culture. The higher level of Subjectivity is what has become capable of resisting the forces of consciousness, symbols, and culture.

Questioning Cosmology Based on a Mind/Matter Binary Opposition: The Cultural Background of This Theory of Subjectivity

My original thoughts on the problem of Subjectivity have arisen from their own historical circumstances. My motivation for pursuing this topic is fourfold. One goal is to demonstrate once again the formula "human = human" (humans are human). The second is a renunciation of the negative component within the traditional cultural system. The third is to question the opposition of mind and matter in a dualistic cosmology prevalent among Chinese scholars. My final motivation is to challenge the currently popular framework of literary theory in China.

Reassertion of the Human = Human Formula In the wake of the Cultural Revolution in China, harsh realities led many intellectuals to the painful conclusion that humans were not allowed to act as humans. A person did not belong to him- or herself, but rather to other people (in particular to official leaders), to organizations, and to external political movements. The original goals of socialism—to eradicate exploitation and classes—were an attempt to emancipate people, but the expounders of socialism in China took socialist nationalization to the extreme by extending it to every possible realm. Consequently, they demanded that not only the economy be completely nationalized, but also that spiritual culture, including the minds of individuals, be nationalized. The slogan "comprehensive dictatorship" was thought to be an advancement of Marxism-Leninism, precisely because it extended proletarian dictatorship from the province of politics and economics to include the spiritual culture of society as well as individual minds. It put human free will under the control and dictatorship of the state machinery and eventually extinguished free will altogether, reducing human essence to mere "screws" in the machinery of the revolution. In this way humans were reduced to things—turned into tools—and they lost the human attribute of Subjectivity.

When spiritual culture and individual minds are nationalized to become the object of a dictatorship, the human function is limited to "obeying" and the Subject is deprived of the right and ability to "choose." It can be argued that the Subject's loss of the right and ability to choose is a significant spiritual phenomenon in twentieth-century China. To take an example from the parlance of daily life, men, mocking themselves, will say that they live in a time of "feminine" dominance over "masculine" decline in which men suffer from spiritual impotence. They are acknowledging the loss of the capacity of the free will to choose and the loss of the kind of personality that possesses this capacity. In the 1950s Chen Yan'ge wrote a poem called "Nandan" that mocked the contemporary Chinese man for having become a "female impersonator," a hapless political actor who has lost the strength to have independent spirit and personality. This loss is what can be referred to as losing human Subjectivity.

There have been countless essays and speeches rationalizing the argument that it is right for a person to become a screw in the revolution. Campaigns to study models such as Lei Feng amount to exhortations, in this spirit, to imitate an appropriate model screw. These writings testify to a formula whereby a human is equivalent to a thing (specifically a screw). As a counterpoint to this formula, I have promoted another formula, "human = human." Pioneers of New Culture Movement exerted themselves to prove this formula during the May Fourth period. They felt that in China a human could not be human, but was the equivalent of a slave or even a cow or horse. They denounced the dehumanizing society and culture, but after a half a century the "human = human" formula has failed to take hold. Instead, the "human ≠ human" (humans are not human) formula has persevered in yet a different form. Thus, a few intellectuals have felt compelled to take up the vital equation and explain it once again, regardless of the risk such an endeavor might incur.

Renunciation of the Deformity of Collectivity in Traditional Cultural Values Around the time of the May Fourth Movement, the New Culture pioneers discovered that in world cultures there were two poles of difference, the Eastern and the Western cultures, and arrived at a crude understanding of the basic difference between these two poles. Western culture, originating in ancient Greece, glorifies individuality, but Chinese culture celebrates collectivity. Two tendencies intrinsic to human nature are revealed in this difference between two cultural traditions. Humanity is forever caught between the pull toward individuality and the pull toward collectivity. Having accentuated individual freedom, Western culture, on the one hand, experiences problems resulting from an exaggerated expansion of individual freedom. The pressure of responsibility on the individual and the deformity of the individual, as a consequence, promote a philosophy that yearns to "escape from freedom." On the other hand, because Chinese culture has emphasized mutual dependence in the collectivity, the individual personality is eliminated. On this cultural foundation emphasis on collective formations such as class and organizations has been carried to such an extreme in China during the second half of this century that individuality can be seen only as corroding highly centralized political authority and not as contributing to the vitality of society. Intellectuals in the 1980s argued, from all different disciplinary perspectives, for the individuality of humans in an attempt to give individuality renewed philosophical justification. It was at this time that the philosophy of Subjectivity regained attention. The emergence of the topic of Subjectivity is the result of this kind of cultural self-reflection.

Questioning the Mind/Matter Opposition in a Dualistic Cosmology The dominant philosophical doctrine in China in the last forty years presents a cosmology in which mind and matter are opposed to each other in a dualistic scheme. In this cosmology there is only one basic philosophic problem, the relationship between mind and matter, consciousness and existence, and spirit and material. In this scheme, matter (or existence or material) is primary and mind (or consciousness or spirit) secondary. The primary determines the secondary. Understanding and describing the world in terms of this order is materialism, but to reverse the order is idealism. The first thing any college student encounters in philosophy class is Ai Siqi's systematization of this philosophical cosmology.

Ai Siqi expounds upon dialectical materialism and historical materialism. Dialectical materialism is actually an improvement over mechanical materialism, because it makes clear that a dualistic philosophy does not mean that consciousness is a mechanical replica of existence, but allows consciousness to act positively upon the world (of existence or material). This capacity is known as human agency and also as subjective agency. However, in the final analysis, dialectical materialism is a naturalist ontology. It still has nature—the objective material world—as its center and does not regard the human (individual human existence) or humanity (total human existence) as of ontological significance. It is incapable of recognizing the human being's position in the world. What, then, is the human ontological position? Chinese intellectuals, who have long lived and breathed in a fixed philosophical model, must confront this problem.

Late in the Cultural Revolution, in order to resolve this problem, the philosopher Li Zehou challenged the cosmology described above with a new interpretation of Kant. His 1978 book *Critique of the Critical Philosophy*[4] and his 1984 article "An Outline of the Kantian Philosophy of Subjectivity" brought up once again the philosophical issue of Subjectivity. The central aim in these works is to replace nature-centered ontology with human-centered ontology and to reassert the primacy of Subjectivity in cosmology. Before Marxist philosophy attained hegemony, Kant had been the most influential philosopher in China. From the beginning of this century, when Kang Youwei, Yan Fu, and Liang Qichao introduced Kant to China, his influence was felt deeply in scholarly circles. But after dialectical materialism took over, Kant's philosophy of Subjectivity was categorically rejected as idealism. His notion of Subjectivity, likewise, was not accepted or understood among Chinese philosophers. Li Zehou was not opposed to Marxist philosophy. On the contrary, he sought to reconcile the concept of Subjectivity with the Marxist philosophy of praxis. Kant's notion of Subjectivity opened a new realm in philosophy, from which Hegel's Absolute Rational Spirit was, in fact, a regression. The emphasis in early Marx on human praxis was a return to Kant's philosophy of Subjectivity. The Subject is a category of praxis in the first place, for it is only in praxis that human Subjectivity can express itself fully.

My conception of Subjectivity transcends, first, the popular framework of traditional philosophy. It also transcends the confines of epistemology. I regard the Subject as something of ontological value on the basis of a distinction between Subjectivity and subjective agency. This distinction has four aspects:

(1) Subjective agency is human cognition of and human reaction to the world. It refers to the activity of human consciousness in the process of reflecting existence. This existence is a function of consciousness and belongs to the category of consciousness.

The Subject is not merely consciousness, however, and Subjectivity is not merely a function of consciousness. Rather, the Subject itself belongs to the category of existence and is not merely an active relationship between consciousness and existence. Subjectivity is first a problem of human beings' ontological existence and then a problem of epistemology. It is only when humans, aware of their human existence, confront the world that they express Subjectivity.

Therefore, subjective agency is merely a function of consciousness and of the human faculty. The Subject, by contrast, is not only a function, but a structure, the very structure of human existence. The structure of the human Subject contains a conscious part, a subconscious part, and an unconscious biological part. Subjectivity is thus not merely the function of consciousness, but refers to the structural characteristics of human existence, the essential force of such existence as well as its Objectification.

(2) Through an ontological grasp of the Subject, we can first determine that the Subject is human ontological existence. The philosophy of Subjectivity can then approach the Subject from the perspective of a theory of value. The theory of value is a system that bases itself on the Subject's needs and its evaluation of the objective world. Philosophical and literary theories prevalent in China have included elements of a theory of value (such as stance or worldview) but they have been socially determined, utilitarian theories of value rather than value from an ontological perspective. These popular theories of value have consistently ignored that behind the various kinds of value is an essential human value, the highest and final value of all. At the same time, they forget that the meaning of existence is existence itself, existence for the sake of existence. The goal of human activity is human. Being human is the highest human aim. Whether humanity exists in the temporal form of the present or the future, the most important measure of value is always relevant to the present existence, that is, to the survival and development of present existence. From this point of view, we can ascertain that the Subject as ontological existence is fundamentally a valuative existence. It is the source of value and also the basic measure of value.

In literature, we can thus ascertain that the Subject, engaged in the practice of literary creation and reception, is itself a kind of valuative existence and a source of value. The essence of literature is as a mode of valuation deriving from the realization of the Subject's needs, rather than as a product of mimesis or merely the product of consciousness' active reflection of the world. In this view we are not limiting literary activities to the confines of epistemology but including them in the domain of value.

(3) Breaking out of the limitations entailed by examining the subject within the boundaries of epistemology does not imply an

elimination of philosophical epistemology itself. I am only opposed to understanding epistemology as passive reflectionism, which treats consciousness as only a reflecting of some substance instead of something that actively creates value. Consciousness actually participates in the essence of life. The activity of consciousness also has ontological significance. Human consciousness not only reflects the objective world but also creates the objective world. (Although traditional philosophy never departed from the tabula rasa, modern psychology has shown that human cognition is a product of the a priori structure of the human mind and its assimilation and equilibration of the Object world.)

(4) Given that the Subject is an ontological category, neither dependent on nature nor a mere vehicle of consciousness, the relationship between humanity and the world is not just a matter of thinking and existence nor a matter of determining and being determined, and Nature cannot be understood in terms of a simple relationship of reflecting and being reflected. In sum, the relationship cannot be characterized as an asymmetric one between primary and secondary nature, but must be seen as an equal relationship between forms of existence. Humans must be seen as total beings that exchange information and energy on an equal footing with the world.

From this philosophical viewpoint, human creative activity, including the creative activity of literature and art, is no longer the activity of consciousness, subsumed within a fixed and unequal relationship between a primary and a secondary nature, but an activity involving an entire existence. This process is the Objectification of the Subject. It is a process in which a total human life finds in the objective world a counterpart in which a homological relationship expresses itself. This view is a fundamental transformation of the common understanding of the nature of literary and artistic practice.

Literary and artistic practices cease to be a cognitive activity (or the function of consciousness), which also includes nonimaginative thinking, but instead are an activity of the total being. They are a comprehensive activity of human life and existence (including conscious, subconscious, and biological sensory systems). The product of literature and art is first a product of thinking, then a product of the entire being, including mental and biological operations (such as smell, hearing, and taste), and finally a product of different levels of consciousness and unconsciousness. In sum, it results from the creativity of the total human existence. Literary and artistic activity is therefore the most comprehensive of human activities. Compared with literary activity, other human activities appear incomplete: material production is largely the function of bodily organs; science and technology are largely an activity of human cognition. Compared with these activities, the practice of literature and art is a total activity, involving all human faculties. It combines the body and the mind, the entire personality, and envelops the material and spiritual realms.

The early works of Marx touched on the problem of the Subject in noting the praxis of labor. When Marx was writing, however, psychology was not yet developed, and Freud's theory had not yet appeared. Marx had no way of incorporating psychology's achievements, and, regrettably, he never investigated the structure of the Subject and certainly not its deep structure. Each human being has a particular existence, and the difference between one human being and another is primarily the difference in the structure of each Subject, particularly their deep structures. The infinite possibilities of humanity stem precisely from the infinite difference every individual's structure exhibits. Only by taking the human as a system of being (and not just as a receptacle for human consciousness) and studying its structure of Subjectivity can we deepen our understanding of humanity.

The challenge posed by the philosophy of Subjectivity to the mind/matter dualism has further changed the basic concern of contemporary philosophy. For traditional philosophers of the classics and the vulgarized philosophy packaged by Ai Siqi, the problem is to set up the dualism and decide which pole is to be primary and which secondary. For the philosophy of Subjectivity the basic problems lie in the meaning of existence and humanity's fate.

A Challenge to the Current Framework of Chinese Literary Theory

The established framework for contemporary Chinese literary theory found in textbooks of literary theory of the past few decades was brought over from the Soviet Union. A cosmology of mind/matter dualism is the philosophical basis upon which a systematic theory of relationships between literature and life, literature and politics, worldview and the method of creation, and form and content was developed. The literary theory thus established finds the nature of literature to be a reflection of social life. Writers and artists are primarily considered instruments engaged in this kind of reflecting. They can hope to have an impact on society, but only by reflecting society. The process of reflection is ultimately seen as a function of consciousness. This theoretical framework completely fails to accommodate the essential freedom and transcendence of literary practice and disregards writers' Subjectivity as well as readers'. It emphasizes cognition but ignores emotion, will, and linguistic forms. As a result, it has given rise to a serious malady: a literary production that is generally formulaic and dogmatic.

The introduction of the philosophy of Subjectivity into literary theory has amounted to a fundamental revolution in the theoretical framework. In an article entitled "The Stylistic Revolution in Literary Criticism in the Eighties," I pointed out:

> Previously, literary criticism and literary theory were built upon traditional philosophy, which was basically structured on a material-centered ontology and reflectionism and, as a result, ignored the Subjectivity of existence itself. In this philosophical system, humans were kept outside of the world, and a reflectionist epistemology took the place of a theory of value. The Subject became an instrument by which the principles and laws of nature and society were understood. It was barred from participating in the creation of the world. Based on this philosophical premise, literary theory naturally negated the Subject and simplistically reduced literature to a mere reflection of reality. Literary theory inevitably became subsumed in vulgar sociology and turned away from exploring the rich possibilities of the spiritual world of the Subject. By contrast, the philosophy of Subjectivity affirms that essential existence is material and spiritual human praxis. It understands the human world as the Object of meaning that the Subject creates and interprets. Literary theory based on the notion of Subjectivity views literature not as a replica of reality nor as mere reflection, but as a mode of free existence. Literature interprets the world in its own way, and it reveals the aesthetic dimension of the human world.[5]

In this way the philosophy of Subjectivity and the study of Subjectivity in literature and art begin to break down the old system of literary theory.

Allowing the philosophy of Subjectivity to serve as the basis of a new literary theory does not eliminate epistemology; rather, it opposes reducing everything to epistemology. The philosophy of Subjectivity is, in fact, a convergence of ontology, epistemology, and a theory of value. Ontology studies the meaning of existence (existence in the sense of the activity of interpretative creation of the world and not existence of the so-called pure object). From an ontological point of view, literary practice can be seen as a mode of existence of the free spirit. This mode of existence goes beyond the "style" of the author and covers the interaction and exchange between the creative Subject, the receptive Subject, and the "text." Ontology also recognizes that the world of meaning revealed in literature is a unique one. This world is not a real existence, but a transcendence. It is an aesthetic intuition of the meaning of existence through its own linguistic system.

From an epistemological perspective, literary practice encompasses cognitive activity on the part of the writer and the reader. The epistemology of Subjectivity further asserts that knowledge is not just a reproduction of objective existence, but a kind of spiritual, creative practice. It therefore also implies Subjectivity. That is to say, the Object world does not reveal itself in a direct, unmediated fashion, but is a world of meaning that has to be discovered, grasped, and interpreted by the Subject. It is a humanized world of meaning embodying the force of Subjectivity. On this point research in modern linguistics and semiotics has shown that interpretations of the world are always dependent on and conditioned by a given linguistic and semiotic system. The system has been conventionalized in human linguistic and semiotic practice through a historical process, so that meaning in the world is presented through the mediation of a symbolic system. The world thus presented cannot be purely objective but always carries the imprint of the linguistic Subject, the imprint of Subjectivity.

As long as literary activity is irrefutably a cognitive activity, literary works will include cognitive content. However, in specific works of literature, this cognitive content is specific only in the surface structure of the text, while the deep structure is a symbolic system that goes beyond a conscious system of symbols. Aesthetic literary activity, although it is also a cognitive activity, has a more basic significance in its creation of values through Objectification. The literary world does include the writer's cognitive understanding of the objective world, but on a deeper, more fundamental level it symbolizes the free spirit of humans, rooted in the Subject's formation of value based on its own need. In literary creation, human Subjective values are more important than scientific values; the principle of purpose or meaning in life ranks higher than the scientific principle of "objective laws." In this unique spiritual space (where literary and aesthetic activity are related to value), cognitive knowledge and reflection are only strategies for survival in life. This view of strategies, too, apprehends the meaning of literature from the point of view of a theory of value.

In the philosophy of Subjectivity, ontology, epistemology, and a theory of value are brought together. Epistemology and a theory of value are an extension of ontology; they help us to grasp the meaning of existence in both its objective and subjective aspects. Clearly, to simplify Subjectivity by relegating it to subjective agency or the spirit of subjective engagement is mistaken. Compared with subjectivism or subjective agency, the concept of Subjectivity is much richer.

Notes

This chapter was translated by Mary Scoggin. Translator's note: The following is a slightly rearranged version of the first part of a much longer work in which the author reviews his overall position upon coming to the United States in 1989. This work originally appeared in the Spring 1990 issue of *Zhishi fenzi* (The Chinese Intellectual).

1. "Wenyi xue fangfalun wenti," collected in *Guanyu wenxue zhuti xing de lunzheng* (*Debates on the subjectivity of literature*) (Nanchang: Jiangxi Association of Literature and Arts, 1987), pp. 82–106.

2. Translator's note: I capitalize the initial letters of certain key terms to indicate that the author uses them in a specialized sense. "Subject," "Subjectivity," "Object," and "Objectification" are used as a kind of philosophical code to distinguish these technical terms in his argument from similar terms in more common parlance.

3. Translator's note: "Object" will be capitalized only when it translates the Chinese term *duixiang*, which in this argument is coordinated with "Subject." It may help the reader to know that in some contexts the word *duixiang* may be translated as "target," "objective," or "goal." The noncapitalized terms "object" and "objective" cover *keguan* and *keti*; the noncapitalized terms "subjective" and "subjectivity" cover *zhuguan* (*xing*) and *zhuguan nengdong* (*xing*).

4. Li Zehou, *Pipan zhexue de pipan* (Critique of the critical philosophy), Beijing: Renmin chuban she, 1984.

5. "Lun bashi niandai wenxue piping de wenti geming" (On the stylistic revolution in literary criticism of the 1980s), *Wenxue pinglun* (*Literary Review*) Beijing, 1989, no. 1, pp. 5–22.

CHING-KIU STEPHEN CHAN

Split China, or, The Historical/Imaginary: Toward a Theory of the Displacement of Subjectivity at the Margins of Modernity

The following analysis deals in very general terms with the ideological attempt of modern Chinese intellectuals at representing or displacing (as one could argue) the "real" (China?). It, in turn, is an attempt to marginalize those modern Subjects of Culture whose most radical obsession was to claim China (the Real) in the utopian moment of what might be called "cultural modernity" that followed a certain climactic stage of "cultural revolution," however that is conceived or realized.[1]

Hence, as I engage myself in this act of reading the splitting of our Identity, there seems to be a double movement in the trajectory of ideological displacement. At stake here is the formation of selfhood as the subject of modernity—the process in which recognition must be realized as misrecognition. Such a split formation of subjectivity is now engaged as an effect of history symptomatic of two desires. First, there is no doubt the utopian desire in a certain May Fourth Imaginary to reread in its cultural formation (and negation) a series of narrative steps and positions accounting for its selfsame misformation (read: identity).

But, ironically, there is also a persistent ideological obsession to rewrite for us—for ourselves as historical subjects of that constituting Culture in our own past (including the stage marked by May Fourth) and for our own future (China! China?)—a subjectivity remixed and relocated with a collectivity that would entail in toto the becoming (the rebirth and rearticulation) of China as modernity.

It seems that the trajectory for this reading of a certain misrecognition of the subject of modernity is capable of opening up a narrative space in which to work through a series of speculative historical and psychoanalytical reorientations in our situatedness as Chinese. For me, the opportunity for such an alternative critical imagination on Chinese modernity is prompted anachronistically by the critique of the Subject disguised as the profane discourse of a certain form of modern Chinese split identity in Mo Yan's *The Thirteen Steps* (1989).[2]

A mesmerizing novel published immediately before the horror of the June Fourth violation and seizure of the Real ("China"), *The Thirteen Steps* is a counternarrative of History itself caught at the threshold of modernity. Given the hegemony of the dominant cultural imaginary to which Chinese today are subjected, it also represents a series of fatal (because historically necessary) narrative steps in the modern Chinese subject's move toward either ultimate freedom or utopian disintegration. With Mo Yan's move we are displaced through a complex of lost desires articulated in a set of lost steps and positions. For in our respective situatedness as Chinese, we are carried away differently by this text, only to be reconstituted involuntarily as lost subjects—I shall argue—remembering History in the distrust of reality and realism, of culture and culturalism; blaming or saving the Imaginary of *China* in the rupture of acts of displacement and misidentification; and articulating subjectivity in positions leading nowhere to a secure order or hierarchy.

China: The Formation of an Identity

> Every belief in the value and worth of life is based on impure thinking and is only possible because the individual's sympathy for life in general, and for the suffering of mankind, is very weakly developed.
> —Friedrich Nietzsche, *Human, All Too Human*

To speak of identity in modern China often entails speaking of China as identity, collectively, in national and cultural terms.

If the identification of "nationality" or "nationness" is to come with the experience and articulation of what Benedict Anderson describes as an *imagined* political community, then the striving for modernity in China must indeed be rooted in the imagination of a Chinese identity that is inherently somewhat limited.[3] Politically speaking, this imagined identity implies that even sovereignty—which constitutes the necessary realization of an autonomous national-cultural identity—would need to be exclusively constituted, i.e., with the selfsameness of that identity delimited through acts of exclusion. For it seems inevitable that sovereignty can be established when the authenticity of a people is secured and its autonomy ascertained through legitimately defined boundaries that enclose and situate, thus identifying, the collective subject within the delimited terrain by severing it from any "identities" outside.

But the Chinese imagination of national identity cannot be taken as the natural or logical result of the discontent of a "nation." Ernst Gellner argues that "nationalism is not the awakening of nation to self-consciousness: it invents nations where they do not exist."[4] Remembering in this context Liang Qichao's call for xinmin (the making new of a people) and the emphasis he put on the social, political, and ethical role of fiction—of the construction of an alternative cultural imaginary—one begins to see how Gellner's claim could actually be applied with some effectiveness to the case of modern China. For, insofar as the making new of the people is concerned, very likely indeed, "it is nationalism which engenders nations, and not the other way round."[5] Thus conceived, the nation has come to be recognized as much more than a mere component of modernity, for if the constitution of nationness as a condition of belonging or a repository of shared values of identity does involve a certain "pre-existent ethnic core," as is often suggested,[6] it also calls for a new and changing relationship of modernity to tradition—that which it is not or is excluded from. This view might well explain why Liang Qichao never did limit himself to describing collectivity as such but always evoked it with the projection of a Chinese modernity—of the modern identity of China—through a call for newness in, or a renovation of, the people.

Identity as Formation

With the coming of the May Fourth Movement, the newness called for by earlier reformists began to take on both material form and a cultural-revolutionary dynamic. A generation of "new youth" in the 1920s witnessed the emergence of a variety of new formations of literature, culture, and thought in an iconoclastic antitraditional current that came to be known as the New Culture Movement. Radical intellectuals led by such prominent figures as Lu Xun, Hu Shi, and Chen Duxiu tried desperately to grasp modernity in their sometimes divergent attempts to turn tradition on its head.[7] In search of a modern identity, May Fourth culture engaged itself in a dynamic that would permit anything but the continual enclosure in the historical prisonhouse of tradition signified unambiguously by, among other things, the old doctrine of Confucius, the old language of *wenyan*, and the old ways of Ah Q.

Hence, if we are to understand Chinese nationality—collectively defined through national identity—as the *formation* of a specific kind of consciousness, then it becomes necessary to speak of identity as the longing for *form*, for the articulation of what Foucault calls a "discursive formation."[8] And given that collectivity in national terms must be taken as a culturally constitutive process, the convergence of two initially separate processes of identity formation—state formation (of modern China as a sovereign power) and the formation of national subjectivity (of the Chinese as a new people)—could now be regarded as the aim and achievement of nationalism as a modern movement.[9]

Indeed, consciousness, as Bakhtin suggests, is always in search of a form, a language.[10] To regard collectivity as a discursive formation of nationality and to see that collective identity through the "imagined community" that is the modern nation—the nation as the political body of modernity itself—is not to downplay in any way the significance of "identity" as a critical and cultural construct, but to stress the urgency of realizing that, as a process—or, in the case of May Fourth, as a movement—it participates necessarily in history and is nothing if not constitutive of historical formation itself.

The category of nation (and its identity, nationness) has been put under rigorous historicization in certain cultural studies (see especially Bhabha). Both discursive formation in general and narrative practice in particular have crucial roles to play in the constitution of identity amid the supposedly dangerous randomization of difference. Hence Geoffrey Bennington's pointed remark: "The idea of the nation is inseparable from its narration: that narration attempts, interminably, to constitute identity against difference, inside against outside, and in the assumed superiority of inside over outside."[11]

The discursive formation of identity, in other words, is necessarily a historical process through and through. It is in this new light that I want to investigate the implications of identity formation and to call for historicizing the search for the cultural modernity of China as the Imaginary, a project that has been engaged since the May Fourth Movement.

The Historical

To historicize is to reintroduce the category of history into the critical practice and cultural imaginary we engage ourselves in—then, now, and in the days ahead. Perhaps I do need to clarify from the beginning that what we do here, if it indeed can be read as a certain longing for a form of historical criticism, is grounded on the recognition, as insisted upon by the new historicist, that "not only the poet but also the critic exists in history; that the texts of each are inscriptions of history."[12] Such an insistence must in turn be recognized within a nontraditional orientation to history, one that stresses both "the historicity of texts and the textuality of history." The latter suggests that "we can have no access to a full and authentic past, a lived material existence, *unmediated* by the surviving textual traces of the society in question—traces whose survival we cannot assume to be merely contingent."[13] The point is that not only would it be unhistorical not to understand the past (by undertaking a critique of tradition, for instance) within the very experience of history itself (thus marking the traces of tradition's break with the present), it is also inconceivable not to admit that the discourse through which both understanding and experience take place is the primary constituent of social formation accessible to the historical subject.

This situation cannot be expressed adequately by a dichotomy like text/context or manifest discourse/deep structure, for historicity cannot be defined as text or context, discourse or structure. No one would feel comfortable arguing that history is exclusively text, that historicity and textuality are but one. Yet there need also be a strong resistance, from the vantage point of critical cultural practice, to seeing history as just context/logic/totality, thus inscribing an irreconcilable gap between the historical and the subjective, and erasing the space for engagement from the realm of the Imaginary.

Indeed one of the most important contributions of contemporary theories to cultural study is an overhaul of the entire critical paradigm we live by today through a reorientation of its relationship to history. Whereas not everyone may want to agree that history, as a story of power relations and struggles, is contradictory, heterogeneous, and fragmented, I think most would accept that it is, in effect, "a tale of many voices and forms of power, of power exercised by the weak and the marginal as well as by the dominant and strong."[14] If we do find it impossible to work on any form of dialectical criticism with the binarism of text/context, a third term may be useful akin to Louis Hjelmslev's category of "purport" or "usage," which describes the oft-neglected level of analysis beyond the usual planes of investigation organized by the dichotomy form/substance.[15]

This category opens our critical endeavor to a dimension in which textual/contextual operations are realized as concrete discursive practice. History, that undeniable logic of necessity informing the events of reality, becomes accessible to us precisely through the practice of the subject in discourse as in consciousness. Jameson recognizes this unerasable logic of History as the absent cause, a logic that is derivative neither of causality nor of essentialism, but one that is informed and governed by an overdetermined sense of constraint and necessity.[16]

In Jameson's view,

> What is dialectical about this more complete structural model is that the third term is always absent, or, more properly, that it is nonrepresentable. Neither the manifest text, nor the deep structure tangibly mapped out before us in a spatial hieroglyph, the third variable in such analysis is necessarily history itself, as an absent cause.[17]

If the cause (that is, History) is constantly absent, there arises a rather different and difficult understanding of "necessity" or "causality." The presence as absence of History (even if it remains a form of totality) brings us to see both "necessity" and "causality" in terms of constraint and overdetermination. For, as Jameson goes on to argue, "the deviation of the individual text from some deeper narrative structure directs our attention to those determinate changes in the historical situation which block a full manifestation or replication of the structure on the discursive level."[18]

Much can be learned from this pointed observation. Specifically, in his attempt to uncover the deeper logic of events blocked by History in the Third World context, Jameson offers to trace the unrepresentable absent cause in the textual narrative and logic of the "national allegory." But critics have argued to the contrary that, for instance, Latin American writers such as García Marquez underscore rather than accentuate the discourse of nationalism and national identity. Claiming that the so-called national allegory is itself complicitous in a legitimizing ideology, Jean Franco reveals alternatively that "it is the private that has become central, a private that cannot be allegorized or transposed into an exemplary national story because there is disjunction between the public and the private."[19] Instead of seeing the fictional text as an allegorization of the national-historical situation, as Jameson has also tried to demonstrate with his reading of Lu Xun's "The True Story of Ah Q" in "Third-World Literature in the Era of Multinational Capitalism,"[20] Franco suggests that the novelistic discourse has been working as "the terrain of conflicting discourses" under the specific historical situation of Third-World society where modernity is being fought for on both cultural and political fronts. Hence, it seems that the national-historical is in effect bound by a provisional and, we may say (after Bakhtin), "dialogical" framework of disconcerting discourses of modernity. In this framework the "nation" disappears, disintegrating and thus reconfirming increasingly its failure in providing coherent, allegorizing, and totalizing systems of meaning, value, and belief. Such a failure inevitably casts a great shadow of doubt over most conventional readings of history—especially those that resist the desire for textuality in history or repress the call for historicity in the text of culture.

Crucial to this infinitely more profane conception of history is the necessary factor/effect of constraint—and subsequently, as we shall see, of displacement—brought about (or so Freud teaches) through the process of repression. But even within the Marxist critical perspective, attempts have been made to understand as dominant ideology nationalism itself, whose coercive social function is clearly to consolidate meaning and belief in the values indispensable to the effective identification of a social group.[21] Conceived in this light and working under specific historical conditions of constraint, the national consciousness would inevitably be organized by a conviction in the value of the "nation" and its "people"; and the ethicopolitical subject that is articulated through this practical consciousness must necessarily be informed by an imaginary whose practice (Hjemslev's "usage") is now socially, ideologically, as well as discursively overdetermined.

The Imaginary

Recognized as a lived world of signification, Cornelius Castoriadis' original notion of the *social imaginary* is thus formulated:

> All that exists within the social-historical is indissociably entwined with the symbolic without, however, being exhausted in it. Real acts, individual or collective—work, consumption, war, love, childbirth—and the innumerable material products without which no society could live for an instant, are not (not always and not directly) symbols. But their existence is impossible outside a symbolic network.
>
> There still remains an essential, and for our purpose, decisive dimension to every symbol and symbolism, at whatever level they are situated. We are referring to the imaginary dimension. . . . The imaginary is distinct from the real, whether it claims the latter's position as its own (a lie) or simply claims its own position (a story).
>
> The profound and obscure nature of the relation between the symbolic and the imaginary becomes apparent as soon as one reflects on the following: the imaginary must utilize the symbolic, not only in order to be "expressed"—this is self-evident—but in order to "exist," to move beyond a merely virtual state of existence. . . . In the last analysis we are dealing with the elementary and irreducible capacity for evolving images.[22]

The identifying moment for the subject of Chinese modernity may indeed be situated in such a cultural imaginary, one that helps sustain the dominant hegemony by reproducing the collective unity of subjectivities engaged on even the most individual level in the lived process of imagination, of evoking images with which the everyday realities of that society (from whatever position it is approached) have already lost touch.

For individuals in a society to participate in and live by this imaginary, it must reconstitute, in the realm of the ideological, for the society its identity with an ensemble of foundational symbols. This ensemble of discourses (called the symbolic) then serves to evoke the selfsame integrity of cultural identity that is registered as a space for desire (called the imaginary).

John Thompson has described this space for the dominant as the central imaginary significations that tie a society together and define what, for the subjects of that given cultural reality, is "real."[23] Reference might well be made to a broader conception of the critical

Marxist notion of "mode of production,"[24] but the implication here for the formation of identity seems to be more relevant to the present purpose. As Thompson argues, symbolic representations of the unity of self and the integrity of culture under sociohistorical constraints result in the projection of "an 'imaginary community' by means of which 'real' distinctions are portrayed as 'natural,' [and] the historical is effaced in the atemporality of essence."[25]

In short, the imaginary as presented by Castoriadis captures an ensemble of social significations through which a people's past is endowed with meaning and their present is organized with a collective and coherent identity distinguishable from the chaos of alternatives and of differences and from the otherness of any nonidentities. Though the signifying practice of the social imaginary necessarily organizes the confines of a coherent and autonomous system of meanings—be it the self-enclosed space of a national-, cultural-, or self-identity—it can never be effectively contained by the logical structure of more conventional forms of totality, and thus it retains the potentially productive and infinitely transgressive power of ideological practice.

There should be little doubt that ideology is "determined by its function, which is the organization of values";[26] I would only insist that its ethicopolitical function be articulated with its semiotic, signifying practice.[27] And yet it is only in ideology that human individuals are constituted and their consciousness articulated as subjectivity. If it is ideology that "interpellates individuals as subjects," if ideology does indeed represent "the imaginary relationship of the individuals to their real conditions of existence," as Althusser claims in his influential essay on "Ideology and Ideological State Apparatuses,"[28] the implication is twofold: (1) individuals do exist as "subjects," primarily as the subject of consciousness in discourse; and (2) individuals are subjected (to discourse, to interpellation), i.e., held to and dependent on the imaginary formation of an identity; in short, individuals are subjected to an imaginary identity, an identity-as-imaginary.

Such a strategy helps summon individuals into existence by subjecting them to the fiction that they are freely creating their own world. But subjects are ideologically defined to the extent that this fiction is constituted by real lived experiences and concrete social relationships. Ideology produces subjects who "work by themselves."

The imaginary does not arise out of "pure" imagination; its experience is, or constitutes, what we ordinarily recognize as "reality."

In other words, the semiotic function of ideology allows it to constitute and institute the "self" as an imaginary subject of freedom in order that it remain subject to the dominance of cultural imaginary and social hegemony. As self-consciousness is being formed through its imaginary subjection, subjectivity is articulated; hence, any practice of ideology addresses itself to individuals in such a way that, despite (and as a result of) their particular response to its interpellation, they become "freely" subjected to it. (Contrary to some arguments, domination by and subjection to the Imaginary is never a matter of real force, but one of real freedom.) And when the self-contained, selfsame identity of the individual is thus represented as part of a split consciousness—the subject now recognized and experienced as a split self—this imaginary self must, in Kearney's words, "die in order for the symbolic other to live."[29]

It is Althusser who, in his very biased rereading of Marx, Freud, and Lacan in their various attempts to articulate history with consciousness and subjectivity, insists that consciousness and subjectivity must first be displaced as the center of history and disarticulated as the origin of discourse.[30] With this critical insight the basic argument can be reformulated. For it is now possible to see that social hegemony works not only as the "effect of history" on the individual subject (or as the effect of what Lacan calls misrecognition, *méconnaissance*, of self), but the Imaginary order is actually functional at the root of humanism in general (read: universal self-orientation) and narcissism in particular (read: obsessive self-representation).

The Mirror Stage

From the standpoint of a feminist psychoanalyst, narcissism can be described as the "love of an image of self, and so [it] demands the image of self which is achieved for the first time in the mirror stage."[31] For Lacan, the mirror stage marks a turning point in the formation of "self" through its *imago*, the mirror image. In his 1949 essay "The Mirror Stage as Formative of the Function of the I as Revealed in Psychoanalytic Experience," Lacan regards the function of the mirror stage as "a particular case of the function of the *imago*, which is to establish a relation between the organism and its reality."[32] In Kearney's exposition: "The human infant first experiences itself as a 'fragmented' body [*corps morcels*]. To overcome its feeling of dispersion it constructs an *imago* of unified selfhood. . . . The imaginary double takes the form of a mirror reflection . . . a reified simulation of what the mother desires the child to become."[33] The mirror stage, therefore, marks the beginning of those crucial moments when "self" is being constituted through a process of signification in the repository of the imaginary, at both the individual and collective levels.

In narcissism, an individual recognizes herself through a mirror image, thus identifying herself and forming selfhood as such. With this formation of the *imago*, the identification of self is mediated by and accomplished through an objective other coming from the external world without which the conception of any sense of collectivity becomes simply impossible. This process must be situated in a historical moment akin to the crucial instant of maturity when the child's newly formed image is simultaneously alienated from itself as an imaginary object and represented for itself as the reality of its own sense of being.[34] It is in the displaced site of subjectivity and the relocated form of consciousness that the "I" is evoked before the mirror. In other words, with the Lacanian mirror stage it is possible to define ego for the first time as a reflexive self capable of narcissistic alienation, for it constitutes subjectivity out of a maturing self in such a way that "the infant who has not yet mastered the upright posture . . . will, *upon seeing herself in the mirror*, 'jubilantly assume' the upright position."[35]

It could be argued that China—and the collective subjectivity under formation as Chinese—has attempted to assume such an upright position in its struggle for identity during and since the May Fourth Movement. If that movement may indeed be said to have marked the mirror stage in the formation of this new and properly modern collectivity, then the crucial point for critical imagination is not so much to locate programmatically this identity as either essence or telos as to grasp and realize its formation in the process of struggle itself.

From our own historical stance, it is certainly important to recognize that through their intellectual endeavor and discursive practice the May Fourth generation has attempted to struggle for identity, for a collective subjectivity that could articulate modernity in China.

Thus, the identity-as-imaginary should after all be captured more in terms of a process of struggle and formation—of a fragmented body's struggling to be formed—than as the fixity of a moment when it is fully registered and permanently contained within the order of the Symbolic. Understood in this specific sense as an identification, the mirror stage that is formative of the modern I of China can be recognized as the drama of revolution that captures what Lacan calls "the transformation that takes place in the subject when he assumes an image."[36]

Hence, like desire, identity is powerful only as form; often taken to be self-consciousness in formation, it occupies neither the position of essence nor that of telos but works most effectively through discourse. Indeed, it is what Williams would call a "practical consciousness."[37] As such, however, the Imaginary under formation can never be comfortably contained (even in China) by the Symbolic, though it is always with the register of discourse that cultural practices have come to articulate and interpellate individuals as cultural subjects on both the private and collective levels.[38]

It is my contention that, with the May Fourth project of modernity, subject positions were beginning to be moved in the cultural-intellectual scene of China. It might even be argued that the movement has worked only insofar as the imaginary function of subject-in-action was put to work. Speaking for a textual politics in modern China, I would like to suggest that what moved were the discourses of identity (discourses that struggled to identify) rather than the closed worlds of individuals (ren) opening up a collective consciousness to the recognition of some pre-Symbolic essence or telos of "identity." Like desire, identity works as a kind of practical consciousness. As consciousness itself, identity never *is*, it *becomes*.

Returning to the mirror stage, we may now be able to see this stage as the phase when the object of desire (the other) is set in dialectical relationship to the self. As when desire is gratified (consuming the other), the subject will no longer be active and consciousness will no longer be practical when its terrain is clearly fixed and the identity of its "self" permanently established.

To our comfort, however, the reality of the mirror stage ensures that this cancellation of the *imago* with the dialectic will not come. With the *imago* fully identified, the upright position of the self can be "jubilantly assumed" and the formation of identity simultaneously secured. Thus, returning to the moment of the May Fourth Move-

Split China, or, The Historical/Imaginary

ment, from which we shall begin our rethinking of the project of modernity in China, it is not the viability of the solutions or options opened by its cultural politics that must be subjected to critique; the very representation of the problem of identity is at stake.

Temporal Dialectic

From this critical position, although Althusser believes that only by abolishing the imaginary order can we begin to construct a theory of the "real object" of history and that the structure of history is still fairly reliable, Lacan's conception of splitting—of identifying other in self and self as *imago*—suggests a more unsettling strategy.[39]

Lacan suggests that the jubilation, the enthusiasm that the subject experiences at the narcissistic moment of identifying with the mirror image is informed by a "temporal dialectic" by which the ego "appears *already* to be what she will *only later* become."[40] In other words, both the present and the future are realized as representations of "pasts." Accordingly, the history of identity formation will have to be understood in the light of such representations. And modernity itself, once rearticulated as a function of the temporal dialectic, becomes instantly dereified.

As a transition from tradition to modernity, the moment of May Fourth can be seen as the mirror stage in the constitution of modern Chinese identity, of China as modernity. Thus conceived, the mirror stage would be a turning point, before which there is no subject of modern China, no possibility for the cultural formation of modern identity, and no historical provision for the constitution of subjectivity. It can be further suggested that the history of modern subjectivity in China is marked by the mirror stage of identification in which the subject's relation to "self" is mediated through a totalizing image—an other, the non-Chinese—that has come from outside,[41] from the world outside China, dominated by another construct of hegemonic identity, the West.

In such a view, the totalization of *imago* in the representation of a collective Chinese identity evident in Lu Xun's depiction of Ah Q would mark the point of origin of the formation of both selfhood and nationhood in modern China.

Elsewhere I have discussed how the formation of the modern Chinese subject is mediated by a collective discourse of desire.[42] It was precisely under the "shadow" of this reified discourse—in this historical realization of lack—that the May Fourth intellectuals articulated their desire for "modernity." It might well be claimed that, before Lu Xun's textual construct of Ah Q, China had produced no subject of modernity or that before Yu Dafu's discursive projection of his narcissistic ego, his other "I," the self of modern China had had no identity (not to mention crisis).

As manifested in the literary works of Lu Xun, Yu Dafu, Ding Ling, Mao Dun, Lao She, and many other new writers of their time, the formation of (the crisis of) modern Chinese identity takes place also in the historical subject's love-hate relationship with both the private and the collective images of the self. Founded on the belief in a projected image of self, May Fourth may be recognized as this moment of constitution of the modern identity. It grew out of and has since grown into a historical moment of despair/desire, of alienation and revolution and counterrevolution—a moment when the Imaginary always articulates collectivity and subjectivity in the same gesture. This moment and this gesture would then be grasped and registered in the Symbolic as the matrix of cultural discourses known today by the name of May Fourth.

As the founding moment of the Imaginary register, however, the mirror stage marks the first instance of what according to Lacan is the basic function of the ego, the classic gesture of the self: identity in misrecognition (*méconnaissance*). But this misrecognition of identity is constituted by and through the temporal dialectic whose proper function is not to mark the self as fictional, but to organize that moment of fictionality as both anticipatory and retroactive. A double violation of chronology is involved here, for retroaction is based on anticipation and vice versa: "the self is constituted through anticipating what it will become, and then this anticipatory model is used for gauging what was before."[43]

In other words, the mirror stage is decisive not only because the self issues from it, but because the fragmented body, the subsequent experience of chaos, and the sense of identity crisis are also derived from it. Insofar as the identification of a new Chinese subjectivity is concerned, this moment of modernity marks the point of origin of both the future (ideal) and the past (tradition) of China. And May Fourth, understood to be that crucial stage in the formation of the modern identity, is taken in this light not as the explanatory origin of causes, but as the historical marker of effects.

As such an instance of "effective history," the mirror stage succeeds in bringing into effect the future through anticipation and the past through retroaction; "yet it is itself a moment of self-delusion, of captivation by an illusory image."[44] Hence, what appears to have preceded the mirror stage (of modernity: May Fourth) is thus a misrecognition by the desiring subjects of the New Culture Movement in their discursive attempt at representing, albeit rejecting, the past as tradition. Both future and past are thus rooted in an illusion, which is subject to the temporal dialectic of identification originated in the mirror stage. "Modernist" in the broadest possible sense of the word, May Fourth dictates that, historically and culturally, there be "nothing on the other side of the mirror"[45] of identification—at which intervention the formation of the subject of modernity is interrupted and reconstituted as a split.

Future/Past

The analysis so far assumes that the May Fourth intellectuals' attempt at representing a new China can be understood as a way of critically representing in its culture both a subjectivity and a collectivity that would entail the coming of modernity or, better, that could signify the rebirth (the rearticulation) of China as modernity.

We have taken as point of departure the question of identity (national identity, cultural identity, collective identity, and self-identity) pertaining to the Imaginary demarcated by the signifiers *China* and *Chinese*. A profane, speculative discourse might indeed allow us to (1) entertain the representation of identity as split, of subjectivity as split; (2) explore the ideological strategies with which the formation of China as identity is exclusively produced at the level of discourse, critical as well as creative; and (3) confront the textual politics through which that sacred and all-pervasive signifier—the unmistakable totalization of the national and cultural collectivity that is China—has been relentlessly transgressed.[46]

In this process of rethinking the project of modernity, it is noteworthy that history has positioned us—qua subjects—in relation to the past, but also the future, from the standpoint of the present. We are all subjected to history because it can virtually be identified as that complex of necessity that situates us in temporal distance/relationship to current events and the logic of events of the past. In this sense, history constitutes the condition of self-formation; hence, even in modernity, the consciousness of self turns out to be nothing if not also a historical consciousness of one form or another.

We may again draw on Lacan's account of the experience of the self/imago in temporal dialectic to suggest some broader implications of the split constitution of self, that the critical moment of identification "decisively projects the formation of the individual into history."[47] As Gallop explains, "What thus occurs in the mirror stage is the formation of what in the future will be antecedent, what grammatically can be called a 'future perfect' "—a tense in which "an anticipation (of the future) precedes a retroaction (of what is anterior to that anticipated future)."[48]

As a decisive turning point in the formation of a modern Chinese identity, May Fourth marks the moment at the threshold of modernity in China when the individual is thus projected—misrecognized—through the formation of its imago, hence, self, into history. Into the complex process thus registered as history, the subject is then formed in the split—imago/self—and articulated into the Real order of things.[49]

Inscribed in the "future perfect," as it were, the self could subsequently be identified as an already anticipated maturity. (Both Lu Xun's first-person narrators in "New Year's Sacrifice" and "Regret for the Past," for example, and Mao Dun's heroines in the *Eclipse Trilogy* and *Rainbow* exemplify such moments of identification in the May Fourth literary discourse. Yu Dafu and Ding Ling might have created individuals troubled by a stronger sense of anxiety and dejection, but their projection of the modern Chinese self must likewise be recognized as part of a historical, rather than atemporal process of maturation.) Yet within the temporal dialectic of the mirror stage, this act of identification serves to articulate the newly formed/split subject with the experience of history, an effort suggested in all the May Fourth discourses of modernity in their various forms of historical representation.[50]

In short, the very process of the "maturation" of the modern Chinese self is decisively affected by the anticipatory function of identity formation (governed by the "future perfect" imperative, as it were)—understood as a controlling function of the Imaginary order, which is never organized according to any natural logic but always inscribed in the real necessity of History.

The Thirteen Steps: Reading the Impossible

In order to read this function of the Historical/Imaginary, let us now try to relive an instance of the effect of the temporal dialectic, imagine ourselves as having been projected into the "future perfect" of history, and consider the necessity, even destiny, of one specific attempt to twist its logic.

As a series of dangerous narrative steps taken in projecting the modern subject's desire for freedom and anxiety about disintegration within the social imaginary of the 1980s, *The Thirteen Steps* is Mo Yan's attempt to articulate the underlying cultural crisis and to organize the fundamental desire and anxiety that inform the hidden danger that is moving the modern subject toward a fatal twist of history. It is conceivable that "the thirteenth step" taken in Mo Yan's 1989 novel has moved the Chinese historical subject of the post–Cultural Revolution generation to the threshold of the unconscious. For it marks not so much the moment of identification, a theme highlighted in the days of revolutionary change throughout the history of modern China, as what I call the displacement of subjectivity at the margins of modernity, beyond which lies the realm where chaos rules and darkness prevails. Hence the danger.

But surely anxiety is also a matter of organization and desire a question of representation. They rely on the violation and transgression of the totalization of the self/imago pairing in the Imaginary, for "that which is not organized or totalized or unified cannot be violated."[51] If anxiety and desire are indeed the effect of retroaction in anticipation, then the following questions remain to be asked: With the ego's jubilation during the process of identification, in what way could the self's history be realized as the future, as destiny? How are the pasts of our future narrativized?

In a nutshell, Mo Yan's thirteen-step organization in his latest novel is dependent on the power of his narrative discourse not only to provide a fantastic version of reality at the verge of disintegration, but also to represent the illusion of an illusion in speaking of the unspeakable, to work with the Imaginary through the Symbolic in attempting to subvert the Symbolic with the Imaginary, and, ultimately, to articulate the Real as the fantastic, the impossible.

This attempt, as we read *The Thirteen Steps*, indeed becomes an impossible one. For in Mo Yan's work, not only is the dominant narrator locked up in a cage, he must also swallow chalk in a gesture to prolong his own life and tell us about the lives of others. Beside the primary speaker there are other narrators who are kept out of the cage. These others, whose point of view is unmistakably presented as "we" throughout the work, have taken it upon themselves to provide the imprisoned storyteller with an ample supply of colored chalk so that he might be able to continue to relate in his never-ending tales the absurd stories of life and so that they (the hungry consumers of tales) might feel reassured of their own lives as they receive and live with the fantasy of destiny created and offered by the madman in the cage.

What is being formed, it seems, is a nightmarish vision of identity rooted deeply in the *Imaginary*, which summons us into conscious being by subjecting us to the fiction that we are compelled to engage ourselves freely in both producing and consuming this world of fantasy.

I pointed out earlier that, when the self identifies itself as the other in the mirror stage, the subject position is being constructed at a moment of illusion, resulting in the identification of the fragmented body with images of reality—with the subrealities of self/imago, so to speak. And yet, paradoxically, it is from this specific subject position, from this situated "fixity," that images are evoked, making it possible for the subject to postulate objects of permanence and identity in the world.[52]

The situation of the storyteller caught in Mo Yan's narrative is notoriously dangerous. Within the novel, he is a lunatic who speaks from behind bars, providing freely a fantastic discourse of the world outside for the world outside. Imprisoned in reality and living in subrealities, he is in pursuit of another kind of freedom, one that could project him outside of the cage of life without his ever having to leave it. But while his imagination soars high as he devours the complicitous supply of chalk offered by the listeners to his tales of the thirteen steps (who are themselves the other narrators of *The Thirteen Steps* on another level of discourse), the imprisoned self remains unable to break free of the iron cage, without which, it gradually becomes clear, the very condition of storytelling would have been impossible.

Dangerous Destiny: Cage of Story, Cage for History

Indeed, the caged narrator must rely heavily on the constraint of the iron cage in his attempt to weave the text of his narrative that constitutes Mo Yan's novel. The cage has become the home of identity and permanence; it houses the repository of images, fragmentary and whole. Paradoxically, it also becomes evident that this cage of narrativity, as it were, has evoked and delimited for the readers of *The Thirteen Steps* the terrain of an Imaginary framed within the Symbolic order, where the one narrative subject must speak unceasingly, while the others (those who listen to tales and those who read about them in novels) are being urged constantly to react to the dominant discourse with discourses of their own. And so, to act upon and resist the power of fantasy with the more powerful narrative of impossible desire: "You too are drawn into the story; together with him [the caged storyteller], you weave the text of its narrative.... You have a feeling that you remain powerless before the movement of the story. There is no way to counter its logic. You feel helpless before the destiny of its ending, you feel that your destiny too is held in the hands of that man in the cage."[53]

The result is your inevitable involvement in and confrontation with the chalk-hungry narrator's logic of discourse. In this struggle, we want to find or invent the strangest and most colorful chalk to draw for ourselves our own cage of the Imaginary: "Now that the caged man is dozing off, his lips stained with chalk powder, we can carry on to weave the cage ourselves" (132).

For we, too, are struggling to be formed, and the cage in question is the "legendary" thirteen steps and ultimately, *The Thirteen Steps* that constitutes them. In the novel, we read:

Dream of the embalmer:

"... 'What did you hear?' she asked. You heard the music of love. 'If you heard the music of love, close your eyes,' she said. You closed your eyes. 'When I count to thirteen, you shall have a sweet dream,' she said. Then you heard amid grandios prestos her clear voice counting: 1, 2, 3, 4, 5, 6, 7, 8, 9, 10, 11, 12.... Now she paused for a while. You could see the twelve numbers just uttered pressed against the gilt sand like twelve unmistakable footprints. 'Thirteen!' It came with a roar. A puff of whirlwind took you by the ear. A hit on your temple, then you became unconscious. You knew you were hit unconscious, and yet your mind remained intact. Smashed was your faculty for action and language." (248)

Dream of the physics teacher:

". . . The story between a man and a woman is ludicrous; nothing much can be done about it. You'd better listen to my dream. 'There is gold in a dream,' so the saying goes. Just a while ago I was lying asleep on the grass when a flaxen-haired woman who smelt of fresh milk said between her splendid big breasts to me, 'There is a beautiful legend. It goes that if anybody sees a sparrow walking on one foot. . . . She said blessed are those who see a sparrow walk like a little chicken: Wealth befalls you who see the sparrow take one step; success for you who see two; romance for three; health for four; best of spirit to you for the fifth step; best of luck in your work for the sixth; your wisdom shall multiply at the seventh step; your wife faithful at the eighth; your fame comes with the ninth; your beauty, the tenth; your wife's beauty, the eleventh; and sisterly harmony between your wife and your mistress at the twelfth. But never catch sight of the thirteenth step, or all the previous treasure of good luck that befalls you will double into misfortune on you!' Then she was gone." (249)

And eventually, at the very end of the novel:

We have taken a fancy for eating chalk. Now we understand you, admire you, but envy you just as much. You've learnt what you've got to learn, taking in an extra amount of chalk. Now, smiling wryly, you accost us through the cage. . . . At last, we are in the same cage. The beautiful sunset in the western heaven arouses us into some unspeakable glory, and while we eat our colorful chalk, we watch the sparrow coming toward us.

In silence we count its steps:

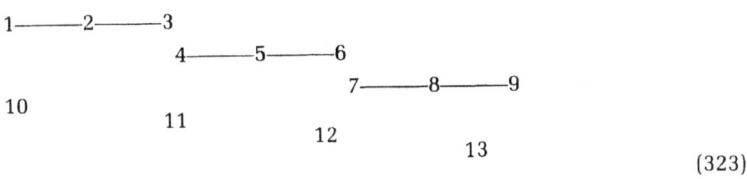

(323)

The hunger for chalk, for sex, for narrative—the desire to represent that which is not representable and to articulate that which would have to be registered nowhere else but in the Lacanian realm of the Real—is to attempt to seize the Real within the order of discourse, the register of the Symbolic. For Lacan, "the Real is that which is already there, and inaccessible to the subject."[54] What is experienced, however, is precisely the reading of identity as Imaginary through the logic of the Symbolic, a logic carried by difference, disjunction, and displacement.

As such, the thirteen steps have to be grasped not as a structure but more as a process that captures and provides a narrative for destiny in an orderly though fantastic movement. This works through an impossible discursive movement that begins and ends always with the cage. It is a process that contemplates the profanation of the language of "fate," realized as the formula for the articulation of both story and history.

The discursive struggle for identity necessarily calls the subject into action and inscribes her in desire (anxiety, despair). In reading through the thirteen chapters of the novel, we follow the illogical steps of destiny, realize its fatal rhythm through our reading, and complete the impossible movement of discourse in our own profane Imaginary—the very cage of narration we weave together with other readers and narrators of our time. Through the textuality of these "steps," we articulate the sense and nonsense of our struggle, thus bringing ourselves constantly to the impossible recognition and misrecognition of the other. We move toward a collective articulation of a story and history through which we could anticipate the future (our modernity) and project the past (our tradition) retroactively.

Split Logic of Displacement: Reading Otherwise in History

But how can we interfere with the dominant discourse? How can we misrecognize and disarticulate the master narratives of our time with minor, fragmentary narratives of our own?

By recollecting subjectivity via the ordering of the Imaginary, we have refrained from identifying the self as the master. We begin to realize that "to 'master' the self, to understand it, would be to realize its falsity, and therefore the impossibility of coinciding with one's self. The moment of 'self-mastery' cannot but be infinitely deferred."[55] The logic is dangerous, but our reading and displacement of it can be dangerous too.

Struggling to be formed, we keep trying to displace the same dominance of structure into a series of different positions, of different ways of situating subject positions, and of displacing eventually the narrative of identity into one of difference. Rhetorically speaking, "This is called 'the transference of pain.' . . . Unless dead, everyone has got to have some bodily pain. So if your ear aches, just pinch your nose; if your nose aches, pluck your eye. For any ache in the eye, the simple way is to cut a toe" (Mo Yan, 13). Displacement generates what I have elsewhere described in a reading of The Thirteen Steps as a "structural imaginary" in which there are "countless illusions, changing only to converge to the same end" (Mo Yan, 31).[56] The displaced "structure" is deep and totalistic, but it is also empty, void: a structure of Lack, an effect of the Imaginary.

Through this process of what we might call the misapplication of power, subjects slide into one another, all indulging fully in dreams of their own, together coping with their impossible lives interchangeably, not being able to survive the fantasy without that Lacanian effect of misrecognition. Hence, in the movement of the thirteen steps quoted above, a man's dream and a woman's dream interpenetrate into one another—tales consuming tales, narratives crossing narratives, steps taking over steps, desires missing desires—as if opposite dreams were moving rigorously for reality during copulation (Mo Yan, 251). And with this misrecognition, obsessions abound: telling stories, eating chalk, consuming stories, feeding chalk, transferring bodily pains, changing dead men's faces, skinning animals, skinning humans, replacing skins, replacing faces, interchanging faces, interchanging names, transferring husbands, transferring wives, displacing sex, displacing desires, remixing life (with death), remixing history (with unconscious). In the end, one is perhaps more than ready to ask: "Whose dream is it anyway?"—only to find the impatient answer drumming endlessly against the fantastic self/imago of an inquiring and desiring subject.

If the call is "Give me back my face!" the inquisition could be "But which face?" For a total misrecognition is now in order. We are confronted with reproductions of reproductions, dreams upon dreams, desires for desires, lies over lies! Having taken off his "original" face and thus changed his "identity," the embalmer teaches the now deceased "people's master": "You must forget that you are you, remembering at all times that you are him [the other teacher]. Your face is his, your tongue is his; your heart his, your bladder his" (Mo Yan, 223).

We have found ourselves plunged into a continuum of sliding movements of subjectivity: As subjects, we witness and experience in us the displacement of faces, appearances, pains, desires, and identities. We are carried into walking the fictional steps toward what is called the structural causality of history[57]—only we have had to walk these steps through an Imaginary structural totality laid down as Mo Yan's alternative narrative of that absent cause that is History (the Real).

If this history is the absent process informing the work of the Imaginary, the subject positions displaced through it must henceforth be organized painfully according to the aphoria of that absent logic. Before it, we remain helpless, transferring pains onto others that are not of our own making and yet contributing to their dissemination through our act of transference in our position as subjects. History constitutes this inevitable and irresistible form—this practical consciousness—whose presence in absence is realized as the notorious thirteen steps evoked in our reading of Mo Yan.

That logic, I submit, we must proceed to work with as subjects of history, in one way or another. One possible step is to "fill in the blanks," as it were:

Question #1. Fill in the blanks (one point for each blank filled in correctly. Two points deducted for each wrong answer).

The "Gang of Four" refers to the anti-Party group that consists of the following:

_____, _____, _____, _____.

Right answer: Jiang Qing, Zhang Chunqiao, Wang Hongwen, Yao Wenyuan.

Twin answer: The headmaster, the Party secretary, the discipline master, Big Mouth Qiu (the cook). (Mo Yan, 60)

The blanks offered are to be filled in by subjects whose articulation will become the realization of emptiness in the structural Imaginary. Articulation thus conceived is nothing if not the practice of void, so to speak, for the Lack of history is at the root of pain for any subject in formation. Thus experienced, pain becomes a symptom as much of history as of the unconscious.

Perhaps one could only work and think, forming consciousness into identities and drawing cages for the self "in between the gaps of the story" (Mo Yan, 222). But in the process of identification as misrecognition, "what does the physics teacher see in the mirror?" (131). For me this might also be the moment of pain registered as history, touched and transformed by the 1-2-3-4-5-6-7-8-9-10-11-12-13 steps of destiny before which we find ourselves instantly impotent. This is not only history unveiling itself without a center, it is also a discursive process engaged in the practice of emptiness. Hence Lacan's point: there is nothing on the other side of the mirror!

For it is not merely a structure that organizes the various discursive parts of the whole but the radical practice of taking steps outside of the binarism of text/context or discourse/structure. It represents the decentering historical process that carries us through the numbers from one to thirteen, and allows us to step freely in an empty frame void of the logic of history but full of the painfulness of its effect.

Inevitably and irresistibly, history makes you realize that you are an impotent subject. Yet a different aesthetic is evolving here. Hence in lack, with full impotence at hand, you gradually begin to feel life, to want to strive for something, to desire, to long for pain, for a radical void, for some logical but dangerous steps on the way to destiny.

And so Mo Yan writes: "Master Zhang Hongqiu is a Chinese" (318). He is the impossible "peoples' master." For the Chinese, to save China, one must first save the self—and vice versa; self-betterment and the betterment of a people must be handled as a single task. But now chalk hunger and pain transfer seem to have formed part of a new, emergent aesthetic and cultural experience, capable of eating into the self-other relationship in the Chinese intellectual's representation of identity on both the private and collective levels.

Split Identity: Mediating the Imaginary/Historical for Difference

The question now remains: Can collectivity still be defined through the formation of a securely organized national-cultural identity? If the answer is affirmative, how? If not, have we been asking the wrong questions all along then? Without a doubt, for any subject, "the past" must now be identified on the basis of "a future that is necessarily an uncertainty."[58] Accordingly, the significance of tradition will henceforth be dependent on revelations made retroactively in the future. If this is the case, we must prepare ourselves, look into the mirror, dream of identifying who we are, and anticipate what our past must have looked like. Let us be historical, in anticipation of the return of the future to constituting our past.

But here it is: history lies impotent before you. You feel it, and a strong sense of futility invades you: the anxiety of impotence overwhelms you. You cannot but choose to transfer it elsewhere, to displace yourself to other logical and illogical positions, and to move along the irresistible historical steps to which you are helplessly subjected.

As a text summing up symptomatically the crisis years of China in the late 1980s, Mo Yan's The Thirteen Steps: "like the monster of dreams, is another imaginary representation of destiny. It used to be able to represent history; this time it suddenly appears as though a prophetic vision of the future had been made. The hands of terror move on to close this album. Never do you want to open it again" (Mo Yan, 107). In that album of history, from which subjects shocked by the terror of destiny slip away through such dangerous steps of narrative, where are you positioned?

For sure, "you" too could be the site of an impossible representation of history, the transference and displacement of pain, and the articulation and misrecognition of desire/despair. And me? "I am a loving enemy and a spiteful friend of yours" (107). Good listeners of tales in the cage of history—you and I—we misrecognize each other while "living in the same cage" (323).

According to this reading of identity-as-formation, the misrecognition of identity as history is the effect of the Imaginary function. "Since the self was founded upon an assumption of maturity, the discovery that maturity was prematurely assumed is the discovery that the self is built on hollow ground."[59]

For the question of subjectivity, particularly after the traumatic historical experience of both the Great Cultural Revolution in the 1960s and 1970s and the new surge of innumerable waves of unrest and discontent culminating in the late 1980s with the Prodemocracy Movement and the June Fourth Massacre, this misrecognition of the "hollow ground" shatters completely the grounding of identity in some fixed, coherent unity of prediscursive "self" and whole, non-fragmented mass of pre-imago "body" that might have served as the foundation of so many different attempts to rearticulate Chinese modernity by calling for yet another "new" subjectivity.

In a way not unlike Mo Yan's invention of "the thirteenth step," the evocation of the Lacanian mirror stage is particularly dangerous for the study of Chinese subjectivity, for it threatens to highlight the impossibility that "the self is an illusion done with mirrors."[60] Significantly, the Lacanian subject thus implied is "almost entirely defined by lack."[61] The implications for the development of subjectivity in modern China and for the understanding of a Chinese modernity on the basis of a logic of progressive idealization of self, history, and the history of self remain to be studied in greater depth.

Lacan suggests that the mirror image could well be taken as "the threshold of the visible world." After the "jubilant assumption" by this specular imago, after the mirror stage is understood as a process of identification, what is left for us to say about the visible world? We realize now that the moment at which the mirror stage comes to an end inaugurates the dialectic process of maturation that will link the I to socially specific situations. This is a decisive moment that "turns the I into that apparatus for which every instinctual thrust constitutes a danger";[62] even though it ought to be part of a natural maturation, the very normalization of it is dependent on a cultural mediation that carries the subject through discursive practice into the register of the Symbolic.

If, as Bhabha recently suggested, a nation did become—"come into being" as—a system of cultural signification, then it would indeed be "one of the major structures of ideological ambivalence within the cultural representation of 'modernity.'"[63] As Bhabha puts it: How do we conceive of the "splitting of the national subject"? "What might be the cultural and political effects of the liminality of the nation, the margins of modernity, which cannot be signified without the narrative temporalities of splitting, ambivalence, and vacillation?"[64]

The subject of discourse—the collective agency of the Chinese people—is split in the discursive formation through which contradiction arises regarding the ethiconarrative authority. The effects remain to be revealed and gauged through what is displayed in the displacement and repetition of such categories as "subject" and "identity"—terms marked by cultural-political boundaries and taken to be "the measure of liminality of cultural modernity."[65]

Indeed, like "nationness" itself, identity must now be recognized as a narrative strategy and an apparatus of power responsible ultimately for the constitution of subjectivity in modern China, for the project of China as modernity.

As Jonathan Rutherford makes clear in his volume titled *Identity: Community, Culture, Difference*, it is always within different kinds of polarities that dominance is established and identity formed. What we need today therefore is a politics of difference to address the question of identity:

> Difference in this context is always perceived as the effect of the other. But a cultural politics that can address difference offers a way of breaking these hierarchies and dismantling this language of polarity and its natural structures of inequality and discrimination.... Such a politics wouldn't need to subsume identities into an underlying totality that assumes their ultimately homogeneous nature. Rather it is a critique of essentialism and mono-culturalism, asserting the unfixed and "overdetermined" character of identities. The cultural politics of difference recognizes both the interdependent and relational nature of identities, their elements of incommensurability and their political right of autonomy.[66]

The form of the Imaginary situates the agency of the self/imago before its entry into the society of discourse. Hence, difference, in the words of the postcolonial artist and critic Trinh Minh-ha, is *"that which undermines the very idea of identity*, deferring to infinity the layers whose totality forms 'I.' "[67] Indeed, it is the irreducibility of Real-differences to Imaginary-identity that we must now persistently recognize, anticipate, and strive for within the Symbolic register of discourse informing the swaying movement at the margins of modernity that will be here and will become China.

It is to be hoped that we never settle into *being* but will be always *becoming* Chinese—a nexus for subjectivity rooted in nothing but radical otherness, a locale for the liberation of difference, disjunction, and displacement.

Notes

1. "Cultural revolution," in the sense in which Fredric Jameson uses it, refers to what he calls the "third horizon" of historical interpretation in which the specific textual object of study is caught by "that moment in which the coexistence of various modes of production become visibly antagonistic, their contradictions moving to the very center of political, social, and historical life" (*The Political Unconscious: Narrative as a Socially Symbolic Act* [Ithaca, N.Y.: Cornell University Press, 1981], p. 95).

2. Mo Yan, *Shisan bu* (The thirteen steps) (Beijing: Zuojia, 1989).

3. Benedict Anderson, *Imagined Communities: Reflections on the Origin and Spread of Nationalism* (London and New York: Verso, 1983).

4. Ernst Gellner, *Thought and Change* (London: Weidenfeld & Nicholson, 1964), p. 169.

5. Ibid., p. 55.

6. Johann P. Arnason, "Nationalism, Globalization and Modernity," *Theory, Culture & Society* 7 (1990), 229.

7. Elsewhere I have discussed the ideology of form in the literary attempts of prominent May Fourth realist writers. See my "Beyond the Cultural Dominant: For a Textual Politics in Modern China," *Tsing-Hua Journal of Chinese Studies*, new series 14:2 (1989), 125–163; "Eros as Revolution: The Libidinal Dimension of Despair in Mao Dun's *Rainbow*," *Journal of Oriental Studies* 24:1 (1986), 37–53; "The Language of Despair: Ideological Representations of the 'New Women' by May-Fourth Intellectuals," *Modern Chinese Literature* 4:1–2 (1988), 19–38; "The Reification of Desire in Modern Chinese Realism: Rereading Mao Dun's *Midnight*," *Journal of Oriental Studies* 28:1 (1990), 1–20; and "Split Consciousness: The Dialectic of Desire in *Camel Xiangzi*," *Modern Chinese Literature* 2:2 (1986), 171–195.

8. Timothy Brennan, in "The National Longing for Form," writes: "The 'nation' is precisely what Foucault has called a 'discursive formation'" (in *Nation and Narration*, ed. Homi K. Bhabha [London and New York: Routledge, 1990], p. 46). Through his own formulation of the "archaeology of knowledge," Foucault defines *discursive practice* as a specific kind of social practice from which a specific kind of social formation, namely, *discursive formation*, is produced. The "rules of formation," in Foucault's sense, are governed not so much by a rigid system of laws as by an order or "regularity" that designates, for each discursive performance, "the set of conditions in which the enunciative function operates, and which guarantees and defines its existence" (*The Archaeology of Knowledge*, trans. A. M. Sheridan Smith [New York: Pantheon, 1982], p. 144). It specifies, in other words, an *effective* domain of appearance not unlike what his onetime mentor Althusser has variously called the ideological field or schema. Yet in at least one major aspect the student diverges from the teacher. For whereas "unity" is often stressed by Althusser in describing the *imaginary* order of the realm of ideology, that space of problematic is usually left dispersive by Foucault to the extent of undermining first the integrity of the field of analysis and soon the employment of the concept of ideology itself. Thus Foucault argues that an "effective" history differs from traditional history in being without constants since it introduces discontinuity into our very existence, uprooting any traditional foundation and relentlessly disrupting any assumed continuity (*Language, Counter-Memory, Practice*, ed. Donald F. Bouchard, trans. D. F. Bouchard and Sherry Simon [Ithaca, N.Y.: Cornell University Press, 1977], pp. 153–154).

9. Arnason, "Nationalism, Globalization and Modernity," p. 213.

10. Mikhail M. Bakhtin, *The Dialogical Imagination: Four Essays* (1934–

38), ed. Michael Holquist, trans. Caryl Emerson and Michael Holquist (Austin: University of Texas Press, 1981), p. 295.

11. Geoffrey Bennington, "Postal Politics and the Institution of the Nation," in *Nation and Narration*, ed. Bhabha, p. 132.

12. Louis Montrose, "Professing the Renaissance: The Poetics and Politics of Culture," in *The New Historicism*, ed. Adam H. Veeser (London and New York: Routledge, 1989), p. 24.

13. Ibid., p. 20. Emphasis added.

14. Judith Lowder Newton, "History as Usual? Feminism and the 'New Historicism,'" in *The New Historicism*, ed. Veeser, p. 152.

15. I am in debt here to Richard Terdiman, *Discourse/Counter-Discourse: The Theory and Practice of Symbolic Resistance in Nineteenth-Century France* (Ithaca, N.Y.: Cornell University Press, 1985), p. 30.

16. "Overdetermination" designates the following essential quality of contradiction for Althusser: "the reflection in contradiction itself of its conditions of existence, that is, of its situation in the structure in dominance of the complex whole" (Louis Althusser, "Contradiction and Overdetermination," in *For Marx*, trans. Ben Brewster [London: NLB, 1971], p. 207). As a "structure of unevenness" often manifested in the dominant forms of condensation and displacement, overdetermination is considered by Althusser "the most profound characteristic of the Marxist dialectic" (p. 206).

17. Jameson, *The Political Unconscious*, p. 146.

18. Ibid.

19. Jean Franco, "The Nation as Imagined Community," in *The New Historicism*, ed. Veeser, p. 207.

20. *Social Texts* 15 (1986), 65–88.

21. See, for example, Leszek Kolakowski, "Ideology and Theory," in *Interpretations of Marx*, ed. Tom Bottomore (Oxford: Blackwell, 1988), p. 295.

22. Cornelius Castoriadis, "The Imaginary Institution of Society," trans. Brian Singer, in *The Structural Allegory: Reconstructive Encounters with the New French Thought* (Minneapolis: University of Minnesota Press, 1984), ed. John Fekete, pp. 7–9.

23. John B. Thompson, *Studies in the Theory of Ideology* (Cambridge, England: Polity Press, 1984), p. 24.

24. See the analyses in Raymond Williams, *Marxism and Literature* (Oxford and New York: Oxford University Press, 1977), pp. 75–135; and Jameson, *The Political Unconscious*, pp. 89–102.

25. Thompson, *Studies in the Theory of Ideology*, p. 25.

26. Kolakowski, "Ideology and Theory," p. 296.

27. See the analyses in Bakhtin, *Dialogical Imagination*; Bhabha, *Nation and Narration* (e.g., Ernest Renan, "What Is a Nation?" pp. 8–22).

28. Louis Althusser, "Ideology and Ideological State Apparatuses," in his *Lenin and Philosophy*, trans. Ben Brewster (London: NLB, 1971), p. 162.

29. Richard Kearney, *The Wake of Imagination: Toward a Postmodern Culture* (Minneapolis: University of Minnesota Press, 1988), pp. 257–258.

30. "Since Marx, we have known that the human subject, the economic, political or philosophical ego is not the 'centre' of history . . . that history has no 'centre' but process, a structure which has no necessary 'centre' except in *ideological misrecognition*. . . . Freud has discovered for us that the real subject, the individual in his unique essence, has not the form of an ego, centred on the 'ego,' on 'consciousness' or on 'existence' . . . that the human subject is decentred, constituted by a structure which has no 'centre' either, except in the *imaginary misrecognition* of the 'ego,' i.e., in the ideological formation in which it 'recognizes' itself" (Althusser, "Freud and Lacan," in his *Lenin and Philosophy*, pp. 218–219, emphasis added).

31. Jane Gallop, *Reading Lacan* (Ithaca, N.Y.: Cornell University Press, 1985), p. 79.

32. Jacques Lacan, *Écrits: A Selection*, trans. and ed. Alan Sheridan (New York and London: Norton, 1977), p. 4.

33. Kearney, *The Wake of Imagination*, p. 259.

34. Cf. Jacqueline Rose, "The Imaginary," in *Sexuality and the Field of Vision* (London: Verso, 1986), p. 173.

35. Gallop, *Reading Lacan*, p. 78. Emphasis added.

36. Lacan, *Écrits: A Selection*, p. 4.

37. See *Marxism and Literature*, pp. 21–71, where Williams develops a moving account of "practical consciousness" as social being in action, drawing from the different ideas of Marx and Engels (pp. 28–30, 58–66), on the one hand, and Vygotsky and Bakhtin/Volosinov (pp. 34–44), on the other.

38. Indeed, the ideological practice of what I have called the imaginary-identity did function through the realist discourse of the May Fourth period; but, as I have argued elsewhere, it also succeeded in disturbing and at times even disrupting the work of the Symbolic order that served to organize all subject positions and desiring positions in that formative stage of modern China. See the works cited in note 7 above, especially "Split Consciousness: The Dialectic of Desire in *Camel Xiangzi*," *Modern Chinese Literature* 2:2 (1986), 171–195.

39. Althusser's delimitation of the imaginary still, in Richard Kearney's words, relies on "breaking the fascination of the *imaginary* so as to allow the symbolic order of the unconscious to speak." Kearney believes that "this transition from *imaginary* self-possession [of identity] to the *symbolic* language of the unconscious amounts to a discovery of the otherness of the self" (*The Wake of Imagination*, p. 260). The image of self-identity would surrender to the unconscious desire, for there is no escape from the symbolic register where is always the Other. For a brilliant discussion of Lacan's polemic, see Gallop's feminist account of the mirror stage in her *Reading Lacan*.

40. Gallop, *Reading Lacan*, p. 78.

41. Cf. Gallop, *Reading Lacan*, p. 79.

42. See Chan, "Split Consciousness: The Dialectic of Desire in *Camel Xiangzi*," and "The Reification of Desire in Modern Chinese Realism: Rereading Mao Dun's *Midnight*," *Journal of Oriental Studies*, 28:1 (1990), 1–20.

43. Gallop, *Reading Lacan*, p. 81.

44. Ibid., pp. 80–81.

45. Ibid., p. 80.

46. In the sense in which Foucault uses it, "transgression prescribes not only the sole manner of discovering the sacred in its unmediated substance, but also a way of recomposing its empty form, its absence, through which it becomes all the more scintillating" (Michel Foucault, "A Preface to Transgression," in his *Language, Counter-Memory, Practice*, p. 30).

47. Lacan, *Écrits: A Selection*, p. 4.

48. Gallop, *Reading Lacan*, pp. 81–82.

49. And, as it were, "thrown forward, in an anticipation that makes her progress no longer a natural development but a 'history,' a movement doubly twisted by anticipation and retroaction" (ibid., p. 83).

50. Identification is "nonetheless a moment *in* the natural maturation process, a moment which projects the individual *out of that process*" (ibid., p. 83).

51. Ibid., pp. 84–85.

52. Rose, "The Imaginary," p. 173.

53. Mo Yan, *The Thirteen Steps*, p. 173 (translation mine). Further page references to the novel will be included in the text in parentheses.

54. Malcolm Bowie, "Jacques Lacan," in *Structuralism and Since*, ed. John Sturrock (Oxford and New York: Oxford University Press, 1979), p. 133.

55. Gallop, *Reading Lacan*, p. 84.

56. See Chen Qingqiao (Stephen Ching-Kiu Chan), "Fangxia tudao chengfo hou, zaicao xiongqi bian chengxian: Mo Yan *Shisan bu* de shuohua luoji chutan," (On the logic of discourse in Mo Yan's *The Thirteen Steps*) *Dangdai*, Taipei: August, 1990, no. 52, 126–137.

57. Cf. Jameson, *The Political Unconscious*, pp. 35–43.

58. Gallop, *Reading Lacan*, p. 84.

59. Ibid., p. 83.

60. Ibid.

61. Kaja Silverman, *The Subject of Semiotics* (New York and London: Oxford University Press, 1983), p. 151.

62. Lacan, *Écrits: A Selection*, pp. 3–5.

63. Bhabha, ed., *Nation and Narration*, p. 4.

64. Ibid., p. 298.

65. Ibid., p. 292.

66. Rutherford, ed., *Identity: Community, Culture, Difference* (London: Lawrence & Wishart, 1990), p. 10.

67. T. Minh-ha Trinh, *Woman, Native, Other: Writing Postcoloniality and Feminism* (Bloomington and Indianapolis: Indiana University Press, 1989), p. 96.

LYDIA H. LIU

Narratives of Modern Selfhood: First-Person Fiction in May Fourth Literature

The notion of the modern can be translated as *xiandai* in modern Chinese.¹ Deceptively simple. Like many of the neologisms imported into the Chinese context at the turn of the century, *xiandai* has acquired meanings beyond the initial translation through translingual practices within the target language.² Rather than being a copy, duplicate, or mere image of the West that always harks back to some "original" concept in its source languages, capable of being measured by the latter, *xiandai* belongs to an intellectual legacy created by the Chinese under the exigencies of national struggle. This legacy in turn defines the meaning of *xiandai*, be it the invention of modern selfhood or that of modern nationhood. In this chapter I study the legitimizing process of the modern within the context of *xiandai wenxue* (modern literature), where the self is often constituted as a privileged site for the contest over the meaning of modernity. I do so by establishing and interrogating the relationship between first-person narration and the imagining of modern selfhood in May Fourth literature. The fiction of Lu Xun and Yu Dafu provides a textual ground for the kind of allegorical reading I undertake below—allegorical in the sense that all criticisms and interpretations are allegorical narratives in relation to a text insofar as they cannot and do not aim to reproduce the same text. My reading seeks to grasp the tensions generated by a mode of writing in first-person fiction that seems to authenticate the narrating subject but undermines the authority of the narrative voice at the same time. The allegorical thrust of my interpretation mainly focuses on the area where history and subjectivity intersect, as mediated through literature. Through reading Lu Xun and Yu Dafu, I will try to tease out the embedded meanings of modernity, self, and writing in the larger context of May Fourth literature in the 1920s.

In his 1907 essay "Moluo shili shuo" (The power of Mara poetry), Lu Xun argued that the decline of a nation was directly attributable to the suppression of the individual voice.[3] Drawing on the Western notion of secular humanism and Romanticism, the early Lu Xun advocated a new literature that would emphasize individualism and emulate the rebellious spirit of Byron and Shelley. When Hu Shi envisioned literary reform in his two seminal essays "Wenxue gailiang chuyi" (Suggestions for literary reform; 1917) and "Jianshe de wenxue geming lun" (Toward a constructive theory of literary revolution; 1918), he called for the rise of the genuine voice of the individual to replace the ancient classical canon.[4] Likewise, Zhou Zuoren argued in "Ren de wenxue" (Literature for humans; 1918) that modern literature must take humanism as its guiding principle. By humanism he meant "subject-centered individualism (geren zhuyi)."[5] Zhou contended that classical Chinese literature failed to live up to humanistic goals and must be discarded.

In creative writing, the privileging of individualism immediately translated into a broad range of experiments with narrative modes borrowed from European fiction. Psychonarration, free indirect style, interior monologue, and so forth, are more than just trendy foreign techniques that Chinese writers try to emulate. They represent the possibility of locating the modern self in a new symbolic context, one in which the protagonist no longer serves as an element in the nexus of patriarchal kinships or in the transcendental, divine schema where premodern Chinese fiction situated its hero or heroine. The protagonist in modern fiction begins to dominate the text as the locus of meaning and is perceived as possessing psychological and moral "truth." It cannot be coincidence that first-person fiction and autobiography written in a "Western" form, one in which the individual takes himself or herself most seriously, asserts his or her absolute rights against society, and possesses an interiority fully representable in narrative, appeared in great profusion in and around the May Fourth period. Modern Chinese writers were immediately attracted to the idea of the individual, because it allowed them to devise a dialogic language with which to attack tradition on behalf of the individual as Lu Xun did in "The Diary of a Madman." But the idea was also fraught with problems, because this individual often turned out to be a misfit in the hostile environment of a rapidly disintegrating society. The "superfluous man" from Russian literature, who figured so prominently in Yu Dafu's works, thus became a perfect embodiment of the dilemma of the modern "man."

If the contest over the meaning of modernity in May Fourth literature came to focus on the question of self, as I have suggested above, it did so because the production of new ideologies and symbolic systems required a massive reconstruction of subjectivity. In other words, the subject must be "interpellated" to legitimate and reify ideologies and be called into position by specific historical discourses.[6] It is not surprising that nearly all the debates on modern literature during the 1920s and 1930s converged on the question of the self within the larger conceptual framework of the nation. One of the issues that was taken up repeatedly in the works and criticism of modern Chinese writers was the relationship between the educated elite and the lower class. In seeking to represent the underprivileged, writers found their own positions increasingly problematized and were driven to question the very notion of the self. By the 1920s, Lu Xun had abandoned his earlier position on individualism and had begun to question the idea of literature for *pingmin* (ordinary people) that his brother Zhou Zuoren had promoted, suggesting that literature for ordinary people was something of an oxymoron, because literary production had always been the sole prerogative of the upper class. "Until workers and peasants themselves are liberated from the dominant ideology of the elite class, there can be no literature for ordinary people in the real sense of the word."[7] Was Lu Xun, then, advocating proletarian literature? We know that as early as the mid-twenties the radical left started to attack individualism and sought to promote a proletarian literature that would replace every form of subjectivity with class identity. Cheng Fangwu, the leading theoretician of the Creation Society, represented this radical view. In an essay entitled "Cong wenxue geming dao geming wenxue" (From literary revolution to revolutionary literature), Cheng called for the "revolutionary intelligentsia" to negate themselves and obtain class consciousness. In order to depict the life of the working class and to produce a proletarian literature, he argued, writers must familiarize themselves with the language of workers and peasants.[8]

A left-wing writer himself, Lu Xun found bourgeois humanism problematic and, in a critique of Zhou Zuoren, disputed his universalistic claim of representing ordinary people. However, he refused to believe with Cheng Fangwu that the problem of modernity—the crisis of the modern intellectual in particular—could be easily resolved by substituting class consciousness for every other form of subjectivity. In fact, some of his later short stories, especially those in the *Panghuang* (Wandering) collection, came to dwell on the precarious condition of the modern intellectual both within and outside the framework of class reference. Lu Xun probably had more skepticism than Marxian critics liked to see, and, in his firm refusal to conform, he became the target of the Sun Society and the Creation Society in the late 1920s. It is interesting that, although he was subsequently involved with the League of Left-Wing Writers in the thirties, he never wrote a single piece of "proletarian literature."

In the case of Yu Dafu, the crisis of the modern intellectual was no less acutely felt. In a 1927 essay entitled "Shui shi women de pengyou?" (Who is our friend?), Yu claimed to have seen through the old and new warlords as well as the bourgeoisie and the intelligentsia, and advocated joining the peasants and workers to serve the majority of the Chinese people.[9] Interestingly, he never acted on this idea, nor did he write anything that could remotely be described as "proletarian literature." Does the discrepancy between his words and his action indicate hypocrisy or self-contradiction? His works seem to indicate that the author was caught in a genuine dilemma about the identity of the modern intellectual. Despite his leftist inclinations, the self, rather than class, was the raison d'être of his literary endeavor. His fascination with the quirks and surprises of the inner being was much too strong to justify its negation for the sake of class struggle. Like Lu Xun, Yu Dafu was interested in probing the inner crisis of the modern "man" and capturing his dilemma, guilt, and self-contradiction through writing rather than providing a global solution to any of those problems. The two authors' willingness to leave the door open for question, indeterminacy, and nonclosure makes them the most interesting of all May Fourth writers.

In order to find a point of textual intersection between modernity, writing, and self, I will take Lu Xun's "Shang shi" (Regret for the past; 1925) and Yu Dafu's "Huanxiang ji" (Reminiscences on returning home; 1923) as exemplary texts for close analysis.[10] My choice of works with first-person narrative is dictated by the manifested concern of the writers with self and its relation to language and also by the inherent complexity of these works as a whole. For in the autobiographical mode—let us leave the generic question of autobiography and fiction aside for the moment—the self is both the narrating I (subject of enunciation) and the narrated I (subject of utterance). The pronoun "I" thus refers to two simultaneously identical and nonidentical subjects. Because of its insistence on the subject and on self-contemplation, this mode of writing openly declares its cognitive and tropological constitution as the self writes itself into being. To borrow the words of Paul de Man, the autobiographical mode "demonstrates in a striking way the impossibility of closure and of totalization (that is, the impossibility of coming into being) of all textual systems made up of tropological substitutions."[11] Since modernity itself often appears as a trope in the literary text, the discursive performance of the autobiographical self probably also reflects on the problematic of modernity as well. Lu Xun and Yu Dafu invented a whole range of first-person narrators to explore the tropological basis of the modern self in a self-reflexive moment. Their writing placed the subject in a complex relationship to self-knowledge that completely eluded the understanding of their leftist critics who tried to introduce a deterministic view of the self in the name of class struggle.[12]

Lu Xun: "Regret for the Past"

> My love gave me a bunch of roses red.
> What did I give her in return?
> —a red-spotted snake for a pet.
> Since then she has put on a long face
> and heeded me no more;
> But why?—better let her go and forget!
> (from Lu Xun, "My Lost Love")

Although Lu Xun wrote his 1924 poem "My Lost Love" as a parody of "Sichou shi" (Four sorrows) by the ancient Chinese poet Zhang Heng, his avowed intention was not to attack traditional literature but to "satirize a large number of poems on unrequited love that were in vogue at the time."[13] The lover in the poem speaks modern vernacular Chinese and, as a mark of modern courtship, he and his beloved exchange gifts that include roses, aspirin, and a gold watch chain. If Lu Xun pokes fun at modern sexual relationships in this lighthearted parody, his story "Regret for the Past" a year later begins to take such relationships seriously and to put them to the test.[14] Ostensibly a story about the disillusionment of romantic love, "Regret for the Past" is in fact a narrative about writing and the modern self. Above all, it allegorizes the "failure" of modernity. When I use the word "failure," I do not presume to stand on the teleological end of history pronouncing a judgment from the enlightenment point of view. Rather, I am referring to the situation set up by Lu Xun's text in which a modern sexual relationship is first established and subsequently undercut by the narrator's own writing.

The narrator Juansheng's autobiographical act in this story is devoted to erasing, exorcising his former love, Zijun, and casting her into the empty space between words. That does not mean, of course, that Zijun never actually appears in his recollection. Precisely because her presence is disturbing, the narrator sets out to overcome her memory in order to restore the confidence of self-knowledge that her death has shattered. Self-narration thus comes across as a therapeutic device for the reconstitution of a coherent self: "Since I am a living person, I must make a fresh start. The first step is just to write down my remorse and grief, for Zijun's sake as well as for my own." . . . "I want to forget. For my own sake I don't want to remember the oblivion I gave Zijun for her burial."[15]

The strange mix of testimony and denial reveals the problematic status of the text. The narrator's forgetfulness as well as his desire to forget disrupt the assumed coherence of his retrospective narrative. This tension comes out most strongly in his digressions on the act of recollection that frequently punctuate the narrative about the past: "I can't recall clearly how I expressed my most sincere and passionate love for her. Not only now—even soon after it happened, my impression grew blurred. At night when I tried to recall the scene, I could only remember snatches of what I had said. During the month or two after we started living together even those fragments vanished like a dream without a trace" (112; Yang 199).

The confession throws into question the reliability of the retrospective narrative. How can the narrator expect the reader to trust him if he has lapses of memory? Interestingly, the event he does remember turns out to be one that he is ashamed to recall, and so he cuts short the narration to prevent further embarrassment. He remembers that, when he proposed to Zijun, he ludicrously imitated a hero courting a heroine in a Hollywood film: "I clasped her hand with tears in my eyes and went down on one knee. . . ." (113; Yang 199). The ellipsis is supposed to suppress a portion of the unpleasant memory, which makes one wonder just how much more the narrator has suppressed.

The retrospective narrative in this story takes place on three levels of temporality, and the act of reminiscence occurs on both the first and second levels. The first temporal level is the process of writing, which places the second and third levels in perspective. The second level consists of the couple's life together as husband and wife up until the time of Zijun's death and Juansheng's writing. During this period, the two are engaged in frequent reminiscences of the days prior to their living together. Zijun seems to indulge in the happy days when they first dated, while Juansheng increasingly longs for his old days as a bachelor. The third temporal level goes farther back, to the period before the couple started living together, and is marked by the absence of reminiscence.

If we take the title "Shang shi" (Regret for the past) as referring to the time of writing (the first level), it is not difficult to see that this title also evokes the second level, as the narrator regrets his involvement with Zijun and mourns for his lost freedom with intense nostalgia: "I had a sudden vision of a peaceful life—the quiet of my shabby room in the hostel flashed before my eyes, and I was just going to take a good look at it when I found myself back in the dusky lamplight again" (115–116; Yang 204).

It would be in line with Lu Xun's position on the question of gender to contend that this tragic story was written for the purpose of debunking the grand illusion of romantic love and female independence prevalent in his own time. The future of a Nora leaving her comfortable home for freedom is unthinkable in Lu Xun's view if the woman has no material means with which to support herself in a male-dominated society.[16] But the story would lose its complexity if interpreted in those terms only, for its critique of the patriarchy also involves a rethinking of the notion of modern love whose male-centered discourse ironically reproduces the patriarchy that it aims to overthrow. It is the narrator who "liberates" Zijun from tradition by feeding her with new ideas from Western literature and who entices Zijun into his project of modern love, known as *ziyou lianai* (romantic love) in the May Fourth period, by using modern rituals of courtship, including the cinematic scene. The two very different occasions on which the narrator brings up the names of Western Romantic poets and Ibsen suggest that the narrator exploits the gender-biased discourse on romantic love as well as women's liberation in his own interest. If he is no less taken in than Zijun by those discourses when encouraging her to live with him, his words ring completely false when he uses the same argument to talk Zijun out of their relationship one year later:

> I deliberately brought up the past. I spoke of literature, then of foreign authors and their works, of Ibsen's *A Doll's House* and *The Lady from the Sea*. I praised Nora for being strong-minded. . . . All this had been said the previous year in the shabby room in the hostel, but now it rang hollow. As the words left my mouth I could not free myself from the suspicion that there was an unseen urchin behind me maliciously parroting all I said. (123; Yang 209)

The project of modern love in the name of foreign literature is aborted in an absurd moment of self-parody. Who is that unseen urchin? Is it the figure of guilt, conscience, or modernity itself? Whatever it is, the narrator's awareness of his own falsehood does not, however, prevent him from carrying out his selfish plan, which shows that hypocrisy may also enlist the service of one's conscience.

Juansheng's "regret" eventually leads to Zijun's death, which in turn engenders the further "regret" that this writing attempts to overcome. The desire to tamper with the past and undo it before and after Zijun's death results in two actions: the banishment of Zijun from his life and the subsequent writing of his "regret" to banish her ghost from his memory. Because of his convoluted motivations, the narrator fails to clarify whether he is writing of his "regret" for his past "regret" or trying to justify it. In any case, the ambiguity works to the advantage of the narrator because, while mourning over the death of Zijun, he nevertheless defends himself against the charge of responsibility by projecting his past "regret" in a sympathetic light. His writing takes advantage of the silence of the dead. When he suggests that Zijun does not understand that "love must be constantly renewed" (115; Yang 202), he is making an accusation from which Zijun cannot defend herself. By suppressing Zijun's side of the story while passing judgments on her, he manipulates the narrative in his own favor. The episode of the pet dog Asui, which prefigures Juansheng's abandonment of Zijun, serves to highlight the point. Seeing that they can no longer afford to keep the dog, Juansheng takes it out and abandons it in the wilderness. On returning home, he is surprised by the tragic expression on Zijun's face. Unable and unwilling to empathize with her feelings, he blames her for what has happened:

> At long last I realized she must consider me a cruel man. Actually, when I was on my own I had got along very well, although I was too proud to mix much with family acquaintances. But since my move I had become estranged from all my old friends. Still, if I could only get away from all this, there were plenty of ways open to me. Now I had to put up with all these hardships mainly because of her—getting rid of Asui was a case in point. But Zijun's understanding has become so obtuse that she did not even see that. (120; Yang 207)

Given that the narrator abandons Zijun soon in the same cruel manner, Juansheng's self-defense appears singularly ironic. Zijun shares the fate of her dog Asui at his hand after all.

Self-contradiction is the crux of a narrative that seeks to establish meaning out of the confused experience of a split self. On the one hand, the narrator describes his past life as if it had been a peaceful haven and turned into hell by Zijun's invasion. On the other hand, a contrary claim is to be found in the opening paragraph, where the narrator recalls, "a whole year has passed since I fell in love with Zijun and, thanks to her, escaped from this dead quiet and emptiness" (110; Yang 197). The discrepant views might well be attributed to a gap in perception between the narrating self and the experiencing self, as the former seemingly discredits the latter. But has the narrating self outgrown his former self? Time, experience, and retrospection might provide the narrator with a unique perspective for self-criticism previously unavailable, but it does not necessarily follow that such self-criticism is unproblematic. In fact, the contradictory statements and carefully wrought images throughout the text point toward an important linkage between the narrating self and the experiencing self. That linkage is established by the kind of escapism that characterizes the narrating self as well as the experiencing self as they both try to flee from self-knowledge, the writing of this confession being just another attempt to escape.

The image of the caged bird, for example, is first used by Juansheng after he loses his job. Making the best of the situation, the narrator compares his previous life as an office clerk with that of a caged bird and welcomes his discharge as freeing him from the routine: "In the office I had lived like a wild bird in a cage, given just enough canary-seed by its captor to keep alive, but not to grow fat. As time passed it would lose the use of its wings, so that if ever it were let out of the cage it could no longer fly. Now, at any rate, I had got out of the cage, and must soar anew in the wide sky before it was too late, while I could still flap my wings" (118; Yang 204). Although there is nothing remarkable about the literary cliché the narrator uses here, it is striking that, in his figurative projection of a future flight toward freedom, Zijun is conspicuously absent. Not only is she left out from this solipsistic picture, but the metaphor, which quickly becomes the narrator's privileged self-image, soon alienates him from Zijun as it frees him from the routine life of a clerk.

With the presence of this metaphor, freedom suddenly becomes the first priority in the narrator's life. He wages his battle for freedom with the help of a vocabulary that successfully unfixes his previous relation to Zijun: "As I sat there alone thinking over the past, I felt that during the last half year lived for love—blind love—I had neglected all the important things in life. First and foremost, livelihood. A man must make a living before there can be any place for love. There must be a way out for those who struggle, and I hadn't yet forgotten how to *flap my wings*, though I was much weaker than before" (121, italics mine; Yang 207–208). The narrator now explicitly condemns Zijun to the role of the cage while giving the superior image of the bird to himself. The metaphor writes off the previous relationship between lover and beloved in order to establish a new one, that of the bird and his cage, so that the narrator can get rid of Zijun with an easy conscience.

In connection with the caged bird, the image of the road is evoked repeatedly by the narrator to embody his yearning for freedom. Harping on the need to make a fresh start, he pins his hopes for the future on Zijun's departure from his life. Lacking courage to initiate a breakup, he decides to speak to her in allusions and metaphors: "I explained to her my views and proposals: we must explore a new path and turn over a new leaf to avoid being ruined together" (123; Yang 209). Insofar as Zijun is concerned, the new path leads to a dead end, whereas the image helps the narrator conceptualize an escape from the immediate reality. This use of the image is a far cry from that in Lu Xun's "My Old Home," in which the road embodies some kind of hope. As Leo Ou-fan Lee points out, the road for the individual in "Regret for the Past" becomes "less certain" as it eventually turns into the sinister image of a grey serpent in the eyes of the narrator.[17] Nevertheless, the narrator decides to take his dubious road of freedom, because, being an individualist, he treats life as a solitary journey and in order to survive alone must rid himself of the obstacle blocking his road.[18] To the experiencing self, that obstacle was Zijun, whereas to the narrating self, it is her ghostly memory that disturbs his peace of mind. If formerly he removed her from his life with speech, the narrator now relies on writing to erase her memory, cast it into oblivion, and assert his authorial control over the story of the past.

The attempt to undo the past binds the narrating self together with the experiencing self in a dubious confessional voice. After Zijun's death, the narrator moves back into the small room he occupied as a bachelor. As he takes up the pen to write, he begins by describing this room to the reader:

> The broken window with the half dead locust tree and old wisteria outside and square table inside are *the same as before*. *The same* too are the mouldering wall and wooden bed beside it. At night I lie in bed alone just as I did before I started living with Zijun. *The past year has been blotted out as if it had never been*—as if I had never moved out of this shabby room so hopefully to set up a small home in Jizhao street. (110, italics mine; Yang 197)

The narrator undoubtedly experiences a profound sense of futility as he surveys the room and contrasts its unchanged look with the turmoil of his own life in the past year. But does that feeling of mourning and regret express a sense of loss because of Zijun's death or does it express self-reproach for having been involved with her in the first place? Perhaps both. In either case, the unchanged room mirrors the narrator's desire to blot out the past. Indeed, when we consider how Zijun is transformed from a lively young girl to a woman and finally to a ghostly memory all within the space of one year, the contrast with the narrator's own condition falls into focus. Since the narrator ends where he started, the time that separates the experiencing self from the narrating self becomes circular. The unchanged space contradicts and, in effect, cancels out the temporal distance installed by the retrospective discourse between the narrator and his former self, so much so that it is impossible for us to take the narrator's regretful mourning or retrospective self-critique at face value.

The complexity of the whole narrative situation is borne out by the narrator's bizarre explanation of his role in Zijun's death. The chief crime the narrator says he is guilty of is his single-minded allegiance to the truth: "I shouldn't have told Zijun the truth. Since we had loved each other, I should have gone on lying to her. If truth is a treasure, it shouldn't have proved such a heavy burden of emptiness to Zijun. Of course, lies are empty too, but at least they wouldn't have proved so crushing a burden in the end" (127; Yang 212). One wonders whether the narrator is not defending more than accusing himself by setting up a spurious dichotomy between "truth" and "love." The false argument is designed to trap the reader in the dilemma of choosing one or the other. However, the story resists being reduced to an abstract, metaphysical lesson, not to mention a false one, for the tragedy of Zijun's death is not caused so much by Juansheng's allegiance to truth as by his rejection of her love and, particularly, his inability to reconcile the claims of love and individualism. If the narrator blames himself for acting like a weakling (127; Yang 212), his cowardice stems from his individualism rather than the inability to live with falsehood. Love is hardly an exception to his escapist view of life. He escapes from boredom via love but flees love as soon as life becomes difficult. In fact, he wants so much to be freed that he even wishes secretly that she would die (124; Yang 209).

The logical conclusion the narrator draws from a spurious discussion of truth and love finally foregrounds the problematic of the entire narrative: "I must make a fresh start in life. I must hide the truth deep in my wounded heart, and advance silently, taking oblivion and falsehood as my guide" (130; Yang 215). One need not accept the above confession literally, for it seems to reinvent the project of modernity by substituting a relatively harmless intellectual discourse—the debate over truth and falsehood—for the deep crisis of the modern subject and by suppressing the dark reality of human relationship affected by that crisis. But even if it were taken at face value, the statement would still profoundly discredit the narrator and the entire narrative at the textual level. Since reminiscent writing is regarded by the narrator as the first step on this new journey, one might ask the following questions: Does it hide the truth? Is it written under the guidance of a falsehood that the narrator embraces?

Yu Dafu: "Reminiscences on Returning Home"

The subversion of the autobiographical self in Yu Dafu's story takes place on a somewhat different symbolic level. Unlike Juansheng, who sets up an opposition between truth and falsehood and gets himself caught in between, the narrator in Yu Dafu's "Reminiscences on Returning Home" comes face to face with the limits of self-representation. The story is marked by the kind of irony that Michael Egan has discerned in most of Yu Dafu's works, that is, Yu's tendency to undercut his hero's sentimental view and to emphasize "the basic absurdity of his self-image."[19] More importantly, it demonstrates the impossibility of self-knowledge in a specular moment. Written in 1923, the narrative consists of ten short chapters plus five additional chapters in a sequel. Very little happens in this story except for the flow of the narrator's disjointed thoughts as he embarks on a homecoming journey from Shanghai to the town of Fuyang.[20] Furthermore, the story questions the act of self-representation as the narrator confesses toward the end: "I shall not dwell on further details about what happened afterwards: how my wife was taken by surprise on seeing me at home, how we shed many tears in commiseration, and what ways we devised to put an end to our lives, because I am afraid of being suspected of dramatizing my plight for the purpose of soliciting people's sympathy."[21]

Unlike in "Regret for the Past," the telescopic act of reminiscence in the above quote is not emphasized in the course of the narrative, for the narrator focuses largely on the experiencing self. But the narrator does not hide the fact that he is *writing* that which he narrates and is fully aware of the limits of this writing. A striking revelation occurs when he describes his arrival at the railway station in Hangzhou. When he comes out of the station, the familiar sights of the red-brick inns, taverns, and teahouses of Hangzhou move and disturb him. As the narrating self tries to pin down the complex emotions he experiences at the moment, he finds himself facing the limits of writing. The result is an interesting digression: "There is no way that this sense of loss and disillusionment can be put down in words. But if I must write it, I shall have to do so in an extended trope. Imagine me in my first bloom of youth when chance threw me into the company of a paragon of beauty."[22] He then proceeds to invent a tropological narrative about the maiden's inconstancy that supposedly has caused his suffering. The curious trope is intended by the "author-narrator" to recapture his nostalgia for the city of Hangzhou after many years abroad, the city being compared to the beautiful maiden and the narrator to her forsaken lover. Admittedly, the fiction (fantasy) is invented to stand in for another text, one that the narrator cannot produce. But one narrative can never quite replace another. Instead of being contained within the figure, the inserted narrative reveals an erotic imagination imbued with repressed desire and a troubled sense of selfhood that the narrator has no intention of divulging (and of which he probably has no knowledge). As the nostalgic narrative takes on the additional one of erotic desire, the invented fiction turns out to be more than an allegory for the narrator's nostalgia for Hangzhou. Rather than seeing the narrator's erotic imagination and fantasized passion as a mere figurative substitute for his attachment to the city of Hangzhou, one may find in it a displaced desire that reinstates itself by means of excessive signification.[23]

Self-fantasizing does much to help sustain the narrator's perception of self, and even suffering has to be invented from time to time with the aid of a hyperactive imagination to cast him in roles that invite narcissistic tears. Strangely though, this kind of fantasizing is always bound up with an erotic subtext in which the female body, a central signifier, plays out the possibility of desire. Take, for example, a scene from the "Sequel to Reminiscences on Returning Home." As the narrator waits to be served at a rundown restaurant, he deplores the fine weather for its indifference to his own plight. He wishes that the sky would be overcast and wet with rain so as to match his dark mood. "If I might wish for a further luxury," says the narrator, "I would also like to have a black-coated coffin placed next to me" ("Houji," 5). From that point onward, he starts to make up a fantastic tale about the death of the women he has loved in order to "swim for a while in the ocean of tears I had myself manufactured."

> After a moment of frantic thought, I came up with a neatly constructed play based on my wish. I saw myself burn some funeral paper offerings and say to the person inside the coffin: "Jeanne [original name in English]! We are heading back home and our boat is about to leave! If you are afraid of being harassed by ghosts, here, take these offerings and use them to bribe the ghosts...." As I came to the last sentence, my voice was choked up, so I buried my head between my hands and bent over the dining table. At this moment I felt something warm coursing down my cheeks. I began to conjure up one after another all the women I had loved in my whole life and saw them, mouths closed, lying hard and cold in front of me. At that I could no longer hold back my tears, so I wept aloud. The woman in the kitchen, thinking that I was pressing her to get my meal, said in a soft tone as if coaxing an infant: "Coming, coming! Dinner will be ready soon. Please be patient for just one more second." ("Houji," 5–6)

The narrator's narcissistic desire takes an odd turn in the presence of a maternal figure, whose contradictory sexual identity as "mother," at once desirable and unavailable, helps locate the libidinous source of the narrator's split self. More importantly, the younger woman in his fantasy has a Western name, "Jeanne," spelled out in English. Is she a Westerner or a Chinese woman with an adopted Western name? Judging from the context, the latter seems more probable, as it was common practice for May Fourth writers to give Western names to their heroines as a mark of modernity, as is evidenced by Sophia, Mary, and Wendy in Ding Ling's fiction.[24] Focusing on male subjectivity, Yu Dafu's story brings out the interesting relationship between modernity and gender.[25] If modernity is a desire for the other, does woman represent the other for the male narrator? Clearly, the invention of the Western female name "Jeanne" by the narrator points in that direction, which poses a question about the whole project of modernity: In whose name is this project invented? Is it just as gendered and patriarchal as the blatantly male-centered slogans of Mr. Science and Mr. Democracy? If so, who is the new father after the demise of the traditional Confucian patriarchy?

Interestingly enough, the purpose of the narrator's trip is to visit his wife, a traditional woman, whose innocence is proportional to his sense of guilt. This guilt represents, as much as it brings into question, a May Fourth discourse that inscribes women as the opposing signifiers of modernity and tradition. Between modern woman and traditional woman, the desiring male intellectual travels, makes free choices, and hopes to work out his own crisis of identity. Needless to say, this act of choice presupposes a male authorial position. May Fourth youths tended to imagine modernity and to invent the modern self through the mediation of desire for a modern woman of their own choice. Yu Dafu's earlier story "Sinking" embodied this desire in a most inflated form, in which the crisis of modernity is experienced by the male protagonist as a crisis of manhood and nationhood. Weakness, impotence, and the loss of national dignity all boil down to the same frustration, as the confused protagonist projects his desire onto the bodies of Japanese women. Yet, as my analysis of Lu Xun's story has shown, the male subject cannot forever postpone facing himself or foreclose the crisis of identity by replacing it with the sexual economy. The mischievous urchin of guilt and doubt seems determined to haunt him at all costs.

"Reminiscences on Returning Home" comes to grips with the

crisis of the modern (male) intellectual by emphasizing the specularity of the narrator's desire. As the narrative foregrounds the tropological construction of woman as modernity or tradition, the fictionality of the narrator's own subject position stands exposed. The following passage vividly portrays the process by which the female body is incorporated into a discourse of male fantasy:

> I turned around and saw that the street was deserted. All of a sudden, I was tempted by a hideous desire: "Break the window and get some money!"
> At that, the hand in my imagination reached out and pushed open that half-closed window with the utmost care. After removing a couple of iron bars from the outside of the window, I jumped over the wall and found my feet inside the room. My mind's eye saw a woman's shoes made of white satin lying underneath the white bed curtain. Together with a black silk skirt was an elegant white silk blouse hanging from the dress stand. As I carefully pulled out the drawer of the dressing table, I discovered a woman's handbag with glittering diamonds around its opening, lying next to a small powder container and an ivory folding fan. Having glanced at the bed a few times, I finally snatched up the handbag. However, as I was making for the window, I felt somewhat ashamed. So I turned around and put the handbag back in the drawer. For the next few moments I lingered on in the room, examining the slim shoes on the floor. All of a sudden, I was seized with a strange desire. So I bent down, picked up one of the shoes, fondled it and inhaled its scent, until I finally made a firm decision to walk away with both the handbag and the shoe. At this moment, my imagination came to a sudden stop. As my consciousness slowly returned to me, I felt my cheeks burning hot and red and my forehead dripping with sweat. I waited till my blurred eyes were completely cleared before hurrying back to my inn near the railway station. ("Huanxiang ji," 31)

The fiction thus staged in the narrator's mind takes an odd turn when the burglar suddenly becomes absorbed in fondling the woman's shoe. Does his fetishizing of the woman's shoes mark him out as a traditional literatus after all? Perhaps. That would explain why the self-conscious narrator who aspires to the modern condition is driven to suppress the inner monster and experiences a profound sense of shame. The intrusion of sexual fantasy in this strange moment calls for a specific expression of desire: voyeurism, as the narrator imagines an urban woman's boudoir being the setting of his burglary. The whole fiction of breaking in and stealing a woman's purse and shoe takes place at a time when the narrator positions himself as a voyeur gazing up at one of the hotel windows. Distanced from the scene, the voyeur stays away from the dangers and disappointments of action while at the same time indulging his imagination in the pleasure of transgression. It is transgression that links the imaginary acts of burglary with eroticism in the scene and produces the accompanying feelings of sin and guilt. What is particularly interesting about our voyeuristic narrator is that he fantasizes a fictional self to fill the role of a transgressor, thus allowing himself to play the role of an *imaginary* voyeur.

Voyeurism here is not just a matter of protest against sexual taboos or a mere display of moral decadence and sexual perversion, as often charged in the author's lifetime.[26] In the context of Yu Dafu's works, it also symbolizes the anxiety of the modern intellectual who desires action but feels excluded from it. The consciousness of his own inadequacy paralyzes the will to act. The image of the voyeur epitomizes this state of loneliness, frustration, and alienation. By the same token, the imaginative literature in which the author is engaged reflects the irony of his voyeuristic deferral of action as the *fiction* of transgression reflects the irony of the narrator's situation. In another revealing moment, the narrator apostrophizes the peasants from a distance: "Oh, upright peasants! You feed the world and deserve to be its masters. I wish to serve you as a beast of burden and toil for you. Would you then let me share your meals?" ("Huanxiang ji," 12–13). The passage appears to eulogize the laboring class, but as the narrator speaks from a certain vantage point—for he is taking a distant view of the rural landscape from the train—the apostrophe comes across as an empty tribute paid by an intellectual who desires to integrate with the working class but cannot go beyond a simile ("as a beast of burden").

The self-contradiction of the modern subject is explored at greater length toward the end of chapter 5, when the narrator contemplates a suicidal jump from the moving train. As he watches the wheels speeding over the railway track underneath his body, his mind is suddenly fascinated by death. The next moment finds him taking hold of the handrail in front of him, closing his eyes, and throwing himself overboard. Chapter 6 begins with the narrator still standing in the same old spot, trying to rationalize his failure to act:

> Oh, the triumph of death! If I had been a bit firmer in my will power, I would have found myself far away from this sad, miserable world, sitting

at the feet of the goddess Beatrice, smiling and picking flowers for her. Unfortunately, when I jumped, I did not exert enough strength. So when I opened my eyes, once more I saw the same old sky, land, rice paddies, and grass fields rushing past my train and heard the same old rhythmic sounds made by the friction of the wheels, and all this while my body had been sitting on top of the handrail like a sick parrot. ("Huanxiang ji," 17)

Far from evoking the image of a tragic hero who is dignified by the moment of death, the image of the sick parrot deflates any dignity and mystery. Like the image of the voyeur, the sick parrot who knows how to prattle finds himself lacking in willpower when it comes to action. Once again the modern intellectual is a hero manqué.

In presenting the individual subject as fissured, unfinished, and indeterminate, Yu Dafu comes closest to Freud, whose psychoanalytical theory shocked the bourgeoisie in the West in much the same manner that Yu scandalized his urban Chinese readers, for they both show that idealism or "the humanist dream of fullness is itself a libidinal fantasy."[27] The sublime thus comes to mean the same thing as the ridiculous. If Yu's narrator contemplates suicide during the day (as in chapters 5 and 6), he is ready to regard himself skeptically by night, as he confesses in chapter 7:

> Walking toward the city, I tripped over the rugged pavement a few times. A nameless fear began to assail my heart. I started to compare this fear with my earlier attempt at suicide during the day and couldn't repress a chuckle. Ah, the presumptuous man calling yourself the noblest of all bipeds, what rationality, what philosophy? What is the human mind and feeling but a chain of contradictions? ("Huanxiang ji," 22)

The fluidity of this subject finds a formal correlative in the narrative mode itself that deemphasizes the act of recollection and focuses on the moment of experience so that the incongruity of the subject is dramatized rather than explained away. This type of narrative is what Dorrit Cohn calls consonant self-narration.[28] The narrator seldom interrupts the flow of the narrative to reflect on a particular moment, nor does he make a consistent effort to establish a retrospective point of view. All the thoughts and feelings expressed in the story supposedly belong to the experiencing self. The narrative aims to recapture the protagonist's fascination with his own psychological incongruities and inconsistencies, leaving the ambivalence and tensions of his personality without corrective hindsight. Consequently, the text relives the spontaneity and complexity of the narrator's psychological experience. Verbal indicators, such as "all of a sudden," "suddenly," "at that moment," "in that instant," in which the story abounds, highlight the grammar of this incoherent text of psychological drama.[29] Just as the text presents itself as hypothetical, suspending coherence and closure, so the subject in this story is deeply problematized. Not only does the narrator lack a fixed identity, but the very notion of the self sometimes threatens to dissolve altogether.

If the quest for the self by the modern intellectual ends in profound disillusionment, does it point to the problematic of modernity itself? The works of Lu Xun and Yu Dafu raise important questions in that regard, yet they were bypassed almost immediately by Marxian critics and proletarian writers of their time, who decided to reject the self in order to implement the project of modernity on a collective basis. However, those questions will not go away, and, with the passage of time, they have become more and more focused: In whose name is the project of modernity conceived? What is the relationship between state politics and the politics of modernity? How and where do the average man and woman fit in? Until the discursive formation of modernity itself is brought into question, the rethinking of the May Fourth tradition will always be dominated by the power of its own rhetoric.

Notes

This paper is based on a chapter from my doctoral dissertation "The Politics of First-Person Narrative in Modern Chinese Fiction," Harvard University, April 1990. Besides the Duke conference, an earlier version was presented at the Fall Regional Seminar at the Center for Chinese Studies, UC Berkeley, November 1990, and at the Symposium on "Representation of the Self" at the Center for Chinese Studies, UCLA, January 1991.

1. The alternative word *modeng* is more of a transliteration than a translation. It also connotes "in fashion."

2. For a discussion of the concept of translingual practice, see my essay "Translingual Practice: The Discourse of Individualism Between China and the West," *Positions* 1 (Spring 1993), pp. 160–193.

3. Lu Xun, "Moluo shili shuo," in *Lu Xun quanji* (The Complete Works of Lu Xun; hereafter *LXQJ*), 16 vols. (Beijing: Renmin wenxue chubanshe, 1981), vol. 1, p. 100.

4. See "Wenxue gailiang chuyi" and "Jianshe de wenxue geming lun," in *Zhongguo xin wenxue daxi* (A compendium to modern Chinese literature), vol. 1 (Shanghai: Liangyou, 1935), pp. 34–43, 127–140.

5. Zhou Zuoren, "Ren de wenxue," in ibid., p. 195.

6. See Louis Althusser, "Ideology and Ideological State Apparatuses," *Lenin and Philosophy and Other Essays*, trans. Ben Brewster (New York: Monthly Review Press, 1971): pp. 127–186.

7. Lu Xun, "Geming shidai de wenxue" (Literature in a revolutionary age), in *Wenxue yundong shiliao xuan* (Research materials on literary movements), vol. 1, p. 451. This essay was originally a speech addressed to the cadets of Huangpu Military Academy on April 8, 1927.

8. Cheng Fangwu, "Cong wenxue geming dao geming wenxue," in *Wenxue yundong shiliao xuan*, vol. 2, p. 21. This essay was written in 1923 and first published in *Chuangzao yuekan* (Creation monthly) in 1928.

9. Yu Dafu, "Shui shi women de pengyou?" (Who is our friend?), in *Yu Dafu quanji* (Complete works of Yu Dafu) (Shanghai: Beixin shuju, 1930), vol. 6, p. 7.

10. In his preface to a subcollection that includes "Huanxiang ji" and other stories, Yu Dafu describes his work as a mixture of familiar prose and fiction. However, when Zhou Zuoren edited the work for *Zhongguo xin wenxue daxi*, he placed "Huanxiang ji" under the category of "familiar prose" and assigned other stories from that collection to the genre of fiction.

11. Paul de Man, *The Rhetoric of Romanticism* (New York: Columbia University Press, 1984), p. 71.

12. Ding Ling's "Diary of Miss Sophia" is another such narrative of modern selfhood. I touch on it briefly in an essay entitled "Invention and Intervention: The Making of the Female Tradition in Modern Chinese Literature," in Ellen Widmer and David Der-wei Wang, eds., *From May Fourth to June Fourth: Fiction and Film in Twentieth-Century China* (Cambridge, Mass.: Harvard University Press, 1993), pp. 194–220.

13. The poem appears in *Yecao* (Wild grass), in *LXQJ*, vol. 2, p. 170. The English translation is from David Y. Ch'en, *Lu Hsun: Complete Poems* (Tempe: Arizona State University, 1988), p. 171. Lu Xun's remarks are from "*Yecao* yingwen yiben xu" (Preface to the English translation of *Wild Grass*), in *LXQJ*, vol. 4, p. 356, as quoted in Ch'en, *Lu Hsun*, p. 256. Lu Xun repeats this idea in another essay entitled "Wo he Yüsi de shizhong" (My involvement with Yüsi from the beginning to end), in *LXQJ*, vol. 4, p. 166.

14. In "Xingfu de jiating" (A happy family; 1924), a story also included in the *Pang huang* collection, Lu Xun ridicules the notion of the bourgeois nuclear family with good humor by depicting a fiction writer who dreams of a modern family consisting only of a happy couple. Not only would they marry for love, but "their marriage contract would contain over forty clauses going into great detail, so that they would have extraordinary equality and absolute

freedom. Moreover they would both have had a higher education and belonged to the cultured élite. . . . Since Japanese-returned students were no longer the fashion, so let them be Western-returned students." See "Xingfu de jiating," in *LXQJ*, vol. 2, p. 36. The English translation is by Yang Hsien-yi and Gladys Yang with minor modifications, *Selected Stories of Lu Hsun* (New York: W. W. Norton & Company, 1977).

15. Lu Xun, "Shang shi," in *LXQJ*, vol. 2, p. 130 (Yangs' translation, p. 215). The romanticization of Chinese names has been converted from Wade-Giles to pinyin. Further references to this work will be included in the text.

16. See Patrick Hanan's discussion of Lu Xun's essay "Nala zouhou zenyang" (What happens after Nora leaves home) in "The Technique of Lu Hsün's Fiction," *Harvard Journal of Asiatic Studies*, 34 (1974): p. 71.

17. Leo Ou-fan Lee, *Voices from the Iron House: A Study of Lu Xun* (Bloomington: Indiana University Press, 1987), p. 88.

18. The solitary journal or "the solitary traveler," as Leo Ou-fan Lee points out, is a prominent image of the individualist in modern Chinese literature (see "The Solitary Traveler: Images of the Self in Modern Chinese Literature," in Robert E. Hegel and Richard C. Hessney, eds., *Expressions of the Self in Chinese Literature* [New York: Columbia University Press, 1985], pp. 282–307). Turning negative here, the image casts doubt on the concept of bourgeois individualism.

19. Michael Egan, "Yu Dafu and the Transition to Modern Chinese Literature," in Merle Goldman, ed., *Modern Chinese Literature in the May Fourth Era* (Cambridge, Mass.: Harvard University Press, 1977), p. 312.

20. In his analysis of the travel imagery in Yu's "A Sentimental Journey," Leo Ou-fan Lee notices the uncertainty that characterizes the traveler's quest for meaning, which he identifies as the "modern" quality of Yu's work. See Lee, "Solitary Traveler," p. 290.

21. Yu Dafu, "Huanxiang houji" (A sequel to reminiscences on returning home), in *Yu Dafu quanji* (Complete works of Yu Dafu), vol. 2, p. 16.

22. Yu Dafu, "Huanxiang ji," in *Yu Dafu quanji*, vol. 2, p. 19. All translations are mine, and further references will be included in the text.

23. Incidentally, this erotic imagination is also reflected in the patriotic fervor of the protagonist in "Sinking," whose troubled love for women and the motherland reveals a Freudian displacement.

24. See Tani E. Barlow, "Introduction," in *I Myself Am a Woman: Selected Writings of Ding Ling*, ed. Tani E. Barlow with Gary J. Bjorge (Boston: Beacon Press, 1989), p. 26.

25. If modernity means the coming into being of female subjectivity for women, Ding Ling's "Diary of Miss Sophia" clearly demonstrates its inherent contradiction, because while modernity gives voice to desire in a female subject like Sophia, it may also defeat that desire by (re)inventing the male

subject in the figure of Ling Jishi, who embodies the male-centered, modern bourgeois ideology.

26. The main source of this charge is his earlier story "Sinking," in which the protagonist peeps at the landlord's daughter bathing and later overhears a couple making love in an open field.

27. Terry Eagleton, *The Ideology of the Aesthetic* (Oxford: Basil Blackwell, 1990), p. 263. Although Freud's influence in China during the first quarter of this century was not nearly as profound as that of Marx, its traces can be readily observed in the works of Yu Dafu, Guo Moruo, Zhi Zhecun, and a number of other writers.

28. Dorrit Cohn, *Transparent Minds: Narrative Modes for Presenting Consciousness in Fiction* (Princeton: Princeton University Press, 1978), p. 153.

29. I owe this reading to Dorrit Cohn's analysis of Knut Hamson's *Hunger*, in *Transparent Minds*, p. 156.

WENDY LARSON

Female Subjectivity and Gender Relations: The Early Stories of Lu Yin and Bing Xin

> Granted that pen and ink are definitely not the business of women, what are we to make of it when they do employ them?
> —Xin Wenfang,
> editorial comment to *Tang caizi zhuan*, 1304

When modern women writers first began to write short stories in the early 1920s, they met with the problem of what to write about and how to grant subjectivity to either their own narrative voices or to the voices of their female protagonists.[1] If they were to write from their own "experience," the women writers had to some extent to reflect the environment within which they were taught to be female: family relations and friendships between girls within an upper-class kinship structure. However, growing up in partially modernized and Westernized areas in the early twentieth century, upper-class girls were often given educational opportunities denied to both their predecessors and to girls whose families were relatively uneducated or without sufficient resources. Thus the modern school was also a context for relationships that used to be impossible or unlikely, and the groups of girls who became friends at school represented a new and sometimes threatening social formation. By writing about friendships among women that developed at school, women writers could be "true" to their backgrounds and experience, work within a mode meaningful to May Fourth reform thought and thus oppose traditional boundaries, and problematize the issue of presenting female subjectivity or giving women agency and a subject position.

One of the main tropes of 1920s romantic fiction, the opposition between the individual and society, was common in the fiction of male writers such as Guo Moruo, Yu Dafu, and Xu Zhimo, as well as women writers. Such stories and novels were translated into Chinese, and their structures and relationships became an inevitable model of modernity for Chinese writers. Writers also had to work within the paradigms produced by local culture to develop a literary discourse of modernity.[2]

To delineate the characters women writers developed or the emphasis on subjectivity they seemed to create as merely the result of their attempts to create modernity through imitation of another economically, militarily, and socially more modern culture does not take into account their maneuvering within the gender definitions they inherited from China's past. Women's participation in the newly emerging literary modernity, in theory on an equal basis as that of men, was made possible by changes in the definition of literature and education that were partially the result of the abolition of the civil service examination system in 1905. Literature, *wenxue*, was a new field created out of changes in the old textual order in which the ability to write poetry (*shi*) and prose (*wen*), but not fiction, was expected in varying degrees from civil servants. Many literary pieces from poetry and prose essays were cornerstone texts in the Qing examinations. The link between poetry and political power was formally broken in 1905 and eroded as a cultural reality in the years following.[3] Only in the late nineteenth and early twentieth centuries did fiction become an avenue for serious literary effort, and eventually fiction rivaled or overtook poetry as the site where the most respected writers did their work. Women were not allowed to participate in the civil service examination and thus were barred from availing themselves of this kind of literary authority.[4] This does not mean women did not write or, in some relatively rare cases, attain fame for their writing. But it does mean that women almost always needed the patronage of a man—generally a father or a brother—in order for their works to be printed or anthologized.[5] In the modern period the politicized, masculine-marked *shi* and *wen* of before, now reformulated as *wenxue*, created a new subject position for women writers.[6] *Wenxue* allowed the possibility not only of women who write, but also of women writers (initially *funü zuojia, nü xiaoshuojia*, or *nü shiren*; by the middle to late 1920s, *nüzuojia*, a modernized woman who has emerged partially through her new relationship with literature).

In one of the earliest articles to theorize the relationship between the new woman (*xin nüzi*) and the new literature (*xin wenxue*), Liu Linsheng establishes this union to be the result of the new stance of the liberated woman, who is "a woman who serves society and can be independent; it can be said that she (*nüxing*) has the means to solve 'human problems.'"[7] It is because women had no independence within their framework of existence, the family, that they could not be independent in literature and only imitated men's works. Although Liu's "women's literature" (*nüzi de wenxue*) should have its own "characteristics" (3), his requirements—realism, clear separation from the old poetry in theme and image, use of the common vernacular, expressed understanding of Chinese and foreign literature—were the same as for literature written by men. In other words, although Liu can and wants to conceive of a positively constructed modern women's literature, it as yet has no characteristics to distinguish it from the "standard" modern literature—that written by men. The woman writer is conceptualized as the modernized woman who writes literature, but exactly what she writes is unclear.

A few years later Zhou Zuoren took this definition further by delineating the kind of literature the new woman should write:

> Because of the many restrictions of the past, women have a major disadvantage: they are misunderstood by others and they generally do not understand others themselves. In this regard the study and writing of literature could have a great effect. There are quite a few women poets or women novelists in the world, but we can say there are almost none who can truly express women's sad song. . . . From this time on women should make use of their own art and literature to express their own true emotions and ideas and get rid of thousands of years of misunderstandings and suspicions.[8]

Because they have been the victims of erroneous portrayal in texts by men, women should not write about society at large, as men do, but should write about themselves and through this process cause the "true" woman to be revealed. This analysis follows the May Fourth discourse on the past: it is a lie in form and content and now must be replaced by a textual truth. In the case of women and literature, the lie is previous representations of women in texts, and the truth is the new literature to be produced by women about themselves.

Thus modern literature proposed a new subject position for women that was gender specific: that of the woman writer. The situation for men writers was different, because although they also took on the task of representing the new self, it was a generalized, modernized self that was not specifically male. The new writing projected a gendered subject for women through its call for women writers to make use of literary romanticism to represent themselves; for the first time, women could write about themselves as writers without being out of place or seriously marginalized. However, this proved to be problematic, at least initially.[9] Before 1925, the stories of the two most prolific women writers, Lu Yin and Bing Xin, that deal with a writer of literature (generally poetry) inevitably posit a male protagonist. At this early stage, when the writings of women writers were insufficient in quantity and had little theoretical base that could be used to produce a "women's literature," the fictional construction of the *nüzuojia* was almost impossible. In other words, since "woman" was not yet the subject (master) of "literature," she could not be the subject (topic) of a literature about itself.

Although, as Nancy Armstrong has shown, women writers in Europe were key players in the development of an essentially gendered novel and in the privileging of "female" subjectivity and sensibility in the construction of a bourgeois modernity, this process did not repeat itself in China. Chinese women writers did not gain a central spot in the development of the modern novel, but took a marginal position that linked women with emotion and subjectivity. This position insisted that women writers veil the "literature" they wrote as diary and letter, and then demoted the diary and letter as an overly emotive, female-gendered, and inferior form. However, this relationship created the *nüzuojia*, and letters and diaries written by woman protagonists within fiction could be literature without directly forcing "literature"—which must maintain the prestige of modernity—to create the *nüzuojia*. Letters and diaries established "female subjectivity" as something to be delved into; through this trope of depth, women came to possess a significant, female-gendered subjectivity, and women writers could take initial steps toward "women's literature" (*funü wenxue, nüxing wenxue*) without directly engaging in "literature" itself.[10]

Before the twentieth century many kinds of literature embodied portrayals of women's interior or psychological states.[11] Writing in 1919, Liu Linsheng points out the melancholic and lustful images of women in the old literature and calls for a new "women's writing" of realism. In the Qing dynasty and before, there were many texts, including the famous *Fuxue* (Women's learning) by Zhang Xuecheng, that outlined the way a woman should be and the boundaries of her activities. Other texts contain references to the incompatibility of women and literary pursuits, yet a "female," vulnerable, erotic subjectivity was a staple of poetic images.

In the twentieth century the discourse on the "women's problem" included a wide-ranging discussion about women and education. Writers attacked the way in which women were educated in the past and demanded that education develop girls not only for marriage, but to function within society. This demand implied a realignment of the relationship between women and textual learning and more generally between women and the text.

Under these conditions women's "subjectivity" as represented in literary texts became a difficult issue. As leftist critique in the late 1920s and early 1930s showed, women as well as men—or even more than men—could be attacked for constructing female characters through reference to what was then viewed as the "traditional" framework of erotic desire, weakness, and passivity. To portray women's subjectivity as existing only as detached emotional configurations produced the "modern" romanticized woman character but ran the risk of linkage with the woman of older poetic images.

Thus all of the ways of being "modern," being a "writer," and being a "new woman" posed their own particular dangers. Like men writers, women who tried to be romantic and modern through their attempts to construct individualistic bourgeois sensibility as the center of literature were eventually branded as socially unaware, uninvolved, and elitist. Those who used the subjective form of diaries and letters to put a woman in the position of holding a literary pen were not only seen as divorced from social problems, but also unwittingly had aligned themselves with the lyricism of old-style poets.[12] And women who disregarded kinship relations to speak of the friendships formed through association at the new-style schools found themselves dangerously on the edge of *yin*: if affection between unrelated girls could not be analyzed within any traditional framework, it could be thought of as a kind of perversion of lust. Sexual relationships between men and women could be turned from their definition as either a husband-wife or a lustful connection toward a "modern" sexual morality, but female-female friendships could not be so easily modernized.[13]

Lu Yin published seven stories in Xiaoshuo yuebao in 1921, another three in 1922, and three more in 1923; Bing Xin published five stories in the first two years and two more in 1923, making these stories the earliest corpus of works by women writers to be published in a famous literary journal of modern China. I will first show how Lu Yin and Bing Xin use stories that feature a male protagonist as writer to identify certain difficulties in the concept of the "woman writer." Then, I will analyze some stories in which Lu Yin and Bing Xin create a woman protagonist who uses either a diary or letters to posit the woman writer (woman's subject position in writing) and to create and privilege female subjectivity as the foundation for a woman writer's creativity. Third, I will discuss two stories in which Lu Yin uses the modern context of the new-style school in order to theorize about the subjectivity of women as a basis of modernity and to construct an untraditional and thus liberating relationship between women.

Literature as Male

In Lu Yin's first story, "Yige zhuzuojia" (A writer), the "writer" has renounced family, friends, and society, and lives alone in a hotel with nothing to comfort him except books and paper.[14] Like many "writers" depicted in fiction at this time, he is sensitive and easily moved by scenery or emotions and so devoted to literature that he prefers books even to a decent quilt. The writer allows his brain to develop at the direct expense of his body. In the three years he has lived in this hotel, he has not so much as received a letter, let alone any corporeal visitors. This existence is shattered only when his former girlfriend, now married to a man with a good job, visits him and expresses her regret for having sold her soul for money. After she leaves, she sickens and dies, and the writer kills himself.

In her famous and widely discussed story "Chaoren" (Superhuman), Bing Xin creates He Bin, a young man who lives alone, pays little attention to anyone else, and keeps nothing but books in his room. When the moans of an injured servant boy keep him awake at night, He Bin gives him money to go and see a doctor, and receives great gratitude. The servant boy writes him a letter thanking him and reminding him that since all people are loved by their mothers, they thus have love in their hearts, no matter how suppressed it may seem. Thus the superhuman is reawakened to love, innocence, and human suffering. Bing Xin furthers the theme in "Ai de shixian" (The realization of love), where a mountain-dwelling poet is able to write only when invigorated by the vision of two lively children who pass by his window. In two 1922 stories, Bing Xin continues to work on the problem of the writer's relationship to "life" or "reality," and in both cases the writer is male. In "Fanmen" (Anxiety), a young student who writes poetry and critiques the poems of his friends expresses doubt about literature in letters to his sister.[15] Even though he feels that everyday life can become "literary material," he would rather sink into "nature," into the hearts of fishing people and peasant women, than write.

In all of these stories, both the study and the writing of literature indicate hypersensitivity, intelligence, idiosyncrasy, and suppressed emotion. Literature is romanticized and detached from common life, but that separation threatens to harm it and its producer. The writer must walk a thin line between immersion in everyday affairs, where he would lose his artistic perspective, and isolation, where he would sharpen his sensitivity but lose vitality. But why must the writer be male?

In their opposition of the writer and the love of a woman (mother or lover), we can see that Bing Xin and Lu Yin associate what is female with what is literary only oppositionally.[16] Even though "literature" is filled with potential for eliciting feeling, in order for it to remain sacred, the writer must contain something cold, isolated, and arrogant. But as an idealized construction, "woman" is warm, nourishing, vital, and powerful merely through her presence, not her own acts. Association with the woman, either the mother in Bing Xin's stories or the lover in Lu Yin's work, can offer the writer a solution to his loneliness and detachment, but then he must avoid becoming just an ordinary person. As long as "literature" must be maintained as an abstracted idealization of suppressed spiritual and emotional depth and sensitivity, "woman" only can take a position as its opposite idealization, as that which makes emotion and spirituality concrete or true.

The hiatus between "text" and "life" that both Lu Yin and Bing Xin formulate so clearly in these early stories can also be seen in early romantic works by Yu Dafu and Guo Moruo. Here, however, the opposition is gendered into a male-female dichotomy, with men assuming the independent if not totally complete role of producers of literature (text) and women taking the subsidiary position of that which makes them whole (life). Thus in "The writer," Lu Yin's female character represents a more human lifestyle for the alienated, estranged writer, and in Bing Xin's "Superhuman" and "Realization of Love," motherly love and its corollary, the lives of children, can move the spirit and make "love" concrete both for the male writer and for his literary text. Woman/literature is not equal to man/literature, because women cannot stand in a subject position against the more powerful object, literature, which is "secretly" gendered as male. In these early modern works, women writers establish a gendered link with literature through their encoding of female characters as supplementary and necessary to the "true" existence of literature. Still, such characters are without the means to pick up the pen themselves.

Female Subjectivity and the Female Subject

In her 1921 article "Chuangzuo de wojian" (My views on literary creation), Lu Yin claims that the "essence of art is subjectivity," and insists on the validity of representing individual experience.[17] The writer is an extrasensitive person who has a responsibility to fight his or her way "out of darkness into light" (21) and avoid driving young people toward suicide. As is clear in the stories discussed above, women cannot be depicted, like men, as spiritualized authors, but they can assume the position of the writer if their role is mediated through the letter or diary. In 1922 Lu Yin published "Huoren de beiai" (Someone's tragedy), and in the same year Bing Xin published "Yishu" (Posthumous letters).[18] Both are fiction in the form of women writing to friends: in "Yishu," the recipient of the letters is "Bing Xin" herself. In both pieces, a woman who is sick writes to a friend, and the letter writer either commits suicide or gets sicker and dies.

Lu Yin's "Someone's Tragedy" characterizes Yaxia, the letter writer, as existing largely through subjectivity, which consists of emotions and passive sensual appreciation.[19] When she sees that her friends who married have divorced, and she herself is not interested in having a love affair either with her married admirer or with the friends of her brother who pursue her in Japan, Yaxia decides life is without significance, something only to be played with. All of her correspondence with old friends indicates to Yaxia that the social world is evil and soiled. She takes action and leaves for Japan, where her brother is studying, but finds Tokyo noisy and irritating and her options for development limited. "Woman" cannot be allied with because her aristocratic, made-up, false appearance in the Association for Far Eastern Peace contradicts the "clean, pure" image Yaxia expected. "Politics" offers little hope, because even though the "socialist" Yaxia and her brother visit is pure and idealistic, his house is surrounded by police; later, another "socialist" who used to be a friend dies, supposedly out of love for Yaxia. "Religion" seems possible, but lack of true belief prevents Yaxia from seeing it as more than a comfort when she is sick. Anxiety makes her ill, but she cannot stop thinking. And even though she wants to write a diary, Yaxia finds herself blocked from writing. Sentiment and intellect fight within her and prevent her from acting; she jumps into a lake and dies, leaving only a book, *Sheng zhi mi* (Riddle of life). Her body is never found.

In Bing Xin's "Posthumous Letters," Yuanyin is convalescing at the seashore in her aunt's house and also finds that she wants to write but cannot; even when she does succeed in writing some scenic description, she usually burns the draft after a few days. More than Lu Yin's Yaxia, Yuanyin is almost pure subjectivity, her body existing only as a sick emblem of her illness and completely without the ability to act. The scenes around her exist only to stimulate her emotions.[20] When her aunt asks her what style of calligraphy she uses, Yuanyin replies that it is her own and comments that writing is only to communicate meaning, thus denying the value of its physical form. In one letter Yuanyin emphasizes the purely subjective nature of her existence and the (ultimately restricted) freedom it brings her in writing:

> You have brought up the issue of "literature," but this topic is too big. I truly am unworthy of discussing it, and even more, I dare not discuss it. Bing Xin, you must firmly remember that when I discuss things, I only use my own personal standard. Of course, this standard is extremely crude and unmeasured. *But in correspondence with close friends, it doesn't make any difference. We can say anything we wish.* (9, my italics)

Not only does Yuanyin lack a well-functioning body, she also must suppress a mind that can produce ideas and concepts, leaving only emotions within her reach. Only through the medium of letters can Yuanyin (and Bing Xin) directly theorize on literature. Standing in contrast to this direct expression of *ideas* is "women's talk" (11), polite and delicate, and the recollection of *impressions* of friends and relatives.

Neither Lu Yin nor Bing Xin creates a woman writer as protagonist, but both construct women letter writers who are far sicker and more subjective than the men "authors" in their stories. Whereas the men authors are lacking something that can be supplied by a woman's presence, the women letter writers have no alternative to mental and thus physical degradation. Walking the line between aloof writer and commoner may be hard for the male writer and he may be forced to neglect his body, but for the woman letter writer the choice is not available. The only way to put the power of "modern literature" into the hands of women is to allow a woman, as a writer of letters, an existence as close as possible to pure subjectivity. Conversely, to put a fictional "woman" in literary creation in a subject position within literary discourse, she must be able to write (if only letters) and to feel. Thus the men authors in stories by women have bodies that are but pale reflections of their mental and aesthetic strength, but Lu Yin and Bing Xin do not develop male subjectivity to the same degree that they do female subjectivity. The women letter writers have bodies that they efface through illness, inactivity, and suicide: not their bodies, but their subjectivities create them as women, and for a woman to have both a subject position and a subjectivity, she must write.[21]

These writers' effacement of the body appears to stand in direct contradiction to the contemporaneous trend of locating the female body and defining its modern significance, and thus privileging it as a means of producing modernity. In the antifootbinding movement, in sanitation, in physical education, and in fashion, bodies—in particular women's bodies—became the object of research, and the resulting profusion of texts was a discourse through which a new group was created.

Whereas women and suicide was a common topic of discussion during the May Fourth period, it generally centered on the suicides of women with "traditional" parents forcing them to marry against their will. In these stories, it is women writers whose bodies are destroyed either through illness or through their own intervention. Actualizing themselves as writers becomes the problem, and it is in the combination *wenxue/nüzi* that women writers efface the female body through suicide, illness, and simple functional inability to act. The bodies of characters who are attempting to write diaries and letters become an impediment to their own actualization as literary creators. The more they write, the sicker they become or the closer they inch toward suicide. The problematic union of women and literature precludes the existence of a healthy, active, functioning body, and because "woman writer" assumes female subjectivity as the proper scope of the *nüzuojia*, the body cannot assume a positive form.

New Associations

In 1923 Lu Yin published two stories, "Lishi de riji" (Lishi's diary) and her well-known "Haibin guren" (Old friends by the seashore), in which she highlights the friendship of women who got to know each other at a new-style school.[22] In the first story, a woman friend of Lishi believes that Lishi died not from a heart attack as the doctors said, but from an illness of the spirit. To prove this, she publishes Lishi's diary. Since the diary is not published by its writer, but only posthumously by a friend, it is doubly mediated: first, as a private form of writing and, second, as writing made public only through the agency of another. Thus the danger of the female-female relationship around which the story revolves is muted by being twice removed from the "writer's" (Lishi's or Lu Yin's) own voice. Only in "Haibin guren" does Lu Yin directly present the lives and emotions of young women.

Lishi is in love with Ruanqing, a woman whom she has known for two years. She calls their love "tongxing de lian'ai," or love between the same sex (11), and this love proceeds through all of the conventions of male-female relationships except for sexual love, which remains undiscussed. Lishi reports her and Ruanqing's excitement and anticipation as they make long-term plans for their life together. They wear the same clothes, and Lishi finds that she lives not for herself, but for Ruanqing. When Ruanqing is told that her mother wants her to marry a cousin, she writes to Lishi: "Why didn't you make yourself up like a man and ask me to marry you before?" (13).

Lishi finds relations with men to be unnatural (11). When Ruanqing finally writes a letter expressing her view that "love between the same sex is not recognized or allowed by society" and urges Lishi to wake up, Lishi decides it is Ruanqing who has sent "that young man, Liwen, whose masculinity is so obvious" to see her (14). She finds his movements coarse and unattractive, herself unlucky in her undying love for Ruanqing, and humans unfortunate in that they are divided into two sexes. All of her friends who have married, women and men alike, have become "degraded" either through the necessity of making money (men) or through devoting all of their time and energy to giving birth to and raising children (women).

In "Old Friends," friendship develops between five classmates, Lusha, Zongying, Lingyu, Lianshang, and Yunqing. Each woman has a distinct personality that is discussed at length. They take advantage of the strikes at school caused by political movements to get together, talk about their pasts, and discuss each other, their classmates, and their favorite topic, qing (sentiment). The discussion often centers on the question of who has the most and truest sentiment (part 1, p. 10). When their parents begin to arrange introductions and marriages for them, these women find that their years of education have changed their ideas, and even though they one by one fall in love with men, they no longer can happily participate in society's definition of "woman." For Lusha, the most prominent character and the woman with the least qing, an ideal life is one without men: all of the women living together at the seashore, some teaching, some writing, each acting according to her interests (part 1, 21). School can be a way to avoid the demands society places on women, but eventually it becomes clear that love between those of the same sex is socially impossible (part 2, 5). Yet when women marry, they change from lively, interesting people into dull creatures interested only in trivial social intercourse (part 2, 8). When only Lusha and Yunqing are left unmarried, they take "refuge" in the study of Buddhist texts and the writing of poetry and divorce themselves from human affairs.

The many articles on "sexual morality" published in *Funü zazhi* in 1920, 1921, and 1922 give witness to the effort of reform-minded intellectuals to reconstitute the discursive meaning of sexual relations, changing them from the "traditional" husband-wife relationship based on subordination within kinship roles into a "modern" alliance based on "love" (*lian'ai*).[23] In 1925, after the debate on love and sex had raged for several years in intellectual journals, an article on love between women in modern schools by Furuya Toyoko was translated and published in *Funü zazhi*.[24] In it, Furuya regards such love a result of new social structures, such as schools and factories, and their new living quarters—the dormitory—where women live together in a way unmediated by kinship relationships. Such love, according to Furuya, is spiritual and lofty, yet actually an imitation of heterosexual relations with the more "feminine" women attracted to the more "masculine" women and vice versa (1069). Furuya also claims that the basis for such love is the teacher-student relationship. Because emotional ties between student and teacher are necessary in order for modern education to be truly successful, these new friendships are an essential aspect of modernity (1067–1068). Furuya is careful to insist that while love relations between men may be "homosexual," between women love relations are spiritual, moral, and nonphysical.[25]

Articles on "singlehood" (the refusal to marry) also appeared regularly in the 1920s. In "Fei dushen zhuyi" (Against singlehood), Peng Daoming claims that singlehood can lead to "same sex love" (*tongxing ai*) and that unmarried women often go insane. While insisting that intense love relationships among women are platonic, Xiao Jiang claims that school promotes friendships among women and that educated women can easily end up as "old virgins" who displace their love for men onto other areas such as a career in science, love for animals, or travel. Furthermore, single women develop a high level of skill in language and have unusually weak bodies—an echo of the weak-bodied woman diary or letter writer that Lu Yin and Bing Xin created. As in the stories of women writers, bodily strength and the ability to speak appear to be locked in a dichotomy, with subjectivity and intellect effacing the strong body but allowing other undesirable tendencies, such as singlehood or strong female-female friendships, to predominate. These articles list the disadvantages of refusing marriage and establish themselves as strongly against "singlehood."

Lu Yin's stories show a double-bind: she perceives the man-woman relationship to be a trap for women, yet the woman-woman relationship at least brings up the possibility of an immoral liaison.[26] The problem with relationships between women is not that they are wrong or bad in themselves, but that they are socially unacceptable. Lu Yin consistently contrasts friendships among women and the lifestyle without men to heterosexual relations and their damaging effects on women. Despite critics' claims about "singlehood," she persists in outlining deep friendships among women as beneficial and natural, validating a possible reconstruction of what previously was possible only within kinship structures.

Conclusion

The early stories of Lu Yin and Bing Xin show that the difficult relationship between women and literature—where women become a supplementary category for men, who are in the process of establishing themselves as the writers—mirrors the socially condoned sexual relationship of marriage, where women are supplementary and disadvantaged. Through the use of the letter and diary forms, Bing Xin and Lu Yin use novelistic conventions to turn women into writers and to elevate gendered subjectivity as the most important literary material. The next step in this line of inquiry is to conceptualize what it would be like to take women out of their supplementary category and give them their own independent role. This role is initially theorized in two ways: without the existence of men, as in Lu Yin's society without men, or without the existence of society. In a slightly later story, Ding Ling's "Sophia's Diary," Sophia lives in one room, rarely emerging, and the reader learns almost nothing about the society in which the room is situated. Here both the woman and the romantic relationship can continue to exist in an abbreviated form as long as they are denied social definition.[27]

Subjectivity as the key to femininity was new neither in China nor in the romantic fiction widely translated in the late Qing and early Republican eras. Poetry had long granted a represented subjectivity to the female voice, and in the widely read if unorthodox *Honglou meng* (Dream of the red chamber), women possess a more pure, true subjectivity than men. The positioning of gendered subjectivity as the means through which a *nüzuojia* is created, however, is a particular response to the specifics of Chinese culture in the 1920s and a key to the way in which women and literature were joined. The tradition of emotive, female-voiced poetry was a double-edged sword, but to some extent female subjectivity could be wrenched away from its weak implications and reinstated as a modern ideology. As 1930s histories and critiques of women writers by women critics show, women eventually tried to recoup the lyricism of Chinese poetry and traditional fiction as essentially feminine and thereby link women with literature in a basic relationship, redefining the nature of the most canonized literature as feminine.[28] Although this strategy usually took the form of an analysis of premodern literary forms, it was based on the link between subjectivity and women that writers like Lu Yin and Bing Xin had emphasized, and it was a strong contrast to the paradigm of leftist critics, which demanded that writers focus on society and the nation. It was not only the new ideologies of love and family entering China through translations and intellectual discussion that triggered the alternative construct of Lu Yin and Bing Xin, but also the changing material conditions of women that placed them in new relationships in factories and schools in urban and semiurban areas.[29]

Notes

My thanks to the Center for the Study of Women in Society at the University of Oregon for support in the research and writing of this chapter.

1. On the means through which modern writers appropriated the concept of "subjectivity" as "the hero's psychological state," which is important to the production of romantic literature, see Marian Galik, *The Genesis of Modern Chinese Literary Criticism* (London: Curzon Press, 1980), p. 107 and the chapter on Yu Dafu; and Leo Ou-fan Lee, *The Romantic Generation of Modern Chinese Writers* (Cambridge, Mass.: Harvard University Press, 1973). For the way in which middle-class writers in England placed gender in a position of primacy by subordinating other social differences, see Nancy Armstrong, *Desire and Domestic Fiction: A Political History of the Novel* (New York: Oxford University Press, 1987). Armstrong shows how novels both illustrated and produced the "project of gendering," which acquired great political influence in the mid-nineteenth century. This privileging of gender was imported into China along with the concept of the modern nation-state. See Peter Zarrow, "He Zhen and Anarcho-Feminism in China," *Journal of Asian Studies* 47:4 (November 1988), 796–813.

My use of "subjectivity" here corresponds to that discussed in Patricia Waugh, *Feminine Fictions: Revisiting the Postmodern* (New York: Routledge, 1989), as she presents a feminist critique of postmodernism: "As male writers lament its demise, women writers have not yet experienced that subjectivity which will give them a sense of personal autonomy, continuous identity, a history and agency in the world" (6). Subjectivity in the works of modern Chinese women writers emphasizes the emotional state over depiction of action or scene.

2. For a revealing discussion of the way in which one woman writer, Ding Ling, constructed a romantic, bourgeois "woman" in her fiction before 1930, see Tani E. Barlow, "Introduction," in *I Myself Am a Woman: Selected Writings of Ding Ling*, ed. Tani E. Barlow with Gary J. Bjorge (Boston: Beacon Press, 1989); see also Barlow, "Feminism and Literary Technique in Ding Ling's Early Work," in *Women Writers of Twentieth-Century China*, ed. Angela Jung Palandri (Eugene: University of Oregon Asian Studies Publications, 1982), pp. 63–110.

3. This discussion is necessarily superficial. For an elaboration of this theory, see my *Literary Authority and the Modern Chinese Writer: Autobiography and Ambivalence* (Durham: Duke University Press, 1991), especially chapter 2; and also two articles by Theodore Huters: "From Writing to Literature: The Development of Late Qing Theories of Prose," *Harvard Journal of Asiatic Studies* 47:1 (1987), 51–96, and "A New Way of Writing: The Possibilities for Literature in Late Qing China, 1895–1908," *Modern China*, 14:3 (July 1988), 243–276.

4. Although there are numerous examples of women disguising themselves as men and taking the exams, the disguise was a necessity, indicating that the exam participant must be designated as male. Such incidents were uncommon in comparison with the legions of men who took the exams.

5. The way in which "woman," in premodern China only a category within kin roles (*funü*), emerged in modern China as a Western-influenced, sexualized being (*nüxing*) at the same time that *funü* evolved into a state concept has been convincingly researched by Tani E. Barlow in two articles. See "Theorizing Woman: Funü, Guojia, Jiating [Chinese Women, Chinese State, Chinese Family]," *Genders* 10 (Spring 1991): 132–160; see also "Introduction," in *I Myself Am a Woman*.

6. In calling *shi* and *wen* "masculine-marked" here, I am referring only to their validation by officialdom and the civil service examination, not to their voice, content, or tropes. Many male poets took the female voice, a fact that was seized upon by women literary historians writing in the 1930s who tried to claim Chinese poetry as basically feminine.

7. Liu Linsheng, "Xin wenxue yu xin nüzi" (The new literature and the new woman), *Funü zazhi* 5:10 (October 1919), 2.

8. Zhou Zuoren, "Nüzi yu wenxue" (Women and literature), *Funü zazhi* 8:8 (August 1921), 8.

9. Wendy Larson, "The End of 'Funü wenxue': Women's Literature from 1925 to 1935," *Modern Chinese Literature* 4:1–2 (Spring–Fall 1988), 39–54; idem, "Nation and Society Versus the Production of Gender: Women and

Literature in China from 1915 to 1926" (paper presented at the Harvard Conference on Contemporary Chinese Literature and Its Literary Antecedents, May 1990).

10. It is precisely the diary and letter forms of fiction that He Yubo identifies as common and detracting from the integrity of the works of women writers. He Yubo contrasts the use of diary and letter forms in women's works, where they are evidence of a lack of literary skill and produce only an "incoherent" and "monotonous" story, with their use in the work of Guo Moruo, where they possess a "clear plot and structure." In other words, He believes that diaries and letters are more commonly a woman's technique and that in women's hands they are a weak and fragmented literary form. See *Zhongguo xiandai nüzuojia* (Modern Chinese women writers) (Shanghai: Fuxing shuju, 1935), pp. 20, 48, 157. See also Nancy Armstrong, *Desire and Domestic Fiction*, passim, for the way in which women's conduct books of nineteenth-century Europe projected a positively constructed domestic woman who bases her power on subjectivity and essence.

11. The construction of the female voice in poetry is investigated by Maureen Robertson in "Voicing the Feminine: Construction of the Female Subject in the Lyric Poetry of Medieval and Late Imperial China" (unpublished paper presented at the Colloquium on Poetry and Women's Culture in Late Imperial China, University of California, Los Angeles, October 20, 1990). Robertson shows how, in poetry, "the dramatized speaking voice is feminine, but the source of this speech is easily given away by the poems themselves, which indicate the eye of the voyeur in their presentation of passive, narcissistic women, romanticized suffering, and their displays and inventories of boudoir furnishings and clothing" (5).

12. He Yubo also criticizes women writers for their incessant reference back to lyric poetry or fiction and links it to their desire to establish themselves as emotional and thus feminine. See *Zhongguo xiandai nüzuojia*, pp. 6–7, 152–153.

13. There were strong statutes against male homosexuality in Qing China but none against female homosexuality. Vivien W. Ng suggests that Cheng-Zhu Neo-Confucianism "imposed a strict code of sexual behavior for men as well as for women—with homosexuality being the male version of female unchaste behavior." See "Ideology and Sexuality: Rape Laws in Qing China," *Journal of Asian Studies* 46:1 (February 1987), 68. Ng postulates that harsher punishments for male homosexuality may indicate that "perhaps male homosexuality was regarded by the Qing government as a worse evil than female unchaste behavior. Iconoclastic men were more subversive to the state than immoral women" (69).

14. Pagination is very erratic in the early volumes of *Xiaoshuo yuebao*; sometimes each story starts with page 1, and other times there are different

sections (such as fiction or poetry) each starting with page 1. I will give page references as they are in each volume.

15. One critic identifies "Fanmen" as a turning point in Bing Xin's stories, the time when she begins to lose the innocence and purity of her earlier works and becomes permeated with sadness and even more unwilling than before to "go out into society." See Pei Wei, "Liangxing jian de daode guanxi" (Moral relations between the two sexes), Xiaoshuo yuebao 6:7 (July 1920).

16. In Bing Xin's stories the "writer" can be inspired by motherly love or by children, but there is always an explicit or implicit connection between children and their mothers.

17. Xiaoshuo yuebao 12:7 (July 1921), 19.

18. Xiaoshuo yuebao 13:12 (December), 7–17; and 13:6 (June), 2–14, respectively. Page numbers for "Huoren de beiai" are from a reprint, Lu Yin xuanji (Selections from Lu Yin's works) (Taipei: Qiming shuju, 1957).

19. Lu Yin also wrote an early story with a male letter writer, "Panghuang" (Wandering). Although the protagonist, Qiuxin, is also melancholy, as a teacher he has a much more physical existence than the women letter writers and must deal with the daily problems of how and what to teach and how to maintain discipline while promoting the "new" idea of democracy. He must even solve physical problems such as where furniture belongs. One reader of this story interprets the story as very subjective but nonetheless basically a discussion of the situation of Chinese education. See Fang Zhuo, "Duhou gan" (Impressions after reading), Xiaoshuo yuebao, 14:3 (March 1923).

20. In her "Lijia de yinian" (A year away from home), Bing Xin's protagonist is a male student who leaves home for school and is very lonely. He frequently writes home to assuage his loneliness but gradually becomes part of his new environment and his loneliness fades. In contrast with Yuanyin, as he makes new friends and participates in new activities, his environment becomes concrete and his physical relationship to this environment overtakes his subjective understanding of it as an alienating or emotive force.

21. For a rethinking of the meaning of guixiupai wenxue (literature of the inner chambers), which calls for an interpretation of the "triviality" of which women writers are often accused, see Rey Chow, "Virtuous Transactions: A Reading of Three Stories by Ling Shuhua," Modern Chinese Literature 4:1–2 (Spring–Fall 1988). Chow claims that "triviality itself should now be seen as an ironic means of exploring patriarchal ideology, whose limits are made palpable precisely through women's so-called private and insignificant sufferings" (85).

22. "Lishi de riji" appeared in Xiaoshuo yuebao 14:6 (June 1923), 7–14; "Haibin guren" in 14:10 (October 1923), 6–23 (part 1), and 14:12 (December 1923), 1–18 (part 2). Bing Xin's story "Meng" (Dream) (Xiaoshuo yuebao

12:11 [November 1921]) is a strong contrast to Lu Yin's radical social analysis. In "Meng," a girl dreams of her youthful life, when she grew up doing "'boys'" activities such as riding horses, meeting with soldiers, and carrying weapons. When she is older, she is forced to be a "girl" and participate in the "trivial and boring" activities of that gender. Her memories of life as a "boy" are vivid, concrete, and extremely physical.

23. For example, see Si Zhen, "Aiqing yu jiehun" (Love and marriage) *Xiaoshuo yuebao* (*XSYB*), 6:3 (March 1920); Pei Wei, "Liangxing jian de daode guanxi" (Moral relations between the two sexes), *XSYB* 6:7 (July 1920); Qin Lu, "Xing de daode de xin qingxiang" (New directions for the morality of sexuality), *XSYB* 6:11 (November 1920); Yu Qifan, "Lian'ai yu xingyu de guanxi" (The relationship between love and sexual desire), *XSYB* 7:6 (June 1920); Zhou Jianren, "Lian'ai de yiyi yu jiazhi" (The significance and value of love), *XSYB* 8:2–3 (January–February 1922); and volume 8 number 5 (May 1922) of *Xiaoshuo yuebao*, a special issue on sexuality.

24. Furuya Toyoko, "Tongxingai zai nüzi jiaoyushang de xinyiyi" (The new significance of homosexuality in women's education), *Funü zashi*, V. 11, No. 6, 1925, pp. 1064–1069.

25. A reader of Lu Yin's "Lishi de riji" is also insistent that the love between the women depicted in the story is lofty and pure and that Lishi is basically a woman of sentiment. This reader interprets the story as a comment on China's sick society. See Tian Xi, "Duhou gan: Lu Yin nüshi de 'Lishi de riji'" (Ms. Lu Yin's "The Diary of Lishi"), *Xiaoshuo yuebao* 14:12 (December 1923), 1–2.

26. This theme gets stronger in Lu Yin's later works. In her 1925 "Shengli yihou" (After victory), Lu Yin investigates the result of fighting the old morality with a modern love relationship: for a woman, the end product is still unequal marriage. The two stories Lu Yin published in *Xiaoshuo yuebao* in 1927, "Lantian de canhui lu" (Lantian's record of remorse) and "Hechu shi guicheng?" (Which way leads to home?), continue along the same lines.

27. In "Ibsen in China: Reception and Influence" (Ph.D. dissertation, University of Illinois at Urbana-Champaign, 1984), Kwok-dan Tam devotes one chapter (chapter 8, pp. 218–259) to "The Nora Theme in Modern Chinese Fiction" and shows how in the 1930s social reform was seen as the *only* way to insure equality for women. However, it is also possible to interpret the 1930s emphasis on social reform as a suppression of gender issues that were developed by women writers in the 1920s.

28. See Larson, "End of 'Funü wenxue,'" pp. 41–45.

29. When documents on feminism and the "women's question" were translated in China, feminism in the West existed in two modes: relational, in which arguments on women "proposed a gender-based but egalitarian vision of social organization," which "featured the primacy of a companionate, non-hierarchical, male-female couple as the basic unit of society," and individual-

ist, in which arguments "posit the individual, irrespective of sex or gender, as the basic unit." See Karen Offen, "Defining Feminism: A Comparative Historical Approach," Signs 14:1 (Autumn 1988), 135–136. Offen shows how feminism is becoming increasingly individualist in the twentieth century yet still is an interplay between the two approaches. In the work of Lu Yin and Bing Xin as well as other women writers such as Ling Shuhua and the early Ding Ling, there is both emphasis on the couple and emphasis on the individual; however, gender as a concept is privileged in both cases, and the significance of the married couple is embedded within the kinship relationships of the family. See Barlow, "Introduction," *I Myself A Woman*, pp. 1–17 for an elaboration of women writers and women in kinship roles.

PART TWO

Representation,

Realism, and the

Question of History

THEODORE HUTERS

Ideologies of Realism in Modern

China: The Hard Imperatives of

Imported Theory

In their proposal for a manuscript based on the proceedings of the 1990 conference on "Politics, Ideology, and Literary Discourse in Modern China," the organizers stressed that "it is high time to engage in a comprehensive reexamination of modern Chinese literature, not only in terms of its local political and ideological traditions and determinations, but also against the larger background of the world historical experience of modernity." There is implicit in this call a sense that a true interrogation of modern Chinese literature from the perspective of what must perhaps be called "world literature" has never been undertaken. One's first reaction is to wonder how this can be true, given that the American sinological establishment has published such substantial amounts of material on modern Chinese literature. But perhaps the notion of the modern that is advanced here contains depths that may explain the sense that modern Chinese literature has been a site largely protected from the harsher inquiry that rigorous comparative study would surely bring to bear.

A clue to the reticence in this respect can perhaps be detected in Naoki Sakai's summary of the scholar Takeuchi Yoshimi's—known in sinology as the preeminent Japanese scholar of Lu Xun—version of the modern: "Modernity for the Orient . . . is primarily its subjugation to the West's political, military, and economic control. The modern Orient was born only when it was invaded, defeated, and exploited by the West. This is to say that only when the Orient became an object for the West did it enter modern times. The truth of modernity for the non-West, therefore, is its reaction to the West."[1] The disadvantageous position of the non-West in this scheme was initially explored by Edward Said in *Orientalism*, and the set of issues surrounding the advent of Western discourses in the rest of the world has since, under the various rubrics of "postcolonial" and "subaltern" studies, gone on to become the fulcrum of one of the most important movements in contemporary criticism.[2]

Students of the Chinese humanities have, however, been curiously passive, if not, until very recently, largely silent on this issue. I will attempt to focus on some of the possible reasons for this silence, first by suggesting historical reasons why certain key issues in Chinese literary studies have rarely been pursued or are pursued in ways that dismay many observers. I attempt to address what it is that these long-enduring encumbrances try to displace, with special attention to the position of literary realism in Chinese literature and literary criticism.

It is probably safe to say that as of about 1980 the study of modern Chinese literature in the West was more interesting (i.e., it had more compelling things to say to noninsiders) than the study of modern Japanese literature. And I think that those of us in the field took compensatory pride in that fact; it was but one of the things that helped to demonstrate to us that our being out of the mainstream of literary theory was more a question of the West's lack of interest in the non-West than a defect in the way we went about our work. C. T. Hsia and Jaroslav Průšek, for example, dealt with literary issues that went beyond the appeal of particular works or the fondness for particular, hyperaestheticized critical response that seemed to characterize American scholarship on Japanese literature at the time. The last ten years, however, have not been good to scholars of modern Chinese literature, and we now find ourselves, much like Ah Q, daily having our heads banged against the wall by the same Japanese Xiao D we were once so contemptuous of.[3]

What has happened here? I would suggest that in the intervening period a new generation of students of Japanese literature has radically historicized the nature of the discourse in that field and thereby forced it onto the broader stage of "world literary studies" (not without resistance from the Europeanists who invented that field and have always dominated it). Specifically, these scholars have begun to focus on the issue of the problematics of the Japanese response to the West (that same old chestnut that has long-since been deemed unfashionable within Chinese studies).[4]

In particular, this new generation of scholars has come to scrutinize the issue of Japan's sense of itself and its otherness from the West and to assess some of the more material consequences of cultural nationalism. Under these premises, hard looks have been given to a variety of written work that reveals itself to be in play between acceptance of Western modes of discourse on the one hand and the displacement of those modes in the name of a return to some essential Japaneseness on the other. The question of the import of the encounter with the West, then, has been transformed. From the sterile pursuit of one-way influence studies, the issue has been reformulated into a series of dynamic interactions within Japanese literary discourse itself. Thus arises the apparent paradox that only through questions raised by the most historically specific features of modern Japanese literary discourse has the field been permitted to raise issues of theoretical interest to those outside the narrow range of professional concern.[5]

We cannot expect to find exactly the same configuration of questions confronting modern Chinese literature. There has, however, since the death of Joseph Levenson in 1969 been a curious and very marked silence concerning the traumatic choices that the coming of the West presented to China. This silence is striking in that modern Chinese literature has traditionally dated itself as beginning in a movement to discard the native literary language in favor of a literary language explicitly based on Western models. It should be even more striking in that, up to about 1917, the literary language was one of the few elements of the tradition not regarded as discredited by conspicuous failure to turn back the challenge presented by Western imperialism. Or, at least, through the late Qing, the old literary language had come to be regarded as the seat of the "national essence," a cultural domain that guaranteed the essential difference of China from the universalizing demands of the modern West.[6]

Perhaps it was the cataclysm of the Cultural Revolution that put the question into abeyance. For, after all, the one premise that made Levenson's project antiseptic enough to pursue was his secure assumption that Chinese culture as traditionally defined had expired (or had been killed off; that the distinction did not seem particularly significant to him was characteristic of the time in which he wrote—

the 1950s) sometime soon after 1895. Perhaps one of the few assertions about the Cultural Revolution that would brook no dissent is that one of its key features was Mao's obsession in the years after 1965 with just how untrue this assumption was. Moreover, Mao's evidently steadfast (and apparently paradoxical) determination to punish both those who claimed the old culture had been supplanted by something new and those who insisted on finding its traces everywhere in contemporary life added an immense charge to this already highly overdetermined issue. Thus it was thought that probing too deeply into the ideological dimensions of the interaction between China and the West would not only be futile but would lead to the most acute sorts of ideological pain.

I suggest that the question of China's reaction to the West will press upon us with an intensity in direct proportion to the extent to which we try to repress it. The coming of literary ideas from the West is a vast topic; a variety of literary schools advocated different genres at different times. Many of these schools shared a determination to minimize the difficulties involved in the absorption or naturalization of Western literary ideas into a Chinese context. Such difficulties as there were were generally attributed to flaws in Chinese literary culture itself. Problems of accommodation were rarely ascribed to any sense that Western ideas—whether realism, romanticism, Marxism, or modernism—had any inherent contradictions either in themselves or in their theoretical suitability to the Chinese context.

This pattern is notably characteristic of the May Fourth period, that short span of years in the late 1910s and early 1920s marked by the inclination to accept Western ideas uncritically. In fact, the discourse on Western literary theory in the May Fourth period is remarkably consistent in making the assumption that such ideas as realism, romanticism, and "neo-romanticism" were universally valid and that any slippage between theory and practice was owed exclusively to factors unique to China.

This attitude toward literary ideas was not unique within the overall structure of May Fourth thought. Ideas about literature were but an important subset of a general discourse on bringing modern, universally valid ideas to China as the general remedy to a backwardness that, if not attended to, would eventually lead to the dissolution of the Chinese polity. In this formulation, the concept of the modern was indistinguishable from the "Western," and it functioned as the major premise lying behind such subsidiary intellectual formulations as democracy, science, self-liberation, and revolution. Literature was regarded primarily as the vehicle by which one or more of these new and liberating ideas would be brought to China. This constellation of modern ideas served as the governing concept for two separate impulses. On the one hand, it encapsulated all aspirations to overcome those elements of the past—and by the May Fourth period these elements had come to be seen as virtually the total set of things traditional—that were perceived as standing in the way of China's universalizing itself in the company of nations. On the other hand, the modern embodied a discourse of national salvation, or, more specifically, a means of salvaging some sense in which China could maintain a specific identity in the face of this same process of a universalizing modernization.

These two formulations were conjoined by modern Chinese writers as if they were two steps of the same process: the abolition of traditional evils, followed by the construction of new and "modern" social and intellectual entities. But what is hidden in this formulation is that both steps are part of a complex of responses to an unprecedented challenge to Chinese thought—the revelation that indigenous institutions and ideas were not capable of keeping the state together in the face of Western incursion. To make a long story short, the second step in the process—building modern institutions capable of keeping China viable—was, in effect, intended to negate the critical impact of the first step—the invalidation of the traditional system. For the very concept of maintaining the preeminence of the Chinese political order lay at the heart of the traditional ideology that had by May Fourth come to be seen as the totalizing force that made social, political, and intellectual progress impossible.[7] In other words, the motivation for trying to resituate China in a new and universal framework paradoxically arose out of a reflex that sought to obliterate the conditions that had necessitated a call for universalism in the first place.[8]

Chinese intellectuals might have dealt with this impasse by claiming that both China and the West had embarked on a simultaneous excursion into a new and modern world, which, for China at least, was marked by its critical position toward all historical formations in both China and the West. As Levenson pointed out long ago, Marxism embodied just such an ideology. More to the point for literary studies, the concept of "modernity" opened the way toward an even more radical critique of all that had gone before. In considering the appeal of Marxism, however, it should be remembered that the predecessor to Marxism as a total explanatory scheme from the West was the concept of evolution, which was envisioned as a universal discourse capable of demonstrating how the world's particulars were actually part of a historical movement that was pulling in a single direction.[9]

The problem with positing such an all-embracing scheme was that the historical particulars embedded within it kept proliferating and precipitating out of each carefully formulated solution. For Chinese critics of the late Qing who looked at the Western novel as the end of a universal teleological process, for example, the differences in linguistic practices between China and the West were evident from the start. In fact, the harder critics tried to show the universal features of narrative language, the more the differences in Chinese practice forced themselves to the fore. The ineradicable fact of Lin Shu's *wenyan* translations of the staples of the English narrative canon, for instance, should have served as an abrupt reminder to the utopian critics of the late Qing who saw vernacular fiction as a ready way to tap into the mainstream of modern life that the particulars of the Chinese tradition were going to complicate the process of universalization. To cite another example, in later years the "realism" that was envisioned as being such a commonsensical category kept escaping from its ostensibly evident definition and revealing subsets that complicated even the most abstract realization of the ideal. Quite aside from the global misunderstanding on the part of Chinese May Fourth writers of the context in which realism had functioned in the West, described so brilliantly by Marston Anderson in *The Limits of Realism*,[10] the eventual permutations—critical realism, socialist realism, proletarian realism, and romantic realism—taken as a whole serve to discount the notion that realism could ever have constituted a discursive category stable enough to provide a source of positive intellectual guidance.

Historical contingency thus intervened with each attribute set forth as an instance of the master narrative of evolution. At each point where anyone tried to attach the evolutionary universal to cultural praxis, particulars from the Chinese past asserted themselves and demonstrated a critical difference. And as each new facet of historical contingency interposed itself between practical experience and the vision of a perfect process of evolution, Chinese intellectuals were reminded of how the "universal" discourse they were conditioned to seek was in fact a cultural artifact of precisely the alien culture that had nullified an earlier unuttered—but all the more powerful precisely because of that silence—assumption that Chinese culture was universal in itself. In the post-Confucian world of modern China, any attempt to recuperate the condition of universal validity that had been assumed under the empire brought sharp reminders of how irretrievable that prior condition of unquestioned universality had become.

Faced with this impasse, post–May Fourth writers overwhelmingly chose not to question the assumption that universal validity was possible. Rather, any anxiety about the possibility of the extension of literary universals to China was displaced into global condemnation of the particular features of Chinese literary practice and history. These features were seen as the devastating impediment to the implementation of universals, which were, after all, imports from the West. Critics and writers thus created for themselves an intellectual framework in which the native product was always at fault for not living up to a new and transcendent ideal. The unfair treatment of traditional literature by modern critics that resulted is well known. What has not been examined, however, are the consequences this ideology of rejection toward all indigenous products, both past and future, was to have on the development of modern Chinese literature.

The contradictions embodied in May Fourth attempts to establish literary universals at the expense of specific features of Chinese literary practice can be seen clearly in the discourse on realism that was a dominant motif of literary criticism in those years. Although realism was the dominant choice for the entry of the "modern" into Chinese literary discourse, from the beginning a few of those who introduced it confessed to serious reservations about the concept. Rarely did these reservations, however, concern whether a literary genre acknowledged to have been developed abroad might have features rendering it unsuitable to Chinese conditions. Instead, they emerged from the opposite perspective, centering on the notion that the Chinese literary tradition had ill-prepared the ground for the introduction of something that has a clearly established and global validity.[11]

There were two principal reasons that realism (or naturalism, a word seen more often, but used in such a way that it appears to be virtually indistinguishable from realism) took pride of place among literary ideas during the time of the May Fourth movement.[12] Both of these reasons were initially part of a general May Fourth reformist discourse and thus were not originally advanced by specialists with literary matters at the forefront of their concern. First, realism was discovered to lie near the top of a Western evolutionary scheme of the progression of genres. Realism was in this sense seen as the natural successor to classicism and romanticism, two genres that Chinese critics saw as variously dominating the long history of Chinese literature. Realism thus became a token of faith that Chinese literature was moving forward along the universal path pioneered by Western literary practice.

The second factor enhancing the appeal of realism was its identification with movements for social reform that had characterized nineteenth century Europe. In a China desperately seeking ways to elevate itself out of social and political backwardness, the literary form most identified with reform movements in the West was hard to resist. That Japan had earlier introduced literary realism and had gone on to prosper as a modern state added significantly to realism's appeal. In fact, this reformist aspect of Western literature had been a powerful draw long before the May Fourth movement, having been noticed with approval even before 1900.[13]

When literary specialists considered realism, they took their bearings from and generally tried to work within the assumptions framing the larger evolutionary and social discourse, even if their discussion of the details tended to be more specific and nuanced. The critic Shen Yanbing (1896–1981), better known as Mao Dun, the pen name he adopted after 1928, was perhaps more than anyone else responsible for the elaboration of the theory of realism in China. Mao Dun, like most everyone else, accepted the orthodox premises on which realism is based, but his ideas reveal a highly complicated relationship with the concept. His decision to opt for naturalism—the term he used most often—instead of some other "universal" genre grew out of a negative evaluation of Chinese literature rather than from a wholehearted commitment to the aesthetic particulars of the form itself.[14] In accepting the principle that naturalism closely "reflects"—he used the English word at one point—society as it actually is,[15] he saw the genre primarily as powerfully distinct from an old Chinese literature written by authors only concerned with self-expression and completely deficient in the capacity to objectively analyze and describe.[16]

But even as Mao Dun saw the need for an augmented capacity for describing reality, he conceded the power of arguments against a purely objective realism. In late 1920 he even advocated a "neo-romanticism" to compensate for the overly mechanistic side of realism or naturalism:

> If one values only analytic expression, then if it is not biased toward the good, it will certainly be biased toward the bad. Romantic writing and naturalistic writing each go to one of these extremes. Descriptions of ugliness do, of course, have artistic value, but they only represent one side of life and they cannot in the end be considered as faultless and faithful expression. The works of Western postrealist neoromanticism are able to combine both observation and imagination, and the resulting synthesis gives expression to life.[17]

Given his acceptance of the universality of evolutionary schemes, Mao Dun's awareness that realism had been supplanted in the West as the mainstream of literary creativity would have been enough to give him pause about its applicability to China.[18] Thus, even in the long essay he published in July 1922 that seems to have been designed as the final and unequivocal embrace of naturalism that he had been unable to give eighteen months earlier, he still spends considerable time acknowledging the force of objections to the form. He sets out six arguments against realism that he has found to be current in Chinese literary circles, four of which are centered on its "mechanistic materialism." Mao Dun considered this materialism to stifle literature within the confines of a rigid objectivity, precluding the application of the kind of subjective energy that would allow literature to escape the confines of either traditional rules or of a passive attitude toward the possibility of individual agents gaining leverage on their own lives.

By mid-1922, however, Mao Dun appears to have finally decided that the disadvantages of realism were no longer significant enough to require a literary ideology that combined the objectivity of realism and the subjectivity of romanticism. One possible reason for this change may have been his immersion into Marxism in the intervening period.[19] But in Mao Dun's writings from this time, one can perceive a reason that may antecede both his turn to Marxism and his conversion to the ideology of realism: His writings of 1921 and 1922 are permeated with an awareness of and dismay concerning an overwhelming subjectivity in traditional Chinese letters vastly more threatening to the future of Chinese writing than the drawbacks of mechanistic materialism.

Exasperation with a subjectivity that inhibits the writer from gaining a comprehensive fix on reality runs through most of Mao Dun's writings from this period. Perhaps his most detailed explanation of the defect occurs in "The Relationship of People to Literature and the Traditional Misperception of the Status of the Writer in China" from early 1921: "[Literature] that belongs only to the occasional [efforts] of a single self and a single period can, in fact, be good and beautiful. But it can only be the literature of the author himself; it cannot be a literature of a period and even less that of a nation. Historically, most of our literature has this flaw." To counter this defect, he goes on to proclaim that "literature that belongs to [one] person's (i.e., the author's) conceptualization is behind us. Literature is not an author's subjective property, it is not one person's, it is not for amusement when one is happy or for diversion when one is disappointed. Quite the contrary, people belong to literature [rather than literature to any individual person]."[20]

Again, Mao Dun acknowledges the argument noted in "Naturalism and Modern Chinese Fiction" that the stifling environment brought to traditional Chinese literature by the Neo-Confucian precept "literature should convey the *dao*" (*wen yi zai dao*) could only be countered by the powerful feelings residing in literary romanticism. He rebuts this argument, however, by asserting that "I think that Chinese literature is not completely without strong feelings. Are not the 'novels of complaint' full of strong feelings?[21] However, it is just because subjective feelings of anger are too strong in them that their [literary] effect is so unexpectedly poor" (p. 398). In other words, a subjectivity that has long haunted Chinese literature and that Mao Dun senses as a continued danger emerges as the core argument pushing him from his earlier advocacy of neoromanticism toward endorsement of naturalism. His anxiety overpowers the two factors that had earlier motivated the move beyond realism: the evolutionary argument that realism had been supplanted in the West and his earlier belief that the mechanistic pessimism of naturalism required an injection of subjective feelings.

As René Wellek makes clear in his important essay "The Concept of Realism in Literary Scholarship" the discourse on realism in the West is replete with concern over the dangers represented by the interference of the personal voice:

"Objectivity" is certainly the other main watchword of realism. Objectivity means again something negative, a distrust of subjectivism, of the romantic exaltation of the ego: in practice often a rejection of lyricism, of the personal mood. In poetry the Parnassians wanted and achieved *impassibilité*, and in fiction the main technical demand of realist theory came to be impersonality, the complete absence of the author from his work, the suppression of any interference by the author. The theory had its main spokesman in Flaubert but it was also the preoccupation of Henry James.[22]

When Mao Dun came to argue a remarkably similar point, however, he made no such appeal to a common realist heritage. Ironically, the universal terms that the Chinese critic had emphasized elsewhere were readily available. The same critique of the excesses of the subjective voice that Mao Dun frames for China existed in the West. Given the general sophistication of his discussion of the history and features of literary terms and the added weight attributed to Western precedents in the May Fourth era, it seems a bit unreasonable to accuse him of ignorance on this score. Yet Mao Dun for some reason casts his argument—and, it should be stressed, it is one that he deems at once key to his case and of the greatest difficulty (if we are to count the number of times it crops up as an objection to realism)— exclusively in terms of the paralyzing defects of Chinese literary discourse rather than looking to features common to all literatures.

In developing this critique, then—no matter how carefully he has anatomized the literary features of naturalism at other points in his text—the particulars of the Chinese case seem to overwhelm any efforts at keeping the argument on a more general plane. Thus although the attractions of realism have all the qualities needed to constitute a "concrete universal"—something valid in both the general and the specific cases—Mao Dun's fomulation of realism breaks down in the end to something unique to China. And so it was to be for realism thereafter. Sensitivity to the personal voice and its social and political implications was to put a rhetorical spin on the concept in the following decades. In this way the realism imported so hopefully after 1918 would become less a site of speculation about the inherent powers that had been its initial source of appeal. It became instead driven by an intensifying anxiety over why local conditions in China prevented the hopes for it from being realized.

The resulting contrast between the hope Chinese critics came to invest in realism and the extraordinary negativity with which these same critics in post–May Fourth China addressed their own literary tradition allowed them to view literature as a space for things absolutely new. The contrast between new universal and old particulars allowed the former to be invested at will with utopian prospects, while the latter became the home of all literary negatives. By leaving the old behind, in other words, anything became possible. It is thus easy to understand how members of the New Culture Movement after 1919, whether they espoused naturalism, romanticism, or neoromanticism, shared a common and rather extravagant vision of what literature could create for China. Less obvious is the possibility that the realists, in seeking to harness individual vision within a framework of social transformation, were the most radical of all the literary schools in laying the groundwork for a thoroughgoing utopian vision that literature could depict. The strong personal voice of the Creation Society's Guo Moruo and his vision of social melioration, for example, had been on the realist agenda from the beginning.

May Fourth critics in their zeal to turn to the new became trapped in a particularly acute set of contradictions when it came to the evaluation of premodern Chinese narrative. On the one hand, they urgently required China to have a tradition of the novel so as to fit May Fourth narrative work into an evolutionary progression. On the other hand, the clear lack of fit between the old vernacular fiction and the historical record of the Western, "universal" novel set up opposing pressures to deny the Chinese genre any validity as part of a live tradition to build on in the twentieth century. The result is a curious critical posture in which the novel is simultaneously praised as an historical artifact and damned in most of its particular manifestations as an unhealthy influence on the present.[23] It becomes, therefore, virtually impossible to decide what theoretical conception of the traditional novel modern Chinese writers worked from when they set about the difficult task of trying to erect something new. Perhaps the exigencies of national emergency and the consequent attraction of Western ideas were simply too great to allow much speculation about the basic ideas lying behind the genre they were trying so hard to reject. Some conjecture about what the differences between the underlying principles of traditional Chinese and Western narrative, however, no matter how repressed or dimly perceived by the participants in the discourse, seems necessary to flesh out the facile rejection of May Fourth critics.

The conclusions of Andrew Plaks concerning allegory in the traditional Chinese novel are suggestive in this regard. In analyzing the different conceptions of allegory in China and Europe, Plaks wrote: "Each isolated element of the Chinese allegory, by virtue of the existential process of ebb and flow in which it is caught up, 'stands for,' or 'partakes of,' *the sum total of all existence that remains invisible only in its extent, and not in essence.*"[24] Mao Dun's objections concerning traditional Chinese narrative's inability to do anything but keep "accounts" of phenomena may be a way of saying much the same thing.[25] In Mao Dun's view, Chinese fiction records things that are "invisible only in [their] extent" or things in a static mode in which the direction of any motion is always already assumed and thus, depressingly, always already known in advance. In other words, according to the Chinese critic, traditional fiction was restricted to setting forth things that were already fixed within a preexisting intellectual horizon. Seeing in Western narrative the power to create things that were truly invisible before they were written into existence, then, became a profound and utopian source of liberation from the dreary inertia that May Fourth saw as perhaps the principal feature of the Chinese past.

The core of this utopianism was a notion of representation that the critics agreed had not been accessible to traditional writers. This augmented conception of representation occupied the ground between two poles, the one being the potential for bringing individual vision to life—the very thing that Mao Dun had finally come out so strongly against—and the other being the potential for literature to create a clean and objective view of a society in transformation. Each pole also expressed a highly complicated notion of the contribution to be made by the individual voice, from something that had to be fostered to something that had to be most tightly reined in. And realism was conceived as something that could provide the perfect fusion between the two poles, as a power that could bring into being things that had never existed before in literature. And the implication was always—such were the terms of the deal, after all—that this literary existence anticipated existence in real life as well.

May Fourth hopes for representation make even more sense in view of the historical junction of their occurrence. The one point on which virtually all facets of the movement were in agreement was that May Fourth embodied the final realization that neither the conventions of the tradition nor its ideological explanations made sense any longer. The seductive properties of theories of representation become evident. At the precise moment that the immanent world ceased to offer any hope of making sense, a way presented itself of imparting meaning to this new opacity: representationalism, or the assumption that some new and meaningful order could be conferred upon the myriad phenomena found at all levels of life. The possibility of thus imagining something into existence was the precise analog to the social crisis that Chinese radicals were facing in the years around 1919: an old and familiar order had suddenly revealed itself to be a set of empty signifiers, and a novel vision was urgently required to create a new order of meaning.

Understanding that realism implied a capacity for literary representation that Chinese critics saw as unprecedented in Chinese letters should help to clarify the vast appeal of literature to May Fourth reformers. When assumptions about the efficacy of realism were set in the context of traditional ideas of the productivity of writing—perhaps given their ultimate persuasiveness by the vivid memory of the examination system and highly influential debates about the nature and function of writing that began in the late eighteenth century—their appeal seemed to carry with it an almost inevitable link to social practice.[26]

The very ease and plasticity of fictionality as introduced into China in the twentieth century carried with it the seeds of a powerful anxiety that even demonizing traditional literature could not wholly suppress. If fictional realism were so universally efficacious, what was the meaning of its absence from the long duration of Chinese literary history? And if it had been absent for so long, what was to guarantee that it could be successfully imported now? If anxiety about writing's fidelity to the world is a feature of all notions of representation, the form this anxiety took in May Fourth China was of a special kind. As I have tried to demonstrate, it becomes a perpetual concern as to whether a literary ideal can be transplanted onto stony Chinese soil. As such, it would seldom lead in the direction of questioning the means of representation themselves, but rather would be displaced into constant apprehension as to whether or not the individual writer could transcend his or her own tradition sufficiently to be faithful to the terms of the new norm. It was precisely this fear that traditional dispositions regarding writing would recrudesce that caused those who advocated realism to be on guard, principally against the danger of that solipsism that seemed to many critics the most enduring legacy of the Chinese literary tradition.

We thus return to the gap between the local effects of the embrace of a theory of representation and the exalted universal goals that provided the master narrative of its adoption into China. Inasmuch as this was to remain a fault line around which much of the particular texture of modern Chinese literary history formed itself, a closer look at some of the detail produced at this site should shed a unique light on some of the practices and results of post–May Fourth Chinese literature. In looking at those literary practices that most evidently clash with the theory that realism has transcendent validity, it should be possible to get a picture of some of the discursive displacements brought about by the failure to match theory to practice.

The idea that one can fabricate something radically other than the means of fabrication themselves has consequences far beyond the local province of literary texts—political implications, in particular. In looking at the relationship of literature and politics from this perspective, one does not dictate to the other, but rather they share an ideal of the powers of representation to bring imagined worlds into existence. This shared ideal also guarantees a perpetual series of encounters and mutual interventions between the two spheres—after all, they both have their eye on the same discursive space. This enduring symbiosis, the predominant link between politics and literature in modern China, has long been overshadowed by concern with the question of how politics has dominated literary discourse. It is as easy to see Marxism, with its narrative of an inevitable coming into being of the imagined, as the culmination of the contradictory hopes embraced by realism as it is to see any of the various offshoots of realism as the result of the embrace of Marxism by the literary world. A hard look at the history of Chinese realism thus should cause us to reexamine our conventional assumptions about cause and effect. Furthermore, many of the most convincing accounts of the genesis of modernism in the West are based on a notion of a crisis of the bourgeoisie, a social class that China was never to have. The aesthetic ideals contained within representationalism, never envisioned as compromised by having become the ideology of state power, were to remain as perpetual goad to a literary imagination mired in the horrible reality of twentieth-century China. As I will attempt to explain below, this ideal remained even when a persistent social conscience obliged writers to rule out of bounds the more utopian elements of the formulation.

A criticism of modern Chinese literature based on Western notions of representation is considerably more than half right. C. T. Hsia, in *A History of Modern Chinese Fiction*, asks questions concerning the representational adequacy of the texts he examines that their authors are begging to be asked. The argument that he is applying an alien standard to Chinese literature cannot apply in a context in which writer and critic alike are doing their best to pursue modes of writing taken straight from the Western canon. But Hsia's determination to pursue issues of successful representation is indicative of the key issues facing modern Chinese letters in an even more important way. His assumption that literary realism is a transhistorical universal mirrors the moves made by its initial advocates within China to mask the crisis in intellectual life brought about by the adoption of a theory of literary discourse so clearly sensed to be of alien origin. Hsia's almost reflexive findings that Chinese realism is inferior to the real thing mirrors May Fourth frustration in discovering the pitfalls lying in the path of successful adaptation.

In that representation seemed to hold out the possibility of something for nothing, it was in itself the perfect image (or device) of the hope that it held out. But given that it was a new graft, adoption of this idea entailed as well a powerful sense of guilt. In other words, how could serious intellectuals accept this utopian vision, this vast justification for the notion of creating something from nothing, without at least entertaining the idea that it just might all be a massive fraud, particularly in light of its foreign origin? Indeed, the term realism itself neatly obscures the core of representationalism's appeal even as it masks its problematic aspects. By being able to label the representation of things that had yet to come into being as faithful transcriptions of reality, Chinese critics of the May Fourth era could both have their cake and eat it. They could indulge utopian possibilities while claiming the most rigorous discipline in recording the real world. However, this very utopianism insured a perpetual series of crises. If the theory of representation embodied the most extravagant of hopes of social amelioration, the texts actually produced under its aegis were bound by realism's most basic tenets to do at least some justice to the dismal actualities of modern Chinese life. Works of literary realism were thus always doomed to provide the plainest illustrations of how remote utopian fantasies were from any hope of practical realization. The eventual adherence of writers to the stark methods of a Marxist-inspired critical realism guaranteed the persistence of a sharp division between theory and practice that came to be a longstanding rebuke to the unfulfilled hopes of critic and author alike.

Lu Xun's early story (completed in January 1921) "Guxiang" (My old home) offers profound meditations on the circumstances of the personal voice in the modern story. The story is a simple account of a journey back home to dispose of the old family mansion by a highly educated man from a family that once occupied the top rungs of the local social ladder. After having been away for about twenty years, the narrator presents an account of his return that is constantly interrupted and complicated by several almost involuntary reminiscences about happier childhood times. Ironically, these recollections center on visions of a boy from a poor peasant family he had once known rather than on memories of wealth and power. These visions contrast so powerfully with the narrator's current perspective as to be a source of great discomfort to him. At the end of the story the narrator makes a final attempt to come to grips with the significance of this contrast but is able to conclude only that it is impossible to rule out either category of perception.

The two worlds contrast with one another as sharply as they can. One is the world the narrator lives in now, a depressingly monochromatic place of harsh grays and dashed hopes: "Since it was now mid-winter, as we approached home the weather turned bleak again. A cold wind blew noisily into the cabin and, looking out through cracks in the awning, one could see here and there a number of desolate villages splayed out under a sallow sky, quite devoid of life."[27] The other, a world of bright colors and gentle possibilities, is explicitly portrayed as being the one in which the narrator does not live, a world of memory and projected hope: "At this time a marvelous picture suddenly flashed into my mind: a round, golden moon suspended in a deep blue sky and under it the sandy verge of the sea, on which was planted an endless succession of jade-green watermelons. In their midst was a boy of eleven or twelve, wearing a silver ring around his neck and grasping an iron pitchfork in his hands" (477). The spectral quality of this place is stressed in the "marvelous" (shenyi de) vision that comes into the narrator's mind, putting into question whether it resembles anything that ever existed or could exist.

The narrator is paralyzed in the dismal world in which he is situated. He can take no meaningful action, nor can he communicate with the people of his hometown. It is only in his fantasies of the other world that problems disabling him in his ordinary life become magically solved. In his imagined world, for instance, he overcomes the class barriers that prevent him from communicating with those around him, an isolation that torments him in his ordinary life and a condition he seems powerless to change. The imagined world is conjured up initially by his mother's mention of the name Runtu, a boy who had once spent a New Year's holiday at the narrator's house as an auxiliary servant in a busy season. At the time, thirty years before, Runtu had told Lu Xun (as the narrator is called in the story) stories of his home by the sea that had seemed magical and quite beyond ken to the narrator. The imagined world thus is, in effect, a refuge from hard reality for the morose Lu Xun.

When these two worlds collide, as they do most dramatically when Runtu appears at the narrator's home in "real" time, the hopeful one vanishes without leaving any residue that could be built upon. In contrast to the close relationship with Runtu that exists in his memory, when Runtu actually appears, he creates an unbridgeable distance between himself and the narrator by referring to the latter as "Master" (*laoye*). For his part, Lu Xun cannot even think of how to begin to talk to Runtu. Only the narrator's mother is able to fashion some means of communication between the two men. The world of memory thus turns out to be utterly illusory. The illusion, far from providing comfort, only serves as an ironic reminder to the narrator of his desperate circumstances and his isolation. He becomes so anxious that when he reenters his imagination toward the end of the story, he confesses, "When I thought of hope, I became afraid." He contrasts his hope with Runtu's belief in idols: "When Runtu had asked for the incense burner and the candlesticks I had secretly laughed at him. I had thought that he had worshipped idols all along and had never been able to put them out of his mind. But now I gained an awareness about my so-called 'hope': was it not also an idol of my own manufacture? The only difference is that his desires are close to hand, while mine are at a vast remove" (485).

The particulars of the narrator's daily life scheme at all times against his general hope. He finally comes to look on his hope as a sort of addiction that has the power to draw the mind off into solipsistic fantasy from where it is painful to return, the narcotic unreality of the place having such allure. As a result, at story's end, the narrator cannot decide whether the category of hope should exist or not. When he compares it to "roads upon the earth," which do not exist until people actually tramp them out, he would seem to be, however, ruling out the sort of metaphysical hope without certain referent in the world that had constituted his memories of Runtu.

If one construes the narrator's illusory memories in "My Old Home" as emblems of the subjectivity that so obsessed Mao Dun in his critical writings from the early 1920s, one can see in Lu Xun's story a powerful metafiction concerning the representation of the individual imagination in modern Chinese literature. The metafiction is clearly a category that the author of the story considers highly problematic, requiring stringent scrutiny to avoid leading the process of creating fictions away from its self-assigned task of being able to come to grips with the full horror of social reality. As Marston Anderson has pointed out, "For realists, the new fiction could authorize itself only through authors' rigorous moral efforts to purge their consciousness of all modes of self-involvement that might inhibit their capacity for social engagement."[28] The problem as Lu Xun presents it in "My Old Home," however, is that it is perceptually and thus intellectually impossible to separate self-involvement from social engagement. For the only thing that moves the story beyond what Mao Dun would have labeled a mere accounting of things observed—a description he used to negatively characterize the traditional novel[29]—is the involvement of an authorial subjectivity inspired by some notion of hope.

In "My Old Home," then, to the extent to which the dream of a new means of representation is just a dream—an individual vision unattached to any practical consequences—it is pure, and dangerous, illusion. Surely the notion that the act of literary representation itself is hedged in all around by dream and delusion is central to this story. The idea of a new literature helping to fabricate a new reality central to Chinese realism thus continually runs aground on the hard facts of Chinese practice. By representing the problem itself, Lu Xun has found rich and moving material. But the space he has created for new literature as a genre in itself is self-canceling. By requiring that hope be something that exists logically only subsequent to praxis—"after many people pass by a road is made" (485)—Lu Xun in effect undercuts any prospect that realist narrative can contribute materially to anything but its sense of its own inadequacy. In "My Old Home," fiction demonstrates itself to be a powerful instrument of representation, but, paradoxically, only if it represents nothing beyond the problems of representation itself.

If Lu Xun's discovery that the individual voice presents a problem that cannot be overcome is deeply embedded in the literary discourse of the years in which he wrote the story, we would not expect to find the issue presented in the same fashion in the 1930s, by which time variously dogmatic theories of the necessity of the objective depiction of reality had dominated literary thought for a number of years. As we have seen, Mao Dun had begun to espouse a theory of the superiority of realism as early as 1922, and his faith in it had only grown stronger by the time he came to write his own narratives.[30] But one can still see embedded in one of the episodes of his 1933 story "Qiu shou" (Autumn harvest) evidence of considerable unease about the possibility of representation. "Autumn Harvest" is the second part of a trilogy Mao Dun wrote about the contemporary Chinese countryside (the first being "Chun can" [Spring silkworms] and the third "Can dong" [Winter ruin]). The overt theme of all three stories is the pernicious effect of market forces, both domestic and international, on the agricultural economy of the quite well developed countryside in the vicinity of Shanghai. The leading figure of "Spring Silkworms" and "Autumn Harvest," the old peasant Tongbao, had been a successful farmer in the days before the internationalization of the agricultural market, but he shows himself in these stories to be no longer capable of dealing with a new world where the market functions under different rules.[31]

The focal point of "Autumn Harvest," the longest of the stories, is a drought that almost wipes out the summer rice crop in the district where Tongbao and his family live. The crops are saved only through the intervention of a new mechanical pump run from a steam launch anchored in the canal beside the farm. The steam launch, as Tongbao is bitterly aware, represents the influx of Western technology, something profoundly alien to the old man that embodies for him all the changes that have disabled his old familiarity with the world. Tongbao can only imagine the water hoisted onto his field as the saliva of the mud-fish spirit that the (to us) mythic animal will soon return for. The use of saliva here is similar to the depiction of moonlight in Lu Xun's "Diary of a Madman." It is indisputably wet (as moonlight is assuredly not dark), but with a spectral wetness that lacks water's virtues in slaking the thirst either of animal or plant. Tongbao, in other words, fears that the water pumped in by Western technology is merely represented and that since it comes from nothing, it can just as easily return there.

The links in these stories between new and spectral objects of representation and the new economic system brought by the West are always situated in the high foreground. The cost of new equipment purchased in the hope of what invariably turns out to be an imaginary return embodies the harsh economic counterpart to the anxiety concerning the potential of representation. Tongbao, initially reluctant to invest money in ventures based on speculation, is always eventually seduced into participation in such ventures by the promise of extravagant returns. Each time, however, some market force intervenes to dash his hopes and to cost him not only his speculative investment, but a portion of his initial capital as well. The irrigation episode provides a case in point. Initially aghast that pumped-in water will cost eight dollars (eight dollars more, in other words, than it had ever cost before), Tongbao quickly shifts his focus to the returns the harvested rice will bring. Should prices even be close to those of the year before, Tongbao will realize a vast return on his eight-dollar investment. But the rice crop that year turns out to be universally bountiful, and the low prices that ensue ruin the family and cause the old man to have a fatal stroke.

I consider this image a central one for May Fourth's aspirations for literary representation, providing the perfect metaphor for the literary dynamic of those years. The trope perfectly embodies the peculiar mix of utopian fantasies alternating with terror that the whole enterprise is fundamentally without value, that everything imagined in this way not only can never come to fruition but will incur crushing unexpected costs as well. Realism, the idea that something virtually tangible can be generated out of nothing, appears itself as part of this trope. It presents itself in the form of a huge gamble that must be taken in defiance of local conditions that inexplicably but persistently manage only to lengthen the odds against eventual success.

This construction of realism offers as payment a vision based on all-or-nothing speculation at a much higher price than any of the traditional genres of Chinese literature had ever demanded. Foreign technology, as the midwife for this fantasy in "Autumn Harvest," is a trope even more fraught with significance. It indicates the extent to which the post–May Fourth notion of literary representationalism could not exist without foreign intervention even as it points to the extent to which its very foreignness renders the whole enterprise doubly uncertain and doubly "marvelous." The resolve of modern Chinese literature to mask its suspicions concerning the foreign origins of realism behind a determined perception of realism as a natural force becomes understandable in this light. Admitting the foreign and discursive origins of the literary dispensation introduced during May Fourth is to openly accept the speculative status of something that it was hoped could stand as the foundation of a new intellectual order. Not admitting it, however, causes the repressed to exhibit its propensity to eternally return.

It would be possible to trace the force of this trope of anxiety concerning the possibility of representation through at least those metafictions that reflect on the condition of modern Chinese literature. But it is in the convulsive status of realism as a critical category where the traces can be discerned most clearly. Yu-shih Chen's brilliant exegesis of Mao Dun's early fiction makes clear the extent to which the theory of "representation" breaks down under critical analysis.[32] When this powerful exegesis is forced to make a choice between reading Mao Dun's texts as explorations of new imaginative worlds or as tabulations of Party history, Chen opts for the latter. This interpretation of Mao Dun's fictions as allegories of the real world rather than as works trying to flesh out the uncertain domains of realism limned in the May Fourth period points out the extent to which guilt over the suspect origins of realism seems to get the upper hand. If representationalism can crumble in the hands of such an astute critic as Chen, it is understandable that it has failed to survive the ministrations of those critics determined to reinscribe it within a state discourse that seeks only the blandest recapitulation of "things as they are."

Notes

1. Naoki Sakai, "Modernity and Its Critique: The Problem of Universalism and Particularism," *The South Atlantic Quarterly* 87:3 (Summer 1988), 496.
2. Perhaps the most far-reaching exploration of the consequences of Western discursive hegemony in the world can be found in Robert Young's *White Mythologies: Writing History and the West* (London: Routledge, 1990).
3. Since 1989 literary scholarship within China has begun to embrace the complex of issues surrounding the impact of Western discourses on modern Chinese thought and writing. A case in point is Meng Yue's ["You Yi"] breakthrough article, "Ye tan bashi niandai de 'xihua,'" (Addressing 'Westernization' in the 1980s), *Jintian* (Today) 1991: 3–4, 30–42, a piece that

brilliantly explores the domestic political consequences of certain discursive assumptions about China's place in the world. As the work on this topic now being produced is very much in the formative stages, however, it is difficult at this time to gain a good sense of its import and direction. As of the initial writing of this article (1990), the scholarship on modern Chinese literature in the United States has been remarkably slow and reluctant to engage the "postcolonial" discourse that has reshaped so much of contemporary criticism.

4. See Paul Cohen, *Discovering History in China: American Historical Writing on the Recent Chinese Past* (New York: Columbia University Press, 1984), especially chapter 1, "The Problem with 'China's Response to the West.'"

5. The "Postmodernism and Japan" symposium originally published in *The South Atlantic Quarterly* 87:3 (Summer 1988) represents a milestone in this development in Japanese studies.

6. Max Weber perfectly captures the subtly nuanced peremptory tone of the Western discourse on universality in the first words of his introduction to *The Protestant Ethic and the Spirit of Capitalism*: "A product of modern European civilization, studying any problem of universal history, is bound to ask himself to what combination of circumstances the fact should be attributed that in Western civilization, and in Western civilization only, cultural phenomena have appeared which (as we like to think) lie in a line of development having *universal* significance and value" (trans. Talcott Parsons [New York: Charles Scribner's Sons, 1958], p. 13).

The parenthetical "as we like to think" gives this statement its real universalizing force, admitting a relativism that establishes within Western thought a capacity for self-reflection that is a signifier of its power and limitless scope.

7. Lin Yü-sheng in his important book *The Crisis of Consciousness: Radical Antitraditionalism in the May Fourth Era* (Madison: University of Wisconsin Press, 1979) gives due stress to the ways in which the radicals of the May Fourth period conceived of the past as a monolithic barrier to progress. His phrase "totalistic iconoclasm" perfectly captures this May Fourth disposition.

8. Although aware of the contradictory nature of the two discourses of particularism and universalism, Levenson seems to have more or less systematically avoided the full implications of that contradiction. See, for instance, his *Revolution and Cosmopolitanism: The Western Stage and the Chinese Stages* (Berkeley: University of California Press, 1971), p. 30: "For China to be both culturally cut down and politically cut up was too crushing to contemplate. And the second of these conditions promised to perpetuate the first." However, he failed to recognize the full opacity of the cultural defense mechanisms that grew out of the first of his two insights. Levenson's failure to deal with the extent to which discourses out of the past still pressed

upon modern China is evident in the way in which his concept of "museumification" was utterly incapable of accounting for the fury of the Cultural Revolution.

9. On Social Darwinism, see James R. Pusey, *China and Charles Darwin* (Cambridge, Mass.: Harvard University Council on East Asian Studies, 1983).

10. Marston Anderson, *The Limits of Realism: Chinese Fiction in the Revolutionary Period* (Berkeley: University of California Press, 1990).

11. C. T. Hsia developed an idea—"obsession with China"—that deals at the thematic level with Chinese literature's sense of its unique burden: "The Chinese writer sees the conditions of China as peculiarly Chinese and not applicable elsewhere." Why Chinese writers have been unwilling or unable to adopt Hsia's prescribed remedy, that they simply see their subjects as part of the common "condition of modern man," is one of the problems this chapter tries to address. Hsia, "Obsession with China: The Moral Burden of Modern Chinese Literature," in *A History of Modern Chinese Fiction*, 2d ed. (New Haven: Yale University Press, 1971), p. 536.

12. Although Chinese writers at various times point out that naturalism implied a more purposeful disposition toward social reform than did realism, in practice the features attributed to naturalism were almost invariably fully applicable to realism as well. Much of Chinese thinking on these issues was inspired by the Japanese critic Shimamura Hōgetsu (1871–1918). See Bonnie S. McDougall, *The Introduction of Western Literary Theories into Modern China* (Tokyo: The Centre for East Asian Cultural Studies, 1971), pp. 100, 168–169, 176, 182, 183. See also Marián Gálik, *Mao Tun and Modern Chinese Literary Criticism* (Wiesbaden: Franz Steiner Verlag, 1969), p. 80.

13. In a long essay published in 1897 explaining why their newspaper, the Tianjin *Guowen bao*, was to begin issuing a fiction supplement, Xia Zengyou (1865–1924) and Yan Fu (1853–1921) mentioned, albeit almost in passing, that the "enlightenment" (*kaihua*) in Europe, America, and Japan had received the "assistance" (*zhu*) of fiction. Xia and Yan, "Guowen baoguan fuyin shuobu yuanqi" (The origins of our [decision] to append a fiction supplement to the *Guowen bao*), in Guo Shaoyu and Wang Wensheng, eds., *Zhongguo lidai wenlun xuan* (Selected essays on Chinese literature through the ages) (Shanghai: Shanghai guji chubanshe, 1980), 4, p. 205. On the influence of Japanese literary thought on China, see Ching-mao Cheng, "The Impact of Japanese Literary Trends on Modern Chinese Writers," in Merle Goldman, ed., *Modern Chinese Literature in the May Fourth Era* (Cambridge, Mass.: Harvard University Press, 1977), pp. 63–88.

14. See McDougall, "Literary Theories," pp. 176–177.

15. Shen Yanbing [Mao Dun], "Wenxue yu rensheng" (Literature and life), in Zhao Jiabi, ed., *Zhongguo xin wenxue daxi* (hereafter *Daxi*) (Compendium of modern Chinese literature) (Hong Kong: Wenxue yanjiu she, n.d.), 2, p. 164.

16. Mao Dun's concern for this issue is indicated by the number of times he comments on it. See, inter alia, "Shemma shi wenxue?" (What is literature?), in *Daxi* 2, p. 170; "Ziran zhuyi yu Zhongguo xiandai xiaoshuo" (Naturalism and modern Chinese fiction), in *Daxi* 2, pp. 391–394; and "Wenxue he ren de guanxi ji Zhongguo gulai duiyu wenxuezhe shenfen de wuren" (The relationship of people to literature and the traditional misperception of the status of the writer in China), in *Mao Dun wenyi zalun ji* (A collection of Mao Dun's essays on literature and the arts) (Shanghai: Shanghai wenyi chubanshe, 1981), 1, p. 23.

17. Shen Yanbing [Mao Dun], "Xin wenxue yanjiuzhe de zeren yu nuli" (The duties and efforts of researchers in the new literature), in *Daxi* 2, p. 162. A slightly different translation can be found in McDougall, "Literary Theories," pp. 181–182.

18. He admitted this in a January 1921 proclamation issued in the name of the "Society for Literary Research" (Wenxue yanjiu hui) announcing the society's plans to reform *Xiaoshuo yuebao* (Fiction monthly). His statement encapsulates precisely the contrast between the "world" universal and the Chinese particular: "Realist literature has recently already shown signs of decline, so from the standpoint of world [trends], it seems as if we should not spend too much time introducing it. From the standpoint of our own literary situation, however, the spirit of realism and the actuality of realism have hardly made an impression [on China]. Therefore, we believe that the introduction of realism is still an urgent necessity." Shen [Mao Dun], "'Xiaoshuo yuebao' gaige xuanyan" (Proclamation of the reform of *Fiction Monthly*), in *Mao Dun wenyi zalun ji* 1, p. 20. See also McDougall, "Literary Theories," p. 173.

19. McDougall seems to accept Gálik's judgment on this point (p. 182). For Gálik's account, see pp. 47–48 of *Mao Tun and Modern Chinese Literary Criticism*.

20. In *Mao Dun wenyi zalun ji* 1, pp. 23, 24.

21. *Daxi* 2, p. 395. Mao Dun separates traditional Chinese fiction into two categories, that of pornographic intent and *fa laosao de xiaoshuo*, which I translate "novels of complaint." By the latter he means fiction written to settle personal scores by putting a particular perspective on a personal dispute into fictional form. He gives no examples but would seem to have in mind those Qing and early Republican novels written with partisan opinions about particular contemporary events labeled by Lu Xun *qianze xiaoshuo*, "novels of censure."

22. René Wellek, "The Concept of Realism in Literary Scholarship," in Stephen G. Nichols, ed., *Concepts of Criticism* (New Haven: Yale University Press, 1963), pp. 246–247.

23. These contradictory feelings about *xiaoshuo* can be traced back to Liang Qichao's seminal 1898 essay "*Yi yin zhengzhi xiaoshuo xu*" (Preface to

the printing of [the series of] political novels in translation), in Guo and Wang, *Wenlun xuan* 4, pp. 205–206, in which Liang praises the idea of the novel in the most glowing terms even as he condemns all extant Chinese examples of the genre. In addition to Mao Dun's early works of criticism discussed above, Zhou Zuoren's "Rende wenxue" (Humane literature) is full of praise for the idea of literary representation while expressing considerable hostility to the traditional Chinese novel, which Zhou condemns as being generally inhumane (*Daxi* 1, 222–223). One can detect the same ambivalence in many of C. T. Hsia's evaluations of the Chinese novel.

24. Andrew Plaks, *Archetype and Allegory in the Dream of the Red Chamber* (Princeton: Princeton University Press, 1976), p. 110; emphasis added. This question of fundamental conceptual differences between Chinese and Western literatures has become an issue on which more heat than light has been shed in recent years. All I am suggesting here is that, for all their confident discourse about universal literary forms, the actual narratives of modern Chinese writers betray a powerful skepticism as to whether imported literary forms can do what they take Western critics to be saying they can do. From the perspective of May Fourth critics, the claims made by the advocates of realism in the West were downright grandiose; anxiety on the Chinese side was correspondingly great.

25. See "Naturalism and Modern Chinese Fiction" in *Daxi* 2, pp. 387–388.

26. A survey of late-eighteenth- and early-nineteenth-century debates about the role of writing in Chinese intellectual life is contained in my "From Writing to Literature: The Development of Late Qing Theories of Prose," *Harvard Journal of Asiatic Studies* 47:1 (June 1987), 51–96. It is my thesis there that "writing" (*wen* or *wenzhang*) took on far greater significance in intellectual life in the years after 1790 than it had before that time. The almost constant series of negative references to the Tongcheng and *wenxuan* schools of prose in a wide variety of May Fourth writing would indicate the continuing resonance of the early-nineteenth-century debates.

27. In *Lu Xun quanji* (Complete works of Lu Xun) (Beijing: Renmin wenxue chuban she, 1981), 1, p. 476. Subsequent references to this text will be given parenthetically in the text. The standard English translation of "My Old Home" is contained in Yang Hsien-yi and Gladys Yang, trans., *Selected Works of Lu Hsun* (Peking: Foreign Languages Press, 1956), 1, pp. 63–75.

28. Anderson, *Limits*, p. 44.

29. "Naturalism and Modern Chinese Fiction," in *Daxi* 2, pp. 387–388.

30. Mao Dun's key documents of Chinese realism, "Cong Guling dao Dongjing" (From Guling to Tokyo) and "Du Ni Huanzhi" (Reading *Ni Huanzhi*) date from 1928 and 1929, respectively. The latter can be found in *Mao Dun wenyi zalun ji* 1, pp. 277–294, while the former, at odds with the leftist literary line over the years, was not included in that collection. It is appended

to Fu Zhiying, ed., *Mao Dun pingzhuan* (Critical biography of Mao Dun) (Hong Kong: Nandao chubanshe, 1968), pp. 341–368. A translation of "From Guling to Tokyo" by Yu-shih Chen is included in the anthology *Revolutionary Literature in China*, edited by John Berninghausen and Ted Huters (White Plains, N.Y.: M. E. Sharpe, 1976), pp. 37–43.

31. All three stories are contained in the Renmin wenxue chuban she set *Mao Dun wen ji* (Literary collection of Mao Dun), published between 1958 and 1961 (rpt., Hong Kong: Jindai tushu gongsi, 1966), 7, pp. 279–360. "Qiu shou" is on pp. 306–338. Translations by Sidney Shapiro can be found in *Spring Silkworms and Other Stories* (Peking: Foreign Languages Press, 1956), pp. 9–95. "Autumn Harvest" is on pp. 39–73.

32. Yu-shih Chen, *Realism and Allegory in the Early Fiction of Mao Tun* (Bloomington: Indiana University Press, 1986).

DAVID D. W. WANG

Lu Xun, Shen Congwen, and Decapitation

In 1906 in Japan, Lu Xun (1881–1936) saw a slide show in which a Chinese crowd idly watched as one of their compatriots was beheaded for spying on the Japanese army in the Russo-Japanese War.[1] What ensued is by now a familiar story. Dumbfounded by this scene of decapitation, Lu Xun realized that, before saving the Chinese people's bodies, he had first to save their souls; hence before practicing ordinary medicine, he had first to cure the spirit of China with the medicine of literature. A slide show of decapitation triggered a crucial moment in Lu Xun's life and thereby set the direction of modern Chinese literature.

Implied in Lu Xun's traumatic experience is a representational chain linking soul and body, body and language, referent and referentiality. For Lu Xun the fiction writer, decapitation would signal not only a barbaric form of punishment conducted and watched by the cannibalistic Chinese, but also the mutilated condition of the meaning system that makes reality what it is.

Lu Xun was not the only modern Chinese writer attracted to the social and literary implications of decapitation. Shen Congwen (1902–1988) also wrote extensively about the bloody form of capital punishment. Dwelling on his benign, lyrical presentation of life in southwestern China, critics have rarely discussed why or how Shen Congwen wrote about decapitation or mentioned its link with lyricism. The subject, nevertheless, merits attention, not only because it constitutes an important part of Shen's recollections of his childhood and military life, but also because it serves as one of the best examples of his radical lyricism. Put side by side, these two writers' stories of decapitation form a dialogue, pointing to one of the major controversies in modern Chinese fiction: what are the ethical and aesthetic limitations of realist writing?

I

In the reported slide show of 1906, Lu Xun saw the more despicable side of the Chinese character. How could Japan and Russia wage a war against each other but choose China as their battlefield? Why were Chinese willing to serve as spies for foreign troops at the risk of decapitation? Why did Chinese show more curiosity than indignation when they were brought to witness one of their compatriots being beheaded? Sixteen years after he first saw the slide show, Lu Xun stated, in *Nahan* (A call to arms): "The people of a weak, backward country, even though they may enjoy sturdy health, can only serve as the senseless material of and audience for public executions.... Our first task was surely to transform their spirits, and I thought at that time that literature could best meet the task of spiritual transformation. I then began to think about promoting literary activities."[2]

The moment of seeing a decapitation in the slide show triggered the most crucial turning point in Lu Xun's life, changing him from a modern student of medicine into a traditional member of the literati. No longer would he adopt the viewpoint of clinical anatomy when faced with a Chinese about to be beheaded. As a convert to the tradition of literature, he saw in the body a representational organism of signs, voicing a complex of meanings about the Chinese character and society—which were cowardly, selfish, callous, and cannibalistic.

The argument as Lu Xun presents it is already a figurative one, dramatizing his anxiety about the primordial loss of origin. Meaning and life are symbolized by the head and loss by the mutilated body. His effort to add retrospectively a beginning, a head, to his literary career itself indicates his anxiety. Critics like Leo Lee have pointed out that the traumatic slide could never be found, and Lu Xun might have fabricated the whole story, giving an allegorical form to his abstract conception.[3] Lu Xun is known to have manufactured or refashioned personal experience for literary purposes. The case of decapitation suggests that fiction and (private and public) history might have become inextricably confused at the (textual) beginning of modern Chinese (literary) history.

Yet Lu Xun's anxiety over decapitation or rupture of meaning did not prevent him from taking advantage of decapitation and rupture in his literary imaginings. Critics have repeatedly noticed that Lu Xun's most engaging works deal not with his reasoning about China's fate but with the "dark side" of his reasoning, not with coherent social and epistemological systems in prospect or retrospect but with the ruptures of those systems.[4] When the representational order of the world he establishes for himself breaks loose, demons, superstitions, and macabre fantasies haunt him. And, strangely, before these dark forces can be exorcised, he is first hopelessly deceived or even charmed by them. Lu Xun's anxiety over decapitation and headlessness serves as the secret fountainhead of his literary inspiration.

One notices an ambivalent adherence to the imagery of dismemberment or mutilation in both Lu Xun's fiction and his essays. For instance, his "Yao" (Medicine), reportedly inspired by the decapitation of the woman revolutionary Qiu Jin, points out the bloody cost of revolution and its gratuitous rewards. Yet the story also betrays Lu Xun's strange fascination with the macabre ritual and cannibalistic superstitions that form part of the ceremony of beheading.

Decapitation is one of the leitmotifs in another famous Lu Xun short story, "Ah Q zhengzhuan" (The true story of Ah Q). Public beheading represents for Ah Q and his fellow villagers both a "heroic" way of death and the most thrilling form of entertainment. But the action culminates in the anticlimax of an absence of beheading, thereby striking the last blow to Ah Q's logic of spiritual victory and mocking his audience's "nostalgia." Stranger yet is the story "Zhujian" (Forging swords), Lu Xun's rewriting of the classical tale about Mei Jianchi's revenge of his parents' murder by the Prince of Qin. In the story, beheading and self-beheading are depicted not so much as a necessary means of revenge as a decadent sport participated in by both the heroes and the villains, in search of sadomasochistic pain and pleasure.

Although critical of the convict about to be decapitated, Lu Xun was more upset by those Chinese in the slide who stood around watching the execution. Lu Xun's onlookers were admitted to the scene to be taught a lesson, to be scared by the death of one of themselves, but Lu Xun could not but notice with resentment that the audience was excited by the rare spectacle and shared a secret sense of a carnival atmosphere. In an essay titled "Changong daguan" (A spectacle of chopping communists), Lu Xun depicts how the crowds in Hunan relished the decapitation of several young women communists with a fervor almost equatable with sexual ecstasy: "One 'crowd' ran from the south to the north [of the town], another from the north to the south. In hustle and bustle, they screamed and yelled . . . their facial expressions showed either that they were longing for a scene of decapitation or that they had already been satisfied by ones they had seen."[5] Literally and symbolically, modern China was a "head"-less country, crowded by spiritually decapitated people whose lives were intensified only by watching beheadings or waiting to be beheaded.

Lu Xun would have shared Michel Foucault's view that classical punishments were often designed with a strong theatrical dimension.[6] Through performing corporal mutilation in public, authorities not only impose torture and humiliation on the convicted victim but also extend their power to those who are watching the execution. But for Foucault, in the public display of bodily punishment there always lurks a threat. Besides fear, the bloody spectacle brings its audience an unexpected thrill that upsets the solemnity of the execution and may even threaten to turn it into a festive occasion. At its extreme, the audience's deviant response to public corporal punishment may threaten the authorities, since it implies either an indifference to or a rebellious consciousness of the power displayed by the mutilated body.[7]

If Foucault has a point in noting the mixed ideological and psychological outcomes of the public spectacle of punishment, a "crisis" can be seen in Lu Xun's treatment of decapitation. Insofar as he expects his readers to read the meaning of beheading more "seriously" than the immediate audience of decapitation, that is to say, to realize the tyrannical power at work behind the scene, he recapitulates better than anyone else the representational meaning imposed by the authorities on the body. On the one hand, though conceptually against the authorities that legitimize the cruel decapitation, Lu Xun shares the same moral and penal *episteme*. On the other hand, Lu Xun reveals his secret alliance with the cannibalistic audience he openly condemns, when he indulges his ironic fascination with the theatrical turmoil and spectacular bloodshed of public beheadings and reveals the cynical knowledge that whatever happens, things remain the same. Stretched between these two contradictory and complementary roles, Lu Xun has put himself in a state no better than poor Xianglin's wife in "Zhufu" (The New Year's sacrifice), who is haunted by the possibility of being dismembered by her two dead husbands in hell yet finds no plausible form of escape.

The way Lu Xun handles decapitation calls for a reconsideration of the problematic of realism. The anguish Lu Xun suffers at the scene of beheading is underlain by an imaginative encounter with a primordial emptiness. Decapitation must signal not only a barbaric form of punishment left by previous generations, a powerful symbol of the Chinese people's state of spiritual dehumanization, but also the mutilated condition of the meaning system that makes reality what it is not. Watching the slide show of the Chinese crowd watching a decapitation, where did Lu Xun situate himself? Reading (watching) Lu Xun watching the Chinese crowd watching the decapitation, how should we readers modulate our moral and intellectual distance from the narrated subject? This vertiginous interplay between authors' and readers' engagement in and detachment from "reality" has become one of the major issues of modern Chinese critical realism.

Marston Anderson once suggested that the realist discourse initiated by Lu Xun prefigures its own formal and ideological gap.[8] Lu Xun (and his followers) explored a discursive form in which the gaps between the text and the world, the self and others, narrated truth and historical reality are supposed to be bridged. Lu Xun led his contemporaries in demonstrating the mimetic power of realism, but his "confirmation" of social abuses and inertia soon proved to be a vicious circle, making him just as much a critic as an accomplice of the forces he had vowed to overthrow. In an effort to reform and "reform" Chinese reality, Lu Xun's own writing remains "severed" from the outset.

But more paradoxical is the ideological mandate that looms ever larger behind Lu Xun's realist discourse. As suggested by his preface to *A Call to Arms* quoted above, Lu Xun believed the task for intellectual reformers was to take over people's minds and that the best way to accomplish this was to inscribe in them a new consciousness as if they were naked writing tablets. But what really fascinated Lu Xun was the representational power of the body and the head. The new, sophisticated rhetorical power of literature in place of the ritual anatomy of torture and decapitation is, after all, derived from the politics of bodies and has its effects on bodies. Spiritual lessons have to find somatic manifestations. At its best, the mind serves as a surface for the submission of bodies to the control of ideas.

Implied in Lu Xun's writing about decapitation is a theory of literature that emphasizes the representational link between mind and body, body and language, referents and referentiality. But Lu Xun's longing for a full-fledged representation of the real ironically nurtures itself on the "break" in this chain of referentiality, as emphatically symbolized by a beheaded body, a split personality ("Diary of a madman," "The New Year's sacrifice"), a living dead man ("Zai jiuloushang" [In the tavern]), or a "speaking" head on a deformed or decayed body ("Mujie wen" [Tomb tablet], "Cong baicaoyuan dao sanwei shuwu" [From Baicao garden to Sanwei study]). It is this break that drives home Lu Xun's imaginary nostalgia for the semantic and somatic plenitude of China. Given Lu Xun's iconoclastic pose, what Lin Yü-sheng calls the traditional "totalistic" mode of thinking permeates Lu Xun's writing, only now as the negative cause, postponing the presence of the real.

Lu Xun's anxiety about the break between the body and the soul motivated a long line of writings in the thirties. In the forties, leftist ideologues took up where Lu Xun left off, giving his realistic problematic a crude and abrupt solution. When Mao Zedong and his literary cohorts asserted that literature should and can openly serve political purposes, writing about reality did bring about bodily discipline or punishment. A literature almost without rupture or anxiety replaced Lu Xun's literature of rupture and anxiety, invoking Lu Xun's name and suppressing Lu Xun's voice.

II

Shen Congwen's references to decapitation can be seen in works like *Wo de jiaoyu* (My education; 1929), "Huanghun" (Twilight; 1934), "Xin yu jiu" (The old and the new; 1935), "Qian xiaojing" (Little scene in Guizhou; 1931), "Sange nanren yu yige nüren" (Three men and one woman; 1930), *Congwen zizhuan* (Autobiography of Congwen; 1934), and *Xiangxi* (West Hunan; 1938). Decapitation is described as a common form of penalty practiced by rural authorities in late Qing and early Republican days even though advanced penal technology was already accessible. In *Autobiogra-*

phy of Congwen, Shen relates how the Miao aborigines were beheaded by the thousands after the failure of their rebellions in the late Qing period, how, on the eve of the Republican revolution, local agitators were arrested and put to death by decapitation, and how this cruel form of execution still went on wherever warlords seized local power.[9]

As a child, Shen saw thousands of heads hung out for display on the city wall or simply dumped on the river bank before family members sorted them out. More appalling is his recollection that soldiers often arrested innocent peasants to fulfill their daily quota, and after a certain number of killings, they let their captives gamble their lives in a lotterylike religious ritual. The winners were set free, while the losers had to resign their lives to fate.[10] Thus, it was not unusual to see in Shen's works an unlucky peasant bidding farewell to his cellmates and asking them to settle for him things unfinished at home ("Twilight"), a sad child carrying baskets containing the heads of his father and his brother, walking home on a mountain path ("Little Scene in Guizhou," *Autobiography of Congwen*), or, more gruesomely, dogs fighting for the decomposed bodies left on the river banks (*Autobiography of Congwen*).

Given the cruelty of public decapitation, one expects a post–May Fourth writer either to lash out at the backwardness of the Chinese penal system or to deplore the callousness of those who participate in such bloody spectacles. Besides Lu Xun, Wang Luyan represents such a case. In his short story "Youzi" (Grapefruit), he bitterly criticizes the "shows" of public beheading in Hunan and ridicules the onlookers as grapefruit buyers.[11] Shen Congwen must have witnessed far more scenes of decapitation than his peers, and he may well have been more qualified to testify to the injustice and inhumanity of the killings. But in the works under discussion, one gets a feeling that his attitude toward decapitation is ambiguous, if not weak. Besides toned-down humanitarian comments, he always seems to have something else to say about the old capital punishments.

The novella *My Education* deals with Shen Congwen's early experience as a soldier; watching decapitation was one of the highlights. The novella contains twenty-three sections; twelve of them contain explicit descriptions of scenes of decapitation. Shen Congwen writes: "Army life is too monotonous; only scenes of decapitation can make strong soldiers excited."[12] After the beheading, some of the soldiers climb to the top of the tower where the heads are hung, playing with the eyes of the dead, some throwing heads at each other for fun. Even Shen himself kicks at the hard skulls and hurts his toes. At night, the soldiers get together. They kill and cook dogs using the same knife they kill people with in the daytime and boast about what they see and do on the execution grounds. But as the days go by, Shen Congwen feels bored even with the spectacle of decapitation. One morning, he walks to the bridge near the execution site. Four headless bodies are still there. "A handful of ashes of paper money looks like a blue chrysanthemum, flecked with dark red traces of congealed blood" (130). Everything is quiet.

Shen is far less worried than Lu Xun about attaching any inherent meaning to the subject of decapitation and headlessness. Where Lu Xun sees in decapitation the stupidity and cannibalism of the Chinese mentality, Shen Congwen finds a complex of coexisting human motives. As in the decapitation scenes he narrates in *My Education*, Shen Congwen is one of the heartless audience, as Lu Xun would have it, scared and thrilled by the bloody scenes. But Shen is also the young soldier dutifully observing daily routine as part of the "war" and the young sensitive artist saddened by the meaningless waste of human life.

Thus, in "Little Scene in Guizhou," the scene about decapitation is like a vignette inserted into a broader picture that is itself an impressionistic slice of life in Guizhou. In "The Old and the New," Shen uses black humor in describing how a professional decapitator loses his sense of value after the technique he has mastered so well is replaced by a more modern method of execution. It is the decapitator, not the decapitated, that wins sympathy. And in *Autobiography of Congwen* and *West Hunan*, as a massive number of people are killed on different occasions, Shen maintains a retrospective posture that combines ironic curiosity and a sense of intellectual and emotional distance.

In "Twilight," Shen Congwen's narrative manifests its lyrical rhythms in weaving varied sensory images from natural and human environments into a fabric and providing correspondences among them. The ever-changing colors in the darkening sky, mothers' dinner calls, a romantic flashback in an old prison warden's mind, prisoners' anguished cries, and the smell of pork on the supervisor's stove are all presented at the same level of narrative proportion, calling for equal attention. Shen Congwen's lyrical imagination originates less with the metaphorical correspondence between the head and the body or the individual and the society than with the method of metonymical replacement, which provides a phantasmal connection between likes and unlikes, between existing phenomena of experience and absent objects of desire.

I am not saying that Shen Congwen lyricizes the horrible decapitation at the cost of social conscience or conferring on Shen Congwen a privileged, transhistorical position. At the readerly level, when a lyrical tone is applied to a scene of cannibalism or when legal injustice and bloody punishment are integrated with casual daily routines like eating and sleeping, Shen's narrative is bound to drive us to question the moral consequences both of the political system that legitimizes decapitation and of a literary mode like lyricism that is used to delineate such a political system.

Shen Congwen's rhetorical strategy makes the urgent subject appear and "disappear" on the same surface of his narrative and renders a discordant harmony among things. In Shen's lyrical agenda, ugly things are neither erased nor reversed as a supplement of the real, but only "displaced," as it were, from their roots, to enact a dreamlike simulacrum. The most human part of his story (like decapitation) is rendered as the most literal, whereas the most insensible part may prove the most allegorical. Instead of reciprocal spontaneity, one finds in Shen's lyrical discourse a complicity shared among characters and between characters and the narrator.

If one senses a strong irony here, the irony stems not so much from Shen Congwen's reversal of the cognitive hierarchy of referents in reality as from his exposure of the figurativeness of referentiality itself in presenting the real. In his decapitation stories, Shen does not erect a symbolic system around the head alone; he builds instead associative relations between likes and unlikes, what exists and what does not.[13] An essential simultaneity is embedded in his poetic vision of the world that demands that readers have multiple perspectives and weave together all sensory impressions. The result is a fundamental undecidability of meaning in his stories. But such a nondefinitiveness or *aporia* should not be understood merely in contemporary critical terms. It takes on a moral and historical dimension ironically by refusing to add another dogmatic voice to the ideology-ridden discourse of modern Chinese literature.

The best example of Shen's view of decapitation is "Twilight." Lacking a clear plot line, "Twilight" tells basically of the daily routine of decapitation in a small town in the mid-Yangtze valley. It opens with an overview of the serene life of a shabby city at sunset: sunshine reflecting the last spectrum of colors in the darkening sky, smoke from cooking fires coming out of the chimneys, and children winding up their games before supper. As part of the late afternoon city scene, a decapitation is soon to be conducted in a detention center. Hearing soldiers' footsteps getting closer, prisoners start to get anxious. Names of those who will be executed are then announced, followed by sighs, cries, and noises of feeble resistance, dragging, and beating. An old warden is standing by, watching the daily turmoil of his job. Moments ago, he was carried away by thinking of the gains and losses of his own life, necessary preparations for his own death, and the wanton adventures of his youth. He can do little with those innocent victims. Shortly, their heads will be cut off and scattered all over the execution site, becoming toys for kids to kick around.

What baffles us here is Shen Congwen's narrator, whose descriptions understate all the scenes in a familiar, casual tone. His use of the iterative style in describing the procedure of decapitation and onlookers' responses especially risks dissolving the temporal and psychological urgency of the particular round of executions about to take place. Besides, the narrator's voice refuses to stay only with the core of the narrative—the prisoners to be beheaded—and shifts from one consciousness to another. One will not forget the prisoner who, when asked for his last words before death, requests that his fellow villagers pay on his behalf a small bill he owes to a painter, nor will one forget the supervisor of execution who loses his temper at the delay of the daily routine by a soldier's misdeed, thinking of the pot of braised pork already well heated on his stove.

As the night finally falls, by the end of the story, the narrator seems to subject himself to the embrace of the impending darkness—the power of the unknown. Human and nonhuman activities are thus gradually diffused into each other. What is important and what is not are no longer distinguishable in the zone of twilight.

One can speak of Shen Congwen's ironic intention that reveals the absurdities of the real world by understating rather than exaggerating them. But I suspect that the real polemical problem with a story like "Twilight" is that it draws readers' attention to it without their having any specific interest in the subject matter supposedly at issue or confidence that the work itself is a definitive treatment of anything. Contrary to conventional wisdom that Shen's lyrical fiction provides an all-embracing aesthetic of consolation, I would argue that Shen's "critical" lyricism leads him to break away from the total (or all-embracing) mode of thinking and writing Chinese reality, a mode that permeates the discourse of modern Chinese realism.

In conjuring up a story where things and creatures *seem* to exist nakedly in resistance of any interpretation, Shen Congwen must have learned a lot from Turgenev. Even his description of the prisoner's honest last wish mentioned above reminds us of the farmer Maxim of "Death," in *Sketches from a Hunter's Album*, who asks his wife and friends to return money he owes to others before his death from a logging accident.[14] Still, since Shen is not bound to a conscious viewpoint like that of the Russian gentleman-hunter, he is left with more freedom to disorient his narratorial position in exchange for an indefinite expansion of perspective. He removes and scatters, as it were, the objects of his story line, and consequently, he offers his readers a mystically "graphic" construction of the scene of decapitation in that the narrated "event" is literally described and the "narrative" event, the language as displayed by Shen Congwen, demands equal attention.

The anti-definitiveness or *aporia* that outlines Shen's lyrical vision takes on a moral dimension, since it refuses to impose a new dogmatic view on a Chinese society already in disorder, while revealing its own expression as a literary and linguistic and therefore a partial, culture-bound practice. Shen Congwen's belief in and "fear of" the pure form of language and its poetic performance should not be seen merely as a predilection for stylistic craftsmanship; rather it must provide a key to his artist's vision of reality.[15] His poetic (or lyrical) worldview demands paying just as much attention to the linguistic surface of a work as to the "deep" meanings behind it.

An arguable "reality" does not represent itself; it is represented. If a literary presentation of life is substantially a rhetorical performance, a formal display of language rather than an outcome of logical or ideological prefiguration (such as the canons underlining "hard-core" realism), then the text can be liberated from the Lu Xunesque "iron prisonhouse" of referential determinism and can gain freedom to express its figurations of the real. By describing Chinese reality in terms of a *lyrical* realism, Shen Congwen questions the privileged position of Lu Xun's kind of realism in representing the world; Shen also redraws the conventional boundary of lyricism. Emphasis on language and poetic expression is also confirmation of a writer's choice in "figuring" out the world. At its peak, Shen's ironic view of text and world dissolves the distinction between realism and lyricism, between prose and poetry, and asserts the fundamentally figured—that is to say, poetic—nature of all language. This may well explain why even when Shen Congwen confronts a pathetic subject directly, he can still manage to transmit a sense of poetic composure.

This special mode is not a Chinese strain of Mallarméan nihilism, nor does it leave its stories *mise en abîme*, as a poststructuralist might have. Shen never makes irony a mode overpowering other modes, as, say, Lao She tends to do in his finest writings. One always has to understand the deep "moral" concern behind Shen Congwen's mixed expression of lyricism and irony, however different his "moral" pose might look from other May Fourth writers'. This moral bearing may stem from the long Chinese tradition that stresses the ethical dimensions of rhetoric (*shi yan zhi*, or poetry expresses one's feeling or will), and it is reenforced by Shen's own existential consciousness of human absurdity and the need to affirm choice against psychological and sociopolitical determinisms.

In welding incongruities of rhetorical form and subject matter, Shen melds human beings' immensely complex emotional capacity to cope with contradiction and the built-in contradictions of any ideal moral-political order. A discourse of lyricism enables him to emphasize the creative force of language and the freedom of human perception, while his sense of irony leads him to bracket, but not to do away with, any lyrical indulgence in life. Only through allowing both narrative modes to illuminate each other, putting one another "under erasure," as conventional critics would have it, can we appreciate that, in a most subtle way, Shen's art expresses the humanism of the May Fourth Movement.

Shen Congwen's rewriting of decapitation with a displaced lyricism thus proposes an alternative to Lu Xun's treatment, a treatment that was overloaded with guilty conscience and moral anxiety. Lu Xun and Shen Congwen share the same kind of repulsion toward social-political abuses and feel the same pathos over the follies and cruelty of humanity. But in search of an artistic expression of their feelings, they demonstrate different approaches. Lu Xun is both horrified by and obsessed with the spectacle of decapitation; the severed body paradoxically "embodies" for him a world broken into pieces; Shen Congwen, who has seen thousands more decapitations than Lu Xun, is engaged not in what the beheading "means" in itself but in how it can be written about so as to let us remember and "re-member" the rest of the world.

Lu Xun attempts to marginalize the human capacity for denial and dismemberment by calling it nonhuman and, in that desperate denial of denial, reaffirms it as inescapably human. He attempts to redefine humanism from a critical position outside history, but the consequence is not humanism but historically understandable rage and self-contradiction. Shen Congwen, in refusing to marginalize the human capacity for denial and dismemberment, writes it into the unbounded space of historical activity. Instead of taking up a position outside history, Shen Congwen takes advantage of all the duplicities of being in a historical moment and invokes a double perspective, of the old China and the new. Shen Congwen's famous lyricism comes from this effect of historical doubling, of the new age knowing the old by remembering it while not being trapped in it. Shen's historical lyricism constitutes a critique from a position that is itself open, one that affirms the human capacity for change, not one that tries to reform humanity by cutting off part of it from the name of "human" (and certainly not a position outside history that praises the past by cutting off cruelty and dismemberment as somehow not "human"). In contrast to the traditional view that juxtaposes Lu Xun's and Shen Congwen's works in recourse to the tired binary model of all-rejecting critical realism versus all-embracing lyricism, I have argued that both writers have faced a mutilated condition of referentiality and reality and that both writers have offered a critique, one metaphysical and one lyrical.

Lu Xun's and Shen Congwen's writings on decapitation inscribed a crucial moment of Chinese writers' search for a discourse of modernity. The final irony is, in the twenties and thirties, when most writers took Lu Xun's decapitation complex seriously, making him the "head" of modern Chinese literature, it was "meek" Shen Congwen who showed how to remove this "head" and break the spell of literary decapitation.

Notes

1. For a full account of this incident in Lu Xun's life, see, for example, Leo Ou-fan Lee, *Voices from the Iron House* (Bloomington: Indiana University Press, 1987), pp. 17–18.

2. Lu Xun, Preface to *Nahan* (A call to arms), *Lu Xun quanji* (Complete works of Lu Xun) (Beijing: Renmin wenxue chubanshe, 1981), 1, p. 417.

3. Lee, *Voices*, p. 18.

4. T. A. Hsia, "Aspects of the Power of Darkness in Lu Hsun," in *The Gate of Darkness* ed. T. A. Hsia (Seattle: University of Washington Press, 1968), pp. 146–162. See also *Voices from the Iron House*.

5. Lu Xun, "Changong daguan" (A spectacle of chopping communists), in *Lu Xun zawenxuan* (Selections of Lu Xun's essays) (Shanghai: Renmin chubanshe, 1972), p. 124.

6. Michel Foucault, *Discipline and Punish: The Birth of the Prison*, trans. Alan Sheridan (New York: Pantheon, 1977), pp. 24–95.

7. Ibid. For a detailed discussion of Foucault's concept of "discipline and punish," see, for instance, Frank Lentricchia, *Ariel and the Police* (Madison: University of Wisconsin Press, 1988), pp. 29–102.

8. Marston Anderson, *The Limits of Realism: Chinese Fiction in the Revolutionary Period* (Berkeley: University of California Press, 1990), pp. 76–92.

9. Shen Congwen, *Congwen zizhuan* (Autobiography of Congwen), in *Shen Congwen wenji* (Works of Shen Congwen) (Hong Kong: Sanlian shudian, 1984), 9, pp. 100–219.

10. Ibid., p. 165.

11. Wang Luyan, "Youzi" (Grapefruit), in idem, *Youzi* (Grapefruit) (Shanghai: Shenghuo shudian, 1937).

12. Shen Congwen, *Wo de jiaoyu* (My education), in *Shen Congwen wenji*.

13. In haste to rejoin head and body, to restore China to its proper self, Lu Xun overlooks the possibility that there are many alternatives to his pharmaceutical imperative (to effect a "cure" to China's spiritual "malaise"). Shen Congwen's moral concern about China is the equal of Lu Xun's, but this moral concern does not give him the guilty conscience that haunts Lu Xun and his followers, sending them in search of a desperate remedy. A moralizing realism has no prior claim to moral realism. Had Lu Xun lived long enough to write novels and stories as abundantly as Shen Congwen, he would surely have found his way into other realisms.

14. Ivan Turgenev, *Sketches from a Hunter's Album*, trans. Richard Freeborn (Baltimore: Penguin, 1967), pp. 129–144.

15. For further discussion, see David D. W. Wang, *Fictional Realism in Twentieth-Century China: Mao Dun, Lao She, Shen Congwen* (New York: Columbia University Press, 1992), pp. 203–206.

TONGLIN LU

Red Sorghum: Limits

of Transgression

Among Chinese experimental writers of the late 1980s, Mo Yan stands out as the transitional figure par excellence. Right after its publication in 1986, his novella Red Sorghum (Hong gaoliang),[1] caused a sensation among Chinese readers and literary critics.[2] A year later, Zhang Yimou, a Chinese director of the "Fifth Generation," adapted Mo Yan's story to the screen. The film, also entitled Red Sorghum, won a Golden Bear Award at the Berlin International Film Festival.[3] Mo Yan became famous before other experimental Chinese writers, most of whom are his juniors. Moreover, his popularity among the general Chinese readership is still much greater than that of his younger colleagues.[4] Because this novella has greatly contributed to his popularity, I have chosen Red Sorghum as my object of study in this chapter in order to situate Mo Yan's success in its particular historical context.

The story is about the romance between the narrator's grandfather, a bandit, and his grandmother, a rich landlady, as well as their participation in the Anti-Japanese War in Gaomi, located in Shangdong. As a teenager, "Grandma" is married to a rich leper by her parents. "Grandpa," her chief sedan bearer Yu Zhan'ao, murders the leper after making love with the bride in the sorghum field. Consequently, Grandma becomes the owner of her dead husband's wine factory; Grandpa becomes a bandit and the owner of the woman. When their son, the product of their romance in the sorghum field, reaches the age of fourteen, the Japanese invade the country. Liu Luohan, Grandma's manager and possibly her lover, is skinned in public by Japanese soldiers. Incited by Grandma's eagerness for revenge, Yu Zhan'ao decides to attack Japanese trucks using rather unconventional methods. At the beginning of the battle, Grandma is killed by Japanese bullets while carrying food for Grandpa and his team in the sorghum field. Her son and her lover, hidden among the sorghum plants, end the battle by killing a famous Japanese general.

On the one hand, Mo Yan's novella differs largely from socialist realist works in its ideological, discursive, and narrative structures. The choice of outlaws and adulterers as Anti-Japanese heroes mocks the Communist Party's self-portrait of the national hero in the Anti-Japanese War. Supernaturalism, which occupies a large space in the story, goes against the basic assumption of socialist realism, namely, faithfulness to reality. The story is narrated by an "I" who presumably never participated in the events of the story. The narration is further complicated by the perspectives of the narrator's father and grandmother, whose reminiscences are intertwined with events situated in an already remote past. This manipulation of complicated narrative perspectives transgresses the convention of a seemingly objective and objectifying narrative framework in socialist realism. On the other hand, *Red Sorghum* remains traditional in comparison with the works of Mo Yan's followers not only because it is more "realistic,"[5] but also because the author's effort to subvert socialist realism is so transparent that it constantly calls attention to itself.

However, the transitional stage in literary history in which the novella is situated largely contributes to its popularity. *Red Sorghum*, emerging at a historical moment when a radical change in Chinese fiction was badly needed, offered an image of change that was not too unfamiliar or too shocking for a readership that, despite its resentment, was accustomed to socialist realism. Furthermore, this apparent familiarity was paralleled by an effort to defamiliarize the reader from socialist realism and to shock him or her by the work's sheer difference. What can be more seductive than this difference that does not require a fundamental change in reading habits? It fulfills the longing for novelty without intolerably provoking the natural resistance to change in the readership.

The transparent linkage to its object of subversion, socialist realism, and its transitional function in Chinese experimental fiction make *Red Sorghum* all the more interesting. Understanding certain devices that work in *Red Sorghum* may help us understand how much Mo Yan and his generation of Chinese experimental writers, despite the apparent influence of Western avant-garde literature, are largely (counter-) products of the communist domination in China.

Nostalgia for a remote past—exemplified by the narrator's exclusive interest in his grandparents' life in *Red Sorghum*—often leads contemporary Chinese experimental writers to the exploration of an origin that is free of any communist influences. Since this origin cannot truly be traced to any remote past, but rather exists in the mind of its author,[6] it may be perceived as a fantasized origin serving as a counterimage or a mirror-image of the communist culture.

Ambivalent and indefinable, this fantasized origin has from the outset been lost. The irrevocable loss of the origin, however, does not hinder Mo Yan's work from being haunted by a more historically situated past, the orthodox Chinese tradition. The ideological and cultural past that is more truthfully connected to a historical origin is totally different from the past that serves as a fantasized origin in Mo Yan's work. The author prefers to reject, or at least to hide, the historical past—which for the sake of convenience I will call the first past. The first past contradicts Mo Yan's belief in the value of an individual self, whereas the second past, the imaginary origin recreated by him, glorifies his belief in individualism.

The implicit image of the first unwanted past exists in *Red Sorghum* by means of a refraction of the communist rejection of China's old traditions. This implicit image exists either as a counterpart to or as an accomplice of communist ideology. Mo Yan's romanticization of the traditional sexual hierarchy through the relationship of the narrator's grandparents functions as a counterpart to the women's liberation movement in Communist China. At the same time, his contempt for traditional ethics and social institutions manifested in the glorification of rebelling forces more subtly acknowledges the legacy of the communist ideology of class struggle.

In the narrator's praise of his grandmother as a "pioneer of individual liberation" (ZGXS, 112), it is the first past—the orthodox Chinese tradition—that Mo Yan rejects as restrictive of individual freedom. After all, the story is about outlaws and adulterers who daringly challenge social structures and marital institutions. In the light of Western individualism and, less conspicuously, of communist ideology, the author considers certain conventions of the Chinese culture backward. But through its misogynistic portrayal of women, by the implicit excuse of subverting the communist ideology of equal rights between the two sexes, Mo Yan's world of fiction reconciles itself to the first past—the traditional Chinese patriarchy. This past still indirectly controls its two rebelling descendants: communists in their political and social hierarchy, and most contemporary experimental writers in their sexism.

Red Sorghum is especially interesting in its contrast between a negatively hidden origin and a positively reconstructed origin, since this stance on "origin" is very common among Chinese contemporary experimental writers. The contrast between the first and second pasts highlights the novella's complicated, often self-contradictory relationship with different axiological systems: Chinese tradition, Western liberalism, and communist ideology.

The Linguistic Subversion of Communist Discourse

In Red Sorghum, Mo Yan attempts to reconstruct the second past in the image of the narrator's home in the countryside, Gaomi. The narrator's description of Gaomi at the beginning of the story reveals the contradictory nature of this reconstruction:

> In the past, I passionately loved my northeastern county of Gaomi, and I also passionately hated it. When I grew up, I diligently studied Marxism. I was finally enlightened: undoubtedly, my northeastern county of Gaomi is the most beautiful and the ugliest, the noblest and the earthiest, the most sacred and the dirtiest, the most heroic and the vilest place on earth, where one can drink and love to one's heart's content. The people of my county love sorghum, and every year they plant a great amount of it. In the eighth month in the middle of autumn, the limitless sorghum field reddens, transformed into an immense ocean of blood. The sorghum is tall, dense, and splendid; sorghum is melancholic and lovely; sorghum is passionate and loving. (ZGXS, 103–104)

What does the narrator's perception of his home county as a paradoxical entity have to do with his "diligent study of Marxism"? At a superficial and literary level, there seems to be a reference to Marxist dialectical materialism, an important component of Chinese Marxist-Maoist discourse. Given that one of Mao Zedong's three major philosophical works is entitled "On Contradictions" ("Maodun lun"), in investing the image of his home county with contradictory values, the narrator apparently is paying his respects to this Marxist-Maoist principle.

However, the "diligent study of Marxism" can be understood as ironic at a different level. Since "Marxism" in China has become a political metaphor for the party line, to study Marxism can be interpreted as a political expression of a person's loyalty to the dominant ideology. Born in a family of "upper-middle peasants," Mo Yan in his writings seems obsessed with his politically disadvantageous milieu.[7] In Red Sorghum the narrator's parents can only be second-class citizens in contemporary China owing to their financial situation as well-to-do peasants in the "old society."[8] In this context, "to study Marxism" implies that, at least for a short period in his life, the narrator tried to reject his milieu—the countryside, which represents the marginalized natural world—by adopting the opposite value system, that of the city, which is also the political and ideological center of the Communist Party.

The narrator's passionate hatred and love for his home in the country metaphorically describes his oscillation between the values of the countryside, or natural earth, and the values of the city. His choice of the earth in the end expresses a return to his original milieu and a deep disillusionment with his experience of "studying Marxism." However, his disillusionment does not prevent him from remaining deeply enmeshed in Marxist-Maoist discourse, in spite of, or because of, his conscious subversion of it. At a deeper level, his literary and ironic identification with Marxist-Maoist discourse comes back to haunt the author of Red Sorghum. His emotional attachment to his hometown as a paradoxical emblem certainly has its roots in Marxism. However, because Mo Yan carefully distances himself from realism or materialism by taking refuge in supernaturalism, these roots cannot necessarily be found in Marxist dialectical materialism, but must be sought in the author's use of language.

Mo Yan's use of language often reveals his contradictory relationship with the dominant discourse. The superlative *zui*, for example, was used frequently by Mao Zedong and his followers. Fifty years ago, in order to establish the norms of socialist realism in China, Mao Zedong, the leader of the Chinese Communist Party, wrote the following passage:

> The source of literature and the arts resides in people's lives. Despite their primitivity and coarseness, these materials are the liveliest, richest, and

most essential. In this sense, they outshine any literature and arts. People's lives are the unique source of literature and the arts, a source that is inexhaustible. It is the sole source, no source outside of which may survive.[9]

In this passage, Mao used zui three times to describe "real life" as the source of literature and the arts: "the liveliest" (zui shengdong), "the richest" (zui fengfu), and "the most essential" (zui jiben). In addition, "unique," "sole," and "inexhaustible" are also superlatives.

The abundance of superlatives exemplifies the logic of the Communist Party, which assumes the role of owner and guardian of the absolute truth. The logic of zui is also the logic of the totalitarian state and of its indisputable authority. Despite his tendency toward dialectical materialism, Mao Zedong hardly allowed anyone to apply dialectical principles to the authority of the "correct" party line, of which he was the permanent personification.

Interestingly, if we go back to Mo Yan's passage, we find that the description of Gaomi conforms to Mao's canon of literary creation in this particular linguistic aspect. The narrator uses zui ten times to describe the open countryside. Nevertheless, the same word creates a different image, owing to the juxtaposition of opposite qualities. Mao's use of zui indicates a single direction, the monological world of the Party further limited by the adoption of its dogmas by his faithful followers, whereas Mo Yan's zui presents a world of insoluble contradictions, disorientation, and fragmentation. The logic that combines "the most beautiful" and "the ugliest" is a logic of paradox and absurdity. The world in which Mo Yan and his contemporaries live is indeed an absurd world. Ironically, the absurdity has been created largely by the Party's logic of zui that has tried to repress differences and oppositions. Under a homogeneous surface, divergences existed more persistently than ever during the three decades of communist domination. During the Cultural Revolution, the Chinese people became deeply disillusioned with the reigning order, because the events of that period amounted not only to a further destruction of traditional culture but also to the self-destruction of the communist ideology through endless fighting between various political cliques.

After the Cultural Revolution, the Communist Party tried to reestablish its credentials by using Western technology in its campaign for "modernization." But contrary to the expectations of most communist leaders, the new program provided a counterreference to the communist ideology: Western bourgeois liberalism. This development shook the ideological foundation of communist China even further. Since the appearance of unity can no longer be maintained, communist China has become ideologically fragmented.

As a result, Mo Yan's subversion of monological discourse is very much caught in linguistic patterns reflecting its current fragmentation. By attributing "the most" (zui) contradictory qualities to his hometown, Mo Yan makes this linguistic feature polemical and disrupts a seemingly closed system of discourse. There is no longer a single highest order. On the contrary, different or, more precisely, conflicting orders exist in the world of fragmentation to the point that the world itself is disoriented. The contrasting values in Mo Yan's description of his hometown can be taken as a metaphor for the China of the 1980s in its dispersal of and disillusionment with the power that has dominated China for more than thirty years. The linguistic disruption of the Party's monological "highest order" can thus be seen as an accurate presentation of the collapse of the communist ideology paralyzed by its exposed contradictions and oppositions. In this respect, Mo Yan's use of the superlative zui as a polemical feature is far more realistic than the conventional language of socialist realism.

Nevertheless, Mo Yan's description of his hometown does not specifically aim at the duplication of the agony of communist ideology in China, but rather intends to create an image of life full of primitive energy and strength. Mo Yan's generation, born after the establishment of communist power, witnessed the dissolution of communist ideology. For them, this image can be found more easily in a past apparently free of communist influence.[10] How could Mo Yan and his generation of writers, experimental or not, recreate this past that is so remote from their own life experiences? More specifically, how could Mo Yan accomplish the reconstruction of the past by using a language that is still heavily saturated with communist discourse? Natural life in Mo Yan's fiction, defined by its object of subversion, largely originates from the fragmentation of the same object, communist ideology. In other words, Mo's original world exists in opposition to the dominant discourse and is determined by its oppositional nature. Mo Yan's notion of original life has little to do with the recreation of a precommunist traditional China. That part of the historical past, which I have been calling the first past, has been lost forever. In that case, what is the second past, this fantasized origin recreated by the author of *Red Sorghum*?

The disintegration of the communist ideology after its years of domination will not bring about a return to the original world. On the contrary, its fragmentation is accompanied by a fragmentation of all of Chinese culture, be it popular or elite, because its domination was established by the violent destruction of the old world. The death of a murderer cannot bring his or her victim back to life; it only settles accounts by reenacting the symbolic death of the victim, in a "radical annihilation of the symbolic texture through which the so-called reality is constituted."[11] In other words, instead of restoring the beauty of the original life in China, the settling of accounts means a second death of the old tradition—death in our memory. Under the communist regime the educational system did not provide an efficient way for young generations to become familiar with traditional culture, the "symbolic texture" through which the nation's past is constituted; with the collapse of communist ideology the memory loses its raison d'être as a form of resistance among certain Chinese intellectuals to the dominant ideology.

In this sense, Mo Yan's reconstitution of the beauty of an original life in the image of the immense sorghum fields is necessarily utopian, because there is no return to the past, but only a negation of modern life. Grandma, who embodies this beauty, has to die in the prime of her life, showing that the return to the past is forever impossible.

The Sorghum Field and the Female Body

To a large extent, Grandma exemplifies the author's impossible desire for a return to an imaginary past. Her name is rarely mentioned at all in the story. Grandma remains her only name, except once when she is named by an old countrywoman reciting a folk rhyme to her grandson about Grandma's contribution to the battle against the Japanese invaders (ZGXS, 112). This folk rhyme is extradiegetic. The absence of her name reveals the paradoxical nature of the author's desire for an eternally desirable female body that is at the same time an efficient tool for the reproduction of male descendants. Because she is less a person of flesh and blood than a conceptualized object of male desire, the heroine must remain nameless. By situating her in a past to which her grandson, the narrator, does not have any access, she is securely free from the contamination of communist ideology. By attributing his father's birth to his grandmother's unlawful romance in the sorghum field, the narrator rejects the family ethics of traditional China. By depriving her of life at the age of thirty, her grandson can desire her well-preserved image of youth and beauty, untouched by the erosion of time.

Like the landscape of his hometown, Grandma's body becomes a location on which the narrator's most contradictory values converge. These values express denials or rejections of other value systems, such as communist ideology and traditional Chinese ethics. However, these contradictions, negations, and rejections miraculously emerge as a positive image of life through the premature death of Grandma. Since her death reconciles past generations with youth, seduction with reproduction, and prolonged sensual desire with its sublimation, Grandma has been transformed into an image functioning as a utopian solution for the author's desire to reconstruct a new world based on the fragments of the old. Furthermore, because Grandma's body is identified with Gaomi, the narrator's hometown, a symbol of natural force and primitive energy, this new world represented by the female body is perceived as an idealized origin, supposedly free of communist influence—which for the sake of convenience I call the second past.

On the verge of death, Grandma remembers the consummation of her passion with Grandpa. Both the memory and the act of remembering occur in the sorghum field. Through her dim eyes, the sorghum field is viewed as a supernatural stage for her dying consciousness. To a large extent, this stage is identified with her body, or more precisely becomes its extension:

> Father left, running. His footsteps were turned into soft and tender whispers and then transformed into the music from the paradise that she had just heard. Grandma heard the voice of the universe coming from the red sorghum plants. She gazed at them. Through her dim eyes, the sorghum plants were marvelously beautiful and had fantastic shapes. They moaned, twisted, shouted, and intertwined. Sometimes they resembled demons, and sometimes they resembled members of her family. In Grandma's eyes, they intertwined like knots of snakes, then, brusquely expanded. Grandma was unable to describe their splendor. They were red and green, white and black, blue and green. They laughed loudly, they cried loudly. The tears they shed, like raindrops, rapped at the desolate

desert of Grandma's heart. Between the sorghum plants, fragments of the blue sky were inlaid; the sky appeared at the same time so elevated and so close. Grandma felt that heaven, earth, human beings, the sorghum plants, everything was woven together, covered by a gigantic shade. (ZGXS, 168)

At different levels, this passage reminds us of the narrator's description of Gaomi. As in the narrator's description of Gaomi, Grandma's vision of the sorghum field is characterized by paradoxes. The difference is that the geographical location Gaomi is described by the narrator as an object. Its contradictory nature is revealed by adjectives—thus, as static qualities. In contrast, in Grandma's description the geographical location of the sorghum field manifests its paradoxical nature through actions.

Both Gaomi and the sorghum field have a symbolic function as the representation of an original world characterized by unsolved contradictions. The difference does not occur at the level of geographical location, but rather at the level of its relation to the two different subjects. For the male narrator, the location is still mainly a stage for actions, such as "drinking" and "loving," shared by his fellow villagers. Since the sorghum plants in the narrator's description are humanized by the use of adjectives (static verbs), such as "melancholic" (qiwan) and "passionate" (aiqing jidang) (ZGXS, 104), the humanized natural world remains passive. Therefore, there is still a clear-cut line of demarcation between the male subject and the landscape. For his female ancestor, however, the sorghum field, humanized by action verbs, becomes a stage for her consciousness, where the sorghum plants, like herself, perform their contradictory actions. In this case, the line of demarcation between the female subject and the objective world is blurred and on the verge of disappearing. In a process of identification, the subjectification of the sorghum plants objectifies Grandma's body by transforming it into a stage for actions. Like Gaomi, the country of the red sorghum, Grandma is the object of "countrymen's love" shared by the narrator (ZGXS, 104).

The sorghum plants are viewed by Grandma as part of the objective world. This objective world, however, is not completely separated from the viewer's subjectivity. On the contrary, the subject and object of viewing become largely identical in a metaphorical world of mutual reflections.

The actions of moaning and twisting that are attributed to plants actually belong to the wounded Grandma on the verge of death. This kind of shift is an intentional manipulation of conventional language and a transgression of socialist realism: combining an inanimate subject with an animate verb or combining an animate subject with an inanimate predicate or verb. In this passage, the positions of things and human beings are reversed. Grandma is reified as a static eye or a theatrical stage, whereas the sorghum plants, humanized, display their activities on this stage. As we see in this passage, they are capable both of dynamic actions—"They intertwined like knots of snakes in Grandma's eyes, then brusquely expanded" (ZGXS, 168)—and of complex emotions—"They laughed loudly and cried loudly." The humanization of sorghum creates a double layer of surrealism by its fantasy and also by its contrast. The sorghum plants are presented not only as human beings, but as more powerful than people, since they can at the same moment perform the most contradictory actions—expanding and restraining themselves—and experience the most conflicting emotions—laughing and crying. The ability to experience the most paradoxical actions and feelings deifies the sorghum plants as the quintessence of the original world.

The deification of the sorghum plants romanticizes Grandma, as plants and her consciousness merge in this world of primitive energy. Both the sorghum field and the female body represent the world of paradox. To a large extent, paradox in Mo Yan's fiction is turned into a symbol of strength, energy, and freedom, since it leads to dynamism, tension, and movement. In this world of paradox, constant motion destabilizes any possible authority. Its breaking of rules and restrictions may explain Grandma's nonconformism and the sorghum field's limitless possibility of actions. Nevertheless, the female body, like the landscape with which it is identified, is largely excluded from the world of dynamic movement. The representation of paradox by her body makes a woman's participation in paradox highly improbable, if not impossible, since the female body mainly serves as a stage for paradoxical actions, not as their agent. As a result, Grandma's first sexual act, even with her lover-to-be, must be disguised as an act of rape. Furthermore, she must die at the very beginning of the battle against the Japanese—mortally wounded by the first Japanese bullet. In the story, this battle is the most important action highlighting the paradoxical nature of the world of the red sorghum—the world of extreme hedonism and heroism in their most basic forms. In both love and war, her body is used as a sacrificial victim—passively representing the action, but not actively participating in it.

The deification of the heroine parallels her objectification. There is a chiasmatic relationship between Grandma and the sorghum plants in this passage. Explicitly, by viewing the sorghum field from a woman's perspective, the reader seemingly is invited to enter Grandma's subjective world. Implicitly, this subjective world is already preempted by nature, represented by the sorghum field. Grandma's consciousness, deified by its reflection of the sorghum plants, is objectified by the same act of reflection. Like the sorghum plants, her actions are devoid of any subjective agent, since they are mainly manifestations of nature.

Grandpa's first lovemaking to Grandma starts as an act of rape. Disguised as a bandit abducting her to the sorghum field, Grandpa begins the sexual sacrifice of the woman by stepping violently on a number of the sorghum plants (ZGXS, 165). This action symbolically unifies the object of sexual violence, the female body, with its sacrificial altar, the sorghum field. The rape of the woman is equal to the violence done to the sorghum plants.

Like Grandma, the sorghum field is portrayed as "marvelously beautiful" in its "indescribable splendor." Like Grandma, it is the object of people's desire, or of "countrymen's" (*fulao xiangqin*) love (ZGXS, 104). The agitations of the sorghum plants metonymically remind us of Grandma's suffering at the last moment of her life. At the same time, they can also be interpreted as her orgasm, echoing her sensuality in their frantic movements of moaning, twisting, shouting, and intertwining. In this sense, not only are the images of the sorghum plants and the woman identical, the images of life and death are also indistinguishable.

In a sense, the desire for the woman's body is also the desire for her absence or her death, because the glorification of the male subject's actions can only be sanctified by the sacrifice of the female body as the object of desire. Grandma's premature death makes her representational value of paradox everlasting. The sacrifice of her youthful body, which has already accomplished its reproductive task by giving birth to a son, eternalizes her function as the icon of male desire. Because of her premature death, her image is glorified in two paradoxical ways. On the one hand, the narrator, her grandson, is a living image of her past, through biological ties and also by his act of story writing. On the other hand, she remains the object of intense male desire. Even her grandson can worship her as a sexual object—safely and glamorously. Nevertheless, even in a remote past, the femininity Grandma embodies is highly contradictory and can be preserved only through the premature death of the heroine in order to reconcile her social function—as son bearer—and her imaginary function—as eternal object of male desire.

The Socialist Realist Legacy

On the surface, the contradictory male desire projected onto Grandma, namely, the desire for a woman who functions both as a mother and as a prostitute, is as ancient as any civilization.[12] In fact, this traditional paradox is further complicated by a desire for woman's subtly limited independence, which may be traced to the socialist realist legacy.

The women's emancipation movement initiated by the Communist Party encouraged Chinese writers to portray women as rebelling, independent, and daring. Be they female students like Lin Daojing in *Song of Youth*,[13] country girls like Chunlan in *Genealogy of the Red Flag*,[14] professional revolutionaries like Jiangjie in *Red Cliffs*,[15] or housewives like Xiaomei in *New Heroic Biographies of Sons and Daughters*,[16] women of socialist realist literature are generally characterized by their outspoken, unconventional, and strong personalities.

The socialist realist novel *Bitter Flowers*, written in 1958 by Feng Deying, is about an oppressed peasant woman, named Mother, who supports her daughters and sons joining the communist revolution and treats everyone in the revolutionary army as her own children.[17] At the beginning of the novel, the chief of her clan reproaches Mother for letting her eldest daughter, Juanzi, participate in social activities.[18] In the old man's eyes, Juanzi's behavior is against Confucian ethics, which forbids women from playing a role outside their households in the name of "three submissions and four virtues" (*sancong side*).[19] In this sense, a woman's participation in the revolution implies independence vis-à-vis traditional ethics, especially Confucianism.

In Mo Yan's *Red Sorghum*, Grandma's independence also subverts Confucian ethics. As a daughter, she disregards her father's arranged marriage. As a wife, she forbids her husband to touch her, in self-defense. Moreover, she commits adultery with the murderer of her legal husband. In other words, Grandma transgresses the rules of the "three submissions" imposed on Chinese women by Confucian ethics. In this respect, Grandma resembles her revolutionary sisters in socialist realist literature. If the chief of the clan in *Bitter Flowers* had lived in the world of *Red Sorghum*, he would have used exactly the same terms to reproach Grandma, Mo Yan's "pioneer of individual liberation," as he did to Juanzi, Feng Deying's woman revolutionary.

However, revolutionary women became independent from traditional social norms in order to serve the communist cause, whereas Grandma gains her independence apparently in order to enjoy sexual freedom. Like the contradictory male desire for a woman who can play the roles of both mother and prostitute, the notion of women's independence in socialist realist literature is inherently contradictory. A woman needs to be independent to serve as an oppressed voice against the old society. But this voice enjoys freedom only to the extent that it depends on the leadership of the Communist Party in order to be heard. In this case, women's independent attitudes toward the old society must be strictly disciplined by the Party, which is basically patriarchal. Mo Yan's portrayal of the sexually "free" woman inherits this contradictory notion of the independent woman in socialist realist literature: Grandma's apparent freedom in *Red Sorghum* must be subject to strict restrictions by masculine power.

Although every heroine of socialist realism chooses her lover or husband according to her personal feelings, her love is always justified by the lover's revolutionary qualities and the collective approval of these qualities. In *Bitter Flowers*, Jiang Yongquan, who has initiated Juanzi into the revolution and is also her leader, talks about revolution enthusiastically. His speech makes Juanzi realize that she is indeed in love with her teacher:

> Every word rapped at Juanzi's kind and tender heart. She became excited, saturated with hatred and love as well as with strength resulting from her passion. She hated—she hated the enemies to death. She loved—she loved these unknown revolutionary companions, these martyrs who had sacrificed their last drop of blood.[20]

Afterwards, Juanzi continues to meditate on her feelings for Jiang Yongquan. She loves him because every revolutionary loves such a good person. She loves him more because he is "her leader, comrade, companion." Her love for his body is instrumental in her love for the revolutionary cause, since her love is not personal but collective, shared by anyone who belongs to this large revolutionary community. Moreover, the object of her love is not only her lover, but every unknown revolutionary who has his qualities. Paradoxically, even though every male revolutionary may have virtually the same qualities, Juanzi must remain loyal to her chosen lover.

Mo Yan's portrayal of Grandma in *Red Sorghum* deliberately transgresses this stereotype of the revolutionary woman in socialist realism. Apparently, Grandma is not concerned with any moralistic values in her choice of Grandpa as her lover. Nevertheless, the evocations of individualism before her death strangely remind us of Juanzi's revolutionary slogans. Grandma proclaims:

> Heavens! What is chastity? What is justice? What is good? What is evil? You have never told me. I have behaved in accordance with my own will. I love happiness. I love strength. I love beauty. My body belongs to me. I am my own master. I am afraid neither of crime, of punishment, nor of your deepest hell. (ZGXS, 167)

Grandma's self-justification on the verge of death by refuting social conventions can be matched by the revolutionary slogans in Juanzi's description of her love in their artificialness and hyperbolism. This overflowing passion and overdramatic language masks a sense of emptiness or of indifference, because the speakers in both cases, instead of being the subjects of their own statements, mainly serve as spokeswomen for other lofty causes. In *Bitter Flowers*, as a teenager from the countryside falling in love for the first time in her life, Juanzi mainly thinks about her passion for all her lover's unknown companions. In *Red Sorghum*, as a country woman who has never been seriously concerned with any ethical values in her life, Grandma on the verge of death spends her precious last moments intellectualizing about the meaning of her transgressive sexual behavior. As Juanzi's expressions of love for her lover illustrate the author's political stance in *Bitter Flowers*, Grandma's confessional voice, which makes a great effort to justify her romance, displays Mo Yan's belief in individualism. Juanzi in *Bitter Flowers* loves Jiang Yongquan because he represents the revolutionary cause. Grandma in *Red Sorghum* loves Yu Zhan'ao because he personifies masculinity by his strength and power. Her "own will" is nothing more than this masculinist ethos to which Grandma must submit. Since the individualism of *Red Sorghum* is based on physical strength, Grandma is condemned as a passive victim or rather as a location on which the brutal masculine power displays its force. In both cases, sexual desire, especially expressed by a woman, must be justified by a more lofty or serious cause, which is the manifestation of the author's ideological stance. To this extent, the individualism in Mo Yan's fiction can be considered a subversive descendant of communist ideology, thanks to commonly shared moralistic forms of slogans and clichés.

This sentimental hyperbolism is revolutionary romanticism, advocated by the former communist leader Mao Zedong. Mao stated that "revolutionary realism must be combined with revolutionary romanticism." As illustrated by the above-quoted passage of *Bitter Flowers*, revolutionary romanticism is characterized by extreme lyricism and passion while remaining impersonal. Thus, the lyricism and passion expressed in literary works must be directed toward a collective cause: revolution. Although in his *Red Sorghum* Mo Yan often maintains the same mood of revolutionary romanticism, his passion and lyricism are individualistic. Naturally, the subject of his individualism must be gendered as masculine.

However, the same kind of exaltation of the self in the mode of "revolutionary romanticism" is not completely absent in previous works of socialist realism, of which Mao Zedong's poems are good examples. His poem "Snow," contains the following passage:

> Mountains and rivers are so magnificent,
> That they attract numberless heroes
> To compete for them at the price of their lives.
> In the past, the emperors Qinshi and Hanwu
> Slightly lacked sophistication.
> The first emperors of Tang and Song
> Somehow needed cultivation.
> Counting every genius
> The best of all still live in modern times.[21]

As is common in romanticism, nature in Mao's poem becomes part of the poet's subjective world. At the same time, nature, represented by mountains and rivers by means of their Chinese connotation of territory, is also politicized. As the modern "emperor," the former communist leader considered himself unique in comparison with his most famous predecessors in Chinese history. In the final analysis, revolutionary romanticism in China is not so different from the exaltation of the self in Western romanticism. However, the only legitimate subject who could *openly* express passion for his individual self in revolutionary romanticism without risking his political life in Mao's China was the leader of the Party or the communist emperor. Mo Yan's *Red Sorghum* certainly democratizes the subject of the self-exaltation by extending it to other men. Nevertheless, the legitimate subject of individualism in *Red Sorghum* is not simply any man. Like the emperors who compete for political control of China's magnificent mountains and rivers in Mao's poem, Grandpa Yu Zhan'ao must also prove his superior masculine power through violent conquest of the female body. Mao Zedong's subjecthood of revolutionary romanticism is reserved for the man who controls the empire, whereas Mo Yan's subjecthood belongs to the man who conquers the most desirable woman. As a result, Mao expresses his individual passion by means of mountains and rivers, and Mo Yan, by means of the female body.

The hero of socialist realist literature does not need to conquer his sexual partner through violence, because the heroine must invariably remain loyal to the lover of her choice. *Song of Youth*, written by Yang Mo in 1959, describes the student movements of the thirties. This novel is considered one of the most influential works of socialist realism during the late fifties and early sixties. After several years of separation from her first Platonic lover Lu Jiachuan, a communist leader of the student movement at Peking University, Lin Daojing, the heroine, learns from a female friend that her lover has already died in prison. In preparation for their future relationship, her potential second lover, Jiang Hua, is carefully described by the narrator as Lu Jiachuan's close friend and comrade, who has the same revolutionary qualities as his predecessor. Because of his unlimited respect for Lin Daojing's feelings for his predecessor, Jiang Hua postpones expressing his love for years. When the two lovers finally decide to make love, the memory of her first lover still creates strong feelings of guilt in the heroine.[22]

Genealogy of the Red Flag is another important socialist realist work of the late fifties and early sixties. The novel describes peasants' lives in the precommunist countryside. Like the revolutionary student Lin Daojing, Chunlan, a country girl, has the same kind of everlasting passion for her lover, Yuntao, who is sentenced to life imprisonment for his revolutionary activities.[23]

On the surface, Mo Yan's heroine differs from these revolutionary women in that she does not *intend* to remain loyal to anyone. On various occasions, the narrator refers to Grandma as a sexually liberated woman (ZGXS, 106, 112). However, this sexual liberation is limited to a verbal and intentional freedom. In fact, from the beginning to the end of the novella, Grandma remains physically loyal to her lover, Yu Zhan'ao, despite the narrator's allusions to the contrary. Female sexuality both in socialist realism and in Mo Yan's *Red Sorghum* serves as an interesting test case of the limits of women's independence.

In socialist realist fiction, women must channel their sexual desire to the revolutionary cause. Like nuns, they are married to their providence, revolution. The ideological marriage desexualizes women's desire. Even the objects of their love, revolutionary men, function primarily as their teachers of communist theory. Lin Daojing in *Song of Youth*, Juanzi in *Bitter Flowers*, and Chunlan in *Genealogy of the Red Flag* become revolutionaries thanks to the teachings of lovers to whom they remain eternally loyal. Thus, their love is turned into a religious devotion to the preachers of communism. Very often, the preachers are inseparable from the cause they preach. Interestingly, despite the pronounced communist ideology of equal rights between the two sexes in China, teacher-student relationships in most socialist realist works are still based on a strictly sexual hierarchy. In this hierarchy, only a politically and ideologically decadent woman like Bai Liping in *Song of Youth* can enjoy sexual freedom. Betraying Luo Dafang, her revolutionary teacher-lover, amounts to betraying the revolutionary cause.[24] Like their sexuality, women's independence is strictly controlled by the Party line. Female characters in socialist realist literature are independent mainly in regard to the traditional norms that differ from communist ideology. Their alleged independence serves as a weapon to be used by the Communist Party against traditional society. Naturally, a weapon has to be carefully guarded in order to avoid hurting its owner.

Since Grandma in *Red Sorghum* is praised as a "pioneer of individual liberation" (ZGXS, 112), it is difficult to expect the same kind of self-censorship in her sexual behavior as in that of her revolutionary sisters in socialist realist works. Nevertheless, her sexuality is not less strictly guarded—not by the Party line, but by masculine power and violence. In exchange for a mule, her father marries her to a leprous husband (ZGXS, 164). On the wedding night, her husband attempts to sleep with her against her will (ZGXS, 163). Yu Zhan'ao, Grandpa, kills her potential rapist, a bandit in the sorghum field (ZGXS, 143), as well as her husband, and he himself rapes her in the sorghum field (ZGXS, 165–166). Her son, at the age of fifteen, tries to shoot a person who expresses sexual desire for his mother (ZGXS, 128). Although she is the successive property of her father, her husband, her lover, and her son, Grandma's loyalty is miraculously preserved for the most physically powerful man, Yu Zhan'ao, by means of his violent struggles. Her "own will" is meaningful only as long as it corresponds to Yu's will—to consider himself the only man who can monopolize Grandma's sexual desire.

In socialist realist works such as *Song of Youth*, *Bitter Flowers*, and *Genealogy of the Red Flag*, sexual relations are often paralleled by teacher-student relations. The knowledge of communist theory is in this context transformed into masculine power that demands women's total submission to a different patriarchal order, the Communist Party. In *Red Sorghum*, however, masculine power appears in a much more naked form, as violence. In both cases, women must submit to masters who are portrayed as their saviors and protectors, regardless of what kind of power they wield. Despite the communist ideology of women's emancipation and Mo Yan's representation of Grandma as a "pioneer of individual liberation," sexual hierarchy remains deeply rooted in communist culture and in Mo Yan's world of primitive origin. In socialist realism, women's independence is a well-controlled weapon used against the enemy of the communists, traditional Chinese society. In the world of *Red Sorghum*, dominated by masculine power and violence, Grandma's alleged sexual freedom can serve either as a harmless decoration for her feminine attraction or as a weapon against communist puritanism—provided that this weapon will not turn itself against its owner, male subjectivity. By treating women as mainly instrumental, both the revolutionary cause in socialist realist literature and Mo Yan's reconstruction of the liberating second past—an idealized and fantasized past—as a counterpart to communist culture, lead to an implicit submission to the first past, the traditional Chinese patriarchy, which both parties apparently intend to reject.

Notes

I would like to thank Elissa Rashkin and Ruth Weil for their careful editing. I am also grateful to Liu Kang, Nancy Mullenex, Maureen Robertson, my friends in the reading group at the University of Iowa, as well as the two anonymous readers for the Duke University Press for their constructive suggestions.

1. Mo Yan, *Hong gaoliang* (Red sorghum), in *Zhongguo xiaoshuo yijiubaliu* (Chinese fiction 1986), ed. Dong Xiao et al. (Hong Kong: Sanlian, 1988). All the translations are mine. In the rest of the chapter, I shall use ZGXS to indicate this book.

2. See for example Zhang Zhizhong's *Mo Yan lun* (On Mo Yan), Beijing: Chinese Academy of Social Sciences Press, (1990).

3. A short article written by Zhang Nuanxin, a woman director, provides a good description of the connection between the novella and the film. See Zhang Nuanxin, *Hongle gaoliang* (Reddening sorghum), *Dangdai dianying* (Contemporary cinema) 1988:1, 55–56.

4. See Zhang Zhizhong's introduction to *Mo Yan lun*.

5. The Chinese critic Li Tuo describes Mo Yan's style in the preface to a collection of the latter's short stories: "Life-style and characters in his fiction are after all lively reflections of realistic life in our countryside" (Mo Yan, *Touming de hongluobo* [Transparent red radish] [Beijing: Zuojia chubanshe, 1985], p. 2). I would like to thank Li Tuo for inspiring discussions concerning his idea of the "Mao style" (*Mao wenti*).

6. See Wang Xiaoming's analysis of this imaginary past in "Bu xiangxin de he bu yuanyi xiangxin de: guanyu sanwei 'xungen' pai zuojia (What one does not believe and what one does not want to believe: concerning the literary creation of three "root-searching writers"), in *Wenxue pinglun* (Literary review) 1988:3, 25.

7. In his "Dry River," for example, a boy from the same family background was beaten to death by his family members. The story ends in a narcissistic note: "By the time people found him, he was already dead. His parents stared blankly, their eyes like those of fishes. . . . Folks with faces as bleak as the desert gazed upon his sun-drenched buttocks . . . as if looking at a beautiful and radiant face, as if looking at me myself" (trans. and ed. Jeanne Tai, in *Spring Bamboo* [New York: Random House, 1989], p. 227). Mo Yan's short story "The Transparent Carrot" talks about a child of the same social origin who tries to create a solipsistically magical world to protect himself from daily mistreatment and torture.

8. See Mao Zedong, "Zhongguo shehui ge jieji fenxi" (The analysis of various classes of Chinese society) (An analysis of the social classes in China).

9. Mao Zedong, "Zai Yan'an wenyi zuotanhui shang de jianghua" (Talks at the Yan'an forum on literature and the arts), in *Lun wenxue yu yishu* (On literature and arts) (Beijing: Renmin wenxue, 1960), p. 64.

10. On this subject, see some of the comments on "root-searching literature" by Chinese critics, for example, Guo Xiaodong, "Muxing tuteng: zhiqing wenxue de yizhong jingshen biange" (Totem of motherhood: a spiritual variation of the literature of educated youth), in *Shanghai wenxue* 1987:1, 90–96. Fan Keqiang, "Xungenzhe: yuanshi qingxiang yu banyuanshi zhuyi" (Root-searchers: primitive tendency and semi-primitivism), in *Shanghai wenxue* 1989:3, 64–69.

11. Slavoj Žižek, *The Sublime Object of Ideology* (London: Verso, 1989), p. 133.

12. Concerning this subject in contemporary Chinese literature, Cai Xiang, a Chinese critic, provides an interesting analysis in his article "Qing yu yu de duili: dangdai xiaoshuo zhong de jingshen wenhua xianxiang" (Conflicts between love and lust: a spiritual and cultural phenomenon in contemporary fiction), in *Wenxue pinglun*, 88:3, 36–43.

13. Yang Mo, *Qingchun zhi ge* (Song of youth) (Beijing: Renmin chubanshe, 1960).

14. Liang Bin, *Hongqi pu* (Genealogy of the red flag) (Beijing: Zhongguo qingnian, 1957).

15. Luo Guangbin and Yang Yiyan, *Hongyan* (Red cliffs) (Beijing: Zhongguo qingnian, 1961).

16. Yuan Jing, *Xin ernü yingxiong zhuan* (New heroic biographies of sons and daughters) (Beijing: Zhongguo qingnian, 1956).

17. Feng Deying, *Kucai hua* (Bitter flowers) (Beijing: Jiefangjun wenyi, 1958).

18. Ibid., pp. 37–38.

19. The three submissions: a woman must submit to her father before marriage, to her husband after marriage, and to her son after her husband's death. The four virtues: woman's probity, language, appearance, and skill (*Houhan shu*).

20. Feng Deying, *Kucai hua*, p. 119.

21. Mao Zedong, "Qingyuan chun: Xue" (Snow).

22. Yang Mo, *Qingchun zhi ge*, pp. 567–568.

23. Liang Bin, *Hongqi pu*, pp. 376–382.

24. Yang Mo, *Qingchun zhi ge*, pp. 355–364.

PART THREE

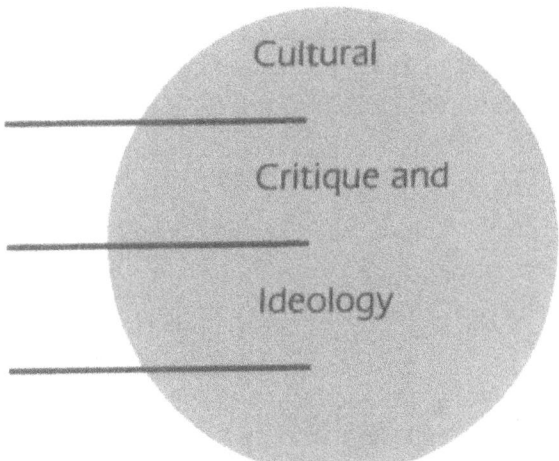

YINGJIN ZHANG

Narrative, Ideology, Subjectivity:

Defining a Subversive Discourse in

Chinese Reportage

Reportage is a special mode of writing in modern China. Although its origin may be traced back to travel literature of the early twentieth century, reportage did not become recognized until the early 1930s, when it grew out of wartime journalism. Since then, reportage has developed a distinct function in providing its readers with in-depth reports on social events. In the mid-1950s experiments with fictional techniques added much to the literary quality of the already popular genre of reportage. From the late 1950s to the early 1970s, however, the tightened control of news media in the People's Republic of China dictated that reportage be a journalistic mouthpiece for official Party policy. It was not until the late 1970s that reportage reemerged as a "literary" genre that focused primarily on individual characters. Since the mid-1980s reportage has turned again to larger issues—historical, sociological, psychological, anthropological, political, ethical, economic—indeed, to virtually all conceivable social and cultural issues.[1] Given the interdisciplinary nature of this mode of writing and its ambition to embrace all subject matter, I propose to approach Chinese reportage not in journalistic terms (e.g., immediacy, accuracy, proximity), nor in literary terms (e.g., narrative structure, characterization, aesthetic effect), but rather in terms of its discursive operation in contemporary Chinese culture.

Aiming at a level more theoretical than descriptive, my study will not be concerned with the formal features of reportage, nor with the development and reception of this journalistic-literary genre before 1980, nor with an archaeology of a specific form like the *texie* (feature story) and its indebtedness to the Russian *ocherk*.² I am interested, instead, in tracing out a cultural logic that shapes the formation of a distinctively subversive discourse in Chinese reportage. Although I may refer occasionally to earlier works, I shall concentrate primarily on reportage writings of the 1980s and particularly on those with considerable appeal to the reading public. I narrow the scope of investigation in order to argue that it is problematic to classify reportage as a by and large conservative genre that unanimously sings praise of the achievements of socialist construction under the communist regime. Classifying reportage merely in such terms as radical, liberal, or conservative does not explain its powerful workings in modern Chinese culture. In a schematic way, my project of defining a subversive discourse in Chinese reportage can be stated as follows: First, this discourse produces a new genre of narrative that cuts across the conventional borders between fiction and journalism, fiction and history, and fiction and politics, and thus invites us to rethink critical concepts such as fiction and history. Second, it highlights the ideological workings of narrative and provides a good place for us to reexamine the social function of literature in contemporary China. Third, it consciously interpellates individuals (writers, characters, and readers) as subjects in their own rights, thereby greatly contributing to a recent intellectual trend toward subjectivity in Chinese culture.³

Negotiating History, Journalism, and Fiction in Reportage

On 14 April 1988 *People's Daily* (*Renmin ribao*) carried in its overseas edition a dialogue between two leading Chinese literary theorists, Liu Zaifu and Li Zehou. Liu told Li that one of the new literary phenomena at that time was the immense popularity of reportage. "Wandering All Over the World" (Shijie da chuanlian; 1988) by Hu Ping and Zhang Shengyou, for instance, sold hundreds of thousands of copies; before it, Qian Gang's "The Great Earthquake in Tangshan" (Tangshan da dizhen; 1986) and Su Xiaokang's "The Revelation of the Flood" (Honghuang qishi lu; 1986) also claimed a great number of readers.⁴ Liu noted that recent reportage had turned away from its previous attention to a single individual or event and had come to investigate all kinds of social problems from a typically panoramic view. The underlying motivation of those new reportage pieces, Liu added, was an "anxiety complex" (youhuan yishi) that had driven the younger generation of writers to rethink history and to reexamine current social problems.[5]

"The Great Earthquake in Tangshan," which certainly belongs to the group of "monumental" and therefore "enduring" works of reportage,[6] exemplifies the tendency to rethink history. Published in 1986, it discloses for the first time and in graphic detail the devastating earthquake that destroyed the entire city of Tangshan in 1976, erasing in a single moment 242,769 lives from the face of the earth and leaving 164,851 seriously injured. In the introduction, which is entitled "About Me and My Tangshan," the author Qian Gang declares first thing that "undoubtedly, Tangshan belongs to me."[7] Tangshan belongs to Qian because he has felt inseparable from the city since he first set foot on the site of the earthquake ruins in 1976. Setting his piece in Tangshan across a span of ten years, Qian turns first to a history book and copies down the "black dates" of 28 July: in 1914 it was the start of the First World War; in 1937, the Japanese occupation of Beijing; and in 1976, the great earthquake in Tangshan. From history Qian then turns to the mournful scenes of the annual commemoration of the dead in Tangshan, where ashes of the burned paper floated in the morning mist like black butterflies. From such an emotionally charged description, Qian returns to history and copies down other devastating earthquakes worldwide in the course of the century: Tokyo, 1 September 1923, casualties estimated at 100,000; Chile, 22 May 1960, casualties about 7,000; 28 March 1964, Alaska, casualties 178. The Tangshan figures speak for themselves, but a number alone cannot articulate what the quake has carved in the heart of the Tangshan survivors. Qian Gang once again turns to the memories—private as well as public—of a series of tragic scenes, and he cannot help declare twice that "this is my Tangshan." Confronted with such a grand scale of disaster, he feels that he can no longer think in terms of "normal conventions" (zhengchang de guifan) and has to experiment with something new in his narrative.[8]

The resulting narrative of Qian's reportage is an admixture of various discourses. In chapter 1 he starts at the exact moment of the earthquake—42′53.8″, 3:00 A.M., 28 July 1976—and then moves back to the previous natural warnings; the climax of this chapter consists of nine witness accounts (recorded and edited by Qian himself) followed by a survey (like a filmic sequence) of the ruined city; crumbled down buildings, twisted train rails, bleeding victims, and piles of dead bodies. To estimate the scale of the destruction, Qian contemplates the ruins from three imaginary positions—those of a historian, an architect, and an economist. In chapter 2, "Tangshan—Hiroshima," Qian narrates the rescue efforts that involved hundreds of thousands of citizens and soldiers. In chapter 3, "Longing for Survival," he reconstructs the stories of a few survivors, some of them miraculously rescued in the fifteenth day. In chapter 4 he tells of the sufferings of special groups of people—foreigners, prisoners, the mentally ill, and the blind. In chapter 5 he reports a number of special events, from the prevention of robbery and pestilence to the continuation of political campaigns. Chapter 6 is devoted to three thousand orphans, and chapter 7 to the National Bureau of Seismology. In the conclusion Qian resolutely disavows *his* Tangshan by declaring that "undoubtedly, Tangshan belongs to humankind."[9] This final declaration is significant not only in that it elevates a private vision to a global one, but also in that it returns Qian's text—a symbolic construct of the actual events through subjective interpretations—to the realm of "the real," a realm that seems to dictate the writing of reportage in the first place.

Qian Gang's text, which incorporates in itself the discourses of history (facts and data), journalism (news items and personal interviews), and miscellaneous others (government documents, personal letters, and statistics), provides us with a good place to examine the current theorizing of reportage. The first theoretic problem arises, to be sure, from the paradoxical term *baogao wenxue* (literally, reportage literature): "reportage" presumably bears on the realm of the real, whereas "literature" pertains to that of the symbolic. The official definition of reportage in China can help us focus on this problematic: "Reportage literature is a literary genre, a type of prose; also an umbrella term for sketches and the *texie*. It is a fast and timely representation, with adequate artistic processing, of *real* people and *real* events that are drawn directly from and regarded as typical of the *real* life. As such it serves the current political agenda and is said to be the 'light cavalry' of literary production."[10] The fascinating image of the "light cavalry" aside (I shall return to its political implication later), the highlighted concept in *Cihai*'s lengthy definition is that of the "real" (zhen)—a concept that bears a distinct meaning in Chinese critical discourse.

Li Zehou and Liu Zaifu, thus conceptualize the real in reportage:

> Li: The key word in the term *baogao wenxue* should be *baogao* (report). Characteristic of *baogao* is a search for the real (*zhenshi*). Truthful and accurate accounts of social issues are of value and will hence endure in history.
>
> Liu: Future historians will probably regard our newspaper and magazine reports today as "official history" (*zhengshi*) and those facts that have been registered in reportage as "unofficial history" (*yeshi*).
>
> Li: Whether treated as official or unofficial history, reportage must be "truthful and accurate" (*zhenshi*). If fictionalized, it becomes fiction, which is then of quite a different nature.[11]

Three points in this dialogue merit close attention: (1) the concept of the real is highlighted and further valorized as the norm of writing (i.e., official historiography); (2) fiction and history are radically dichotomized, leaving little room for negotiation between the two; and (3) reportage writings are restricted to "truthful and accurate accounts" of the real and, as such, are not to be fictionalized.[12] The position of Li and Liu, I would contend here, represents a fallacy in Chinese literary theory—a false belief in the referentiality or transparency of language. Their dialogue seems to suggest that a reportage writer, merely by "truthfully and accurately" recording historical facts or actual events, will automatically transpose the intangible "real" to the discursive realm of narrative. The point at issue here is that the manner of such "recording" or "reporting" is left unexamined.

In this respect, Chinese literary theory can benefit much from recent Western critical theory. In the second half of the twentieth century, language has occupied a central position in the critical inquiry of Western theorists, and concepts such as history, narrative, and fiction have been reinterpreted and reformulated. "History," indeed, refers to two concepts simultaneously: one is the "real," "the flow of events itself," and the other "the intellectual form," the historical narrative of that real.[13] Concerning the writer's relation to the former, Robert Scholes takes an extreme position in claiming that "in life, we do not attain the real. What we reach is a notion of the real."[14] Obviously, a notion of the real is not the real itself, but rather a mediated, conceptual projection of it by the knowing subject. Mediation thus arises ineluctably between the subject and the referent, and creates the following epistemological dilemma: on the one hand, without a "fictive" paradigm (a narrative structure) that enables us to perceive actual events and order our experiences, we can hardly make sense of the real;[15] on the other hand, whenever we attempt to fix the real in narrative form, it is already receding into a distance (of time and space) from us. With regard to this dilemma, Fredric Jameson presents a dialectic proposition: "that history is not a text, not a narrative, master or otherwise, but that, as an absent cause, it is inaccessible to us except in textual form, and that our approach to it and to the Real itself necessarily passes through its prior textualization, its narrativization in the political unconscious."[16]

The Western distinction between history as narrative (i.e., historiography that is already present) and history as the real itself (an entity that is always "absent") throws light on the problematic of history and fiction in Chinese reportage. Theoretically speaking, reportage, as a narrative written in the medium of language, can never be the real itself; at best, it can "only approximate [it] in asymptotical fashion."[17] The same holds true for history and journalism. All of these forms of narrative, in other words, are just different types of symbolic (fictionalized) constructs, each residing in its specific locus along the asymptotic line toward the real.

My challenge of the history/fiction dichotomy in theoretical terms is predicated on ample evidence from reportage writing in China. For one thing, the "facts" reported in reportage writings are often openly objected to or rejected as being "distorted" or "untruthful" for various ideological and political reasons.[18] For another, writers sometimes frankly admit to the fictive elements in their works. They choose to do so either directly in the texts, as does Hu Ping at the beginning of "The Eyes of China" (Zhongguo de mouzi; 1989), or more discreetly, as Liu Binyan does concerning his invention in "The Inside News of the Newspaper" (Benbao neibu xiaoxi; 1956).[19] Whatever they do—and they do it with absolute confidence—Chinese writers realize that reportage is a useful genre of narrative situated between fiction and history (or fiction and journalism); with this realization they further claim "the best of both worlds—the freedom to invent and generalize from the former [fiction]; and the prestige of truthfulness, the actuality, and the wide distribution from the latter [journalism or history]."[20]

Returning to Qian Gang's text, we can now see more clearly how "The Great Earthquake in Tangshan" makes use of the combined advantage of fiction and history in reportage. The success of Qian's narrative, on closer analysis, depends as much on its skillful use of narrative techniques (i.e., fictional means) as on its sheer appearance of truthfulness and actuality of the events in question. Among the techniques Qian effectively employs in his text are (1) the detailed description of scenes (e.g., that of the annual commemoration of the dead), which serves to work up emotions in the reader; (2) the careful reconstruction of dialogue that will fit the personality of each eyewitness—a technique, understandably, to secure both vividness and credibility for the narrative; (3) the rearrangement of the casual and isolated incidents before the disaster into a sequence of causally linked events that culminate in the climax of the quake—the purpose of which is to set up dramatic suspense. Effective as these "conventional" techniques may be, however, they are not sufficient for Qian Gang's professed ambition to write an "epic" narrative "to offer to today's and tomorrow's anthropologists, sociologists, seismologists, medical researchers, psychologists. . . . Not only to them, but also to peoples all over the world, I want to offer a true account of the holocaust, a true account of men and women in the catastrophe, the historical truths that have not yet been officially endorsed, and also my reflections and questions."[21]

In order to fulfill that ambition, which outgrows "normal conventions" of narrative, Qian Gang decides to resort freely to discourses of anthropology, sociology, seismology, psychology, medical research, and official memoranda. What is more, since mere factual accounts of the disaster will not suffice, Qian is compelled to create an imaginary space for his "reflections and questions" (e.g., his own hypotheses and arguments as articulated from the perspectives of a historian, an architect, and an economist). The narrative that results from such an integration of miscellaneous discourses is a special account of that historical event as seen from numerous different angles, an account of the real experienced from its *multifarious layers of manifestation* (physical as well as imaginary).

Through this reading of Qian Gang's text, I have demonstrated that an insistence on a clear-cut distinction between history and fiction is a problematic position to maintain in the first place and that such a rigid position does not advance our knowledge of reportage much further. It is worth recalling that, historically speaking, a blurring of the lines between history and fiction in narrative is nothing new in either Chinese or Western cultures. So far as the historical narrative is concerned, fiction is always recognized as a constitutive element in classical Chinese historiography,[22] just as prior to the French Revolution, historiography was conventionally regarded as a literary art in the West.[23] So far as fiction is concerned, its emergence in China was closely connected to the practice of historiography;[24] similarly, the rise of the English novel was traced to the practice of a special journalistic form in England, "the news/novels discourse." Yet, just as the English novel's early insistence on a connection to reality need not be taken for granted,[25] so the claim to truth in Chinese reportage must be investigated from a perspective other than the dichotomy of history and fiction.

A clue to the workings of reportage in modern China is discernible in Qian Gang's text: "The Great Earthquake in Tangshan" was written with an aim to providing the public with "the historical truths that have not yet been officially endorsed." In other words, Qian deliberately situates the text as "unofficial history" in opposition to "official history," thereby gaining a critical edge that would otherwise be unavailable. If read against the backdrop of the meager and distorting official coverage of the Tangshan earthquake in *People's Daily* in 1976, sprinkled with political slogans and boldface quotations from Marx and Mao Zedong,[26] Qian's text will emerge as a critique of Chinese state policy of the 1970s, which ignored individuals' sufferings while championing a strict censorship system. The trenchancy of Qian's critique is best expressed in a section in chapter 5 entitled "The Political 1976," where he cites a selection of sympathetic news reports issued by foreign media in 1976 and contrasts them, quite dramatically, with the egoistic words of a then top Chinese leader: "Foreigners want to come and help us; yet our great People's Republic of China doesn't need others' intervention, it doesn't need others' aid."[27]

Thus historicized, the ideological workings of Qian's text come to the fore. In fact, when he qualifies his account as truths "not yet officially endorsed," Qian already implicitly acknowledges that his writing can be read as a counterreport to the distorted official coverage in *People's Daily*. It is in this special sense that Qian's text joined the rank of the "light cavalry" of literary production and participated in current sociopolitical issues in a "fast and timely" manner, as *Cihai*'s definition has it. Qian Gang's text, furthermore, confirms

A Ying's characterization of reportage from 1932: "The greatest force of reportage lies in its reporting of true events. But this reporting is not a linguistic presentation of reality in the same mechanical way as a camera registers an object; rather, it necessarily contains certain purpose and tendency."[28] The "certain purpose and tendency" in question, needless to say, are ideological in nature. From this perspective, I venture to assert that the decision to write a reportage text in China is definitely an ideological act, ideological in the sense that such a decision will inevitably define the writer's position in an overhomogenized political culture in modern China.

Situating Ideology, Hegemony, and Antagonism

One of the earliest attempts at theorizing reportage, in addition to that of A Ying, is found in Bo Chuan, who published an essay in 1931 summarizing a seminar on reportage organized by the Association of Young Writers in Beijing. Bo Chuan defines the purposes of reportage writing in the following terms: "to expose the enemy's corruption and shamelessness, to criticize our own mistakes and shortcomings," and "to correct the distorted media coverage."[29] Given those purposes, reportage must prioritize values of ideological struggle over artistic values, so that it can serve as the light cavalry in the field of literature. The content of reportage should be of public concern and should be provocative; as for the form of reportage, it could contain the author's own opinions and could dispense with any central protagonist. One last thing that Bo Chuan emphasizes is the author's ideological identification with the oppressed.

Bo Chuan's position, part of which has been adopted in the official definition of reportage in *Cihai*, highlights the ideological workings of reportage rather than its problematic relationship to the real. From Bo Chuan's perspective, it is easier to understand why Xia Yan's "Contract Labor" (Baoshengong; 1936) was later set up as a "model" of reportage writing.[30] By means of exposing the bloody exploitation of innocent country girls who were contracted—actually sold—to work in the Shanghai textile industry, Xia's piece propagates an emerging proletarian ideology against the capitalist ideology then dominant in Shanghai. It is interesting to note that Xia's text is valued in terms not so much of its truthfulness as of its identification with the oppressed. The same kind of evaluation applies to Qu Qiubai's travel account, *My Private Thoughts in the Red Capital* (*Chidu xinshi*; 1924). Although it contains miscellaneous modes of writing—poems, sketches, lyrical prose, a dream sequence, and a political treatise—Qu's book is classified as reportage mainly because, for the first time in Chinese literature, it identifies itself conscientiously with the emerging ideology of communism. This ideological tradition in Chinese reportage and its continuation in contemporary society, therefore, deserves investigation at a theoretical level.

Louis Althusser offers this succinct definition of ideology: "Ideology represents the imaginary relationship of individuals to their real conditions of existence." "What is represented in ideology," Althusser continues to argue, "is not the system of the real relations which govern the existence of individuals, but the imaginary relations of those individuals to the real relations in which they live." Accordingly, the real is rendered seemingly inaccessible to individuals; as a result of the "imaginary" nature of ideology, all the available representations of the real are always already "necessarily" distorted. Hence Althusser's formulas "ideology = illusion" and "ideology = misrecognition."[31]

Althusser's theory of ideology as a necessarily imaginary distortion is susceptible to critique from various perspectives.[32] For the purpose of this chapter, however, I shall adhere to Althusser's observation of distortion as a specific outcome of the workings of ideology, for the simple reason that this view is particularly pertinent to the workings of Chinese reportage. The question of distortion can be better grasped in relation to Althusser's distinction between the State Apparatus (SA) and the Ideological State Apparatuses (ISAs). The State Apparatus includes government, administration, army, police, courts, prison, and so forth, while the ISAs are subdivided into religious, educational, familial, legal, political, communicational, and cultural (literature and arts) apparatuses. The basic difference between the SA and the ISAs is that the former functions predominantly by violence or repression and only secondarily by ideology, whereas the latter functions predominantly by ideology and only secondarily by repression. Moreover, despite their diversity and contradictions, all the ISAs are to be ultimately united beneath the ruling ideology. Although the ruling ideology is realized and realizes itself through the installation of the ISAs, once realized, it demands and commands an "absolute" hegemony. The totality of the SA and the

ISAs, therefore, is envisioned by Althusser as a stable and self-stabilizing structure.

The relevance of the concept of hegemony to a reading of modern Chinese culture can be further elaborated. As Althusser argues, "No class can hold State power over a long period without at the same time exercising its hegemony over and in the State Ideological Apparatuses."[33] This argument is certainly true for China's sociopolitical situation. Even before the Communist Party obtained state power, its attempt at a unifying ideology was remarkably documented in Mao Zedong's "Talks at the Yan'an Forum on Literature and the Arts" (1942), which laid down the fundamental Party line—"Literature and the arts are subordinate to politics."[34] Since the establishment of the People's Republic in 1949, a quick succession of cultural and political campaigns has been launched to consolidate the Party's power by purging dissident voices: first the Anti–Hu Feng campaign (1954), then the Anti-Rightists campaign (1957), the Socialist Education campaign (1963), and the Cultural Revolution (1966–1976), and most recently several Anti–Bourgeois Liberalism campaigns (1986, 1989). All these campaigns were conducted at the level of the ISAs, to be sure, and they worked predominantly by ideology (e.g., the endless sessions of political study throughout the country) and only secondarily by repression (e.g., the exile and imprisonment of the rightists in the late 1950s). Whenever the ISAs fail or are about to fail in their ideological workings, the State Apparatuses (the army and the police) are quickly brought in for a violent repression. The best illustration of the violent intervention by the SA is the Tiananmen Incident of 4 June 1989, which suppressed the emerging ideology of democracy and freedom at the expense of hundreds of innocent lives.

There is little doubt that Chinese ruling ideology was realized by installing and manipulating various ISAs. A recognition of the "supremacy" of the ruling ideology, however, does not necessarily entail a total elimination of difference or antagonism in a given society. Recent social theorists have questioned the Althusserian concept of determination (or, rather, over- and predetermination) in many ways. Ernesto Laclau, for one, insists that "the order of society is the unstable order of a system of differences which is always threatened from the outside."[35] In fact, threats may even emerge from inside, from what was once installed in the ISAs. The sheer "necessity" deemed by the Chinese Communist Party to launch endless campaigns against various "dangerous" ideologies suffices as evidence for the persistent emergence of difference and antagonism either from within the otherwise hegemonized ISAs or from outside (e.g., in underground journals, many of them literary in content). To venture one step further, it can be argued that, since literature is often the first target and writers among the first scapegoats of political campaigns in China, literature in a sense constitutes one of the most subversive forces in contemporary China.

Seen in this light, the ideological workings of Chinese reportage become clearer. Given the necessarily distorted representation in the ruling ideology, reportage finds an indispensable mission to redress distortion, if not with an altogether truthful transcript of the real (which is by definition impossible), at least with a reconstructed account that will come closer to reality (or truth for that matter) than the official versions. Historical evidence has confirmed this theoretical hypostatization of the built-in ideological program in Chinese reportage. Bo Chuan's observation that reportage serves to correct the distorted media coverage is one example; another example is the function of Qian Gang's text in exposing the hitherto distorted facts of the Tangshan earthquake. The claim to truth—a truth that is not yet officially endorsed in Qian Gang's case—forcefully spells out an ideological position ingrained in reportage writing—a conscious, though perhaps sometimes inarticulate, distance or resistance to the ruling ideology.

The potential subversive force of reportage is best exemplified in Liu Binyan's "The Inside News of the Newspaper." In this fictionalized *texie*, Liu creates an idealized woman journalist, Huang Jiaying, who dares to articulate her own views that are at variance with Party policy. The story begins with Huang sitting on a train lost in thought. Her assignment at Jiawang Mine was cut short, presumably because she had personally participated in the miners' boycott against endless political meetings. She has not quite followed the instructions of her senior editors, and she knows that is why two out of five stories she wrote over the past three years ended up as "inside news" (i.e., news stories that are deemed unpublishable for overt criticism of government bureaucracy). At twenty-five, she is upset that she is not yet a Party member. Only recently has she recognized her crucial mistake: she did not approach the Party on her own, but rather waited for the Party to come and recruit her.

In the course of the story, Huang remains an "outsider" at the official *New Light Daily*. It is this outside position, however, that empowers her to retain a vital connection to reality as experienced by the masses and to challenge the otherwise homogenized news agency to report the truth. Huang tends to question the conservative editorial policy of the *Daily*, and her questions gradually attract the attention of some of her colleagues. With her conscientious efforts, Huang is finally able to effect considerable change in the "inside" of the newspaper. By the end of the story, the managing editor, who used to be the servile mouthpiece for "a despotic and ignorant editor-in-chief" and who was "interested only in saving his own skin,"[36] decides to speak out. "Can one be regarded as a Communist if one has no brain?" he raises this serious question at a Party meeting; and further on: "How can we divorce militancy and creativeness from Party spirit?"[37] Ironically, the meeting that was to discuss Huang Jiaying's eligibility for Party membership ends up debating whether the *Daily* should lend a voice to the public sentiment against Party bureaucracy.

The ideological message of Liu Binyan's reportage becomes explicit in the final scene: the inside of the Party system is highly bureaucratized and needs supervision from the outside (i.e., by the masses), and the newspaper ought to be an effective channel for such supervision. This "inside-outside" demarcation in Liu's text can be further elaborated at two levels. At the level of institutions (like *New Light Daily*, a title inviting ironic interpretations), the inside is depicted as a closed hierarchical system championing leadership, organization, and discipline, whereas the outside is where the subversive, or at least "corrective," forces come from. At the level of news reports, on the contrary, what is outside (i.e., public) is the "shining" surface of a continual eulogy of Party achievements that conceals real socioeconomic problems, whereas what is inside (i.e., unpublished or unpublishable inside news, like that written by Huang Jiaying) often turns out to be more truthful than the published news.

The ability to expose the inside as well as the outside is attached to an image of the scout intimately associated with Liu's texie.[38] This image, resonant with the metaphor of the "light cavalry" in *Cihai*'s definition of reportage, again highlights the militancy and subversiveness of reportage, for both images of scout and cavalry presuppose the existence of an "enemy" camp and, furthermore, probably also imply the necessity of an offensive attack—at least on a "discursive" level. To be sure, Liu's most articulate attack on evil Party practices is in a work published twenty-three years later, after he was rehabilitated from his "rightist" status. "People or Monsters?" (Ren-yao zhijian; 1979), in a more daring and more militant manner than Liu's earlier *texie*, exposes an unbelievably large scale of government corruption in the case of Wang Shouxin. Throughout the entire text, innocent common people are placed in opposition to corrupt Party officials. The subversive force of "People or Monsters?" reaches its climax at the end, where Liu Binyan appeals directly to the reader:

> The case of Wang Shouxin's corruption has been cracked. But how many of the social conditions that gave rise to this case have really changed? Isn't it true that Wang Shouxins of all shapes and sizes, in all corners of the land, are still in place, continuing to gnaw away at socialism, continuing to tear at the fabric of the Party, and continuing to evade punishment by the dictatorship of the proletariat?
> People, be on guard! It is still too early to be celebrating victories.[39]

Liu Binyan's direct call for intervention on the part of the reading public (people) to correct the wrongs in the Party system is echoed in Su Xiaokang's "The Revelation of the Flood" (1986). Unlike Qian Gang's text, which is focused on the graphic details of the natural disaster itself, Su's text follows Liu Binyan's tradition in exposing the seemingly more disastrous aftermath of the flood brought about by human factors. Since August 1975 Zhumadian District in Henan Province had been plagued by flooding, which had destroyed farming and housing facilities across the district and severely threatened the subsistence of a million people. Famine spread over the land every year; in one county alone, more than twenty thousand people left their hometowns and begged their way to the south in 1984. The local government, however, covered up the real conditions of people's lives, because they did not want to lose their chance to profit from government subsidies. In two separate chapters "Natural Disasters or Human Errors?" and "The County Magistrate and the Common People," Su Xiaokang narrates a number of events that testify to various forms of government corruption: profiteers made fortunes on government funds and grain storage; local officials bulldozered common people's houses to reconstruct the town according to their own blueprints; and a local tyrant whose dog was killed by a car punished someone else by parading him around several villages. At the end of his text, Su Xiaokang confesses that he was haunted by these common people's tragedies to such a degree that he had to write the stories down and to sing an "elegy" on behalf of the poverty-stricken and voiceless people in Henan.

Both Liu Binyan's and Su Xiaokang's texts confirm my thesis that a subversive discourse is fully at work in reportage—a discourse that articulates resistance or antagonism against the distorting representations in the ruling ideology. Given this subversiveness, Chinese reportage does not conform to the model of hegemony in Althusser's theory of ideology. A theoretical account of antagonism is provided by Chantal Mouffe, who firmly believes that hegemony is never established conclusively in a society. Mouffe's reflection on the source of antagonism is worth quoting: "An antagonism can emerge when a collective subject . . . that has been constructed in a specific way, to certain existing discourses, finds its subjectivity negated by other discourses or practices."[40]

Constructing Subjectivities in and through Reportage

Althusser's thesis that "ideology has always-already interpellated individuals as subjects"[41] implies a virtually predetermined outcome that individuals, owing to their given subject positions in society, are always to be interpellated into subjection to the "Subject"—the ruling ideology. The applicability of his theory of subjectivity to a study of Chinese reportage can be contested, as I show in the following analysis of two recent texts on the Cultural Revolution.

Hu Ping and Zhang Shengyou's "Historical Reflections" (Lishi chensi lu; 1987), dedicated to their "contemporaries dead and alive,"[42] is about the Red Guards' 1966 pilgrimage to the Jin'gang Mountains. In the early part of the text, Hu and Zhang dramatically demonstrate to what extent Mao Zedong's ideological interpellation of millions of Red Guards as the bravest revolutionary force in China had succeeded in mobilizing young students to a nationwide campaign, later known as the "Great Proletarian Cultural Revolution." In their enthusiastic subjection to the Maoist ideology, the Red Guards traveled all over the country and flocked in millions to Tiananmen Square in Beijing to pay homage to Chairman Mao. At the same time, millions of them went on pilgrimages to various "sacred" sites of the Chinese revolution, among them the Jin'gang Mountains. Within a short period between 29 May 1966 (when the first Red Guard group was organized by children and grandchildren of senior Party officials in Beijing) and January 1967, about one million Red Guards visited the mountains. At one time, two hundred thousand people crowded into the space of just three square kilometers waiting for a much anticipated visit by Chairman Mao—who, of course, did not show up. A number of the Red Guards died of hunger, infectious disease, or traffic accidents. It is only after twenty years that the authors, who personally participated in the manic homage, are finally able to reflect on the Red Guards' hypnotized subjection to a godlike Subject, Chairman Mao.

Thus far, the Althusserian theory of subjectivity seems to fare all right, for the religious ferment in the Red Guards' subjection to the Maoist ideology certainly testifies to the power of interpellation. To be sure, in just a couple of years after 1966, the Red Guards succeeded in dismantling those government agencies that Mao had designated as the "headquarters of the bourgeoisie" (with such incredible results that the president of the People's Republic, Liu Shaoqi, was thrown out of office, put in secret custody, and eventually died under a false name). Yet the glorious victory of the Red Guards was immediately followed by fierce battles (many of them involving machine guns) among their various factions. From 1968 on, as the number of casualties increased and no better use could be made of them in cities, the Red Guards were sent to mountain areas or to the remote countryside. At the beginning they naively believed in the official endorsement of their new mission as settling down in "a vast world with much more to be accomplished" (*guangkuo tiandi dayou zuowei*). Years later, however, these former Red Guards, removed from the center of political struggles and estranged in alien environments, gradually awakened to the cruel realities of the Cultural Revolution. Some of them realized that their presumed subjectivity as the agent of a cultural revolution was actually nonexistent and that they were but mere puppets in a set of grand-scale political schemes.

The story of a former Red Guard commander in Ganzhou City, Jiangxi Province, invites critical attention in this respect. In "Historical Reflections," she was given the name Li Lian, because the authors were not sure of her true identity at that time although they could not forget the alleged brutality of her execution: Li was forced to undergo a surgical operation without anaesthesia just before her execution; her kidney was cut out and hurried away to a local hospital where a patient was waiting for an organ transplant.⁴³ A reader's feedback following the publication of this fictionalized account led the authors to the real identity of the tragic heroine and to other victims in related cases. In "The Eyes of China," a sequel to "Historical Reflections," Hu Ping retells the haunting story of Li Jiulian.

The story begins with a bloody battle on 29 June 1967, the earliest one in the history of the Red Guard movement. Facing 168 dead bodies on the streets, the local Red Guard commander Li Jiulian swore that she would never participate in a second "Cultural Revolution." The "revolution," however, went on with more ferment and claimed more victims. In February 1969, working in a Ganzhou factory, Li began to question in her diary entries the legitimacy of the Cultural Revolution. She naively mailed a letter to her soldier boyfriend in which she praised President Liu Shaoqi and expressed her suspicion of Lin Biao, then a Chinese leader second only to Mao Zedong. Her boyfriend betrayed her, and Li was soon arrested. After the death of Lin Biao, whose jet plane crashed while he was fleeing Mao's persecution, Li was released in 1972 and assigned to work in a mine. Seeking to redress her case in 1974, Li resorted to "big-character posters" (*dazibao*) that questioned a whole series of government policies. She was arrested again as a "counterrevolutionary," but this time her arrest entailed a public demonstration that involved two thousand people. Inside the prison, Li continued to write political treatises that challenged the political legitimacy of Mao's regime, and knowledge of her case reached as high as the "Gang of Four." In 1975 she fasted for seventy-three days in protest against the injustice of the legal system. In what might be a great political puzzle, after the downfall of the "Gang of Four" in October 1976, Li Jiulian was sentenced to death on 14 December 1977 in a public meeting attended by ten thousand people. She was shot to death and left at the execution site until later that evening a retired factory worker cut off her breasts and genitals and brought them home to satisfy perverse sexual desires. It might seem more incredible that, as late as in April 1978, Zhong Haiyuan, a woman who was imprisoned merely for her signature on a public poster that protested against the injustice to Li Jiulian, was also sentenced to death. Her execution resembled what is described in "Historical Reflections"—her kidney was removed before she was dead—but in "The Eyes of China," Hu Ping is able to provide an eyewitness account—full of horrifying details—by one of the executioners.

Li Jiulian's case was not redressed until March 1981, after piles of letters had reached the desks of Central Committee members. The injustice of the legal system in China that brought about thousands of tragic deaths in the past decades has been denounced in many recent reportage pieces (e.g., Mai Tianshu and Zhang Yu's "Land and a Local Tyrant" [Tudi yu tuhuangdi, 1987] and Su Xiaokang's "A Memorandum on Freedom" [Ziyou beiwang lu, 1989]). My present concern is to search for a theoretical model that will account for the radical shifting of subject positions: in Li Jiulian's case, from a formerly unreflecting "individual" who was hypnotized by the official ideology to a conscious "subject" who was firmly engaged in defiance against Party authorities. Li Jiulian's case, in this respect, is a good place to test various theories of subjectivity.

Owing to its over- and predeterminism ("always-already interpellated") and its insistence on "subjection" ("*There are no subjects except by and for their subjection*"),[44] Althusser's model cannot adequately account for Li Jiulian's shifting of positions. What is problematic in Althusser is his disregard for the impact of multifarious discursive practices on the construction of subjectivity. These discursive practices—which might not always be in keeping with the ruling ideology—are close to Teresa de Lauretis' formulation of "experience":

> Through that process [i.e., experience] one places oneself or is placed in social reality, and so perceives and comprehends as subjective ... those relations—material, economic, and interpersonal—which are in fact social and, in a larger perspective, historical. The process is continuous, its achievement unending or daily renewed. *For each person, therefore, subjectivity is an ongoing construction*, not a fixed point of departure or arrival from which one then interacts with the world. On the contrary, it is an effect of that interaction ... and thus is produced not by external ideas, values, or material causes, but by one's personal, subjective engagement in the practices, discourses, and institutions that lend significance (value, meaning, and affect) to the events of the world.[45]

The pertinent points of de Lauretis' formulation to the study of Chinese reportage are (1) her restoration of the sociohistorical dimension to the concept of subjectivity and (2) her recognition of the importance of everyday practices in the construction of subjectivity. This more subtly construed theoretical perspective can better explain what provided the conditions for the former Red Guards' shifting of subject positions.

Settled down in mountain areas or in the remote countryside, or employed in factories in cities that might or might not be their hometowns, millions of former Red Guards experienced what Chantal Mouffe calls "a negation of subjectivity or identification."[46] Those who were sent to the countryside realized with utter astonishment that their glorified position as "subjects" acting in a revolution had been virtually replaced by a new position as objects of reeducation (zaijiaoyu)—thus a new but ironic designation was reserved for them, "educated youth" (zhishi qingnian). In "Historical Reflections" Hu and Zhang list some of the basic rights that were stripped from those Red Guards turned "educated youth": (1) the right of school education, (2) the right of employment in the city, (3) the freedom of intellectual life, and (4) the freedom to love or to be loved.[47] Such a realization of their negated subjectivity was a major source for the former Red Guards' increasing antagonism against the official ideology, which was expressed in underground literature during the 1970s. In the case of Li Jiulian and those who worked in the cities, their new positions in factories or mines prompted them to rethink their pasts, and to rethink them from a few discursive positions available to them at that particular historical moment. The negation of their subjectivity had taken the form of the negation of their basic right to speak, to articulate their own political views. The brutal violation of this basic human right had resulted in Li Jiulian's and Zhong Haiyuan's tragic deaths.

Another source of antagonism is a "contradictory interpellation," defined by Mouffe as "a situation in which subjects constructed in subordination by a set of discourses are, at the same time, interpellated as equal by other discourses."[48] Huang Jiaying in Liu Binyan's "Inside News" best exemplifies this situation. As a candidate awaiting official approval of her Party membership, Huang is interpellated into subordination to all of her seniors, whose orders she is to follow blindly and subserviently; yet as a journalist who pledges her allegiance to truth, she is called on to expose the wrongdoings within the bureaucratic system and to do so in spite of potential damage to the glorified Party image. In an antagonistic spirit typical of Liu's "scouts," Huang resolutely chooses to give priority to her professional calling—which represents a higher kind of loyalty—and thereby negates her subjectivity-in-subordination.

At this point, my usage of the terms "individual" and "subject" needs some qualification. Generally speaking, the term "individual" refers in this chapter to a person not yet defined by the specific ideological positions he or she is to assume; the term "subject" refers not to a single fixed position, but rather to "what is actually the series of the conglomeration of positions, subject-positions . . . into which a person is called momentarily by the discourses and the world that he/she inhabits."[49] In my analysis above, I have identified—with regard to the ruling ideology—a number of such positions: the subject-in-subjection (the Red Guard), the subject who challenges the authorities (Li Lian or Huang Jiaying), and the subject who reflects on history (Hu Ping, Zhang Shengyou, and a number of former Red Guards mentioned in their texts). Because of the diversity of subject positions, contradictions and competitions among them are common, and only a few of these positions—under certain conditions (like the cases of negated subjectivity analyzed above)—will lead to antagonism. For the antagonistic position attainable to a subject, the term "agent" is suggested by Paul Smith to designate "the idea of a form of subjectivity where . . . the possibility (indeed, the actuality) of resistance to ideological pressure is allowed for."[50]

Having differentiated between the terms used to describe the construction of subjectivities, I now recapitulate major findings with regard to the ideological workings of Chinese reportage: through its strategic deployment of narrative techniques of history and fiction, Chinese reportage can manage to resist the hegemony of the ruling ideology by virtue of (1) awakening readers out of ignorant or hypnotized subject positions and (2) placing them in an alternative—often critical—perspective, whereby a particular form of subjectivity that allows for independent thinking can be constructed. To be more precise, the ideological workings of reportage (i.e., interpellating individuals not just as ordinary subjects but as potential "agents" in the making of history) occur at three different levels. First, at the level of the author, Chinese reportage as a specific cultural discourse interpellates writers to assume a subject position outside that of the ruling ideology, a position that will empower them to penetrate into forbidden territory (thus the images of the "scout" and "light cavalry") or to correct distortions in the official representations (thus the image of a historian or sociologist).[51] Second, at the level of the textual strategy, the flexible discursive position of reportage between history/journalism and fiction enables the writer to manipulate various kinds of narrative elements and to select or create the desired characters and situations that will achieve an optimal ideological effect. Third, at the level of the reading public, reportage readers are interpellated not just as connoisseurs of rare literary expertise or sensational news, but rather as eager participants who feel obliged—at least for a time being—to think and to act on their own, often with little or no regard for what is dictated by the ruling ideology. Hence, in the wake of the publication of "People or Monsters?" many Chinese readers responded actively to Liu's call for intervention by writing letters to the author and to newspapers pledging their support for the exposure of government corruption.[52] No doubt, it is through such "fast and timely" interpellation of its readers into active confrontation with the false or distorted representations of the hegemonized ISAs that reportage comes to fulfill one of its essential ideological functions—as a subversive discourse in China's cultural and political arena.

Defining a Subversive Discourse in Chinese Reportage

In Foucaultian terms, the recent emergence of subjectivities in China can be seen as the outcome of specific institutional and discursive practices. On the one hand, institutional practices (such as school education and family influence) and discursive practices (such as exposure to the media and literature) specify the number of subject positions that are available at a particular time and place, and thus determine to a great extent the shape of the subjectivity that is to emerge. When the Red Guards in the late 1960s were interpellated as the bravest revolutionary force in China, they took heart and willingly inserted themselves into the symbolic order of the official ideology by renouncing all of their individual specificities (family, education, and even gender). The subjectivity—or, more precisely, subjectivity-in-subordination—of the Red Guards, therefore, is a predetermined product of the Maoist ideology. On the other hand, however, individuals, through their own social praxis, also endeavor to transform powerful institutional discourses. For example, the antagonism implicit in much of the post-Mao literature of "educated youth" (i.e., the literature written by the former Red Guards since 1976) challenged the self-righteousness of the previous official lines and contributed a great deal to a subsequent negation of the Cultural Revolution as a whole. The widespread democracy movement in 1989, moreover, is so far the most daring endeavor that successfully enlisted support from a wide range of ISAs (the educational, the cultural, and the communicational). Given the tight control over the news media and the state educational system in China, literature turns out to be the most productive field in which Chinese writers manage to articulate their own ideologies or, in many cases, counterideologies. It is no coincidence that the best and most memorable reportage pieces are generally not to be found in official newspapers in China, but rather in literary journals.

The special institutional affiliation of reportage with literature rather than journalism should be further contextualized in political and cultural specificities in contemporary China. For the purpose of such contextualization, I briefly examine below aspects of a cultural logic that shaped the formation of a subversive discourse in reportage. To highlight reportage's ideological workings, I conduct this examination in terms of what He Xilai discerns as the three types of rationality (*lixing*) in Chinese reportage: enlightenment rationality, historical rationality, and critical rationality.[53]

Enlightenment rationality (*qimeng lixing*) is evident in what I defined above as the typical function of reportage—that of bringing "light" to the dark areas of the covered up or distorted representations in the ruling ideology and thereby awakening readers out of their hypnotic states of subjection. The relation of reportage to official journalism in contemporary China accounts much for its rapid development in an antagonistic direction. At the 1988 colloquium on Chinese reportage,[54] Li You maintained that it is owing to the "countereffects of the stagnant journalism in China" that reportage has emerged as an important cultural discourse; in other words, Chinese reportage comes to fill a seeming vacuum in the official news channels by providing the public with a unique access to what happened and what is still going on. At the same colloquium, Liu Binyan forwarded a more radical proposition—that Chinese reportage has in a sense replaced the newspaper's function in terms of reporting true events to the public. Liu's exaggeration notwithstanding, Chinese reportage does possess an enormous power to compete with official journalism in terms of its depth of investigation, its scope of coverage, and particularly its enormous impact on the reading public. It is appropriate that a number of recent reportage pieces should bear in their titles the word "revelation" (*qishi lu*), a word that presupposes the previous concealment of truths.

As an alternative source for more reliable information, Chinese reportage often maintains a critical posture vis-à-vis official representation—a posture necessitated respectively by its questioning of the latter's reliability or legitimation, by its exposure of the latter's superficiality or even falsehood, and, in most cases, by its supply of a corrective to the latter's distortion. Reportage's *critical rationality* (*pipan lixing*), therefore, defines its antagonistic, subversive function. This critical rationality also explains two related postures of the reportage writer: (1) a "participatory" (*canyu*) posture that reveals the writer's willingness to take part in cultural production in contemporary society, and (2) an "interventionist" (*ganyu*) posture that testifies to the writer's determination to fight against social injustices.[55] In connection with the first type of rationality, it may be argued that the mission of "enlightenment" can be better achieved by developing a "critical" perspective to illuminate certain sociopolitical issues that would otherwise be kept in darkness.

A few words are here in order for a clarification of the typical antagonistic position inherent in Chinese reportage. In spite of—or rather because of—its built-in ideological program and its function as the "light cavalry" in Chinese literary production, reportage may also be easily made into an effective instrument of compliance for the ruling ideology. During the 1960s, for instance, when the Chinese Communist Party achieved its most stabilized hegemony in all the ISAs, many reportage texts were indeed devoted to unreserved praise of officially endorsed "socialist heroes," such as Lei Feng and Jiao Yulu.[56] However, since these reportage pieces were actually "dictated" by the official propaganda machine in the first place, their literary and journalistic value was quickly lost in the subsequent nationwide political campaigns (for instance, the campaign "to learn from comrade Lei Feng," as Mao Zedong himself put it); as a result, none of them quite survived as reportage texts in the public memory (in other words, they were regarded more as "news reports" [*xinwen baodao*] than as reportage texts). On some occasions, furthermore, a reportage text that at first sight conforms to the official ideology may in fact turn out to contain a subtext of a rather critical nature. The reportage pieces that eulogized the achievements of Chinese scientists in the late 1970s fall under this category.[57] These cultural products were as much a response to the government's call for the "Four Modernizations" as a product of the writers' indignation that most scientists not only suffered inhuman treatments under the previous—and by then officially pronounced "erroneous"—Party poli-

Narrative, Ideology, Subjectivity   **233**

cies, but were in fact still neglected or misunderstood by the present regime (to such a tragic extent that many of the internationally known scientists died in their forties). In many reportage pieces of this kind, the elements of exposure usually outweigh those of eulogy, and an underlying thrust of subversion tends to pierce through a deceiving surface of compliance.

The reason why subversiveness has become a dominant feature of Chinese reportage may be traced to the third type of rationality—a *historical rationality* (*lishi lixing*) that is deeply ingrained in this mode of writing. Although history remained a central concern throughout the twentieth century, it was not until the 1980s that Chinese reportage came to claim the historical rationality that makes it a unique discourse in the field of cultural critique. Many reportage writers of the 1980s display in their writing a "historian's consciousness" (*shiguan yishi*), a self-reflectiveness applied not just at the level of individuals, but also at the level of the Chinese nation and Chinese culture. Qian Gang's eloquent articulation of the purpose of his writing (quoted in the first section) is one acknowledgment of such a historical mission. Arguably, the historian's consciousness—coupled with an "anxiety complex"—so overwhelms many reportage writers that they feel it their duty—regardless of potential political danger—to redress the distorted representations of the ruling ideology and to disclose covered up historical events to the reading public. In Hu and Zhang's words, "History . . . may sometimes be covered up or misinterpreted."[58] It follows from this observation that it should be incumbent upon reportage writers, among other Chinese writers and intellectuals, to pledge "a higher kind of loyalty" (in Liu Binyan's words) to historical truth and therefore to restore history to its more "truthful"—if not absolutely "true"—manifestations.

To be sure, the commitment to history is doubly invested in Hu Ping and Zhang Shengyou's text: in the original Chinese, the title "Lishi chensi lu" can equally mean "Historical Reflections" (in which case individuals are interpellated as the subjects to reflect on a specific historical event) and "History's Reflections" (in which case history seems to reflect in and by itself). It must be admitted that history is evoked in many recent reportage writings as a transcendental concept, always eloquently articulated but never fully defined.[59] In this sense, it differs from the two Western concepts I discerned above—history as an incessant flow of events and history as an intellectual form of narration. In the context of recent Chinese reportage, history is often conceived of as an ultimately justifying force that transcends the various imaginary distortions in the ruling ideology and therefore legitimates the writer's antagonistic position and further endorses a subversive discourse of reportage in the contemporary Chinese cultural arena. It is in the name of history that reportage writers proceed to incorporate the absent truth in their narratives in the first place and to return their symbolic constructs to contemporary society as an actual—and at times actually powerful—force of intervention.

Owing precisely to the potential power of a subversive discourse in Chinese reportage, the entire subgenre of "problem reportage" (or "social problem reportage") was censored in the wake of the 1989 Tiananmen Incident. It is not a historical coincidence that two leading reportage writers—Liu Binyan and Su Xiaokang—became leading political dissidents who were forced into exile abroad. In late 1990 an article by Fang Hui appeared in the restructured *Literary Review* (*Wenxue pinglun*). On the one hand, it denounces bourgeois liberalism, which is held responsible for portraying "negative images of Party members" in problem reportage; on the other hand, it hails the "reappearance" of reportage pieces that eulogize "positive" heroes in socialist construction.[60] In fact, the eulogizing mode of reportage never ceased to exist in the 1980s; it just rarely attracted attention. If my view of the cultural formation of a subversive discourse in Chinese reportage can be sustained, sooner or later the subversive discourse in reportage will regain its momentum and reclaim its functions in the realms of narrative, ideology, and subjectivity.

Notes

I would like to thank Maureen Robertson for supervising my M.A. thesis at Iowa that marked the beginning of my reportage project in 1988. I am also indebted to Liu Binyan for referring me in summer 1988 to a number of recent reportage texts discussed in this study. In addition, this chapter has benefited from the comments of my mentors at Stanford, John Bender, Regenia Gagnier, and Herbert Lindenberger; my colleagues Xiao-mei Chen, Liu Kang, and Xiaobing Tang; and a Duke University Press reader, Marston Anderson.

1. This is a very brief outline of the development of reportage in modern China. For a comprehensive history of Chinese reportage, see Zhao Xiaqiu, *Zhongguo xiandai baogao wenxue shi* (A history of modern Chinese report-

age) (Beijing: Renmin daxue chubanshe, 1987). The nineteen-volume *Zhongguo baogao wenxue congshu* (An anthology of Chinese reportage) (Hubei: Changjiang wenyi chubanshe, 1981–1982) contains a wide selection of representative works of Chinese reportage, among which the following are worth mentioning: Qu Qiubai's *Exiang jicheng* (A travel report from the land of hunger; 1922) and *Chidu xinshi* (My private thoughts in the red capital; 1924, reprinted in vol. 1, part 2); a collection of reportage writings on the 1932 Shanghai Incident (reprinted in vol. 1, part 3); Xia Yan's "Baoshengong" (Contract labor; 1936, reprinted in vol. 1, part 1, pp. 265–277); Fan Changjiang's *Saishang xing* (Travels to northwestern China; 1937, reprinted in vol. 2, part 1, pp. 211–392); Liu Binyan's pieces from the mid-1950s and late 1970s (reprinted in vol. 3, part 3); and reportage that eulogizes the achievements of individual scientists during the late 1970s (reprinted in vol. 3, part 5). Major reportage writers since the mid-1980s are Qian Gang, Su Xiaokang, Jia Lusheng, Mai Tianshu, and Hu Ping. Most of their texts are classified as "social problem reportage," and I shall mention some of them later in the study. For a collection of critical essays, see Wang Ronggang, ed., *Baogao wenxue yanjiu ziliao xuanbian* (Research materials on reportage), 2 vols. (Ji'nan: Shandong renmin chubanshe, 1983); for some reportage writers' own comments, see Zhang Deming, ed., *Zhongwai zuojia lun baogao wenxue* (Chinese and foreign writers on reportage) (Kunming: Yunnan renmin chubanshe, 1985).

2. These aspects of reportage have been studied respectively in Yin-hwa Chou, "Formal Features of Chinese Reportage and an Analysis of Liang Qichao's 'Memoirs of My Travels in the New World,'" *Modern Chinese Literature* 1:2 (Fall 1985), 201–217; Xiao-mei Chen, "Genre, Convention, and Society: A Reception Study of Chinese Reportage," *Yearbook of Comparative and General Literature* 34 (1985): 85–100; and Rudolf Wagner, "Liu Binyan and the *Texie*," *Modern Chinese Literature* 2:1 (1986), 63–94.

3. By subjectivity is meant, in this chapter, a particular "subject position" that will empower a subject to reflect independently on his or her relations to the world. The subject, in this sense, is the subject of knowledge. As for the recent intellectual trend toward subjectivity in China, I have in mind the controversy centering on Liu Zaifu's theory of "literary subjectivity," which attempts to construct a system of literary theory and literary history that places humans at the center of his thinking (see his "Lun wenxue de zhutixing" [On the subjectivity of literature], *Wenxue pinglun* 6 [1985]: 11–26 and 1 [1986]: 1–15). Since the Chinese theory of subjectivity is a large topic that merits a separate study, I confine myself in the present study to those issues relevant to the workings of reportage. I shall also have more to say on the recent formulations of subjectivity in Western critical theory.

4. See Hu Ping and Zhang Shengyou, "Shijie da chuanlian" (Wandering all over the world), *Dangdai* 1 (1988): 4–32; Qian Gang, "Tangshan da dizhen" (The great earthquake in Tangshan), *Jiefangjun wenyi* 3 (1986): 4–107;

and Su Xiaokang, "Honghuang qishi lu" (The revelation of the flood), *Zhongguo zuojia* 2 (1986): 144–159.

5. See Li Zehou and Liu Zaifu, "Wenxue yu yishu de qingsi" (Feelings and thoughts on literature and the arts), *Renmin ribao* (Overseas Edition), 14 April 1988, 4.

6. These words are from Zhu Jianxin, "Miandui fangxing weiai de baogao wenxue shijie" (Facing the world of blooming reportage), *Wenxue pinglun* 2 (1988): 31.

7. Qian Gang, "Tangshan," 6.

8. Ibid., 9.

9. Ibid., 103.

10. See *Cihai* (Thesaurus), one-volume edition (Shanghai: Shanghai cishu chubanshe, 1979), p. 679, emphases added.

11. Li and Liu, "Wenxue," 4.

12. The freedom to "fictionalize" in reportage writing is regarded on another occasion as a serious political issue; such freedom must be renounced so as to conform to the Party's principle of "firmly adhering to the truth." See, for a typical example, Huang Gang's 1979 criticism of Xu Chi in "Baogao wenxue de shidai tezheng jiqi bixu yanshou zhenshi de dangxing yuanze" (Reportage: its historical characteristics and its necessary adherence to truth according to the Party's principle), reprinted in Wang Ronggang, *Baogao wenxue*, vol. 2, pp. 335–382.

13. See Murray Krieger, "Fiction, History, and Empirical Reality," *Critical Inquiry* 1:2 (1974), 339.

14. *Fabulation and Metafiction* (Urbana: University of Illinois Press, 1980), p. 7.

15. This is the basic argument in Hayden White's reinterpretation of Western historiography. A statement from his *Tropics of Discourse: Essays in Cultural Criticism* (Baltimore: Johns Hopkins University Press, 1978) is worth quoting here: "The older distinction between fiction and history, in which fiction is conceived as the representation of the imaginable and history as the representation of the actual, must give place to the recognition that we can only know the actual by contrasting it with or likening it to the imaginable" (98).

16. *The Political Unconscious: Narrative as a Socially Symbolic Act* (Ithaca: Cornell University Press, 1981), p. 9.

17. Fredric Jameson, "Imaginary and Symbolic in Lacan: Marxism, Psychoanalytic Criticism, and the Problem of the Subject," *Literature and Psychoanalysis: The Questions of Reading Otherwise*, ed. Shoshana Felman (Baltimore: Johns Hopkins University Press, 1982), pp. 388–389.

18. A recent example is the furious attack launched by *Xinzhou bao* (28 April 1987), a newspaper controlled by the local government, against the "antisocialist" and "counterrevolutionary" ideology in Mai Tianshu and

Zhang Yu's reportage text "Tudi yu tuhuangdi" (Land and a local tyrant), *Zhongguo zuojia* 1 (1987): 73–100. This attack exemplifies my thesis that reportage constitutes a subversive discourse in contemporary China.

19. Hu Ping explains at the beginning of "Zhongguo de mouzi" (The Eyes of China) (*Dangdai* 3 [1989]: 7–8) why he and his coauthor Zhang Shengyou had to alter the name of a former Red Guard in their previous text, "Lishi chensi lu" (Historical reflections) (*Zhongguo zuojia* 1 [1987]: 128–163). Compared with Hu's local tactic, Liu Binyan's 1956 strategy was more daring. During a visit to Iowa City in August 1988, Liu told me in person that the story of "The Inside News" is pure fiction. He did not seem bothered by this "confession," but rather readily justified himself by enlisting support from his precursor, the Soviet writer Ovechkin, whose *ocherk*—the prototext of Liu's *texie*—was purposefully fictionalized in order to intervene in current sociopolitical affairs. It should not be a surprise, therefore, to read C. T. Hsia's classification of Liu's piece as an "example of revisionist fiction" (see Hsia, "Residual Femininity: Women in Chinese Communist Fiction," *Chinese Communist Literature*, ed. Cyril Birch [New York: Praeger, 1963], p. 177).

20. Wagner, "Liu Binyan," p. 73.

21. Qian Gang, "Tangshan," p. 9.

22. This is particularly evident in J. R. Hightower's refined taxonomy of Chinese historical narratives: pseudohistory, fictionalized history, euhemerized history, fictionalized biography, historical fiction, imaginary oratory, invention, fiction treated as history, genuine history with an admixture of fiction, and anecdotes. See chapter 3 of his *Topics in Chinese Literature: Outlines and Bibliographies* (Cambridge: Harvard University Press, 1953).

23. This is an observation made by Hayden White, who further clarifies the point as follows: "More specifically, it [historiography] was regarded as a branch of rhetoric and its 'fictive' nature generally recognized" (*Tropics of Discourse*, 123).

24. See, for instance, Kenneth DeWoskin, "The Six Dynasties *Chih-kuai* and the Birth of Fiction," in *Chinese Narrative*, ed. Andrew Plaks (Princeton: Princeton University Press, 1977), pp. 21–52.

25. This is because, according to Lennard Davis, "the reality they [the novels] reported was largely one they were in the process of creating. That is to say, the reality of the news/novels discourse was an ideological one in that it was created as a system of signification rather than as a virtual reproduction of material reality" (*Factual Fictions: The Origins of the English Novel* [New York: Columbia University Press, 1983], pp. 221–222). The same can be argued for Chinese reportage.

26. On 29 July 1976 *People's Daily* published the text of the telegram of condolence sent by the Party's Central Committee to the people of Tangshan, urging them to defend themselves against the natural disaster under the

guidance of Chairman Mao's revolutionary thought. On 31 July a report on how the people of Beijing fought the disaster appeared on the front page. A selection of telegrams of condolence sent by foreign leaders were printed on 1 August, most of them from the socialist countries. On 2 August *People's Daily* carried an editorial, and another editorial appeared on 11 August under the title "Continue Criticizing Deng Xiaoping, Recover from the Disaster." During those two weeks, few details of the disaster were disclosed, and the only photos that appeared in the paper showed people back to work in the fields and factories—there were absolutely no visual images of the crumbled buildings or broken power lines.

27. Qian Gang, "Tangshan," p. 75.

28. See Zhang Deming, *Zhongwai zuojia*, p. 6.

29. Bo Chuan, "Baogao wenxue lun" (On reportage), *Wenyi xinwen* 18 (1931), reprinted in Wang Ronggang, *Baogao wenxue*, vol. 1, p. 39.

30. In a 1937 article on reportage, Mao Dun argues against setting Xia Yan's piece as "the model" for reportage writing (see Zhang Deming, *Zhongwai zuojia*, p. 25).

31. These quotations are taken from "Ideology and Ideological State Apparatuses," in Althusser's *Lenin and Philosophy and Other Essays*, trans. Ben Brewster (New York: Monthly Review Press, 1971), pp. 162, 165, and 183.

32. See, for instance, Terry Eagleton's critique of Althusser's theory of ideology as "functionalist," "economistic and technicist," "structuralist," "empiricist," and finally "idealist" ("Ideology, Fiction, Narrative," *Social Text* 1:2 [1979], 62–63). For more details on the debate, especially in connection with E. P. Thompson's anti-Althusserian polemic, see Perry Anderson, *Arguments within English Marxism* (London: Verso, 1980), pp. 15–58.

33. Althusser, "Ideology," p. 146.

34. See Bonnie McDougall, *Mao Zedong's Talks at the Yan'an Conference on Literature and Art: A Translation of the 1943 Text with Commentary* (Ann Arbor: Center for Chinese Studies, University of Michigan, 1980), p. 75.

35. Ernesto Laclau, "Metaphor and Social Antagonisms," in *Marxism and the Interpretation of Culture*, ed. Cary Nelson and Lawrence Grossberg (Urbana: University of Illinois Press, 1988), p. 254.

36. These words were used by Liu Binyan himself in his *A Higher Kind of Loyalty: A Memoir by China's Foremost Journalist*, trans. Zhu Hong (New York: Random House, 1990), p. 66.

37. Liu Binyan, "The Inside News of the Newspaper," in *Literature of the Hundred Flowers*, ed. Hualing Nieh (New York: Columbia University Press, 1981), vol. 2, pp. 460–462; the original Chinese text, "Benbao neibu xiaoxi," appeared in *Renmin wenxue* 6 and 10 (1956).

38. Here are some qualities of a journalist/scout: "fact orientation, nimbleness, astute powers of observation, independent decision making and

investigation, and the freedom to choose any means necessary to get at the facts and convey them" (Wagner, "Liu Binyan," p. 79).

39. Liu Binyan, *People or Monsters?* ed. Perry Link (Bloomington: Indiana University Press, 1983, p. 68; the original text, "Renyao zhijian," appeared in *Renmin wenxue* 9 (1979).

40. Mouffe, "Hegemony and New Political Subjects: Toward a New Concept of Democracy," in *Marxism and the Interpretation of Culture*, ed. Cary Nelson and Lawrence Grossberg (Urbana: University of Illinois Press, 1988), p. 94.

41. Althusser, "Ideology," p. 175.

42. "Lishi chensi lu," p. 128.

43. See ibid., p. 159.

44. Althusser, "Ideology," p. 182.

45. Teresa de Lauretis, *Alice Doesn't: Feminism, Semiotics, Cinema* (Bloomington: Indiana University Press, 1984), p. 159; emphasis added.

46. Mouffe, "Hegemony and New Political Subjects," p. 94.

47. "Lishi chensi lu," p. 157.

48. Mouffe, "Hegemony," p. 95.

49. See Paul Smith, *Discerning the Subject* (Minneapolis: University of Minnesota Press, 1988), p. xxxv.

50. Ibid., p. xxxv.

51. These two images—the scout and the historian/sociologist—may be better understood in relation to two types of rationality I shall discuss in my concluding section: critical rationality and historical rationality. For the "scout" type of reportage texts, which exposes various kinds of social injustices, see most of Liu Binyan's pieces; Mai Tianshu and Zhang Yu's "Land and a Local Tyrant"; Mai Tianshu's "Huoji" (A live sacrifice) (*Baogao wenxue* 5 [1989]: 2–51), which narrates the event of a public demonstration against the removal of a reformist Yueyang mayor from his office; and Su Xiaokang and Zhang Min's "Shensheng yousi lu" (Noble reflections) (*Renmin wenxue* 9 [1987]: 4–22), which caused a heated discussion on a current crisis in China's education. For the "historian" type of reportage texts, which usually presents—either for the first time or from a new perspective—certain covered up or little-known historical events, see Qian Gang's text on the Tangshan earthquake; Wen Shulin's "Nanjing da tusha" (The slaughters in Nanjing), *Jiefangjun wenyi* 7 (1987): 87–97; Da Ying's "Ziyuanjun zhanfu jishi" (Reports on the captured soldiers of the Chinese Volunteers Army in Korea), *Kunlun* 1 (1987); 156–238; and Li Hui's "Wentan beige" (A tragic song from the literary arena), *Baihuazhou* 4 (1988): 4–193. For the "sociologist" type of reportage texts, see most of recent writings by the following writers: Su Xiaokang (e.g., *Ziyou beiwanglu—Su Xiaokang baogao wenxue jingxuan* [A memorandum on freedom: selected reportage by Su Xiaokang] [Hong Kong: Joint Publishing Co., 1989]); Mai Tianshu (e.g., "Aihe hengliu" [The river of

love is flooding], *Zhongguo zuojia* 5 [1987]: 191–220; and "Xibu zai yimin" [The immigrations to Western China], *Renmin wenxue* 5 [1988]: 49–77); Jia Lusheng (e.g., "Kongzi yu Zhongguo" [Confucius and China], *Kunlun* 5 [1986]: 174–206; "Gaibang piaoliu ji" [A gang of drifting beggars], *Zhongguo zuojia* 3 [1987]: 41–65; "Nanyi zouchu de muxie" [Those graves from which people have difficulty walking out], *Zhongguo zuojia* 4 [1988]: 38–52; and Jia Lusheng and Lu Wa's "Beishenpan de jinqian yu jinqian de shenpan" [The trial of money and the trial by money], *Baogao wenxue* 9 [1987]: 1–23); as well as Hu Ping and Zhang Shengyou.

52. See Liu Binyan, "Guanyu 'Renyao zhijian' da duzhe wen" [A Response to the readers of "People or Monsters?"], *Renmin wenxue* 1 (1980): 99–101; and "Cong 'Renyao zhijian' yinqi de" (Consequences of "People or Monsters?"), *Renmin wenxue* 12 (1980): 86–90.

53. He Xilai's argument can be found in Ai Ni, "Nongchaoren de qiusuo: wenti baogao wenxue yantao hui gaishu" (The reformers' quests: seminar on social problem reportage), *Wenxue pinglun* 3 (1989): 67.

54. For a report on the colloquium, see Zhu Jianxin, "Miandui fangxing weiai de baogao wenxue shijie," 31–38.

55. Li Yunzhuan classifies these terms—anxiety complex, critical rationality, historical rationality, and participatory posture—in recent reportage writings under one general term, "modern consciousness" (*xiandai yishi*), which he defines as consisting of "social obligation and historical commitment in the modern sense of the words"; see his contribution to "Baogao wenxue fazhan quxiang bitan" (Written comments on the directions of reportage), *Wenxue pinglun* 2 (1988): 40.

56. Lei Feng was an ordinary army soldier who was always ready to help the needy; Jiao Yulu was a county Party chief who devoted his whole life to hard work and eventually died of illness. During the 1950s and 1960s, nationwide campaigns to learn from these two heroes were launched by the government, with Mao Zedong and other top leaders issuing their directives in the form of calligraphy. The report on Lei Feng's life—"A Good Soldier of Chairman Mao: Lei Feng"—was cowritten by Zhen Weimin, Tong Xiwen, and Lei Ruming, and published in *People's Daily* on 2 February 1963; the report on Jiao Yulu—"The Model of the County Party Secretary: Jiao Yulu"—was cowritten by Mu Qing, Feng Jian, and Zhou Yuan, and published in *People's Daily* on 2 February 1966 (reprinted respectively in *Zhongguo baogao wenxue congshu*, vol. 3, part 1, pp. 477–497, and vol. 3, part 4, pp. 445–453). It is significant that, after the 1989 crackdown on the prodemocracy movement, the Chinese government once more staged propaganda, and these two heroes were set up again as models of self-sacrifice and absolute compliance to Party authority. Screen versions of the lives of these two heroes were released in 1964 (*Lei Feng*) and 1990 (*Jiao Yulu*).

57. For example, those reportage pieces collected in Xu Chi's *Gedebahe*

caixiang (Goldbach conjecture) (Beijing: Renmin wenxue chubanshe, 1978), and in Li You's *Ta you duoshao haizi* (How many children does she have?) (Beijing: Renmin wenxue chubanshe, 1980).

58. "Lishi chensi lu," p. 130.

59. It is interesting to see what is included in this rather vague notion of history. In Qian Gang's text, the premonition of the earthquake in the natural world (animal, birds, the lake, the weather, and so forth) and the Western news coverage after the quake are all listed as belonging to history. In Hu and Zhang, the Roman Pope's 1966 warning against a "personality cult" (presumably that of Mao Zedong) is deliberately—and abruptly, in terms of textual coherence—inserted into the authors' frame of reference to history; at the same time millions of Red Guards (among them both authors) are situated in "real" history without any ability to comprehend the actual historical happenings and thus all fall victim to Mao's ideological interpellation.

60. See Fang Hui, "Baogao wenxue 'xinchao' zan" (Praising a "new wave" in reportage), *Wenxue pinglun* 5 (1990): 142–144. A sample of Fang Hui's targets may be found in the following two recent collections of "social problem reportage," both edited by Zhou Ming and Liu Yin: *Xuanzhuan de Zhongguo* (China on a carousel) (Beijing: Zuojia chubanshe, 1988); and *Zhongguo dangdai shehui wenti jishi* (Records of social problems in contemporary China) (Beijing: Guangming ribao chubanshe, 1989). The social problems "recorded" in those reportage pieces include—in the order of the contents—inflation, ballroom dancing, economic crimes, city planning, organized beggars, teenage problems, college entrance examinations, overseas studies, matchmaking, divorce, abortion, law versus power, early deaths of middle-aged intellectuals, single women, cohabitation before marriage, sex and sexuality, gambling, ravaging of ancient tombs, housing shortages, and smoking.

YUEJIN WANG

Anxiety of Portraiture:

Quest for/Questioning Ancestral

Icons in Post-Mao China

In 1981 a gigantic portrait caused a stir in China. Titled *Father* (1980), it portrayed in a frontal close-up the weather-beaten wrinkled face of a turbaned old peasant, holding a bowl of water, his almost toothless mouth half-open, his eyes blandly looking into nowhere, beads of sweat twinkling on his face (figure 1).[1] It was painted by Luo Zhongli, age thirty-two, an artist from Sichuan.[2] The whole country raved. Many wept before the canvas.[3]

The tears came from eyes that had been tuned to Mao's frontal portraits for decades. The visual culture of the Maoist era as an age of icon is best paraded in Sun Zixi's *In Front of Tiananmen*, an oil painting executed in 1964 (figure 2). It solicits the viewer's devotional piety by regimenting the figures in a manner typical of the *sacra conversazione* ensemble. Implied in the choreography is a proper attitude toward the central icon: Mao's frontal head portrait— the so-called Helmsman's Portrait—hung on Tiananmen Gatetower in the heart of the country's symbolic center.[4] That such a snapshot setup should deserve a serious academic oil painting at all suggests the place of honor Mao's portrait occupied in the public imagination and the popular allegiance to it. Toward the end of the 1960s, copies of the Mao portrait flooded the whole country. Slight damage to a portrait meant scandalous iconoclasm which would lead to an immediate punishment or persecution. The practice imbued the square frontality of the portrait with a devotional imperative.

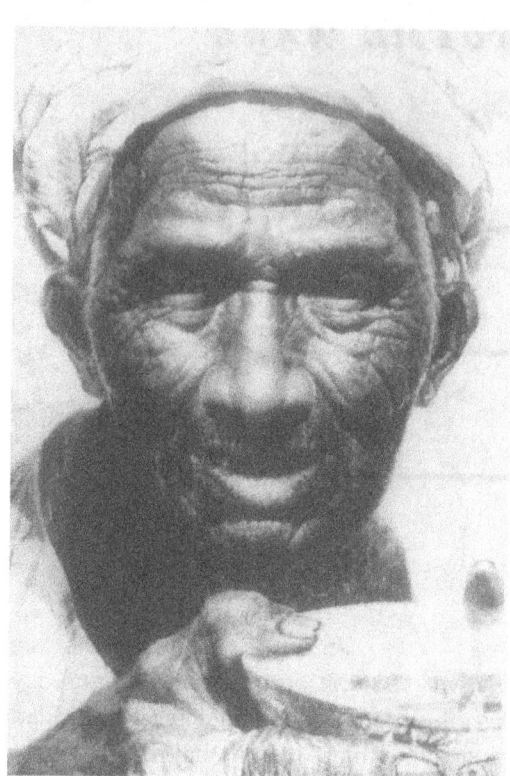

Figure 1. Luo Zhongli, *Father* (1980). (The National Gallery of Art of China)

Figure 2. Sun Zixi, *In Front of Tiananmen* (1964). (The National Gallery of Art of China)

The death of Mao marked the end of the age of icon. Though Hua Guofeng, Mao's hand-picked successor, legitimized his enthronement by propagating his own frontal portraits in the exact format of the Helmsman's Portrait, the use of the icon was soon dismissed by Deng Xiaoping, the more powerful contender for power, whose pragmatism called for iconoclasm and a dismissal of, ironically, the "personality cult."

Luo's *Father* portrait appeared four years after Mao's death. The artist's use of the format of the "Helmsman's Portrait" was self-conscious.[5] And the public was quick to get the message. An art critic wrote on Luo's *Father*:

> Has anyone seen a two-meter tall head portrait of a peasant? No, not a single precedent in the world history of art. This is the first time in art exhibitions in our country. At the first sight, it was mind-boggling that the image of a "plain" old peasant should deserve such a gigantic portrait like the Helmsman's Portrait often seen in the great halls. It would have been a crime during the reign of the Gang of the Four. When you come to think about it, the "Father" that has raised the whole Chinese race, how could he not deserve such a dignified format? We revere our Helmsman, but we should not forget our hard-working "father."[6]

Putting an anonymous old peasant into a Helmsman's Portrait on a gigantic scale—2.4 × 1.6 meters—implies both the sacralization of a new subject (the anonymous sitter) and consequently the desacralization of the form (gigantic portrait format).

This double movement was unsettling. The format traditionally reserved for the Helmsman icon now featured an anonymous, earthy, and sagging old peasant. The face is wrung awry; the deep-cut wrinkles accidentally spell out contingent suggestions of ambiguous expressions. The heavy-knit brows over the deep-seated and darkly shaded eyes border on anxiety; the expression could also be a scowl, an ugly cry, or simply a blank. The portrait is something of a pictorial monstrosity. Not surprisingly, it was controversial at the time. There were those who were unable to come to terms with the work. The portrait was deplored by some as "numb, idiotic," "passive, resigned, pessimistic," "ugly and deformed," "an unenlightened old-fashioned peasant," and "dark, dim, and insipid, like a drug addict."[7] The apologists resorted to the vocabulary of a Soviet-processed Marxist art criticism: that it was "synthetic and typical" of our age.[8] The quarrel boils down to a spatially structured dichotomy: backward versus forward, depressing versus uplifting, with the moral/aesthetic priority given to the forward/upward move. In hindsight, all these are irrelevant. It is not that the viewers of the time lacked perceptions; rather it was the way they articulated their perceptions that was hopelessly mired in the entrenched categories. Their visual perception was structured by these categories. The whole language of the time was enmeshed in limited descriptive terms that were unable to accommodate a new visual rhetoric.

The artist's self-apology, sincere and unpretentious, does not help much. The emotional formula of Millet's earthy pathos and quiet grandeur, the pictorial recipe of Chuck Close's photorealism, matched with his own intimacy with the rusticity of Dabashan—these are allegedly what come to bear upon his canvas.[9]

That the portrait thrives on photorealism is a mild irony. Luo asserted the "choice of this medium in which all my passion and thoughts could find the most powerful articulation."[10] Passion and thoughts were shunned by photorealists in America, who sought visual directness, emotional distancing, and a "literalness of the imagery" that remains "psychologically unmotivated." The "poster-like deadening of the surface" would spell out an eternal present to mock the *a priori* order and *a posteriori* significance. "No ideas but in things" was the credo.[11] Once Luo executed his work in the photorealist form, he borrowed not only the form but the zero-degree effect with its underlying or attendant values: a denial of commitments and a refusal of moral propensities. Luo may indeed have wanted to "speak" for peasants, for the beloved father. Instead, the image "spoke" its own confused messages. The artist did not foresee the real significance of his portrait.

Four years after the success of Luo's *Father* portrait, *Yellow Earth* (1984), a pioneering Chinese New Wave film, stunned the world with its brooding cinematography and bittersweet lyricism. Curiously, there are moments when the film aspires toward the condition of still photography and the self-conscious, studied mannerism of close-up portraiture. Even more curious is that such moments focus on the screen presence of a father—equally old, weather-beaten, wrinkled and earthy—with his eyes hidden behind a screen of shaded blandness. Several times in the film, the camera is held deadly still in a frontal extreme close-up of the father's face. The dim lighting scheme accentuates the figure against a dark background, much in keeping with the generic scheme of portraiture (figure 3). The image produced

Figure 3. Close-up of the father's face. From *Yellow Earth*, a film directed by Chen Kaige, 1984. (Still provided by Beijing Film Archive, with permission)

is surprisingly close to Luo's *Father* in modeling, iconography, and above all, in mood. We recall the "stupefied, numb look" that gripped Luo's memory and translated into his portrait;[12] we find in *Yellow Earth* the camera's riveted gaze at the father's stupefied face.

Moreover, the structuring imagery of *Yellow Earth* echoes that of Luo's oeuvre. Parallels or counterpoints between the two are striking. Such scenes in the film as the marriage processions zigzagging through the barren rocky hillside, half-naked peasants praying for rain, and the *suona* player blowing away on a sour tune had all occupied Luo's pictorial imagination. It is as if *Yellow Earth* had taken cues from Luo's oeuvre and fleshed them out into cinematic spectacles and a coherent narrative.[13]

The auteur of *Yellow Earth* may have been aware of Luo's portrait. Luo's works were exhibited in Beijing in 1981; the *Father* won the National Grand Prize for Young Artists that same year; Zhong Dianfei, then the leading Chinese film critic, wrote a review rhapsodizing about Luo's *Father* while deploring the absence of similar efforts on screen;[14] Zhang Yimou, the cinematographer of *Yellow Earth*, had an ardent passion for still photography—he sold blood to get a camera—and his ardor would leave no stone unturned, let alone Luo's spectacular photorealism. Yet the iconographical and stylistic indebtedness of the portraits in *Yellow Earth* to Luo's work is all but a lesser issue, if not totally irrelevant, than the iconography itself. If the film were cast under the spell of Luo's work, why did this type of paternal icon continue to be fascinating? If the film did not borrow from Luo's iconography, why did the film unwittingly coincide with Luo's work in fashioning such a paternal icon? The crucial questions are two: (1) why did the icon of the weather-beaten father in a close-up portrait matter so much to the Chinese imagination of the 1980s? and (2) why did the genre of frontal portrait—and its cinematic equivalent, frontal close-up still shots of a face—take on such an urgency?

"Civilization," says R. F. Thompson with regard to Yoruba, "is *ilaju*, face with lined marks."[15] Commenting on R. Avedon's photographic head portrait of William Casby, a black slave, Barthes writes:

> Since every photograph is contingent (and thereby outside of meaning), photography cannot signify (aim at a generality) except by assuming a mask. It is ... what makes a face into the product of a society and of its history ... the mask is the meaning....[16]

For all the artist's self-effacing modesty and the blandness of photorealism that cancels all a priori meanings, the fact that many wept before Luo's *Father* portrait suggests that meanings have been read into the portrait; that it caused controversies suggests tensions and contradictions internalized in the pictorial texture. The earthy, weather-beaten face in a portrait-like close-up in *Yellow Earth* derives its meaning from the narrative context. The affinity of Luo's *Father* portrait with *Yellow Earth* in turn allows us to infer possible subtexts underlying the portrait.

Yellow Earth shows the numbed senses of the old, mired in poverty and aridness, and tells the story of the young, frustrated in their burgeoning aspirations. Old father—harrowed by hardship, he appears much older than he actually is—marries away his daughter to a man much older than she is. Most of the time, he remains mute, as if half-dead, and he becomes frantic only when he prays for heaven to bless the arid yellow earth with rain.

The paternal icon in *Yellow Earth* is invested with certain moral antinomy. The father's grim and austere face furrowed by deep wrinkles correlates with the dry yellow earth (hence nature) and the basic mode of rural existence in central China, at once unyieldingly barren and unfailingly nurturing. Yet he acts on behalf of a traditional inertia that has nullified him into a languorous apathy and a moral blindness. He ruins his daughter's life—which is to say he stifles human nature. The marriage procession—the bitter moment of coercion and apathetic sacrifice—externalizes the father's will; the praying for rain—massive blind faith—headed by the father shows the father's blindness. *Yellow Earth* at once acknowledges our linkage with the paternal earth and questions its vitality. The yellow earth—emblematized by the paternal face—nurtures as its stifles. The face is both profundity and stupor writ large.

This ambivalence toward the father was visually prefigured but conceptually repressed by Luo Zhongli. The artist was one day struck by the sight of an old man who was safeguarding the manure in the Luo family's latrine, as manure was good fertilizer for farming in China and therefore jealously guarded in Luo's area. The old man huddled beside the latrine in the bitter cold from morning till night. Elsewhere there were firecrackers as it happened to be the eve of the Chinese New Year. Yet there he was, the lonely old man shivering in the biting wind, forlorn, unobtrusive, and tenacious. The artist was overwhelmed. An onslaught of received images flooded his mind. A mixture of emotions overtook him. The artist has never since been able to free himself of the memory of that "stupefied and numb look (*daizi, mamu de shenqing*)"

> . . . and his eyes, a pair of eyes, like those of a cow or a lamb, riveted on the manure pit, as if cornered in an impasse, he would protest against nobody; he only wanted to keep himself alive. I was overwhelmed with an inner storm. Compassion, pity, and all kinds of mixed feelings engulfed me into a violent whirlwind. Yang Bailao, Xianglin Sao, Runtu, and Ah Q . . . a medley from real life, literature, and things foreign all huddled in front of my eyes.[17]

Luo was apparently experiencing a pricking sense of rediscovery and an awakening of cultural conscience. The guilt was the collective forgetting. The encounter with the old man awakened in him an awareness of certain traditional Chinese traits: self-denial, forbearance, and quietism in suffering. These he found moving but never scrutinized. Overwhelmed by the poignant sight, he never rationalized beyond that poignancy. At the level of the subconscious, however, it was another story. The fictional figures that swarmed his mind in his initial inspiration come from Lu Xun's repertoire: Runtu and Ah Q—characters whom Lu Xun disposed of with scathing criticism. They carried traits that Lu Xun deplored as the diseased numbness plaguing our national character. It is these disturbing "ghosts" that adumbrated Luo's private associations. A second thought on these figures whom he associated with the old man would have disconcerted him. Consequently, his confessional pen halts at the point where Ah Q is mentioned: "Yang Bailao, Xianglin Sao, Runtu, and Ah Q . . ." Why is there ellipsis after the naming of Ah Q? The associative mind halts at the point beyond which his emotional imperative and moral consciousness will not allow him to tread. There is no question about his love for the peasant; hence, the father. But Ah Q, that despicable wretched Ah Q bitterly portrayed by China's most sensitive cultural critic of the century? Never.

Such is the tension. The paternal icon was made not out of filial piety but out of pity, which always carries some moral detachment, if not superiority. Might it be that deep in Luo Zhongli there couched an impulse, a subconscious prompting that twisted an otherwise straightforward representation? Should we suspect that Luo, for all his admiration for rustic simplicity and gratitude for the nurturing father, was already troubled in the early 1980s by ill-defined qualms, vaguely dark thoughts, and nagging skeptical impulses? He could not *name* it; he *painted* it. Where words could have failed or frightened him, he reconciled himself through pictures. What was mumbled in speech translated into a pictorial eloquence on canvass. Moral antinomies and conceptual contradictions find their symbolic reconciliation in a smooth visual logic.[18] The verbal language of the time failed to supply the categories to formulate the emotional experience; visual language accommodated well.

Any speculation on the private thoughts underlying Luo's work, however, can only hinge on a leap of faith in the psychoanalytical algebra. A more fruitful question is not what the father portrait means by itself or what the private meaning entertained by the artist is, but what the image/icon means to the public and how that meaning has changed over the past decade. The portrait was originally titled by the artist as *My Father*. It was renamed *Father* by the jury of the National Youth's Art Exhibition.[19] The change in name is significant. It marks a transformation from private emotional expression to a public monument.[20] Luo, for all his private thoughts that motivated the painting, was from that moment on, *disowned* the meaning of the painting. It was and was not anyone's father; it was a collective father.

A rhapsodic poem written in 1981 in immediate response to the portrait reads:

> How I wish to become the bowl you're holding
> Inseparable from you all my life!
> The crude bowl with fish patterns on it,
> Ancient as the unearthed relics,
> I would receive the sweat from your forehead,
> And suck it clean;
> Only your sweat can melt
> My hardened heart like unearthed relics.
> The heart that was the Qing Dynasty,
> The heart that was the Han Dynasty,
> The heart that was the Tang Dynasty,
> And perhaps, the heart that is the Republic.
>
> Who can count how many times you have died!
> Father, my father!
> That year you rolled into the dark depths with the rocks you carried,
> The local hearth nevertheless holding the torch, spurring the hordes
>   maddeningly on.
> Before your bones could be collected
> Your body already torn by jackals beyond recognition . . .
> That year you leaned against the earthen wall,
> Would never wake up even under the sun's caress,
> With yellowish green saliva oozing from your drooping mouth,
> Your hand clasping a handful of weed seed . . .
> That year you tore a wasteland into a patterned Dazhai field, your head
>   bent over,
> Pulling the plough, the tow-rope gnawing into your shoulder.
> After you smoked your last pipe filled with dried peach-tree leaves
> Fell down only to wake stars billions of years old.
> Father, my father!
> How many harvests have you watered!
> You can't leave behind the patch of gold!
> Turn around, quick! Quick!
> The gold belongs to you! You are the master!
> Master! Do you see that, master?
> Oh, father, my father!
> I am praying for you, for you.[21]

It is by Gong Liu (1927–), a veteran Chinese poet. Over the decades, the poet has always dwelled on the paternal metaphor. Early in the 1950s, he swore "to the nation, I am like a filial son";[22] he addressed the Yellow River as "our stubborn and tempestuous father" whose proper "temperament should be benign and modest."[23] After suffering political persecutions for more than twenty years, he still sang of the father, though in a vein of cult mingled with pathos, reverence coupled with poignancy. The emotional structure became more complex, but the father was still on the pedestal.

Years later, there was another rhetorical response to Luo's *Father*, this time through the medium of painting. But the tone had changed. Cai Feng's *A Window with a Mirror*, an engraving with polemic immediacy and topical urgency, directly "quotes" Luo's *Father* (figure 4). Multiplied images of Luo's *Father* portraits are aligned along four sides in an artificially constructed corridor space receding toward a vanishing point. The direct grafting of Luo's image disclaims ownership of any private meaning by the original author and puts Luo's image into a public space. The visual conceit is not difficult to grasp: the multiplication of Luo's "father" constructs a pictorial space of historical past. The father is the past, the past is the father. History is understood in terms of lineage and an emotional umbilical cord. The present is cast under the tyranny of paternal surveillance and enclosure. The emotionally compelling frontality of Luo's image is now obliquely foreshortened on receding planes so that gripping emotional urgency and sensual palpability are avoided. If Luo's *Father* was mired in emotionalism, it has now been put in a rational perspective, with orthogonals being drawn to indicate the construction of linear perspective—the grid of rationality.

The critical edge of Cai's work can be illuminated by some contemporary works, for example, Du Jianxin's *Untitled* (figure 5), a pair of paintings. In each there are two identical portraits plotted along a grid indicating linear perspective. The subject of the portraits within the picture is deliberately blurred, leaving only a contour. The two pictures are identical in setup except that in the second picture a muscular human body dives across the space, piercing the portrait canvases of both portraits. On the table of the second picture, the telescope is replaced with a book: Kant's *Critique of Pure Reason*. The evocation of a linear perspective as the grid of critical rationality is reiterated also in a more dashing work—titled *Big-sized Painting of Patriarch in Yellow Tone Painting* (figure 6) on canvas (1989). The

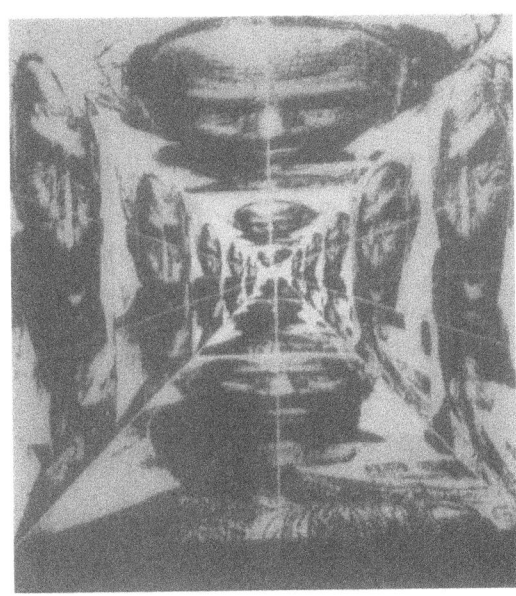

Figure 4. Cai Feng, *A Window with a Mirror* (1989). (Reproduced from *Meishu* 258: 6 (1989): 37)

vision is even more grim; "Patriarch" came under a direct attack—not a coincidence in the wake of 1989 Tiananmen event.

From Gong Liu's infatuation with the father icon to Cai Feng's critical scrutiny, the change of mood is apparent. The concern with the father icon is not confined to individual artists' private contingencies, but shared by the collective imagination. From Jia Pingwa's "Tiangou" (1985) to Liu Heng's *Fuxi fuxi* (1988), for example, we see a trajectory plotted along the same master scenario laid out by the changing reception of the *Father* portrait.[24] Both stories seem to lend themselves to a conspiracy with Cai's vision. Or, Luo's father portrait and Cai's critique merged in Jia's and Liu's texts.

Jia's story is about a love triangle among a disabled well digger, his wife, and his apprentice. The well digger is treated as a paternal figure, reinforced by the use of the Chinese guild nomenclature *shi fu* (master-father). The wife is referred to in the story as *shi niang* (master-mother). The story is provocative in its bold exploration of an ambiguous relationship bordering on the incestuous. The outcome of the father figure's suicide and the hinted union between the master-mother and the apprentice is all but a playing out of the Oedipal ur-narrative. The story assumes an ambivalence toward the father figure. Physically disabling him in the middle of the story and disposing of him by suicide toward the end of the story are two symbolic

Anxiety of Portraiture **253**

Figure 5a.
Du Jianxin,
Untitled
(1987).
Part I.

Figure 5b.
Du Jianxin,
Untitled
(1987).
Part II.

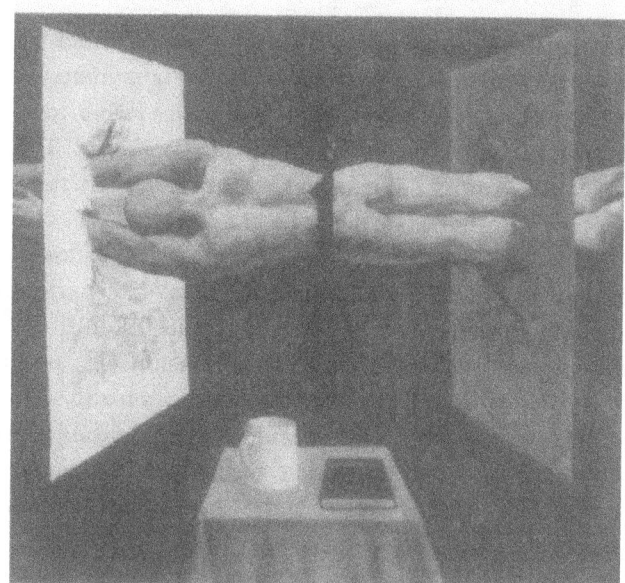

(Both reproduced from *Zhongguo gaodeng meishu xueyuan zuopin quanji: bihua nianhua lianhuanhua* [Complete works from High Academies of Fine Arts of China: Murals, Spring Festival paintings, and narrative pictures] Changsha: Hunan meishu chubanshe, 1989, not numbered)

Figure 6. Mao Xuhui, *Big-sized Painting of Patriarch in Yellow Tone.* (1989) (Reproduction provided by Rubel Collection of Asian Art, with permission)

acts on the part of the author. But the acts are timid, correlating the guilt-ridden semi-incestuous setup, a hesitant tampering with a taboo, with the unthinkable. There is an allegorical overtone, masking both a subterranean desire to write off the old and the attendant sense of guilt and pity.

Toward the end of the decade, this Oedipal drive found a bolder incarnation in *Fuxi fuxi* (1988), a novella by Liu Heng, later adapted to the screen as *Ju Dou*, directed by Zhang Yimou. The setup of the relationship is surprisingly similar. Only now it has two tension-ridden triangles: that among an impotent dyehouse master, his young wife, and his nephew apprentice; and that among the wife, the nephew, and the son of their illicit affair. The story is thus structured around two sets of father-son relationships, the second one being more sinister. More provocative is the symbolic act of making the father (that is, the nephew) illegitimate. He lives under the son's questioning eyes:

Anxiety of Portraiture

> Everywhere he goes, Tianqing [the nephew] sees his own son's stern eyes. Relentlessly, the son subjects him to the name of father. That breaks his heart. He was once dying to throttle the little bastard, but millions of times he ends up dying to throttle, drown, and hang himself.[25]

The "illegitimate" father in *Fuxi fuxi* is beset by the ubiquitous presence of his son's "multiple" questioning eyes. In Cai Feng's picture, it is the multitude of father images the viewer has to face. The two—the story and the picture—are mirror images of the same scenario: the questioning of the father. Such is the cultural anxiety in 1980s' China.

In spite of the poet Gong Liu's elegiac reading, Luo's *Father* portrait does not have any internal pictorial cue for death. The artist reserves his elegy for maternal figures. His *Spring Silkworms* (*Chuncan*) (figure 7) is filled overwhelmingly with an old woman's bent-down head crowned over with silver-white hair. As a pictorial trope, it draws on a classical poetic line, "The silkworm exhausts its *si* (silk) at the moment of death," with the "*si*" as a pun meaning both "silk" (*si*) and "thinking of; thought" (*si*).[26] Equally poignantly elegiac but subtler is his *Years* (*Suiyue*) (figure 8). A sagging white-haired old woman, presumably drawn on the same model, surrounded by an interior darkness, sits in the doorway, looking outdoors. On this side of the threshold is a quern, a symbol of endless cycles of back-breaking grinding toil and consuming years, and a litter of chicks, signs of burgeoning life. Intimation of imminent death charges the picture with an elegiac pathos.

Taken at its face value, *Years* is a genre painting saturated with the rustic pathos of a Millet. But it is more than that. In the preparatory cartoon, the view is kept more distant (figure 9). The woman sits with her legs planted outside of the door frame. Our point of view is slightly more oblique than the near frontality of the finished picture. Miscellaneous accessories fill the picture frame. The final version (figure 8) eliminates these accessories so that we are less certain about the painting being about a world out there. The old woman is completely contained *within* the door-frame which runs squarely in a parallel fashion against the outer picture frame. The door frame looks like a picture frame. The woman is seen in a frontal view, framed by the door-frame, set against a flat darkness which is analogous with the shrouding darkness conventionally surrounding a por-

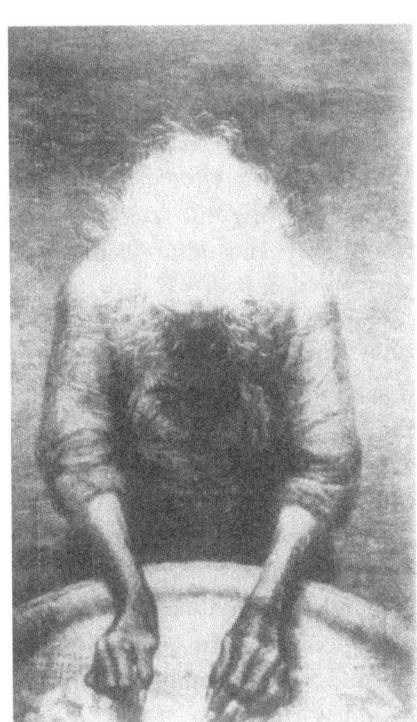

Figure 7. Luo Zhongli, *Spring Silkworms*. (Courtesy of Luo Zhongli)

Figure 8. Luo Zhongli, *Years* (1982). (Courtesy of Luo Zhongli)

trait subject. Here is, so to speak, a *portrait in the picture*. The picture borders on a threshold between the world of illusionistic realism and an ambiguous world of artifice. It turns self-referential; it evokes the idea or artifice of a portrait. The picture therefore is not so much about the aging woman as about the implications of having an old woman turning into a portrait image. Luo's tapping of the generic resources of portraiture brings up again the question raised earlier: why portraiture at all?

Ancestral portrait is an old traditional pictorial form in China. With its origin rooted in remote antiquity, it gained its currency during the Tang Dynasty (618–907) and was much in vogue during the Ming (1368–1644) and Qing (1644–1911) periods when almost every household would have a *xianbei de yixiang* (ancestral portrait).[27] It evolved into an entrenched cultural practice. The portrait subject is typically stiffly seated, *en face*, drawn before or after death by an artisan painter (figure 10). The portrait is then shown in funeral ceremonies and afterwards in *citang* (sacrificial offering hall) both for soul-summoning and for the living offsprings to pay reverence.[28] As such, ancestral portraits are memorial objects. They perpetuate memory.

Attending portraits is thus an emotional experience. It is consequently seized, formulated, and set up, by literary and theatrical conventions to become a wordy affair, at times long-winded. In other words, a portrait as a cultural construct is also a *discursive form*. Frontal head portrait *en buste* is closely attended by confessional apostrophes and monologues. There are compelling mis-en-scenes in classical Chinese fiction and drama in which one addresses a portrait to evoke or lament the absent beloved or the deceased.[29] The much dramatized legend of the Emperor Ming Huang of Tang Dynasty lamenting the loss of his beloved concubine, for instance, lives in popular imagination through the heart-rending scene of "ku xiang" (addressing the portrait in tears). The matter is treated in Tang texts without involving portraits. Bai Pu (1226–1295), a playwright of the Yuan period, fashioned the dramatic conceit as a way of mourning for the dead lover in the hope of summoning up her wondering soul in *Rain Over the Parasols* (*Wutong yu*).[30] The conceit jellied into a dramatic convention with a popular following.[31] Its currency suggests its appeal to the popular imagination. The portrait form thus gathers unto itself several associative features: an elegiac strain, a discursive intensity, and the rhetorical trope of apostrophe.

Figure 9. Luo Zhongli, preparatory cartoon for *Years* (1981). (Courtesy of Luo Zhongli)

Figure 10. Lu Danrong, *A Portrait of Yuan's Mother Han Ruren* (1742–1781). Eighteenth century. Nanjing Museum (Reproduced from Nanjing Museum, *Ming Qing renwu xiaoxianghua xuan* [Selected figure paintings and portraits of the Ming and Qing periods] Shanghai: Shanghai renmin meishu chubanshe, 1982, pl. 52)

Anxiety of Portraiture   **259**

Stylistically, the traditional portrait may well be a thing of the past; the traditional *way of attending to* ancestral or dead portrait, however, has sedimented in our response to portraits. This is precisely what the poet Gong Liu, as cited earlier, does with the *Father* portrait. The poet assumes an I-thou relationship with the portrait subject. For all the sensual palpability of the image, the Father is evoked not as a living one, but as a *dead* one recollected in the collective memory of past turmoil. He becomes an elegiac object and a figure of History, as "History always tells us how we die, never how we live."[32] The portrait is all but an unfailing receptacle for a rhapsodic language. It exists to be addressed. As such, it induces an anxiety:

> Endlessly I sustain the discourse of the beloved's absence; actually a preposterous situation; the other is absent as referent, present as allocutory. This singular distortion generates a kind of insupportable present; I am wedged between two tenses, that of the reference and that of the allocution: you have gone (which I lament), you are here (since I am addressing you). Whereupon I know what the present, that difficult tense, is: a pure portion of anxiety.[33]

This anxiety over the Other's oscillating presence/absence status defines well the emotional structure underlying Luo's *Years*. The old woman is seen in a frontal view, framed by the door-frame. She is set against a flat darkness which lends itself to an analogy with the shrouding darkness surrounding the portrait subject. The door-frame looks like a picture frame. Accordingly, the old woman appears both as a real presence within the door-frame and a mere image within a picture frame. The aging woman is presented both as a bodily presence and a portrait within the picture. As a bodily presence, she will fade into the past; as a portrait image, she is the *past*. In other words, past is around the corner, imminent. Conceptually, this is an oxymoron; pictorially, it is not.

The painting therefore embodies a peculiar kind of nostalgia: the nostalgia not for what has already become the past, but for what is soon to become the past. By evoking the artifice of portrait, by an unwitting conceit of self-referentiality, the picture compounds two temporal modes into a single space: the past and the present. The picture invites two modes of viewing. We either see that old woman as a *body* in space or view her as an *image* flattened on a picture surface framed by the door-frame as a picture frame. If the grandma figure were to be seen in a world out there, then we are there seeing the old woman in the present; if we were to see the old woman as existing in a picture frame (suggested by the door-frame), then we have a glimpse of an ancestral portrait whose subject once lived in the past. The two modes of viewing, hence two modes of time, are not mutually exclusive. We are both seeing the old grandma and remembering her; we both address her and recall her. The grandma image is both a mimetic presence and a mnemonic construct; she will turn into a mere portrait image. So the tone invested in the picture is both a gnawing regret and nagging nostalgia: regret that she will soon become a thing of the past; nostalgia in the sense that she is the past and the portrait therefore warns against our forgetting.

Hence the anxiety: the enshrined darkness surrounding the old woman in Luo's portrait already foretells a hermetic enclosure, an unfathomable interiority, and eternal sealing of secrets. With the grandma's wrinkled face imprinted in our memory, thereby surrogating as the totality of past, the historical mysteries surrounding her past become an untold tale.

This mnemonic efficacy of portrait symbolically formalizes an anxiety of historical epistemology: the anxiety about knowing the past, or the uncertainty about its knowability. Leyuan (Paradise) (1989), a novella by Lu Yuan, begins with that anxiety. The narrator of the story yearns to know the dark mystery surrounding his legendary grandmother. Yet all that registers in his memory is the image of his grandmother's wrinkled face at her dying moment: "I was at her deathbed, gazing at her face that had withered like a patch of furrowed and cracked dark soil on a dry river basin." The narrator frets about the woeful absence of a photographed portrait:

> There is no way of verifying the accuracy of my portraiture. Grandma lived a whole life without leaving a photograph behind, not even a yellowed black and white picture. All that is available for my reference is this deathbed face.[34]

Lu Yuan's anguished yearning for a photo portrait in Leyuan (Paradise) is a symbolic gesture; it is a longing, a quest for the origin of his family, which is to say, the origin of his present existence. He wants to press the image for clues to the mysteries about the family genealogy, as the whole story begins with a puzzle:

> It is said that my uncle is a Japanese bastard. Even Grandma on her deathbed did not reveal whose offspring my uncle is. No one in our clan

> therefore knows the secret of my uncle's birth. Grandma finally took that secret with her into her tomb, and it will rot together with the mummified body that weathered the climate of the world.[35]
>
> I have been obsessed by this question, my mind racing like hell, burning out lots of cerebral cells. If this secret could be unraveled, then my inquiries into mankind, maternity, womanhood, *even into our national character* may find some clues.[36]

The reading of maternal physiognomy is thus charged with an interrogative urgency. Likewise, the narrator in Mo Yan's "Ecstasy" (*Huan le*) reads the face of his mother, who "all of a sudden appears mummified, lifeless, senseless . . ."[37]

> Look at the mother's murky and benign eyes, like those of an old dog's, her face burned by high fever. Mother is also a woman. She was a young woman. She may have been . . . may have once been a loose woman; then I am the son of that loose woman, born with dirt over my head . . . Oh . . .[38]

The moral angst consequently finds the apostrophe, a rhetorical trope, vis-à-vis a portraitlike presence, a most compelling means for the urgent interrogative impulse. It also gives anxiety an order: what Barthes sees as an essential paradox—addressing someone absent—is bypassed with the portrait as a presence, as a substitute for the dead: my addressing you presupposes your presence; yet you are absent, dead long ago. A portrait, your substitute, remains the umbilical cord that leads back to the origin. It then lends itself as a depository site for an outpouring of questions, doubts, speculations, and imagination directed toward the historical past. Insofar as these doubts are vaguely shaped and privately harbored, there is a need for an unmediated space of intimacy to keep these disturbing thoughts private. The frontal close-up portrait fulfills that need. It galvanizes questions while suppressing answers; it is the umbilical cord that goes back to the past, yet is lost in the past. *Formally*, portraiture as a mode of discourse *bridges* the gaping gaps between past and present, absence and presence, I and thou; *epistemologically*, it *separates* them. It is a symbolic act on the past.

The grandmother in *Years* will, as Lu Yuan describes in his novel, "take that secret with her into her tomb, and it would rot together with her mummified body that had weathered the climate of the world."[39] The tell-tale face offers only a flat muteness. The suffering of past years and the complexity of the past experience have only vaguely registered in the Grandmother's forehead in the hermetic form of wrinkles. If there has been too much collective forgetting in the previous decades, ancestral portraits then redeem that collective forgetting by calling for remembrance, an unfulfilled remembrance at that. Therefore they induce the anxiety of remembrance, even the frustration of failed remembrance.

Addressing the portrait thus becomes a mode of historical memory which may range, as we are told, from *Erinnerung* (recollection) to *Gedachtnis* (memory). Both address the past, yet one is "the inner gathering and preserving of experience," whereas the other is "the learning by rote of names, or of words considered as names, it can therefore not be separated from the notation, the inscription, or the writing down of these names. In order to remember, one is forced to write down what one is likely to forget."[40] When one makes a point of recalling, it already presupposes the de facto forgetting, the fear for, and the effort of overcoming, the forgetting.

Attending to ancestral portraits in the mode of *recollection* is dramatized in *Red Sorghum*, a film adapted from Mo Yan's novel by Zhang Yimou. The film begins with *a head portrait en face*. From a dark screen, the space of the inward-looking mind, breaks in the voice-over: "I would like to tell you some stories of my grandpa and grandma. It was quite long ago, so some now do believe it and some don't."

Fade in. A young woman's face emerges from the darkness and remains absolutely static, held by a stationary camera. "This," says the voice-over, "is my grandma." The body/image duality is at work here. The screen presence of the female figure, motionless, appears both as a conjured image and a living body. The visual image (the young maid) and the verbal referent ("my grandma") come into a head-on clash. The spectator has to mediate between the palpable visual immediacy of the young woman and its repudiation by the voice-over insisting on calling her "my grandma." Throughout the film, the voice-over time and again breaks in to reiterate that calling, or naming—"my grandma"—so that the visual presence, a fresh and young woman, is linguistically invested with and dogged by this name "grandma." Since she is presented in a frontal close-up, the young woman as grandma is never free from the dogging gaze of her future grandson: the I-narrator-voiceover. All this historical drama of passion and desire is packed with imagination—the historical fantasy of the present "I." It is the grandson/narrator who *wills* her appearance in the first place.

This visual rhetoric of naming versus viewing is the structure of historical imagination played out in the novel. Throughout, the narrator's grandmother is simply and persistently referred to as "grandma." Even in the primal scene when she is first sexually ravished by the hooded man later known as "my grandpa," the addressing/naming is none the less emphatic:

> Yu Zhan'ao ruthlessly tore apart grandma's brassiere and let the cascading sunshine dance on her cold and taut breasts on which squirmed swarms of tiny gooseflesh. Under his powerful wriggling, Grandma cried out in a low and husky voice: Oh, heaven! And she fainted.
>
> Grandma and Grandpa made love in the vibrant sorghum field. The two hearts, unbridled and scornful of all mundane laws, were closer to each other than their delightful bodies. They tilled and showered in the sorghum field, painting a trace of red onto the history of our Gaomi in the northeastern countryside.[41]

It is an imagined scenario of historical voyeurism: the grandson peeping into the primal scene of his grandparents. Historical illusion is insistently punctuated by the intruding gestures of calling and recalling—even in the most ecstatic and private moment—the young maiden "Grandma." The grandson/narrator, the voyeur of the historical primal scene, is only half self-effaced, brazenly and boldly asserting his voice, as if his presence had preceded the copulation that caused him, as if he reserved the right to christen his grandmother, as if he had the choice of seeing his father (not even himself) to be born or not to be born. As a grandson he would have no choice; as a narrator he has the power to opt for the otherwise.[42] In this symbolic act, history is mastered, for, as Barthes rhetorically asks: "Is History not simply that time when we were not born?"[43]

This emphatic trope of historical recalling by way of apostrophic calling illuminates the *raison d'être* of the portrait prefacing the whole film—the slow fade, the portraitlike posture of the young woman/grandmother, the intimate and unmediated relationship with the camera/I. The maternal icon is all but a mental portrait retrieved from historical memory. I call you, "grandma," therefore you are.

The film ends also with such apostrophes. Grandmother has been shot down by a hail of a Japanese machine gun fire. The furious Grandpa and his gang blow up the Japanese truck at the cost of their lives. The little child—"my father"—tries to shake "my grandpa" who has by now turned into something resembling a stone statue. The screen is awash with bloody red after the bloodbath. The camera swoons across a field strewn with stacked fresh corpses amidst which grandmother's young body lies in prominence. The drum starts to roll on the soundtrack. An overwhelmingly atmospheric red color slowly wipes out the field and covers the screen. The child, now appearing as if afloat on a sea of red color starts to chant at the top of his lungs:

> Mom, Mom, go to the west!
> The long, long boat . . .

The ritualistic chant reverberates in the space of an echo chamber—down the corridor of our memory. As the film ends, the piercing tune of the *suona* bursts out, the very *suona* that plays both marriage and funeral tunes. Thus is closed a cycle of birth and death. The film ends with an ancient Chinese ritual, that of soul-summoning, which also attends ancestral portraits.

The film is therefore an extended play-out of the "I-thou" relationship with the ancestral portrait. It is tantamount to the symbolic structure of "the wooden reel with a piece of string tied round it" played by Freud's grandson who, through the symbolic act of *fort-da* game, learns to live with the experience of loss and regain by letting go of the reel and subsequently retrieving it.[44] Through this symbolic act is overcome the poignancy of Mother's absence. Translated into traditional Chinese cultural terms, it reverts to the ritual of soul-summoning.

Red Sorghum shows the limitations of actual portraits beyond which it goes far afield as a film. At the same time, it also brings out the potentialities of a single portrait by stretching it in a cinematic way. As an extended reading of an ancestral portrait, it demonstrates well the interlocking relationships involved in the experiencing of a portrait: living/dead, present/past, I/thou, and child/grandma. The yearning is toward the past. The burden of the past hangs, however, heavily on the present. Portrait is as much an act of *self will* on the part of the living as it is a commemoration of the dead. The anxiety over the ancestral portrait—such as what Lu Yuan's narrator feels—is the anxiety about the present.

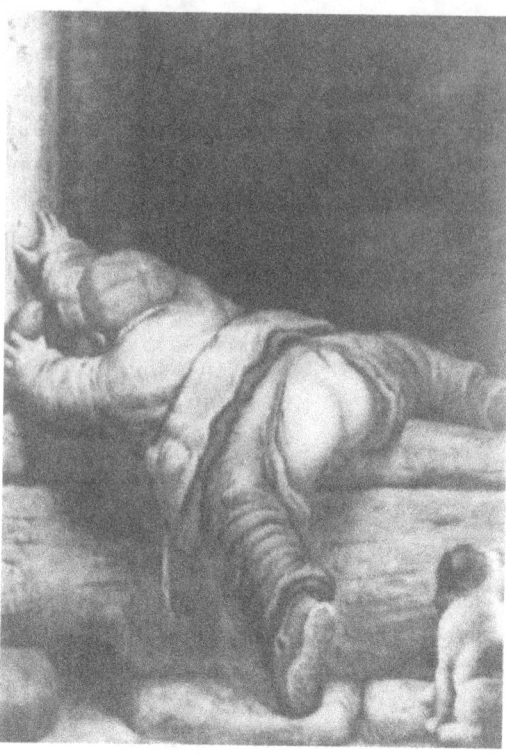

Figure 11. Luo Zhongli, *Climbing the Threshold* (1983). (Courtesy of Luo Zhongli)

This marks Luo's maternal portrait off from the conventional old woman in oil cast in a portrait format which has its attendant formal or generic implications. Any reading of such portraits could easily lapse into the way the Renaissance portraits are attended to, highlighting their preoccupation with age and aging. Giorgione's *Old Woman* with the wrinkled face and a self-referring gesture is a classical example. It tells a moral tale: *vanitas vanitatum, et omna vanitas*. The pathos is about the transience of life, the ruthless fate of aging, and the inevitability of the destructive Time that devours beauty and claims our life. The portrait is an allegorical warning.[45]

Death indeed hovers around Luo Zhongli's maternal portraits. Earlier versions of *Suiyue* (*Years*) placed the old grandmother alongside either a tomb-mount or a coffin.[46] The preoccupation with death is obvious. But the sentiment has a different edge. It is hardly a morality tale about the transience of life. Giorgione's portrait works by *semblance*: what befalls of the old woman applies to me; it alerts the viewer to the transience of life. Luo's portraits work by *difference*—the old woman's death confirms my living—it calls for an awareness of how to come to terms with my ancestor's imminent absence. It is no coincidence that Luo's grandmother portrait should not go by itself. It coexists with a companion piece titled *Climbing the Threshold* (figure 11). The similar point of view—the close frontal view of the doorway—and the same setting relate this painting narratively, or contextually, to *Years* (figure 8). A child is shown, as if caught by an unseen camera, in a strenuous effort to climb over a high wooden threshold. The sympathetic tenderness of the moment, highlighted by exposing the child's bare bottom to the viewer, is touching. But beyond the cuteness there is an acute poignancy. The coming into the world of the child correlates to the grandmother's eternal absence. Conceptually the threshold is the same one that encloses the old woman in the dark house in *Years*. The space that used to hold the old woman becomes a vacant tomblike darkness. In climbing the threshold, the child is also covering a temporal distance, reaching into a space that used to hold the historical other.

The child figure is a familiar visual trope in the rhetorical structure of portraiture. The child in Ghirlanddaio's portrait (1490) gropes for an old man as if to verify the ontological status of the old man's existence both as a portrait image and a real sitter.[47] The child in the opening sequence of Bergman's *Persona* (1966) caresses a huge portrait of the mother as if to call the mother into existence. Luo's innocent child also unwittingly enacts a fumbling and groping quest for the portrait space once occupied by the now absent mother/grandmother. It looks ahead to the grandson/narrator of *Red Sorghum*.

So what is exactly the present anguish in the form of anxiety over the ancestral portrait? Does it follow that desiring/mourning the missing mother, or the mother-to-be-lost, suggests, according to a psychoanalytical logic, a disappointment with the "failure of the paternal metaphor"?[48] One views and confronts the paternal icon while mourning the maternal icon. Though the scene fits the Freudian scenario snugly, it is more of an ambivalence toward the past: an urge both to detach from, and attach to, the past, a desire to reject the past and the fear of being rejected by history and disowned the heritage, a wish to come into one's own while questioning whether there is such a thing called "one's own." There is a resignation to being condemned to be the "sons" and "grandsons" of fathers and mothers. Questioning the father and nostalgia for the mother become different ways of defining and coming to terms with the self. Such is the way the poet Wang Xiaolong, who writes about the father-son tension, addresses the dead father.

> You look at me from the mirror.
> Father, we really look alike, you and I, don't we?
> After all, all I have been loathing is myself.
> When I want to make peace with you, you disappear.
> How can one befriend oneself?
> After all, I have been acting you and acting myself.[49]

The question "who are you, father?" finally boomerangs to become "who am I?" And the question "who am I?" is necessarily overshadowed by a nagging prompting: how can I be other than those who gave birth to me? If we cannot disown our father, we cannot disown that part in us. The son in *Fuxi fuxi*, who has refused to acknowledge his father's fatherhood, finally confronts his father's dead body. "With his bold eyes finally fixed on the part where the thighs parted, . . . he studied its nature," and finally recognized "the narrow passage he himself had trodden through, and the primitive and mysterious habitat that had given birth to him."[50] The narrator in Mo Yan's "Ecstacy" (*Huanle*), addressing himself as "you," is revolted by the imagined sight of fleas hopping over his mother's genitals; in his final ecstatic suicidal moment, however, he envisions his own painful passage from the maternal womb "through this dark tube" into the world.[51] The pain is turned into ecstasy. The death of the self is accompanied by the birth of the self—a return to the origin, the maternal body.

So all the ambiguities and ambivalence inscribed in the paternal and maternal portraits are what constitute the viewer as the son/grandson. To view them is to view us. What we find disturbing about the portrayed image is what we reflect about ourselves. The whole cultural revisionism in 1980s China is ultimately about how to be the son/grandson vis-à-vis the Other—call it father when skepticism sets in; call it mother when nostalgia overwhelms. Portraits are mirrors.

Notes

1. The painting was reproduced as the cover picture of *Meishu* 157:1 (1981).

2. See Tao Yongbai, "Youhua fuqin yu zuozhe Luo Zhongli" (*Father*, an oil painting, and Luo Zhongli, the painter), *Guangmin ribao*, Jan. 14, 1981. All translations appearing in this text are mine.

3. See Dong Wei, "Qingzhu xinxue hua fuqin" (Putting himself all out in painting the *Father*), *Zhongguo qingnian bao*, Feb. 26, 1981; "*Dianran qianjin de huoju* (Light up the marching torch)," *Renmin ribao*, Jan. 15, 1981.

4. For an excellent discussion of the use of Mao's portrait hung on Tiananmen Gatetower, see Wu Hung, "Tiananmen Square: A Political History of Monuments," *Representations*, 35 (Summer 1991), 85–89.

5. See Xia Hang, "*Sichuan qingnian tan chuangzuo*" (Young artists from Sichuan on creation), *Meishu* 157:1 (1981), 44.

6. Zhang Fangzheng, "Yao zhuzhong xingshi tansuo" (More attention to the formal experiment), *Meishu* 165:9 (1981), 53.

7. Shao Yangde, "Chuangzuo, xinshang, pinglun—du fuqin" (Creation, appreciation, and criticism: a reading of *Father*), *Meishu* 165:9 (1981), 56–59.

8. Zheng Jinchu, "Hua shenme, zenyang hua, mei zai nali (What to paint, how to paint, and where is the beauty?)," *Meishu* 159:3 (1981), 23.

9. Luo Zhongli, "Wode fuqin de zuozhe de laixin" (Letter from the painter of *My Father*), *Meishu* 158:2 (1981), 4–5; Luo Zhongli, "Nongmin he wode hua" (Peasants and my paintings), *Zhongguo Meishu*, February 1981, 28–33.

10. Luo Zhongli, "Wode fuqin de zuozhe de laixin," p. 4.

11. See Linda Nochlin, "Realism Now," in *Super Realism*, ed. Gregory Battcock (New York: E. P. Dutton, 1975), pp. 111–125.

12. Luo Zhongli, "Wode fuqin de zhuozhe de laixin," p. 4.

13. One sweltering day Luo was about to add a drop of sweat to the Father's nose on this canvas when from outside the room came the sound of children: "It's raining! It's raining!"

> If there is such a thing as inspiration, I certainly experienced it. My mind was electrified. All of a sudden, through the storm outside, it was as though I saw Dabashan and the peasants of Dabashan standing on the drought-cracked land.... I quickly jotted down this fleeting image: in a cracked dry field stood a half-naked peasant, his head raised, his eyes closed, his arms spread. A long-denied gratification showed on his face.... I was trying to illustrate the relationship between nature and man.

And on his meditation over the spectacle of marriage procession, we read,

> Those who have seen the mountaineers' marriage ceremony will never forget the scene. For others, the sight of a palanquin borne into the mountain is unforgettable.... [The procession] zigzagged along the boulder-ridden barren hillside for miles to begin a life, to reproduce, to accomplish one of life's major imperatives.

It is as if Luo were visualizing the film script for *Yellow Earth*. See Luo Zhongli, "Nongmin he wode hua," pp. 30–32.

14. Zhong Dianfei, "*Fuqin yu dianying*" (The *Father* and cinema)," *Wenyi bao* 395:23 (1981), 46–48.

15. R. F. Thompson, "Yoruba Artistic Criticism," in *The Traditional Artist in African Societies*, ed. W. L. d'Azaredo (Bloomington: Indiana University Press, 1973), p. 35.

16. Roland Barthes, *Camera Lucida: Reflections on Photography*. trans. Richard Howard (New York: Noonday Press, 1989), p. 34.

17. Luo Zhongli, "Wode fuqin de zhuozhe de laixin," p. 4.

18. On the symbolic solution to social tension, see Fredric Jameson, *The Political Unconscious: Narrative as a Socially Symbolic Act* (Ithaca: Cornell University Press, 1981), pp. 77–83.

19. Dong Wei, "Fang quanguo qingnian meizhan yideng jiang huodezhe Luo Zhongli (An interview with Luo Zhongli, the winner of the National Young Artists grand prize)," *Xinhua wenzhai*, May 1981, 198.

20. The painting was referred to by some critics as "a monumental portrait." See, for instance, Shao Dazheng, "Yetan fuqin zhe fu hua de pingjia" (More about the assessment of *Father*), *Meishu* 167:11 (1981), 15.

21. Gong Liu, "Du Luo Zhongli de youhua fuqin (Reading Luo Zhongli's *Father*, an oil painting)," in *Zhongguo xinshi cui 1950–1985* (New Chinese poetry, 1950–1985: a selection) ed. Xie Mian and Yang Kuanghan (Beijing: Renmin wenxue, 1985), pp. 353–355.

22. Gong Liu, *Gong Liu Shixuan, 1945–1985* (Selected poems by Gong Liu) (Nanchang: Jiangxi remin chubanshe, 1987), p. 142.

23. "Oh, Yellow River, our stubborn and tempestuous father, / Change your temper right now, / You should be benign and modest!..." Gong Liu, "Ye du huanghe" (Crossing Yellow River at midnight) in *Gong Liu Shixuan* (Selected poems by Gong Liu), p. 131.

24. Jia Ping'wa, "Tiangou," *Shiyue* 38:2 (1985), 6–29.

25. Liu Heng, "Fuxi fuxi," *Beijing wenxue* 307:3 (1988), 37–38.

26. Li Shangyin (ca. 813–ca. 858), "Untitled," in *Quan Tang shi* (Collected Tang poems), (Beijing: Zhonghua shuju, 1960), 539:6168.

27. Nanjing Museum, *Ming qing renwu xiaoxianghua xuan* (Selected portraits of the Ming and Qing periods) (Shanghai: Shanghai renmin meishu chubanshe, 1979), p. 2.

28. For a brief history of the ritualistic use of Chinese ancestral portraits, see Eli Lancman, *Chinese Portraiture* (Rutland, Vermont; Tokyo, Japan: Charles E. Tuttle, 1966), pp. 39–40. For a more recent work on Chinese portraiture, see Richard Vinograd, *Boundaries of the Self: Chinese Portraits, 1600–1900* (Cambridge and New York: Cambridge University Press, 1992).

29. See, for example, the episode in which Ximen Qing laments Li Ping'er, his dead lover, through her portrait in Xiao Xiao Sheng, *Jin Ping Mei cihua* (Golden Lotus) *xinke xiuxiang piping jinping mei* edition (Taibei: Xiaoyuan chubanshe, 1990), p. 882.

30. Bai Pu, *Tang Ming Huang qiuye wutong yu* (Emperor Ming of Tang in a rainy autumn night), Act. 3, in *Zhongguo xiqu xuan* (Selected Chinese plays) ed. Wang Qi (Beijing: Remin wenxue chubanshe, 1985), pp. 84–89.

31. See, for example, Hong Sheng (1645–1704), *Changsheng dian* (The palace of immortality), Act 32, in *Zhongguo shi da gudian beiju ji* (Ten great classical Chinese tragedies), ed. Wang Jishe (Shanghai: Shanghai wenyi chubanshe), pp. 702–706.

32. Roland Barthes, *Michelet*, trans. Richard Howard (New York: Hill and Wang, 1987), p. 104.

33. Roland Barthes, *A Lover's Discourse: Fragments*, trans. Richard Howard (New York: Noonday Press, 1978), p. 15.

34. Lu Yuan, "Leyuan" (The Paradise) *Shiyue* 65:5 (1989), 36.

35. Ibid., p. 36.

36. Ibid., p. 37.

37. Mo Yan, "Huanle" (Ecstacy), *Remin wenxue* 328–319:1–2 (1987), 13.

38. Mo Yan, "Huanle," p. 26.

39. Lu Yuan, "Leyuan," p. 36.

40. Paul de Man, "Sign and Symbol in Hegel's Aesthetics," *Critical Inquiry* 8 (Summer 1982): 772.

41. Mo Yan, *Hong Gaoliang jiazhu* (The Red Sorghum Family) (Beijing: Jiefangjun chubanshe, 1987), pp. 81–82.

42. Such a mapping of an I-thou relationship onto a past/present scheme is implicitly played out in the film. "My grandma" stretches out in the sorghum field with "Grandpa" kneeling over her. The camera zooms back, craning upward toward a bird's-eye view of the sorghum field with the copulating couple as tiny figures on the ground. The camera enacts the transition from the past tense to the present, from the mode of "being there" to the mode of *reflecting* "being there." Mo Yan's meditation ("Grandma and Grandpa ... tilled and showered, painting a trace of red onto the history ...") occurs as an afterthought, leaving behind the imaginary primal scene. The upward craning camera enacts that afterthought.

43. Roland Barthes, *Camera Lucida: Reflections on Photography*, p. 64.

44. Sigmund Freud, *Beyond the Pleasure Principle*, trans. James Strachey (New York: Liveright Publishing Corporation, 1950), pp. 14–17.

45. David Rosand, "The Portrait, the Courtier, and Death," in *Castiglione: The Ideal and the Real in Renaissance Culture*, ed. Robert W. Hanning and David Rosand (New Haven and London: Yale University Press, 1983), pp. 113–114.

46. The originally conceived version of *Years* was charged with even more macabre overtones: the old grandmother was shown herding cattle on a tomb-ridden hillside. Luo's initial proposal was rejected in a group discussion: it was regarded as too distressingly obsessed with death. The second cartoon is closer to the final work we see except that beside the old grandma

is placed a coffin. Again it was rejected by Luo's mentors on the grounds that it was too close to the macabre. In the final work, the foreground is littered with lively chicks. See Wei Chuanyi. "Sichuan meishu xueyuan qiqiji biye chuangzuo jiaoxue" (Supervising the creations of the graduating class of 1977 of Sichuan Fine Art's Academy) *Meishu yanjiu* 3 (1982) 19.

47. I owe this point to Professor John Shearman's lecture on Italian Renaissance Painting and Sculpture c. 1260–1600, Harvard University, 1991.

48. Jacques Lacan, *Écrits: A Selection*, trans. Alan Sheridan (New York and London: W. W. Norton, 1977), p. 215.

49. Wang Xiaolong, "Ni yiwei ni mei bei wo banyan guo ma?" (You think I have not played your part?) *Zuopin yu zhengming*, 88:44 (1988), 55.

50. Liu Heng, "Fuxi fuxi," p. 43.

51. Mo Yan, "Huanle," p. 41.

LI TUO

Resisting

Writing

Although there are many kinds of writing, each kind has its established rules. When a writer becomes addicted to writing—for whatever reason—he or she must select one set of rules from the existing assortment. A majority of writers (the word "majority" is really inadequate, because it does not do justice to the actual number of such writers) are not aware of this limitation. They congratulate themselves on the choices they make and frequently exaggerate by representing these choices as pioneering creations. They are like the monkeys in the ancient Chinese fable "Three in the Morning and Four in the Evening."[1] Perhaps I am being ironic, but to me the greater irony is that, after witnessing the drive to recognize the limited nature of writing evident in the writings of people such as Roland Barthes, Michel Foucault, and Jacques Derrida, many have begun to understand this limitation (although the majority still do not), but they still feel compelled to write.

There might yet be a way to satisfy the desire to write and at the same time preserve the dignity of writing itself; that is to use writing in order to resist it. This method is not so easy to carry out, and its results can be questionable. For example, in my own recent writings, I have been careful to avoid using superlative modifiers such as "the most," "extremely," and so forth. I do this because several years ago I suddenly discovered that these superlatives had found their way into my writing without my knowledge, and no matter whether it was fiction, miscellaneous essays, literary or film criticism, or even personal letters to friends, these modifiers were everywhere. However, when I resolved to eradicate these words from my own lexicon, my already laborious writing became even more laborious. I had used these words unconsciously to classify the world. It was nearly impossible for me not to use them whenever I encountered something in which I felt I had a stake (even if the stakes were entirely abstract). It was as though I had to classify matters in which I had an interest with written words—the "best," the "worst," the "absolutely right," or the "utterly wrong"—before I could rest easy. Removing these modifiers felt like depriving myself of the potential benefits and the important right (here I refrain from saying "the most important" right) to pass judgment, for which I have struggled. To forego the right to pass judgment would mean renouncing not only my own long-held values related to this right, but also the system of ideas that generates and sustains such values.

Some might accuse me of exaggerating either deliberately or inadvertently; after all, the use of an expression is only a matter of style, so what's all the fuss? But the question of style is what I am driving at. I have pointed out in several articles the enormous impact the long and prolific writing career of Mao Zedong has had on contemporary China. (Mao thoroughly integrated his writing career with his political career. It can even be said that he combined his writing and political activities so that the two became indistinguishable, and he developed them into a special kind of praxis. In this respect Mao's writing is very different from writing in general and has become a separate genre in itself.) The discourse and style found in China today both have their origin in Mao's own writing. I have called this style the "Mao style," and it is a unified system of language style that has extended a solid grip on all realms of discourse. The widespread use of words such as "the most" and "extremely" (I am only one of the victims) is but one specific example of the widespread dominance of the Mao style in writing and speech.

I have at hand a booklet by Zhou Yang published in 1948, "Defining the New Era of the Masses." As I casually flipped through the pages, this passage on page 81 caught my eye: "Comrade Mao Zedong in *Talks at the Yan'an Forum on Literature and the Arts* provided a new direction for revolutionary literature. This talk represents a new epoch in the history of revolutionary literature and thought. It is the most broadly accepted and most concrete summary of Marxist policy and science regarding literature and the arts, and therefore it is the best textbook of Marxist literary science and policy." Turning the page I found: "The central concept running through the entire work can be summarized thus: literature and the arts come from the masses, and to the masses they must return. This concept is also central to Mao Zedong's thought overall. His greatest contribution is that he provided the most correct solution to the problem of how to return to the masses." A cursory sweep through various publications in China in the last several decades would furnish anyone who might be interested in this problem with numerous similar examples, even in works that make no mention of Mao Zedong. Thus, resisting words such as "the most" and "extremely," although it might appear trivial, in fact means resisting an entire system of writing (that is, resisting the Mao style). This kind of resistance can hardly be easy, because what is resisted is far more than just writing itself.

In the 1980s resistance against the Mao style became a widespread movement. (Unfortunately, few people have noticed. Even among those who are engaged in it, few see it as resistance.) It has engulfed many fields, including literature, philosophy, and historiography. The movement has led to the emergence of a new range of phenomena. There are several indications of this ground-breaking movement, including various peripheral discourses that challenge the centralizing forces of the Mao style from within and a rivalry between various different styles. Moreover, there has been a profound transformation in the modern Chinese language, induced by the sudden onslaught of new vocabulary (largely as a result of the introduction and translation of twentieth-century Western works in the humanities and social sciences). These changes have fundamentally affected literary and cultural circles in China, creating a climate that is chaotic but full of vitality. Although the reprisals stemming from the political upheaval in 1989 may have dealt a grave blow to this burgeoning environment, the vitality cannot be completely obliterated. Mao discourse has already been overthrown. Although the Mao style still enjoys powerful political backing, it has been reduced to one common kind of discourse among many kinds in China today—particularly from the perspective of writing. (For evidence of this diversity, take a look through any periodical published in mainland China in the past year or so.) Despite their resistance to the Mao style, authors have not yet come to a clear understanding of writing. On the contrary, new dangers emerge from this kind of resistance.

One of the new dangers is that many writers, consciously or not, have taken the easy way out of the Mao style by simply taking over (or inhabiting) some other ready-made discourse and using it in writing. This is the most prevalent approach to writing in China at present. "Introducing" "new" Western theories and applying them in the analysis of various issues in contemporary China seems to be a way of evoking "modernization."

The real danger does not lie in how crude or careless these "introductions" might be. It is not how unsystematic or fragmentary they are, nor is it the misreadings, misunderstandings, or distortions of those who introduce and use these theories. (Misreadings are not only inevitable but also, in a certain sense, necessary.) Poor writing can be improved, given time. As for the misreadings and distortions, they are only a problem if the "misreading" or "distortion" does not pass muster by somehow producing meaningful discourse, discourse that can resist the discourse at the center. Rather, the danger is that many authors, in their renditions, descriptions, and applications of these "new" theories, attribute some kind of universality to them and believe that they are applicable to any historical or cultural discursive context. They fail to take into account that any theoretical discourse embodies specific ideologies and is produced, as a text, in a specific historical and cultural context, and contains interpretive strategies that imply an interpretive "will to power." As an example of how such an interpretive will works, in the last two years there has been a continuous stream of people using one or another theoretical discourse having to do with Western modernism to interpret the new literary phenomena of the last decade in China. They assert that a modernist literary movement has in fact emerged in China, whether it was deliberate or not. This assertion is no more than a reiteration of the notion that "modernity" in Europe and America is the universal model for all humankind to follow. Those who believe in this model are unable to imagine that history today or tomorrow could ever be different.

Writing is an enticing venture, but it is also humiliating. When you have the sense that you should resist writing with writing, just when you think you are resisting, you find that you are again captive. I often feel this way, but other than heaving a sigh, I have not come up with any way to deal with it.

Note

Translated by Mary Scoggin.

1. In the *Qi wu lun* book of Zhuangzi: "The monkey king was distributing *mao* grass to all the monkeys. He said, 'Three in the morning and four at night.' All the monkeys were angry. Then he said, 'Four in the morning and three at night.' All the monkeys were content."

XIAOBING TANG

The Function of New Theory:

What Does It Mean to Talk about

Postmodernism in China?

To answer the question above in a relevant and meaningful fashion, let us first read a text. In a recent issue of the journal *Theorists of Literature and Arts* (February 1990), we can find a brief article bearing a fairly heavy title—" 'Recoding' and Contemporary Chinese Literature." The intent of the essay, as the author makes it abundantly clear at the outset, is to point a way out for the contemporary situation in which literature has allegedly suffered from an identity problem, a "loss" or some "confusion." The conclusion reached rather hastily in a space of less than four pages reads as follows: "For Chinese literature to get out of this difficult situation, the only way available is a return to the principle of realism; for the Chinese writer (or even the entire literati) to rid himself of the fate of being ignored or left out in the cold by the nation, the only thing to do is go back to the altar of moralism." The opposite of "realism," according to the writer, is a self-obsessed "modernism," which is neatly diagnosed as the cause of the going astray of contemporary Chinese literature and is rather conveniently condemned as a mere replay of medieval mysticism in the West in the first place. More specifically, the nature of realism, at least in the version the author requests, is prescribed as "the construction of a new set of ethical and moral values that meets the demand of modern society."[1] In short, it is high time that men and women of letters in China give up literary innovation and cultural criticism and once again commit themselves to a positive, if not leading, role in a society anxiously waiting outside the gate of modernization.

Judging from the time of its appearance, that is, at a moment when a bankrupt ideological orthodoxy has rolled back to reassert itself with sheer force and terror, this article and its ardent call for a renewed and ever explicit subjugation of literature to the political establishment should come as no surprise. What is amazing (I was going to say "amusing") is the author's unsuspicious use of something that happens to be profitably available. The entire essay draws on the notion of "recoding," which is briefly acknowledged as a term borrowed from a certain Frenchman named Deleuze. By faithfully applying the Deleuzian model of reinterpreting human history into a metalinguistic continuum of "coding—overcoding—decoding (recoding)," the author happily puts together his own theory that contemporary Chinese literature and indeed culture in general needs some sort of "recoding," a resumption of traditional, moral-oriented values. His access to Deleuze, nevertheless, is through some other introductory interpretation, namely, Fredric Jameson's Chinese book *Postmodernism and Theories of Culture*, which the author of the essay in question quotes profusely without, as is customary, taking the trouble to indicate so. Since there is no other material on or by Deleuze readily available, he cannot but at the same time accept Jameson's illustrative translation of Morgan's *Ancient Society* into Deleuzian terms.[2] Thus by means of an effortless transplantation, the poststructuralist hero, with all his imaginable schizophrenic exasperation, is willy-nilly brought to rationalize the imposition of a subservient moralizing discourse as well as an "immanent and despotic" Urstaat that he dreads only too much. In the meanwhile, Jameson's interpretive reading of Deleuze, together with his critical remarks about poststructuralism, is left unacknowledged and undifferentiated.

The purpose of our reading this article here, however, is not exactly to lament a typical lack of intellectual rigor and scope nor to seek to do justice to the original texts through some intertextual tracing. Rather, such a piece of writing gives us a good chance to bring together a number of important theoretical issues that either signal or constitute a predominant ideological and cultural difficulty in the Chinese situation. It is, in other words, a text that demands a symptomatic reading. First, there is the now age-old and facile "realism/modernism" opposition. The debate over which of the two should be the politically correct choice is bound to be fruitless because, just like the even more ancient "Chinese principle vs. Western application" squabble, the terms involved here have over time acquired their own specific cluster of referents and abstractions. Both "realism" and "modernism," like many other loaded catchwords, are less meaningful as terms describing a certain aesthetic style or cultural logic than as rigid epithets for a political alignment and power distribution. As a result, the discourse as a whole is exhausted and has long stopped generating any intellectual enthusiasm or indeed fresh thinking. In a sense, such a ritualistic controversy can itself be taken as a gigantic signifier, its moving in and out of the discursive field infallibly indicating fluctuations in a given political and cultural equilibrium. In the past decade, as part of an ideological readjustment, two intellectual debates duly took place, the first about the validity of either realism or modernism and the second over the desirability of either Chinese or Western culture. Themselves a repetition of a number of previous efforts, these two closely related debates accurately record a historical trajectory that moves from a more specific literary rethinking to a general reexamination and critique.[3] Of course, there is never such a thing as simple and mechanical repetition in the realm of history. On the contrary, an apparent return to an old problem should always call our attention to the complex and, most likely, violent movements of history.

The palpable movement of history captured in this otherwise extremely boring attempt to reinstate a bankrupt official doctrine, therefore, has to be the rather outlandish appearance of an already transformed Deleuze. In fact, the wishful appropriation of a poststructuralist theoretician in the text, no matter how perfunctory and random it may be, unmistakably points to a much larger and more problematic context of the local discursive economy. This is the paradox: on the one hand, the production of a fashionable text endorsing a highly specific and contingent policy (governmental or ideological) is somehow compelled to derive its legitimacy from a nonindigenous and high-brow theory. The subsequent discursive circulation and consumption also surreptitiously depends on the authority and marketability, because he is new and "contemporary," of a Western theorist. The point of reference is therefore always placed on an exogenous, preferably global-spirited, source. On the other hand, the transplanted theory or discourse is cynically twisted and put to a manipulative use in order to rationalize the political need of a dominant power. The theory itself is consequently deprived of all its own historical specificity. The imported language remains truncated and causes considerable textual gaps and inconsistency, while at the same time the current local problem is not readdressed in any critical way but on the contrary double-proved to be absolute and perpetual. In other words, the unwieldy new language of universal significance is not utilized to reformulate or shed light on the old contradictions, but only to prolong and fortify them as such. No paradigm shift is introduced, no new insight gained, and the two discursive orders, the newfangled and the home-made, the exogenous and the native, the exotic and the conventional, are arranged in such a clear hierarchy that they remain strictly apart. There is no ambiguity, of course, over which order constitutes the paradigmatic precedent and meaning system. In the end, what gets impoverished is both the new theoretical discourse and an understanding of the real issue at hand.

However, such an unproductive use of a newly introduced theory, as I have suggested, is more a symptom of the political and ideological backlash that has been scrambling to reentrench itself on all fronts than an indication of what the general function of New Theory has been in literary discourse. The sudden (which does not mean unexpected) and forced retreat to a dysfunctional and openly challenged political system necessarily prescribes a refurbishing of the badly worn-out ideological state apparatus, and the last thing needed is any creative probing. For instance, the recent resurrection of Lei Feng, an enormously good-hearted soldier of the early 1960s who came to be deified as Mr. Good after his early but timely death, tells of how desperate the regime is in seeking to dress up the blood-stained image of the army, on the one hand, and to return to the old practice of mass deception and control through a rhetoric of idealistic heroism, on the other. Indeed, any innovative thinking and unorthodox, not even necessarily revolutionary, language poses a fundamental threat to a regime that secures its absolute hegemony through relentless ideological homogenization, rigid social stratification, and political terrorization. Nonetheless, the profound irony here is that only with such a historical given, namely, a politically illiberal situation, will New Theory, a broad enough term for all the discursive formations that are exogenous in their origins and obligatorily marginal, acquire its subversive force despite its expressed intention. The very form of New Theory becomes historically progressive and often outweighs its manifold content. But with a weakening or metamorphosis of this repressive grip, either due to an inability of the system itself to exercise control as it would like to or, more probably, because of the pervasive intrusion of something called the market, the revolutionary thrust of New Theory would rapidly evaporate and lose its social relevance, very often to the confusion and despair of those who are accustomed only to resisting a prohibitive power, an external or internalized police that says no. This, as I will argue, was actually the complex situation in which New Theory found itself in the second half of the 1980s in China and which can be characterized as postmodern.

To reconstruct a history of how New Theory has fared recently in the Chinese context is already an enormous job, because so much introduction, translation, application, and expansion has been done in so little time and so rapid a succession. Here we are going to agree with some other critics and specify New Theory as that part of contemporary Chinese literary discourse which "has its basic content derived from representative literary theories of the twentieth-century West."[4] Around 1985–86, with the economic reform program carried out steadily and continually broadened, there erupted a widespread interest in literary methodology. Overnight almost everyone in the business felt compelled to employ some idiosyncratic and sufficiently scientific-sounding terms or concepts in talking and writing about literature. Much complaint and even personal vexation, understandably, was expressed, especially by the older generation of critics or so-called literary workers. But the "methodology fever" got enough bureaucratic acquiescence, at least no outright rejection, partially for the reason that such a discursive shift corresponded to and implicitly endorsed the official ideology of modernization, of catching up with, in every way possible, the strange modern world of science and technology. Preceding this attention to a new critical language, we need to recall, there had been some other theoretical controversies conducted largely within the perimeter of the Party doctrine, such as the then sensitive one over whether literature should serve Party politics or the more extensive debate about the existence of an aesthetics in classic Marxist writings. The title of one of the first defiant articles (*Shanghai Literature*, April 1979) gives us a good idea of the flavor of these preliminary arguments: "Rectification of Literature and Arts—a Critical Response to the 'Literature Is an Instrument for Class Struggle' Doctrine." Now from historical hindsight, those debates appear to be the first and uncertain tidings of a whole new wave of rethinking.[5]

Out of these initial ideological skirmishes and methodological experiments, and perhaps more importantly, alongside new literary experiences such as the "Misty Poetry" and "Stream of Consciousness" fiction, grew what came to be called "theory of literary ontology" or "subjectivity of literature," its major proponent being Liu Zaifu, an established Lu Xun expert as well as creative writer. In 1985, Liu Zaifu published a manifesto-like essay calling for a shift in the general literary discourse: "Literary Studies Should Have Human Beings as Its Central Conceptual Category." There he echoed Hegel's plea for philosophy to return to itself in order to achieve fuller and purer development and announced that "writers in our time have felt the same as Hegel did; therefore they are trying to regain the essence of literature itself."[6] Following that, Liu Zaifu published a series of lengthy essays elaborating his thesis and described the general tendency of contemporary literary studies as a movement "from outside to inside, from homogeneity to heterogeneity, from micro-analysis to macro-review, and from a closed to an open system."[7] Step by step he built up a theoretical system pivoted around the core concept of an irreducible individual subject as both agent and thinker. As a slogan, "return to literature itself" in search of its own inner logic and autonomy expectedly caused much more debating and thinking. The shock waves stemming from Liu Zaifu's ever forceful elaboration on the "subjectivity of literature" ran fast and deep. Not the least of the immediate reactions were charges that such a move would obscure the ideological nature of literature and deviate from the accepted notion that literature is a reflection of social life.[8] It was readily brought home that a return or retreat to Literature or Human Being [ren] posed a radical challenge not only to an institutionalized literary practice but also to an entire tradition of social thinking and organization. As one critic put it, the difference between Liu Zaifu and his opponents in the debate was about more than some specific aesthetic topics in literary theory; it pointed to a "profound divergence of opinion as far as epistemology, methodology, and historical conception are concerned." It thus suggested the incompatibility between the old and new literary theoretical systems.[9] Soon, Liu's thinking as a complex would be studied by a younger generation of critics as the "Liu Zaifu Phenomenon" and he himself would be taken as the embodiment of a dynamic Faustian spirit in contemporary China, representing a transfiguration of the classical, in particular German, humanist tradition. In fact, a profound affinity between twentieth-century Chinese intellectual life and that in early nineteenth-century Germany is in general perceived to be neither surprising nor inexplicable.[10] This situation, combined with the fact that nineteenth-century Russian literature strikes an endearing note of familiarity for the middle-aged pool of writers, of course owes as much to the massive introduction and study of Marxism as to the simultaneous erasure of other historical experiences.

The significance of Liu Zaifu's intervention is many-sided and its historic impact on contemporary Chinese culture still remains to be fully examined. Various assessments have been made of his theory from different perspectives, either tracing its philosophical genealogy or speculating about its practical implications. One point that is easily overlooked, especially with a theory that explicitly focuses on literature as an autonomous object with a validity of its own, is the strong historical consciousness that Liu Zaifu exhibits throughout his writing. Human subjectivity, according to him, should include two components, a practical subjectivity and an intellectual one. "To emphasize subjectivity in literary creation, it has two basic implications: one is to place human beings as the practical subject within a historical movement . . . the other is to draw critical attention to human intellectual subjectivity, to the activity, self-autonomy, and creativity of the human spiritual realm."[11] In the essay referred to above, Liu Zaifu bases his theoretical proposal on first describing the present as a peculiar moment, a moment of entering a new historical horizon. The broad cultural background against which a new form of literary studies becomes necessary is characterized as: (1) the ongoing historic change and its Zeitgeist are bound to affect the field of literary studies; (2) with this transition, "every and each department of spiritual production" demands to proceed according to its own laws and nature; (3) the rich discoveries of natural sciences will inevitably influence the thinking of social sciences; (4) as a result of the "open-door policy," the scope of literary workers is broadened, and (5) finally, new literary phenomena, both Chinese and worldwide, bring up new theoretical problems that go beyond the conventional conceptual framework. The new historical situation clearly shows the inadequacy of traditional methods and thinking, and we are therefore forced to search for a new approach. Thus the decision to embrace an autonomous literature is more a reaction to or indeed a courageous rebellion against a reductionist ideology and practice than a product of serious examination of the new reality and its new problems. The new reality is such that very soon the heated discussion of "literary subjectivity" and the entire myth of an individual heroically contemplating history will be rendered not as solemnly tragic or exciting or, ironically, as relevant.

This new historical reality is what Liu Zaifu and his contemporaries, of whatever ideological camps, cheered as the New Period of openness and economic reform. The process of marketization marched at such a swift speed and on so large a scale in the second half of the 1980s that the traditionally politically sensitive and responsive readership quickly dispersed and preferred not to be diverted solely by some plainly ideological, if not scholastic, argumentation, no matter how radical or conservative the engaged parties might be. The immediate concern of the public was turned away and absorbed by other much more mundane matters. What had been an all-important "ideological front" was compelled to undergo an unhappy transformation through which, so to speak, the line was redrawn to shift the front to the background. In the meanwhile, numerous journals mushroomed, mass culture irrepressibly returned as a forgotten form of commercialism, literary production was accordingly professionalized, and with the now steady outpouring of graduates from universities and colleges, literary criticism necessarily became a serious business. All this of course did not go without causing much confusion, anxiety, and bitterness, because such a radical reorganization of society around the market had to cost some people something, either their authority and privilege, or an easy job and livelihood, or simply an accustomed way of thinking. Thus, on the one hand, novelist and historian Zhang Chengzhi, for example, gave full vent to his frustration with a rampant commodification and professionalization when he observed that a "print waste" was mounting daily only to block the true and lively development of pure science itself. His nostalgic sentiment was widely echoed, not least by publishers and editors of those journals that deemed themselves serious and scholarly.[12] On the other hand, so-called "popular literature," consisting of either semi-legal imports straight from Taiwan and Hong Kong or hasty renditions of sensational mysteries and soft pornography from all sources possible, stormed in, and with a force not seen for quite a while, took over the book market and left many writers, who had reached their maturity by taking writing assignments, at a well-nigh total loss. All of a sudden, the reading public was no longer to be educated but to be entertained, a choosy customer rather than a faithful, only less cultivated, fellow comrade.

Amidst this pervasively unsettling reorientation, however, literature and literary studies also find themselves in an unfamiliar and yet very tempting territory. Sensing that they do not have as much ideological constraint, innovative young writers write to explore all the possible frontiers and start turning out large quantities of rebellion-spirited and experimental novellas and short stories. Their writings thus acquire two outstanding characteristics: they are first a challenge against the ideological orthodoxy and at the same time have to feed on the imagination of a reading public that is all too hungry for anything that smacks of "modern" or "contemporary." Not only is what now gets told greatly expanded to include the primitive and exotic, a bustling and estranging urban space, a deviant inner mind, and a tumultuous history, but the form of the story, the narrative itself is also subjected to all sorts of playful experimentation. Brief new waves constantly gather to surge and overshoot a previously clamorous tide. From Liu Suola to Su Tong to Wang Shuo, from Mo Yan to Ge Fei to Yu Hua, to name just a few fiction writers, the cycling of divergent literary pursuits and styles goes on at an ever faster speed. To one critic's sensitive mind, these young writers do more than mere creative writing: they "in a carefree manner invite the reader to dance disco with them—upon all the glittering bits and pieces of what used to be the sacred." Yet the same critic is no less bewildered by what she sees is going on in new fiction and criticism and, with dead seriousness, she asks "What else can we have?" in the wake of all these sacrilegious plays, dismantling, and almost masochistic exposure.[13] This uneasiness with and distrust of an emerging literary production that pursues "shock effect" as a market value more than anything else is in fact quite representative. Calling it a doomed counterculture, another critic does not hesitate to condemn as a self-inflicted "failure" Mo Yan's violent use and abuse of language goaded by his desire to always reach new territories of experience.[14]

At the same time, however, with the market economy increasingly penetrating into all realms of social life and consumption starting to manipulate and generate desire, other cultural activities also quickly adapt themselves and accord themselves new roles. A thundering concert by rock star Cui Jian deliberately dances on a thin line

Figure 1. Cui Jian performing "A Piece of Red Cloth." Courtesy of Pan China Media Ltd. (Hong Kong)

between the accepted and the unsayable, bringing into a game of parody both the officially endorsed and the rejected (figure 1). A fifth-generation film will either pointedly reconstruct and project refreshing imagery of history and minority culture, or simply portray a wildly energetic and restless present. In this new genre (or generation) of films, political struggle, historical memory, sexuality, and desire all become mixed up to build up an ideological representation of the contemporary. Successful avant-gardist attempts, despite unrelenting censorship, are constantly carried out in contemporary drama to first break down the classical three-unity principle and then pose fundamental questions of reality and representation. Examples that readily come to mind are the parodic play *Pan Jinlian* and the series of works by Gao Xingjian. In the field of art, furthermore, the prevailing spirit of innovative rebellion gives simultaneous rise to philosophical reflection in the modernist tradition and a postmodern playfulness and fascination with floating and disorienting signifiers. The most striking instance of the latter tendency is of course artist Xu Bing's industrious invention of senseless Chinese characters, in the ancient form of a thread-bound book and perfectly according to the principle of ideographic composition (figures 2 and 3).[15] All this does as much to popularize an emergent cultural presence as to distract attention to literature per se. The still vibrating argument for a "literary subjectivity," in this light, appears all but distantly elementary and, indeed, so embarrassingly modernistic. Xie Mian, the most eloquent defender of the Misty Poetry, cannot help letting out a deep sigh over what he calls a "beautiful chaos," directly reminiscent of the bursting "terrible beauty" that struck W. B. Yeats in another place and at another time. While the generation of Liu Zaifu and Xie Mian have not quite disengaged themselves from the exhausting battle against a repressive political order under the banner of "humanism," some young theorists, in the words of one commentator, already "turn to worship Foucault, Derrida and Lacan as the hero and set out to deconstruct 'Truth'."[16]

For a number of reasons, that "beautiful chaos" fails to loom as frightening when it struggles to get born in the field of literary criticism. First of all, if a now multifarious cultural life attracts various critical responses but also gives the unmistakable impression of vitality and creativity, an erratic theoretical discourse will only rub in its own superficiality and even incompetence. This is to a large extent what happened to New Theory. With all the different and more often than not conflicting theories introduced en masse, critics, anxious to try them all, write to produce a confusing hybrid of discourses. From New Criticism, Psychoanalysis, Structuralist Poetics, Semiotics, Reception Aesthetics, Reader's Response, Hermeneutics, Archetypal Criticism, Deconstruction, and Poststructuralism, all the way to Feminist Theory, Western Marxism, and Postmodernist Cultural Critique, the entire course of literary criticism in the twentieth-century West and more is frantically crammed into scores of introductory essays, dozens of translated selections, all in a matter of a few years.

Since the preoccupying concern is to do away with the traditional critical vocabulary and catch up with the new trends, critics find themselves faced with two uneasy tasks in their writings: on the one

Figure 2. A page from Xu Bing's *A Book from the Sky*, Photograph by Howard Y. F. Choy. (Courtesy of the artist)

Figure 3. Xu Bing's work at exhibit in the Elvehjem Museum of Art, University of Wisconsin-Madison, November 30th, 1991–January 19th, 1992. Photograph by Howard Y. F. Choy

hand, they have to constantly explain and define unfamiliar concepts such as "unconscious" or "sign" so as to make some sense in the following argument; on the other hand, employing the new theoretical apparatus, they have to convince themselves as well as the reader that it is desirable and superior to what it comes to replace. In connection to all this, practitioners of New Theory, as ardent defenders and interpreters of the New Wave in fiction, see it as a historic duty to develop a new reading public. Thus they sometimes have to assume a pedagogical role. It is then no wonder that we should occasionally come across essays with a neatly packaged title like "Read for Meaning in Old-fashioned Stories, but Read the Sentence Structure in New-style Fiction."[17] But with limited access to the original texts, because most of the active critics depend on translation, and those who know a foreign language have difficulty in obtaining foreign books anyway, introduced theoretical models are too easily uprooted and put to uses that are not necessarily in accordance with what they were designed for in the first place. The "recoding" essay we just looked at can serve as an extreme example here. Arbitrary application like this inevitably turns the borrowed theories into a metaphysical truth system. The works of Derrida, for example, have been widely referred to and quoted and contended over, but, as far as I know, there is still no serious and systematic translation of the French philosopher whose remarks about the Chinese language seem to have inspired quite a few while offending some others.

Secondly, and more telling of our historical situation, is the ambivalent relationship between New Theory and the Old or dominant theoretical establishment. As an emergent discourse, New Theory in literary criticism, even though it is still fashionable to do and has been attempted continuously, remains a theoretical practice largely relegated to the margin. Contrary to enthusiastic claims that a whole new open theoretical structure has been set up to liquidate the hegemonic orthodoxy,[18] the new literary discourse, either creative fiction or theoretical exploration, retains its defiant posture and, partially because of the tremendous presence of popular literature, its offensive thrust is increasingly weakened. While it is counterhegemonic in its intention as well as effect, New Theory is in one way or another mandated to be apologetic about its existence. This is an impression regularly gathered from reading any of those balanced introductions, prefaces and postscripts attached to translations. The rationale for introducing or translating is to magnanimously familiarize oneself with the "new knowledge" and the purpose for using New Theory is to "enrich" or "augment" our current understanding of literature and arts. Indeed this seems to be the well-trodden path for any discursive interventions. "The origination and development of New Theory has not," it is critically observed, "shaken the conceptual premises of the traditional theory. Up to now, the traditional theoretical structure still possesses its systematic integrity and authority, and continues to be the philosophical basis for all administrative decisions about major theoretical issues." A fundamental reason for this impotence of New Theory is shown to be that, because it is contingent on an unstable political environment and its practitioners are not exactly well equipped, New Theory could not accomplish a rigorous and necessary negation of the old structure in order to assert itself without compromise.[19] Part of the "emergent" culture, it challenges the center by constantly creating new discursive spaces which nevertheless turn out to be fragile and severely restricted.

In other words, the traditional "ideological front," backed up by a still mostly intact institutionalized political power, now amounts to a stubborn final resistance to the general social and cultural reconfiguration. This time lag between a historical reality and its intellectual reflection, between advanced forces of production and outmoded relations of production and legitimizing ideology is at the heart of a Marxist understanding of history. The ideological front is where people become conscious of and fight over the economic and social transformation that has already taken place. (In *The German Ideology*, Marx and Engels analyze a possible historical situation in which an earlier form of social intercourse ousted by a "later interest" "remains for a long time afterwards in possession of a traditional power in the illusory community (State, law) . . . a power which in the last resort can only be broken by a revolution."[20]) In a situation tightly guarded by an "illusory" but still dominant ideological orthodoxy, New Theory may enjoy some innocuous fancy excursions into a foreign land but is never allowed to reach the base or center of control. All those ingenious theories and deconstructions of Truth or Power, therefore, can be easily wiped out overnight. In addition, society itself, the ideological hegemony practiced in everyday life, is never allowed to become a legitimate object of analysis and critique. This vulnerability of New Theory and in fact of all ideological transgressions has of course been given bloody evidence in recent history. The impossible situation of serious oppositional cultural critique, on the other hand, explains why Althusser, as a thinker engaged in critique, the Frankfurt School, and other Western Marxists, together with Foucault and Derrida have tremendous attraction for young Chinese critics and intellectuals. Significant or not within their own social milieu, these Western critics are believed to have at least a chance to express their discontent and oppositionality in a bourgeois society. So their voluminous writings and apparently unrelenting analyses serve only to inspire a general longing, just as in Eastern European countries, for a liberal "civil society" as both a solution and a preferred form of social existence and administration. The sad irony is that the best weaponry offered by Marx himself is very often painstakingly avoided due to a prolonged abuse and discrediting by a self-proclaimed Marxian discourse which, incidentally, has now been identified as a "Mao Style" with its peculiar power mechanism.[21]

Thirdly, as a result, New Theory, or rather the general intellectual effort to translate the text of contemporary China into a supposedly world language, proves to be a twofold mission that keeps canceling itself. It is a deeply troubling situation: while on the one hand the counterhegemonic enterprise of instituting a new theoretical framework has to challenge political repression by resorting indiscriminately to classical humanism, liberal pluralism, or a postmodern ideology of heterogeneity, the haunting specter of a market economy, on the other hand, hardly appears any more charitable or desirable when it reveals its mercantile face and elects to ignore all those intellectual concerns. Between political unfreedom and market indifference there is no real choice for the better. Between an elevating but duly persecuted heroism and a self-gratifying but equally impotent radicalism, there persists the same frustrated desire for action and fulfillment. Before it gets around to standing on its own feet, so to speak, New Theory finds itself already engaged in a two-front battle of which there will be no winner. This only indicates an even deeper cultural predicament. Alternating between a moral-oriented social order and an economic system in pursuit of profit, indeed, any efforts at constructing a comprehensive legitimizing ideology or in fact Meaning itself have to be deflated and self-contradictory. It appears that these two value systems, that of morality and that of profitability, are as mutally exclusive as they can be complementary, at least as a conceptual hypothesis, to each other. As philosopher Gan Yang perceived without any ambiguity toward the end of 1988, "for traditional culture, we have our criticism and negation, but we are also nostalgic and see its positive aspects; similarly, for a 'modern society,' we certainly have our longing and requests, but at the same time we sustain a deep suspicion and anxiety." For a long period of time in the future, he predicted, "Chinese culture will most likely have to develop itself in this complex situation with all antagonistic forces caught in tension."[22] With this understanding of our present, Gan Yang periodized contemporary cultural consciousness and its strategies into two succeeding phases—Rebellion followed by Confusion. What Tzvetan Todorov was to describe as "Post-totalitarian Depression" in the wake of a most dramatic 1989 was already present in Gan Yang's vision of history.[23]

This deep historical anxiety is of course not entirely new. The same experiential dilemmas have plagued intellectuals all over the world who happened to be caught in a painful moment of violent historic transformations and emerging realities. In China, the late Qing intellectual debate about the superiority of Eastern or Western learning reflected a simultaneous longing for and resistance to a wholesale acceptance of the modern capitalist mode of production and its accompanying social values. What substantiates this anxiety, needless to say, is the historical precedency set up by capitalism developed first in Europe and then in some other parts of the world, such as North America and Japan. All the consequences of this historical development, positive as well as negative, have been fully experienced, looked into, and documented. Any humanist optimism about laissez-faire capitalism and the market is a historically precluded illusion. Unless shielding themselves with bad faith, the advocates of free enterprise and its legitimizing ideology of liberalism, even though they may represent an emergent and productive social force in a national context, will never enjoy the same masterful confidence as those Enlightenment giants who, in revolt against political absolutism, resolutely stood up to call for an age of reason and individual freedom. In short, any form of utopia, within the boundaries of a nation-state, now becomes a categorical impossibility; or, in other words, a utopian discourse is bound instantaneously to reveal its gross ideological underpinnings and agendas.

Such is the historical situation facing contemporary Chinese culture in general and New Theory in particular; it also no doubt constitutes a persistent dilemma for all so-called Third World countries, not excluding Eastern Europe, where searching to avoid a historical repetition is certain to become a cultural obsession, because it directly translates into a question of national identity and, no less painfully, a problematization of "future" as a meaningful concept. The determination to avoid a historical repetition, it is helpful to remind ourselves here, was the primary goal of the first generation of Chinese socialists, represented by Sun Yat-sen and his followers, who believed that socialism would help China rid herself of all the evils of modern capitalism. Chinese socialism, in fact, has always taken itself, and to a considerable extent must be deemed, as a massive experiment, a grand project of surpassing modern capitalism which, let us also clarify, there has never been the likelihood of simply "restoring."[24] Thus in a postsocialist period (I borrow this term from Arif Dirlik), when two supposedly opposing value systems have been sufficiently debunked, one through irreplaceable historical experience and the other by means of no less convincing ideological analysis, any intellectual activity, either assuming a serious constructive approach or engaged in a wholehearted negative critique, faces tremendous difficulty. A self-important discursive production can be immediately subjected to irony because the situation is such that any positive value has already been thoroughly dismantled or made mockery of. Furthermore, a coercive political power helps neither fully discredit the dissension nor legitimize its own hegemony. The same moment "Mao Style" itself becomes an object of satire and repudiated as repressive, it can also be utilized, if its literal meaning is doggedly carried through, as a handy and often powerful weapon against the official endorsement of the market and even the political establishment itself. In fact, as critic Wang Bing observes, what now has the most direct comic effect among a Chinese audience or readership is precisely a derision or mockery of "Mao Style."[25]

Reinforced by political cynicism, this peculiar, but historically wrought absence of cultural normativity, which, by the way, is not the same as political hegemony, makes irony the dominant mode of writing and reading. All discursive practices are now caught in an ironic tension and yield no constructive discussion or consensus. Subsequently, a general uneasiness with its largely negative sense of irony expresses itself through an extensive debate on a "cultural crisis." Attention to the "culture crisis," as well as any remedy prescribed for it, on the other hand, somehow serves only to make irony all the more unavoidable. Such a disintegrative cultural environment certainly reminds one of the historical background from which Western modernism emerged, only to diversify itself right away and pursue separate cultural politics. It also strikes one, especially now, as helplessly reminiscent of the fin-de-siècle mentality. To be sure, there are self-consciously modernist sentiments and schools in art and literary production, and once in a while there can be heard no less strong apologies for modernism as a preferable cultural alternative.

It is postmodernism, however, as a general description of being simultaneously modernist and modernist manqué, that best characterizes contemporary Chinese culture which, due to the lack of any legitimate normativity or rather because of a synchronic juxtaposition of different, if indeed incompatible, modes of production, gives continuous rise to irony and displaces all efforts to stabilize meaning. The postmodernist wariness of uniformity and of any facile utopian expectation echoes only too well with the specific experience of recent Chinese history. At the same time, the postmodernist obsession with intertextuality and the floating signifier leads to a happy rediscovery of the deconstructive force of the Chinese language. As a matter of fact, New Theory has already offered adroit postmodernist interpretations of contemporary New Fiction and Film by underscoring a new mode of writing. In New Fiction, where a historical happening is systematically turned into a narrative signifier detached from its signified, "the prestructured meaning," as Li Tuo phrases it, "is canceled and the habitual recirculation of meaning gets broken down." This he calls a writing of "antimeaning" that is revolutionary in displacing the authoritarian Mao Style.[26] On the other hand, giving direct recognition to a postmodernist ingenuity and indifference in writers like Ye Zhaoyan and Yu Hua, critics notice a merge between mass culture and elitist literature in New Fiction. "Postmodernism does not radiate idealism, nor does it dish out predetermined critiques of reality," state Wang Zheng and Xiao Hua, two prolific critics of the younger generation. And they go on to observe that when violence or mystery as a form is deployed by young writers, when playfulness and parody enter the narrative, New Fiction chooses to identify itself with popular literature and in a verifiable "postmodern" gesture "conveys its attitude toward the world—detachment, distrust, and irony." In the end, they call for critical attention to the postmodernist wave rising in China.[27]

Admittedly, as a general social discourse about cultural production, postmodernism in China remains in the margin and is very often confused, purposely or not, with the poststructuralist theoretical discourses. But it is an energetic cultural practice that meets the demand of a society perennially caught in political instability and social reorganization. To talk about postmodernism, to engage in an intellectual activity that prolongs a productive and diversifying, although occasionally agonizing, "culture crisis," is necessarily a political choice. No matter how vague or controversial it may be, postmodernism, as a periodizing concept first of all, turns out to be a discursive formation conveniently in the service of a counter-hegemonic commitment. Let us make no mistake about it, postmodernism in China is not something that the neo-Stalinist bureaucrats would spread and promote among the young students and the public.[28] On the contrary, the Chinese conception of postmodernism has to include at once a rejection of the repressive political order and a critique of the rapid process of commodification. While opening up the past to parody and laughter, postmodernism in China is also bound to strip the future of its mystifying halo. The apparent incompatibility of these two critical thrusts will only enrich our understanding of our own time and shape contemporary Chinese culture with its own historical specificity. Like it or not, the function of postmodernism is here precisely to dismantle various master-narratives about modernity and create a new field of uncompromising demystification. Finally, to return to the essay we read at the beginning, I have to say that, quite contrary to the grave intention of its author, it is a text that cries for an ironic reading because, when placed in a larger historical context, it appears as no less than a parody of all those vacuous cultural signifiers such as "realism" and "modernism" and demarcates, through omission, a postmodernist territory for cultural critique.

Notes

1. Zeng Xiaochun, "'Recoding' and Contemporary Chinese Literature," *Wenyi lilunjia* (Jiangxi: Nanchang), February 1990, 15–18.

2. *Houxiandai zhuyi yu wenhua lilun*, tr. Tang Xiaobing (Xi'an: Shanxi Normal University Press, 1986). The passages about Deleuze and his "coding" theory are on pp. 20–22. For Deleuze's own presentation of the "three social machines," see his *Anti-Oedipus: Capitalism and Schizophrenia*, with Félix Guattari, tr. Robert Hurley et al. (Minneapolis: University of Minnesota, 1983), esp. 260–262.

3. Two important essays may testify to the trajectory outlined here: Gao Xingjian, "Belated Modernism and Contemporary Chinese Literature," *Literary Review* [Wenxue pinglun], 1988, no. 3, 11–15; and, more pertinently, Gan Yang, "Some Issues in the Culture Debate of the Eighties," *Cultural Consciousness in Contemporary China* [Dangdai Zhongguo wenhua yishi], ed. Gan Yang (Hong Kong: Joint Publishing [H.K.] Co., 1989), 1–35, first published in the journal *Culture: China and the World* [Wenhua: Zhongguo yu shijie] (Beijing), 1987, no. 1.

4. Xin Xiaozheng and Guo Yinxing, "The Situation of New Theory," *Review of the Contemporary Writer* [Dangdai zuojia pinglun] (Shenyang), 1988, no. 6, 4. This is a very helpful article, and I shall return to it shortly.

5. For a good summary of the history of literary criticism in the 1980s, see Yan Zhaozhu, "The Rising and Confusion of Literary Ontology—A Survey of the Literary Theory of the Ten Years of the New Period," *Literary Studies* [Wenyi yanjiu], 1989, no. 4, 197–201.

6. *Selected Essays by Liu Zaifu* [Liu Zaifu lunwen xuan] (Hong Kong: Dadi Book Co., 1986), 230–239. The text originally appeared in *Wenhui bao*, July 8, 1985.

7. "The Expanding of the Space for Literary Thinking," *Selected Essays by Liu Zaifu*, 1–36. The text first appeared in the journal *Reading* [Dushu], February 1985.

8. Ding Zhenhai and Li Zhun, "A Brief Essay on Several Examinations of the Law of Development of Literature in Recent Years," *Literary Theory and Criticism* [Wenyi lilun yu piping], 1986, no. 1. Quoted in Yan Zhaozhu, 202.

9. Lin Xinzhai, "Literary Theory of Our Time—Review of Liu Zaifu's Recent Works and Discussion with Chen Yong," pt. 2, *Reading*, January 1987, 150.

10. Chen Yan'gu and Jin Dacheng, "Critique of the Liu Zaifu Phenomenon—The Faustian Spirit in the Cultural Movements of Contemporary China," *Literary Review* [Wenxue pinglun], 1988, no. 2, 16–30. On p. 25, for instance, the historical situation of Liu Zaifu is compared to that after the French Revolution in which Hegel found himself contemplating philosophical issues. Xin Xiaozheng and Guo Yinxing's essay makes a similar point. See op. cit., 4.

11. "On the Subjectivity of Literature" ["Lun wenxue de zhuti xing"], *Selected Essays by Liu Zaifu*, 265.

12. Zhang Chengzhi, "The Dirt of Disciplines and the Gold of Science," *Reading*, April 1988, 25–30. The "Notes from the Editor" of the same issue highlights Zhang's point and expresses doubt whether uncurbed competition and commercialism will really bring the best out of scientific and cultural activities. See p. 160. *Reading* was a vanguard journal in the 1980s in introducing new reform-oriented books and ideas (in the first half of 1987, for example, it carried a series of five dialogues about the "New Economic

Liberalism") to the Chinese intellectual readership, but in the last couple of years its "Notes from the Editor" constantly complained about price hikes and the financial difficulties it was experiencing.

13. Ye Fang, "What Else Can We Have?—Demand for New Fiction and New Criticism," *Literary Review*, 1988, no. 3, 16–22.

14. Wang Gan, "The Failure of Counter-Culture—Critique of Mo Yan's Recent Fiction," *Reading*, October 1988, 12–18.

15. For a very good historical survey of both art and cinema in the 1980s, see Gao Minglu, "The Movement of Contemporary Chinese Art," and Yao Xiaomeng, "New Cinema in China: From the Perspective of Ideology," both collected in Gan Yang, ed., *Cultural Consciousness in Contemporary China*, 36–97, 193–221.

16. Zhang Yiwu, "The Field of Confusion," *Reading*, July and August 1989, 95–101. Zhang's article is a review of Xie Mian's 1988 book *The Green Revolution in Literature* (Guiyang: Guizhou People's Press). Although this book review did not come out until after the June Fourth Massacre, it was dated as written in February 1989, the heyday of that "beautiful chaos."

17. Jiang Yuanlun, *Zhongshan*, 1990, 3 (no. 66), 147–150. As its title suggests, this essay offers a postmodernist justification for the disappearance of narrative in contemporary fiction.

18. See, for instance, Ji Hongzhen, " 'Seeking Roots' in Culture and Contemporary Culture," *Literary Studies*, 1989, no. 2, 69–74, esp. 73–74.

19. Xin Xiaozheng and Guo Yinxing, op. cit., 4–5.

20. Ed. with intro. C. J. Arthur (New York: International Publishers, 1970), 88.

21. Li Tuo is one of the first who brought up this concept and is currently working on a book about the institutionalization of the "Mao Style" and the power mechanism at work in it. Zhang Ning, in her review of Mo Yan's novel *Thirteen Steps*, gives a preliminary definition of "Mao Style" in a summary of a general discussion. See her "Subversion of Literary Language and the Disorientation of Value Precepts—Mo Yan's Novel *Thirteen Steps*," *Dangdai* (Taiwan), June 1990, no. 50, 148.

22. "Preface by the Editor," *Cultural Consciousness in Contemporary China*, iii. Gan Yang's formulation in the "Preface" contributes to the point I am making here. The phrase he uses for "all antagonistic forces caught in tension" is a much more vivid *quanya jiaocuo*, which literally means "interweaving of dog teeth."

23. Todorov's extremely moving essay "Post-totalitarian Depression," appears in *The New Republic*, June 25, 1990, 23–25, translated from the French by Carol Cosman.

24. For a good discussion of this point, see Arif Dirlik, "Socialism and Capitalism in Chinese Socialist Thinking: The Origins," *Studies in Comparative Communism*, vol. 21, no. 2, Summer 1988, 131–152.

25. Li Tuo, Zhang Ling, and Wang Bing, "The Revolt of 'Language'—The Phenomenon of the Last Two Years' Fiction," *Literary Studies*, 1989, no. 2, 79. As a cultural phenomenon, it was indeed not surprising that, during the "democracy movement" of spring 1989, the gigantic portrait of Mao Zedong hung over Tiananmen should have been defaced at the same time other demonstrators were carrying his portraits, calling for an end to official corruption. On the other hand, there was a lot of literalization of a revolutionary, if not utopian, discourse that had been mass produced by the official propaganda but now readily served the cause of the students and civilians.

26. Li Tuo, Zhang Ling, and Wang Bing, op. cit., 75–80.

27. "Complementary Youth Consciousness: Things Having or Not Having to Do with Su Tong," *Reading*, July and August 1989, 106–107.

28. It disturbs me to see Terry Eagleton, whom I have always admired and learned a lot from, write the following when he is engaged in criticizing postmodernist cultural politics. "I write this article while the Chinese students and workers are still massing outside the Great Hall of the People; and I find it rather hard to understand why the neo-Stalinist bureaucrats have not, so far anyway, moved among the people distributing copies of Derrida, Foucault and Ernesto Laclau. For the Chinese students and workers to learn that their actions are aimed at a 'social totality' which is, theoretically speaking, non-existent would surely disperse them more rapidly than water cannons or bullets." "Defending the Free World," *Socialist Register 1990*, ed. Ralph Miliband et al. (London: The Merlin Press, 1990), 91. Let me simply say this here: not only would Derrida and Foucault *not* be able to disperse—on the contrary, they would encourage—the assembling in Tiananmen Square, but Eagleton's own radical bashing of Derrida and Foucault, for the very fact that his writings can be and are published in book form and in London, would give the students and workers still another reason to continue their quest for civil liberties.

LEO OU-FAN LEE

Postscript

              The contributions to this conference volume are mostly by young scholars, particularly scholars from the People's Republic of China who some years ago took the initiative at Indiana University in establishing the American Association for Chinese Comparative Literature. The chapters of this volume are from the first annual conference of this scholarly organization at Duke University (the second was held at UCLA). It was my privilege to serve as a discussant at the conference's concluding session and to offer my congratulations to all the "newcomers" of this budding field whose research and "rethinking" (largely as a result of their American academic training in Western literary theory) has already brought about what Liu Kang has called a "paradigm change" in modern Chinese literature studies. It would be redundant for me to add more self-congratulatory words in this postscript. The present volume, as a whole, abundantly demonstrates that the much-talked-about "paradigm change" in our field is no longer mere wishful thinking or hot air. It provides us with convincing examples of what some new directions and subjects of investigation may be, and what reading strategies we could apply to old, familiar texts. It is a volume with which the next generation of students of modern Chinese literature will have to come to terms.

    So instead of commenting on each chapter included in this volume, the intellectual substance and theoretical richness of which defy any easy summation, I would like, if I may, to take this opportunity to recapitulate one small point of my commentary at the conference's final session, what many might consider to be an untimely polemic—a purposeful, even willful, defense of a significant tradition in contemporary Chinese literature that is all but forgotten. Looking back beyond the saga of the Cultural Revolution, I wish to recall specifically the Soviet- (now Russian-) influenced revolutionary legacy of the 1950s, a legacy embodied in the experiences and writings of a whole generation of conscientious Party intellectuals (mostly castigated as "rightists" following the termination of the Hundred Flowers campaign): Liu Binyan, Wang Meng, Qin Zhaoyang, Yang Mo, the later Ding Ling, and many others. The pronounced absence of their ideological profile in this present volume bespeaks a peculiar kind of memory lapse, if not historical forgetfulness. I find it slightly ironic that, in a conference devoted to the theme of ideology and politics in modern Chinese literature, there is hardly any discourse, deconstructive or otherwise, of revolutionary literature.

Why do I choose to bring up this rather unsavory and unfashionable topos of a country's past "national allegory"? It is certainly not because an outsider like myself (whereas many at this conference were insiders, "born," as they say, "under the Red Flag") can harbor any personal affinities with such a revolutionary tradition. Nor do I wish to advocate an overt political position. My concern remains scholarly, stemming perhaps from certain "chronological" biases of a conventional literary historian. It seems that the textual landscape of these chapters leaves an obvious lacuna: it is as if nothing had happened in creative writing between the May Fourth period and the post-Mao era. In a way it may have indeed been the case if one adopts a high modernist artistic pose or a post-1985 avant-gardist perspective. Likewise, at a recent conference at Harvard that had as its central theme the May Fourth legacy in contemporary Chinese literature and film, little was said about the revolutionary interregnum. Yet this is precisely the ideological background against which most of the current writing in the People's Republic of China can be considered a purposeful artistic revolt. And for better or worse, such a corpus of work did exist, with all its utopian sound and fury. What is there for a postrevolutionary critic to do, aside from pronouncing its demise?

Should we attempt to fit these works into Althusser's definition of "ideological state apparatuses"—a grand revolutionary illusion or imaginary "distortion" that nonetheless captured the minds and hearts of a whole generation? Leaving aside those writers who started their revolutionary careers in the mid-1940s in Yan'an or the "White areas" during the war, by the time the People's Republic was formally established in 1949, a kind of collective "social imaginary" (here I borrow Charles Taylor's phrase from a different context) was already in place consisting of a set of clearly articulated values as canonized in a limited number of key revolutionary texts: *The History of the Soviet Communist Party (Bolshevik)*, *The ABCs of Communism*, *How the Steel Was Tempered*, to name a few, in addition to some of the basic texts by Marx and Mao. A majority of such texts (or textbooks) are originally Russian—not only in intellectual content but in form as well, and not only in the familiar Soviet brand of socialist realism but in such unique genres as literary reportage (for which Liu Binyan's direct mentor is Ovechkin and his *ocherk* form of investigative prose) or such popular novels as Nikolaeva's *The Director of the Machine Tractor Station and the Chief Agronomist* (a text that enters directly into Wang Meng's famous story "Newcomer in the Organization Department"). It is not my place to give more examples, since a brilliant and thorough analysis has been provided by Rudolf Wagner,[1] a renowned German scholar with a revolutionary past of his own. Is it then pertinent to ask whether such a legacy is no longer relevant to the theoretical sensibilities of the present generation of American-educated Chinese scholars—even as a subject of study? Or are there other layers of the Chinese "political unconscious" that remain to be uncovered?

To be sure, confronting such a past "master narrative" is by no means an easy task, especially in view of the current distrust of all master narratives in postmodernist theory. It also entails painstaking reading and research of materials no longer palatable to a Derridean bent of mind. But still I would like to present it as a challenge in a plea for committed scholarship in modern Chinese literature studies: the Revolution is dead, long live the revolution!

Note

1. Rudolf Wagner, *Inside a Service Trade: Studies in Contemporary Chinese Prose* (Cambridge, Mass.: Harvard-Yenching Institute Monograph Se-

ries, 1992). I was pleased to learn, while writing my brief postscript, that Xiaobing Tang, one of the editors of this volume, had just completed editing a collection of essays in Chinese that deals precisely with the tradition of revolutionary literature: *Rereading: People's Arts and Ideology* (Hong Kong: Oxford University Press [H.K.], 1993). I certainly hope that this publication indicates a growing willingness, in the Chinese-speaking community, to confront the revolutionary heritage.

INDEX

Adorno, Theodore, 42
Aesthetics, 25, 38, 40, 43, 44. See also Politics
Ai Siqi, 61, 65
Alienation, 28, 35, 45, 83
Allegory, 102, 115, 159, 168, 182, 266, 302
Althusser, Louis, 17, 35, 44, 79, 82, 97 n. 8, 99 n. 39, 225, 228, 239 n. 32, 292, 302–3; "Contradiction and Overdetermination," 98 n. 16; "Freud and Lacan," 99 n. 30; "Ideology and Ideological Apparatuses," 54 n. 45, 78, 98 n. 28, 121 n. 6, 220–22, 234, 239 n. 31, n. 33, 240 n. 41, n. 44. See also Ideology
Anderson, Marston, 19, 165, 178, 235; *The Limits of Realism: Chinese Fiction in the Revolutionary Period*, 14, 19 n. 3, 152, 170 n. 10, 172 n. 28, 187 n. 8
Anti-Japanese War. See Sino-Japanese War
Armstrong, Nancy, 127; *Desire and Domestic Fiction: A Political History of the Novel*, 138 n. 1, 140 n. 10
A Ying, 219

Bakhtin, Mikhail, 73, 76, 99 n. 37; *The Dialogical Imagination: Four Essays*, 97–98 n. 10, 98 n. 27
Barlow, Tani E.: "Feminism and Literary Technique in Ding Ling's Early Work," 139 n. 2; *I Myself am a Woman: Selected Writings of Ding Ling*, 122 n. 24, 139 n. 2, n. 5, 143 n. 29; "Theorizing Woman: Funü, Guojia, Jiating [Chinese Women, Chinese State, Chinese Family]," 139 n. 5
Barthes, Roland, 248, 262, 264, 273; *Camera Lucida: Reflections on Photography*, 270 n. 16, 271 n. 43; *A Lover's Discourse: Fragments*, 271 n. 33; *Michelet*, 271 n. 32
Bhabha, Homi K., 73, 95; *Nation and Narration*, 97 n. 8, 98 n. 27, 100 n. 63, n. 65
Bing Xin, 14, 127, 129–38; "Ai de shixian" [The realization of love], 130, 131; "Chaoren" [Superhuman], 129, 131; "Fanmen" [Anxiety], 130, 141 n. 15; "Lijia de yinian" [A year away from home], 141 n. 20; "Meng" [Dream], 141–42 n. 22; "Yishu" [Posthumous letters], 131, 132

305

Bo Chuan, 219, 222, 239 n. 29
Body, the, 13, 15, 27, 80, 87, 174–87, 260; female, and the male desire, 195–200; in Lu Xun, 174–79; in Mo Yan, 16, 195–200; in Shen Congwen, 179–86

Cai Feng: *A Window with a Mirror*, 252, 253, 256
Castoriadis, Cornelius, 77, 78; "The Imaginary Institution of Society," 98 n. 22
Chen, Xiao-mei, 19, 235, 236 n. 2
Chen, Yu-shih, 168, 173; *Realism and Allegory in the Early Fiction of Mao Tun*, 173 n. 32
Cheng Fangwu: "Cong wenxue geming dao geming wenxue" [From literary revolution to revolutionary literature], 104, 105, 121 n. 8
Chow, Rey: "Virtuous Transactions: A Reading of Three Stories by Ling Shuhua," 141 n. 21
Collective, the, 14, 16, 17, 202; collectivity, 60, 80, 84, 93, 95
Communism, 23, 39, 190–206; Communist Party, the, 23, 31, 43, 44, 48, 189, 192, 193, 201, 203, 211, 221, 224, 233, 237 n. 12, 238 n. 26, 282, 302
Confucianism, 24, 26, 41, 53 n. 29, 73, 116, 153, 200–1; Neo-Confucianism, 140 n. 13, 156
Consciousness, 9, 25–28, 33, 58, 61, 62, 64, 73, 76, 78, 85, 105, 118, 183, 197, 284
Critical theory, 18. *See also* New Theory
Cultural critique, 9, 18, 24, 25, 30, 38, 49, 74, 278, 288, 291
Culturalism, 25, 40
Cultural reflection, 16, 17, 40, 46
Cultural Revolution, the (1966–1976), 16, 23, 24, 31, 35, 43, 48, 59, 62, 70, 94, 149–50, 170 n. 8, 193, 221, 225–33, 302; post-Cultural Revolution China, 46, 86

Cultural theory, 24, 48
Culture, 25, 40, 59, 60, 294–96, 285, 288, 294
Culture fever, 9, 31

de Lauretis, Teresa: *Alice Doesn't: Feminism, Semiotics, Cinema*, 228, 240 n. 45
Deleuze, Gilles, 279–280; and Félix Guattari, *Anti-Oedipus: Capitalism and Schizophrenia*, 296 n. 2; *Kant's Critical Philosophy*, 52 n.22
de Man, Paul, 106; *The Rhetoric of Romanticism*, 121 n. 11; "Sign and Symbol in Hegel's Aesthetics," 271 n. 40
Democracy Movement, the (1989), 51 n. 17, 94, 231, 299 n. 25. *See also* Tiananmen Incident
Deng Xiaoping, 44, 245
Derrida, Jacques, 55 n. 53, 273, 288, 290, 292, 299 n. 28, 303
Ding Ling, 14, 83, 85, 116, 139 n. 2, 143 n. 29, 302; "Shafei nüshi de riji" [The Diary of Miss Sophia], 121 n. 12, 122 n. 25, 137
Dirlik, Arif, 18, 294; *The Origins of Chinese Communism*, 50 n. 2; "Socialism and Capitalism in Chinese Socialist Thinking: The Origins," 298 n. 24

Eagleton, Terry, 42; "Capitalism, Modernism, and Postmodernism," 55 n. 55; "Defending the Free World," 299 n. 28; "Ideology, Fiction, Narrative," 239 n. 32; "From *Polis* to Postmodernism," 55 n. 55; *The Ideology of the Aesthetic*, 53 n. 27, 54 n. 43, 123 n. 27
Engels, Friedrich, 34, 35, 40. *See also* Marx, Karl
Enlightenment, 39, 46, 48, 170 n. 13, 232–33, 293; May Fourth project of, 12, 24, 25, 26, 38–39

Feminism, 1, 8, 13, 14, 79, 138 n. 1

Feng Deying: *Kucai hua* [Bitter flowers], 200–1, 203, 205, 206, 208 n. 17, n. 18, n. 20
Fifth-generation film, 287. *See also* New Wave film
Foucault, Michel, 73, 177, 231, 273, 288, 292, 299 n. 28; *The Archaeology of Knowledge*, 97 n. 8; *Discipline and Punish: The Birth of the Prison*, 187 n. 6, n. 7; *Language, Counter-memory, Practice*, 97 n. 8, 100 n. 46
Franco, Jean, 76, 98 n. 19
Frankfurt School, the, 34, 36, 39, 43, 292
Freud, Sigmund, 4, 36, 41, 42, 53 n. 29, 54 n. 41, 55 n. 53, 65, 76, 79, 99 n. 30, 119, 122 n. 23, 123 n. 27, 265, 267; *Beyond the Pleasure Principle*, 271 n. 44

Gálik, Marián: *The Genesis of Modern Chinese Literary Criticism*, 138 n. 1; *Mao Tun and Modern Chinese Literary Criticism*, 170 n. 12, 171 n. 19
Gallop, Jane, 85; *Around 1981*, 1, 2; *Reading Lacan* 99 n. 31, n. 35, n. 39, 100 n. 40–n. 41, n. 43–n. 45, n. 48–n. 51, n. 55, n. 58–n. 60
Gan Yang, 292–93; *Dangdai Zhongguo wenhua yishi* [Cultural Consciousness in Contemporary China], 20 n. 5; 298 n. 15, n. 22; "Some Issues in the Culture Debate of the Eighties," 297 n. 3
Gao Xingjian, 287; "Belated Modernism and Contemporary Chinese Literature," 297 n. 3
Gong Liu, 251–52, 253, 256; "Du Luo Zhongli de youhua fuqin" [Reading Luo Zhongli's *Father*, an oil painting], 270 n. 21; *Gong Liu shixuan, 1945–1985* [Selected poems by Gong Liu, 1945–1985], 270 n. 22, n. 23
Gramsci, Antonio, 4, 6, 51 n. 11
Guo Moruo, 123 n. 27, 125, 131, 140 n. 10, 58

Habermas, Jürgen, 36, 52 n. 27
Hegel, Georg Wilhelm Friedrich, 27, 29, 32, 35, 37, 44, 46, 62, 283
Hegemony, 27, 51 n. 11, 62, 219–20, 230, 281
He Xilai, 232, 241 n. 53
He Yubo: *Zhongguo xiandai nüzuojia* [Modern Chinese women writers], 140 n. 10, n. 12
Historical, the, 16, 74–76. *See also* the Imaginary; Lacan, Jacques; the Real; the Symbolic
Historical materialism, 61; in Li Zehou, 32–37, 40–43, 46. *See also* Li Zehou
History, 16, 33, 45, 70, 71, 82, 92, 97 n. 8, 99 n. 30, 103, 212, 252, 264, 280, 291; and historical narratives, 10, 71; rethinking, 17, 213
Hsia, C. T., 15, 148, 172 n. 23; *A History of Modern Chinese Fiction*, 162, 170 n. 11; "Residual Femininity: Women in Chinese Communist Fiction," 238 n. 19
Hu Feng, 12, 24, 25, 26–30, 47–48, 50 n. 2, n. 5, 51 n. 9, n. 11, 221; *Lun minzu xingshi wenti* [On the question of national forms], 51 n. 14, n. 15; "Lun xianshi zhuyi de lu" [On the Path of Realism], 29; "Wenyi gongzuo de fazhan ji qi nuli fangxiang" [The development of literary and artistic works and the objectives of their endeavors], 51 n. 6, n. 10; "Xianshi zhuyi zai jintian" [Realism today], 51 n. 8; "Zhishen zai wei minzhu de douzheng limian" [Situating ourselves in the Struggle for Democracy], 28, 50 n. 4, 51 n. 7, n. 12–n. 13. *See also* Subjective fighting spirit
Humanism, 23–24, 79, 103, 105, 116, 151, 186, 284, 288, 292
Hu Ping, 17, 236 n. 1; "Zhongguo de mouzi" [The eyes of China], 216, 238 n. 19
Hu Ping and Zhang Shengyou, 241 n. 51; "Lishi chensi lu" [Historical re-

Hu Ping and Zhang Shengyou (*cont.* flections], 225, 229, 234, 238 n. 19, 240 n. 42, n. 43; "Shijie da chuanlian" [Wandering all over the world], 212, 236 n. 4

Hu Shi: "Jianshe de wenxue geming lun" [Toward a constructive theory of literary revolution], 103; "Wenxue gailiang chuyi" [Suggestions for literary reform], 103

Huters, Theodore, 15, 26; "From Writing to Literature: The Development of Late Qing Theories of Prose," 139 n. 3, 172 n. 26; "Hu Feng and the Critical Legacy of Lu Xun," 50 n. 3; "A New Way of Writing: The Possibilities for Literature in Late Qing China, 1895–1908," 139 n. 3

Identity, 6, 14, 71–74, 85, 104; collective, 12, 71, 82; crisis of, 83, 116; cultural, 77, 78; national, 72–74, 78, 93; split, 70–101

Ideology, 27, 78–79, 97 n. 8, 99 n. 38, 138, 140 n. 13, 141 n. 21, 147–73, 182, 192–95, 211–35, 279–80, 281, 283, 285, 286, 291, 292, 302; dominant, of the modern nation-state, 14, 76, 222; and State Apparatus and Ideological State Apparatus (*see* Althusser, Louis)

Imaginary, the, 45, 70, 71, 74, 77–79, 84–96, 303. *See also* the Historical; Lacan, Jacques; the Real; the Symbolic

Individual, the, 13, 14, 24, 103

Individualism, 60, 103–4, 108, 190, 202–3

Intellectuals, 5, 10, 12, 13, 23, 31, 46, 48, 53 n. 34, 59, 60, 61, 70, 73, 83, 105, 151, 195, 284, 292, 293, 302

Internalization, 35, 42

Jameson, Fredric, 18, 42, 52 n. 27, 75, 76, 216; "Imaginary and Symbolic in Lacan: Marxism, Psychoanalytic Criticism, and the Problem of the Subject," 54 n. 41, 237 n. 17; *Late Marxism: Adorno, or, The Persistence of the Dialectic,* 54 n. 40; *Marxism and Form,* 51 n. 9; *The Political Unconscious: Narrative as a Socially Symbolic Act,* 19 n. 3, 96 n. 1, 98 n. 17, n. 18, 100 n. 57, 237 n. 16, 270 n. 18; *Postmodernism and Theories of Culture,* 279

Japan, 154, 174. *See also* Sino-Japanese War

Japanese literature, 148–49

Jia Pingwa: "Tiangou" [Celestial dog], 253–55, 270 n. 24

Journalism, 214, 232. *See also* Reportage

June Fourth Massacre, the, 94. *See also* Democracy Movement; Tiananmen Incident

Kant, Immanuel, 32–33, 35–38, 41–42, 44, 52 n. 22, 53 n. 27, n. 29, 62; *Critique of Judgement,* 53 n. 30; *Critique of Pure Reason,* 252

Lacan, Jacques, 36, 42, 79, 82, 84, 89, 91, 93, 95, 99 n. 39, 100 n. 54; *Écrits: A Selection,* 53 n. 29, 54 n. 41, 55 n. 53, 99 n. 32, n. 36, 100 n. 47, n. 62, 272 n. 48, 288; mirror stage, the, 79–82, 84, 87, 94–95; "The Mirror Stage as Formative of the Function of the I as Revealed in Psychoanalytic Experience," 79. *See also* the Historical; the Imaginary; the Real; the Symbolic

Laclau, Ernesto, 221, 299, n. 28; "Metaphor and Social Antagonisms," 239 n. 35

Lao She, 83, 185; *Luotuo Xiangzi* [Camel Xiangzi], 97 n. 7, 99 n. 38, 100, n. 42

Lee, Leo Ou-fan, 18, 111, 122 n. 18, n. 20, 175; "The Crisis of Culture in China," 52 n. 19; *Lu Xun and His Legacy,* 50 n. 3; *The Romantic Generation of Modern Chinese Writers,*

138 n. 1; *Voices from the Iron House: A Study of Lu Xun*, 122 n. 17, 186 n. 1, 187 n. 3
Lei Feng, 60, 233, 241 n. 56, 281
Levenson, Joseph, 149, 151; *Revolution and Cosmopolitanism: The Western Stage and the Chinese Stages*, 169 n. 8
Liang Bin: *Hongqi pu* [Genealogy of the red flag], 200, 204, 205, 206, 208 n. 14, n. 23
Liang Qichao, 62, 72, 236 n. 2; "Yi yin zhengzhi xiaoshuo xu" [Preface to the printing of [the series of] political novels in translation], 171–72 n. 23
Lin Shu, 152
Lin Yü-sheng: *The Crisis of Chinese Consciousness: Radical Antitraditionalism in the May Fourth Era*, 19 n. 2, 50 n. 1, 169 n. 7; and Li Zehou, *Wusi: duoyuan de fansi* [May Fourth: pluralist reflections], 50 n. 4; on "totalistic" iconoclasm, 10, 169 n. 7, 179
Ling Shuhua, 141 n. 21, 143 n. 29
Li Tuo, 16, 18, 207 n. 5, 295, 298 n. 21; critique of "Mao Style," 16, 18, 275–76; with Zhang Ling and Wang Bing, "The Revolt of 'Language'—The Phenomenon of the Last Two Years' Fiction," 299 n. 25, n. 26
Liu Binyan, 17, 225, 229, 232, 234, 235, 236 n. 1, n. 2, 238 n. 19, 240 n. 51, 302, 303; "Benbao neibu xiaoxi" [The inside news of the newspaper], 216, 222–24, 239 n. 37; "Cong 'Renyao zhijian' yinqi de" [Consequences of "People or Monsters?"], 241 n. 52; "Guanyu 'Renyao zhijian' da duzhe wen" [A response to the readers of "People or Monsters?"], 241 n. 52; *A Higher Kind of Loyalty: A Memoir by China's Foremost Journalist*, 239 n. 36; "Renyao zhijian" [People or monsters?], 240 n. 39
Liu Heng: *Fuxi fuxi*, 253, 255–56, 268, 270 n. 25, 272 n. 50; and *Ju Dou*, 255. *See also* Zhang Yimou
Liu Kang, 12, 235, 301
Liu Linsheng, 126, 128; "Xin wenxue yu xin nüzi" [The new literature and the new woman], 139 n. 7
Liu Zaifu, 12, 18, 25, 44, 51 n. 17, 58; *Guanyu wenxue zhuti xing de lunzheng* [Debates on the subjectivity of literature], 68 n. 1; and Li Zehou 16, 24, 25, 26, 29, 31, 44, 47–49, 212–15 (*see also* Li Zehou); and Lin Gang, *Chuantong yu Zhongguo ren* [Tradition and the Chinese person], 46, 54 n. 47; on literary subjectivity, 24, 25, 43–47, 283–85, 288; *Liu Zaifu lunwen xuan* [Selected essays by Liu Zaifu], 283, 297 n. 6, n. 7; "Liu Zaifu Phenomenon," 283; "Lun bashi niandai wenxue piping de wenti geming" [On the stylistic revolution in literary criticism of the 1980s], 69 n. 5; "Lun wenxue de zhuti xing" [On the subjectivity of literature], 43, 54 n. 46, 56, 236 n. 3, 297 n. 11; on philosophical dualism, 46–47, 55 n. 52; "Wusi wenxue qimeng jingshen de shiluo yu huigui" [The loss and recovery of the enlightenment spirit of May Fourth literature], 50 n. 4; *Xingge zuhe lun* [On dual composition of literary character], 47, 55 n. 52; *Xunzhao de beige* [Tragic songs of quest], 47, 54 n. 51; "Zailun wenxue zhuti xing" [The subjectivity of literature revisited], 12, 54 n. 50; "Zhongguo xiandai wenxue shi shang dui ren de san ci faxian" [Three discoveries of humanity in modern Chinese literature], 54 n. 48, n. 49; "Zouchu duduan lun: Zhongguo dangdai wenxue pinglun shiji mo de zhengzha" [Beyond totalitarianist theories: the fin-de-siècle struggles of contemporary Chinese literary criticism], 54 n. 44

Li Zehou, 12, 25, 30, 32–43, 44, 52 n. 22, 62; critique of Western Marxism, 34–35; on historical materialism, 25, 32–37, 40–43 (see also National salvation); "Ji Zhongguo xiandai san ci xueshu lunzhan" [Notes on three scholarly debates in modern China], 50 n. 4; and Liu Zaifu, 16, 24, 25, 26, 29, 31, 47–49 (see also Liu Zaifu); *Pipan zhexue de pipan* [Critique of the Critical Philosophy: A Study of Kant], 32–42, 52 n. 20, n. 24, n. 26, 53 n. 28, n. 30–n. 32, 54 n. 36–n.37, n. 41–n. 42, 62, 69 n. 4; on practice and praxis, 34, 38, 62; and Schwarz, Vera, "Six Generations of Modern Chinese Intellectuals," 53 n. 34; on sedimentation, 35, 36, 42; *Zhongguo xiandai sixiang shi lun* [Essays on modern Chinese intellectual history], 50 n. 4, 51 n. 16, 53 n. 34, n. 35; *Zou wo ziji de lu* [Take my own path], 52 n. 25, 53 n. 29, n. 35

Li Zehou and Liu Zaifu, "Wenxue yu yishu de qingsi" [Feelings and thoughts on literature and art], 237 n. 5, n. 11. See also Liu Zaifu

Lukács, Georg, 24, 27, 28, 51 n. 9

Luo Guangbin and Yang Yiyan: *Hongyan* [Red cliffs], 200, 208 n. 15

Luo Zhongli: *Chuncan* [Spring silkworms], 256, 266, 267; *Climbing the Threshold*, 266, 267; *Fuqin* [Father], 243–56; "Nongmin he wode hua" [Peasants and my paintings], 269 n. 9, n. 13; and photorealism, 17, 246; *Suiyue* [Years], 256–62, 266, 267, 271–72 n. 46; "Wode fuqin de zuozhe de laixin" [Letter from the painter of *My Father*], 269 n. 9, n. 10, n. 12, 270 n. 17; and *Yellow Earth*, 246–48

Lu Xun, 13, 15, 44, 73, 83, 102–13, 116, 163–66, 171 n. 21, 174–79, 180, 184, 185, 187 n. 13, 283; "Ah Q zhengzhuan" [The True Story of Ah Q], 73, 76, 82–83, 148, 176, 249–50; "Changong daguan" [A spectacle of chopping communists], 177, 187 n. 5; "Cong Baicaoyuan dao sanwei shuwu" [From Baicao garden to Sanwei study], 179; "Geming shidai de wenxue" [Literature in a revolutionary age], 121 n. 7; "Guxiang" [My old home], 163–65, 172 n. 27, 249–50; "Kuangren riji" [Diary of a Madman], 104, 166, 179; "Moluo shili shuo" [The power of Mara poetry], 103; "Mujie wen" [Tomb tablet], 179; *Nahan* [A call to arms], 175, 178, 187 n. 2; *Panghuang* [Wandering], 105; "Shang shi" [Regret for the Past], 13, 85, 105, 106–13, 114, 120 n. 15; "Xingfu de jiating" [A happy family], 121–122 n. 14; "Yao" [Medicine], 176; *Yecao* [Wild Grass], 121 n. 13; "Zai jiulou shang" [In the tavern], 179; "Zhufu" [New Year's Sacrifice], 85, 178, 249; "Zhujian" [Forging swords], 176

Lu Yin, 14, 127, 129–38; "Chuangzuo de wojian" [My views on literary creation], 131; "Haibin guren" [Old friends by the seashore], 134, 135, 141 n. 22; "Hechu shi guicheng?" [Which way leads to home?], 142 n. 26; "Huoren de beiai" [Someone's tragedy], 131; "Lantian de canhui lu" [Lantian's record of remorse], 142 n. 26; "Lishi de riji" [Lishi's diary], 134, 141 n. 22, 142 n. 25; "Panghuang" [Wandering], 141 n. 19; "Shengli yihou" [After victory], 141 n. 26; "Yige zhuzuojia" [A writer], 129

Lu Yuan: *Leyuan* [Paradise], 261–62, 265, 271 n. 34–n. 36, n. 39

Lyricism, 246; lyrical realism, 184–86 (see also Romanticism: revolutionary); in Shen Congwen, 174–75, 179–86

McDougall, Bonnie S.: *The Introduction of Western Literary Theories* into *Modern China*, 170 n. 12, n. 14, 171 n. 17, n. 19; *Mao Zedong's Talks at the Yan'an Conference on Literature and Art: A Translation of the 1943 Text with Commentary*, 239 n. 34

Mai Tianshu, 236 n. 1; "Aihe hengliu" [The river of love is flooding], 240–41 n. 51; "Huoji" [A live sacrifice], 240 n. 51; and Zhang Yu, "Tudi yu tuhuangdi" [Land and a local tyrant], 228, 237–238 n. 18, 240 n. 51

Mao Dun (Shen Yanbing), 15, 50 n. 5, 83, 154–60, 239 n. 30; "Can dong" [Winter ruin], 166; "Chun can" [Spring silkworms], 166; "Cong Guling dao Dongjing" [From Guling to Tokyo], 172 n. 30; "Du Ni *Huanzhi*" [Reading *Ni Huanzhi*], 172 n.30; *Hong* [Rainbow], 85; Naturalism and modern Chinese fiction, 156, 172 n. 25; "Qiu shou" [Autumn harvest], 166; "The relationship of people to literature and the traditional misperception of the status of the writer in China," 156; *Rishi sanbuqu* [Eclipse trilogy], 85; "Shemma shi wenxue?" [What is literature?], 171 n. 16; "Wenxue yu rensheng" [Literature and life], 170 n. 15; "Xin wenxue yanjiuzhe de zeren yu nuli" [The duties and efforts of researchers in the new literature], 171 n. 17; *Ziye* [Midnight], 97 n. 7, 100 n. 42

Maoism, 2, 30, 33, 35, 40, 43, 44, 225

"Mao Style," 207 n. 5, 274, 292, 294, 295, 298 n. 21; revolt/resistance against, 18, 275–76 (see also Li Tuo); Maoist language, 193

Mao Zedong, 23, 24, 26, 149, 179, 192, 218, 239 n. 26, 241 n. 56, 243–45, 269 n. 4, 274–75, 303, 299 n. 25; and the Cultural Revolution, 24, 49, 225–33, 242 n. 59; "Maodun lun" [On Contradictions], 191–92; post-Mao China, 6, 17, 30, 31, 35, 43, 52 n. 18, 231, 243–72, 302; "Qingyuan chun: Xue" [Snow], 203; "Zai Yan'an wenyi zuotanhui shang de jianghua" [Talk at the Yan'an forum on literature and the arts], 26, 30, 50 n. 5, 208 n. 9, 221, 274 (see also Yan'an Talks), "Zhongguo shehui ge jieji de fenxi" [The analysis of various classes of Chinese society], 207 n. 8

Marxism, 2, 32, 43, 45, 65, 155, 161, 282, 284, 291; Chinese, 24, 35, 51 n. 11, 52 n. 17, 56; critical theory of, 8, 76, 78; cultural dimension of, 6, 40, 48, 245, 275; Leninism, 59; Marxist literary thought, 24, 26, 43, 44, 45, 47, 49, 105, 120, 162; in the May Fourth Era, 23, 151–52; theory of subjectivity in, 6, 32, 33; Western, 24, 34, 39, 51 n. 9, 150, 288, 292 (see also Li Zehou)

Marx, Karl, 35, 42, 52 n. 24, 53 n. 29, 57, 79, 99 n. 30, 123 n. 27, 218, 292, 303; *Economic and Philosophical Manuscripts*, 35, 37, 45, 52 n. 23

Marx, Karl, and Engels, Friedrich, 99 n. 37; *The German Ideology*, 291

Maternal icon, the, 256–68

May Fourth Movement, the, 13, 23, 50 n. 1, 60, 70–74, 80, 81–82, 108, 126, 133, 150–68, 302; intellectuals, 10, 39, 84, 105, 116–20; literature of, 26, 102–23, 185; post-May Fourth China, 153, 158, 161, 167, 180; project of cultural enlightenment, 12, 24–25, 28–30, 40 (see also Enlightenment); project of modernity, 81, 124; realism, 29, 48, 50 n. 5, 97 n. 7, 99 n. 38. See also New Culture Movement

Mirror stage, the. See Lacan, Jacques

Misty Poetry, 283, 288

Modernism, 16, 102, 150, 276; and postmodernism, 48, 288, 295 (see also Postmodernism)

Modernity, 9, 11, 12, 13, 16, 17, 102, 106, 116–20, 124–43, 276, 296. See also Postmodernity

Modernization, 2, 4, 5, 23, 30, 35, 193, 279, 282
Mouffe, Chantal, 225, 229; "Hegemony and New Political Subjects: Toward a New Concept of Democracy," 240 n. 40, n. 48
Mo Yan, 6, 15, 286; celebration of the body in, 16, 195–200; and the film adapation of *Red Sorghum*, 263–65, 271 n. 42 (see also Zhang Yimou); *Hong gaoliang jiazu* [Red Sorghum], 15, 188–208, 207 n. 1, 263, 271 n. 41; *Huanle* [Ecstasy], 262, 268, 271 n. 37, n. 38, 272 n. 51; *Shisan bu* [Thirteen Steps], 13, 71, 86–96, 96 n. 2, 100 n. 53, 100 n. 56, 298 n. 21; *Touming de hong luobo* [The transparent carrot], 207 n. 7

Narcissism, 79–80, 115
National culture, 4, 5
National forms, 26, 29
Nationalism, 3, 7, 72–73, 76, 149
National salvation, 30, 38–39
Naturalism, 27, 37, 57, 61, 154–56, 170 n. 12
Nature, 33, 35, 37–42, 58, 61
New Culture Movement, 24, 60, 73, 84, 158. See also the May Fourth Movement
New Theory, 6, 10, 18, 278–99. See also Critical theory; Postmodernism
New Wave film: *Ju Dou*, 255–56; *Red Sorghum*, 188, 263–65, 267; *Yellow Earth*, 246–47, 269 n. 13. See also Fifth-generation film; Zhang Yimou
Nostalgia, 16, 176, 190, 293; for history, 17, 260–61, 268

Object. See Subject, object relations

Paradigm, 9, 40, 281, 301
Paternal icon, the: and filial piety, 248–50; in *Father*, 243–72
Piaget, Jean, 35, 36, 40, 41, 42, 52 n. 27, 53 n. 29, 54 n. 41; *Genetic Epistemology*, 52 n. 26; *The Principles of Genetic Epistemology*, 52 n. 26
Plaks, Andrew, 158–59; *Archetype and Allegory in The Dream of the Red Chamber*, 172 n. 24
Politics, 3, 11, 25, 26, 43, 47, 49, 81, 96, 132, 212, 302; cultural, 295, 299 n. 28; depoliticization, 1, 43, 47; and literature, 15, 45, 161, 279, 282. See also Aesthetics
Postmodernism, 1, 6; in China, 18, 278–99. See also Modernism: and postmodernism
Postmodernity, 10
Poststructuralism, 16, 42, 185, 279–80, 288, 295–96; and postmodernism, theories of, 9–10
Průšek, Jaroslav, 148

Qian Gang, 17, 234, 236 n. 1; "Tangshan da dizhen" [The great earthquake in Tangshan], 212–13, 217–18, 222, 224, 236 n. 4, 237 n. 7–n. 9, 238 n. 21, 239 n. 27, 240 n. 51, 242 n. 59
Qing Dynasty, the, 128, 140 n. 13, 152, 179, 180; late, fiction of, 137, 139 n. 3, 149, 171 n. 21
Qu Qiubai: *Chidu xinshi* [My private thoughts on the Red Capital], 220, 236 n. 1; *Exiang jicheng* [A travel report from the land of hunger], 236 n. 2

Rationality. See Enlightenment; He Xilai; Kant, Immanuel; Li Zehou
Real, the, 14, 45, 85, 87, 89, 92, 182, 214–15. See also the Historical; Hu Feng; the Imaginary; Jameson, Fredric; Lacan, Jacques; the Symbolic
Realism, 14, 24, 26, 27, 28, 147–73, 175, 178; critical, 14, 15, 152; lyrical (see Lyricism); and modernism, 14, 278–80, 296; socialist, 16, 43, 152, 189–206. See also Naturalism
Reality, 10, 13, 15, 24, 25, 28, 178
Red Guards, the, 225–33, 238 n. 19, 242

n. 59. See also the Cultural Revolution
Reportage, 17, 303; defined as a subversive discourse, 211–42; and texie, 212, 222–24. See also Journalism
Revolution, 2, 16, 59, 83, 151
Romanticism, 103, 150, 154; revolutionary, 203–6 (see also Lyricism)
Rousseau, Jean-Jacques, 37
Rutherford, Jonathan: *Identity: Community, Culture, Difference*, 95–96, 101 n. 66

Said, Edward, 8, 18; *Orientalism*, 148; "Secular Criticism," 20 n. 6; "Traveling Theory," 19 n. 1
Sakai, Naoki, 147–48; "Modernity and Its Critique: The Problem of Universalism and Particularism," 168 n. 1
Sartre, Jean-Paul, 6, 32, 35
Scholes, Robert, 215
Sedimentation, 35, 36, 42
Self. See Subject
Shen Congwen, 174–75, 179–86; *Congwen zizhuan* [Autobiography of Congwen], 179, 180, 181, 187 n. 9, n. 10; "Huanghun" [Twilight], 179, 180, 181, 182–84; lyrical realism of, 181–86 (see also Lyricism); "Qian xiaojing" [Little scene in Guizhou], 179, 180, 181; "Sange nanren yu yige nüren" [Three men and one woman], 179; "Wo de jiaoyu" [My Education], 179, 180–81, 187 n. 12; "Xin yu jiu" [The old and the new], 179, 181
Sino-Japanese War, the (1937–1945), 24, 25, 27, 188, 189, 211
Su Tong, 17, 286, 299 n. 27
Su Xiaokang, 31, 235, 236 n. 1; "Honghuan qishi lu" [The revelation of the flood], 212, 224–25, 237 n. 4; and Zhang Min, "Shensheng yousi lu" [Noble reflections], 240 n. 51; "Ziyou beiwang lu[A memorandum on freedom], 228; *Ziyou beiwang lu: Su Xiaokang baogao wenxue jingxuan* [A memorandum on freedom: selected reportage by Su Xiaokang], 240 n. 51

Subject, the, 7, 13–14, 31, 42, 45, 56–69, 70, 80, 102–23, 182; collective, 7, 57, 71, 225; decentered, 6, 12; subject-object relations, 29, 41, 57–58, 197
Subjective fighting spirit, 12, 24, 27–30. See also Hu Feng
Subjectivism, 24, 57, 61, 62, 283
Subjectivity, 6, 7, 11–14, 23–55, 56–69, 103, 197, 283–85, 288; displacement of, 70–101; and gender, 116–20, 122–23 n. 25, 124–43; in reportage, 17, 211–42
Symbolic, the, 86–90, 95, 96, 99 n. 38, 214. See also the Historical; the Imaginary; Lacan, Jacques; the Real

Tang, Xiaobing, 18, 51, 235; *Rereading: People's Arts and Ideology*, 304 n. 1
Tao Yongbai: "Youhua fuqin yu zuozhe Luo Zhongli" [*Father*, an oil painting, and Luo Zhongli, the painter], 269 n. 2
Texie, 212, 222–24, 236 n. 2, 238 n. 19. See also Liu Binyan
Theory, 2, 14, 18, 66, 215, 288; imported, 147–73. See also West, western theory
Third World, the, 5, 76, 293
Tiananmen Incident, the (June 4, 1989), 8, 31, 49, 71, 221, 235. See also Democracy Movement
Turgenev, Ivan: *Sketches from a Hunter's Album*, 18, 187 n. 14

Utopianism, 159, 161, 162, 196, 293

Wagner, Rudolf: *Inside a Service Trade: Studies in Contemporary Chinese Prose*, 303 n. 1; "Liu Binyan and the Texie," 236 n. 2, 238 n. 20, 239–40 n. 38, 303
Wang Meng, 302; "Newcomer in the Organization Department," 303

Wang Xiaolong: "Ni yiwei ni mei bei wo banyan guo ma?" [You think I have not played your part?], 268, 272 n. 49
War of Resistance. *See* Sino-Japanese War
Wellek, René: "The Concept of Realism in Literary Scholarship," 156, 171 n. 22
West, the, 12, 37, 38, 119, 280; western influence in China, 5, 38, 40, 147–73; Westernization and modernization, 10, 11, 40, 124, 150, 276; western literature, 103, 108, 149–52, 156, 218, 275; western theory and theorists, 5, 9–12, 18, 215, 176, 280, 293
White, Hayden: *Tropics of Discourse: Essays in Cultural Criticism*, 237 n. 15, 238 n. 23
Williams, Raymond, 6, 81; *Marxism and Literature*, 98 n. 24, 99 n. 37
Wittgenstein, Ludwig, 35, 40, 52 n. 24
Women's literature, 124–43

Xia Yan: "Baoshengong" [Contract labor], 219–20, 236 n. 1, 239 n. 30

Yan'an Talks, 26, 30, 50 n. 5, 221, 274. *See also* Mao Zedong

Yang Mo, 302; *Qingchun zhi ge* [Song of youth], 200, 204, 205, 206, 208 n. 13, n. 22, n. 24
Yu Dafu, 13, 83, 85, 102–20 123 n. 27, 131, 138 n. 1; "Chenlun" [Sinking], 116, 122 n. 23, 123 n. 26; "Huanxiang houji" [Sequel to reminiscences on returning home], 115, 122 n. 21; "Huanxiang ji" [Reminiscences on returning home], 13, 113–20; "Shui shi women de pengyou?" [Who is our friend?], 105, 121 n. 9

Zhang Chengzhi, 285; "The Dirt of Disciplines and the Gold of Science," 297 n. 12
Zhang Yimou: *Ju Dou*, 255; *Red Sorghum*, 188, 263–65, 267; *Yellow Earth*, 247–48. *See also* Fifth-generation film; New Wave film
Zhou Yang: "Defining the new era of the masses," 274
Zhou Zuoren, 104, 105, 121 n. 10, 126; "Nüzi yu wenxue" [Women and literature], 139 n. 8; "Ren de wenxue" [Literature for humans/Humane literature], 103, 172 n. 23
Žižek, Slavoj: *The Sublime Object of Ideology*, 208 n. 11

CONTRIBUTORS

Liu Kang is Assistant Professor of Comparative Literature and Chinese at the Pennsylvania State University, University Park.

Xiaobing Tang is Assistant Professor of Chinese at the University of Colorado, Boulder.

Ching-kiu Stephen Chan is Lecturer of English at the Chinese University of Hong Kong.

Theodore Huters is Professor of Chinese at the University of California, Irvine.

Fredric Jameson is William Lane Professor of Comparative Literature and Director of the Graduate Program in Literature at Duke University.

Wendy Larson is Associate Professor of Chinese at the University of Oregon.

Leo Ou-fan Lee is Professor of Chinese at the University of California, Los Angeles.

Li Tuo is a prominent Chinese writer, film and literary critic, and member of the editorial board of the literary journal *Today*.

Liu Zaifu, former Director of the Institute of Literature at the Chinese Academy of Social Sciences, is now a Visiting Professor at the University of Stockholm, Sweden.

Lydia H. Liu is Assistant Professor of Chinese and Comparative Literature at the University of California, Berkeley.

Tonglin Lu is Assistant Professor of Chinese at the University of Iowa.

David D. W. Wang is Associate Professor of Chinese at Columbia University.

Yuejin Wang is a Ph.D. candidate at the Department of Art History, Harvard University.

Yingjin Zhang is Assistant Professor of Chinese at Indiana University.

Library of Congress Cataloging-in-Publication Data

Politics, ideology, and literary discourse in modern China :
theoretical interventions and cultural critique / Liu Kang,
Xiaobing Tang, editors ; foreword by Fredric Jameson.
   p.   cm.   Includes index.
ISBN 0-8223-1403-7. — ISBN 0-8223-1416-9 (pbk.)
1. Chinese literature—20th century—History and criticism. 2. Politics and literature—China. 3. Communism and literature—China. I. Liu, Kang. II. Tang, Xiaobing.
PL2303.P65 1993
895.1'09358—dc20   93-4448 CIP

www.ingramcontent.com/pod-product-compliance
Lightning Source LLC
Chambersburg PA
CBHW070751230426
43665CB00017B/2326